PRECIPICE

THE LEFT'S CAMPAIGN *to* DESTROY AMERICA

NICK DEIULIIS

REPUBLIC

BOOK PUBLISHERS

Paperback: 9781645720607

Ebook: 9781645720591

For inquiries about volume orders, please contact:

Republic Book Publishers

27 West 20th Street, Suite 1103

New York, NY 10011

editor@republicbookpublishers.com

Published in the United States by Republic Book Publishers

Distributed by Independent Publishers Group

www.ipgbook.com

Book designed by Mark Karis

Printed in the United States of America

This book is dedicated to the four generations of women who nurtured, inspired, challenged, disrupted, and supported me through my life.

CONTENTS

Introduction   1

The Awesomeness of Creators, Enablers, and Servers
      and How to Define the Leech   13

The Leech Mothership: The Deep State   39

Leech-Targeted Callings Beyond the Government Bureaucrat   69

Training Grounds Part 1: Who Runs Academia   119

Training Grounds Part 2: Hijacking STEM   173

Funding Sources Part 1: The Fed   201

Funding Sources Part 2: Unwitting Retirees
      (aka "Other People's Money")   227

Leech Power Centers: Urban Hell   257

Profile #1: Pope Francis   303

Profile #2: Bono   331

Profile #3: Jeffrey Sachs   351

Epilogue: Defiling the Noble Lie   365

Author's Note   370

Endnotes   377

DISCLAIMER

ALL OPINIONS DISCUSSED IN THIS BOOK ARE THOSE OF NICK DEIULIIS ALONE, IN HIS PERSONAL CAPACITY, AND NOT OF ANYONE ELSE.

INTRODUCTION

"As my intention is to write something useful for discerning minds, I find it more fitting to seek the truth of the matter rather than imaginary conceptions."

NICCOLÒ MACHIAVELLI, *THE PRINCE*

"The further a society strays from the truth the more it will hate those who speak it."

GEORGE ORWELL

THIS AUTHOR'S BACKSTORY

Growing up, two things were important to me: Pittsburgh, my beloved hometown, and my Italian heritage. Italians are one of God's gifts to the world, I believe. Forgive my bias, but Italian food, art, and civic pride are an inspiration to me. Christopher Columbus, despite his flaws and being far from perfect, should be celebrated as the greatest navigator of his age who achieved the then unimagined feat of crossing the Atlantic in three ships without maps. Along with Columbus discovering the New World, what other nationality can point to the great contributions of the Roman Empire, the Renaissance, da Vinci, and the *Godfather* film epic (Parts I and II only, of course)?

Pittsburgh is where my heart is, and where it will remain. There are many reasons for this. It's the place where I struggled, won and lost battles, and became the person I am today. In addition to my heart, I suppose Pittsburgh also holds my soul.

I've chosen to live my entire life within a tight five-mile radius of the Steel City. I've been fortunate to travel the world, but no matter how beautiful the locales and exciting the trips were, the best part of every journey was the day I returned home. Pittsburgh stands for so much: the American ideal of a city built upon true industry and populated by an immigrant class; a place where you arrive with nothing but your name and work ethic, and you make a life. Yes, a place where Dennis Miller once quipped, "The good thing about Pittsburgh, it's a good place to be raised . . . it doesn't tolerate assholes. You're either a good guy or a bad guy."[1] Pittsburgh simultaneously exemplifies where the traditional values of this nation yielded remarkable results and where our society is threatened.

Pittsburgh's position in our nation is a principal factor that affects the psyche of Pittsburghers themselves. Pittsburgh's people, history, culture, and future have more in common with upstate New York, eastern Ohio, and West Virginia than with Philadelphia or the East Coast. Pittsburgh is the capital of Appalachia, and Appalachia has so much going for it: a booming energy industry, industrious people, a strong manufacturing base, natural beauty, low crime, and inexpensive cost of living. Yet coastal elites love to look down on Appalachia, while shallow-minded elites within Pittsburgh desperately try to make the Steel City into something it will never be: a Boston, San Francisco, or whatever other shiny new place these self-described sophisticates discuss at their cocktail parties and social clubs.

The dynamic of arrogant coastal elites looking down on and trying to control independent-minded and industrious Appalachia has been part of our history since the Founding Fathers. Appalachians and people from western Pennsylvania, the greatest people you will ever meet, have never taken kindly to such snobbish and intrusive oversight. President Washington found that out during the Whiskey Rebellion in the 1790s when the new federal government decided to tax a core industry of Appalachia at the time, whiskey production. Western Pennsylvania farmers revolted, and the federal government raised a militia of thousands to put down the insurrection. The more times change the more things stay the same: today the coastal elites and the federal government continue to look down on regions like Appalachia and work to tax and squelch the lifeblood of the region. Back then it was whiskey tax; today it is an array of draconian regulation, a de facto carbon tax, and policies aimed to help major urban coastal areas at the expense of flyover regions like Appalachia. This dynamic creates a chip-on-the-shoulder mentality of western Pennsylvanians, the author's shoulder included.

I'm a dad, a son, and a husband. Those three challenges are quite different, but all three roles share the ultimate prize if you deeply commit to them: unconditional love. They start to get you thinking about things out there beyond yourself and the here-and-now.

I'm a businessman by job classification and W-2 but an engineer at heart. Growing up, my family was somewhere between working poor and middle class. Today, I now live in a world of so-called executive privilege. This journey didn't happen overnight. It included a progression through the middle and upper classes, which has given me a unique perspective across these classes of society.

But my core experience was set at an early age in a family and community consisting of a lengthy line of blue-collar members. If you sat perched above the chip on my shoulder during my formative years, you would've observed a family and community of great people in the working-class who struggled all their lives for what relatively little they had. Fear was a constant motivator, economic reality was often harsh, and pleasures were simple. There was no such thing as "work-life balance" and many worked in professions that physically broke them down over time. Thick clouds of job security trepidation constantly hung in the air. No one was a four-year college graduate, yet every parent had dreams of the kids going to college and breaking out into a higher socio-economic caste.

As I get older, I realize the experiences in the earlier parts of my journey, from lower-middle-class urban to middle-class suburbs, have defined my habits and preferences more so than any recent experiences. To this day, I am more comfortable in a t-shirt and jeans than khakis and a polo shirt, let alone a suit and tie. And I prefer to cut that grass and pull those weeds in my yard on weekends or to roll out that pizza dough on a Saturday evening.[a]

Born Catholic, I attended a Catholic grade school, served as an altar boy, and dutifully headed to church every Sunday morning with my dad and brother. Jesus understood that what we consider today as socialism was bad. That's why in the Parable of the Rich Fool, when a man asked Jesus to pressure the man's brother to share an inheritance, Jesus responded, "Man, who made me a judge or a divider over you?" (Luke 12:14).

Yet increasingly, I don't subscribe to what I hear coming from the pulpit these days. That may make me a struggling, remedial Christian just like Johnny Cash described himself. I struggle regularly with the tug and pull of feeling on one hand the responsibility to be a good parent and take the kids to Mass, while on the other hand the sense of duty to talk afterwards about how much of what they heard the past hour simply doesn't square with today's world. Add to this on the ride home, opinionated young adults with thoughts of their own, and you can imagine the debate that ensues on a regular basis. Should we continue to go to Mass and focus on what still resonates? Are we better off just contemplating things outside of Mass and skipping the event altogether? Should we find a parish and priest preaching the core foundations and beliefs of the faith?

This internal struggle is intensifying and contrasts with my youth. Catholics are often going through the same struggles, which inspired a book chapter on Pope Francis. After reading the chapter, fellow Catholics may find me guilty of the sin of giving scandal.[b]

I'm currently a registered Republican and a historical Democrat,

---

a   I subscribe to the Henry Rollins view that, "pizza makes me think that anything is possible."

b   The Catechism of the Catholic Church defines scandal as an attitude or behavior which leads another to do evil.

which means I'm a fiscal conservative and a social liberal. As Ronald Reagan once famously said, "I didn't leave the Democratic Party. The party left me."[2] If we could only take about two-thirds of the Republican Party platform and about one-third of the Democratic Party platform, there would be no stopping the United States. Undeniably, that's part of the attraction so many of us felt toward Donald Trump in the 2016 election.

Most middle-class Americans voted for President Trump in 2016, because they realized the Democratic Party had abandoned them long ago in favor of something sinister. The people left behind who turned to President Trump were succinctly and eloquently defined by the great orator but politically flawed Mario Cuomo as, "the middle class, the people not rich enough to be worry-free, but not poor enough to be on welfare; the middle class—those people who work for a living because they have to, not because some psychiatrist told them it was a convenient way to fill the interval between birth and eternity."[3] These people, people I love, are smart enough to realize when self-described liberal elitists pay them nothing more than lip-service for votes and then abruptly abandon them once elected. Cognizance of the elites' arrogance does not make the middle-class racist, bigoted, stupid, or abusive; just astute.

Philosophically, I'm a libertarian, who values personal freedoms favored by modern liberals and economic freedoms favored by modern conservatives. Today, neither of the major parties is for anything other than more government; that is, more government intervention into people's lives, bedrooms, and wallets in innumerable and fantastic ways. In the famous words of Edmund Burke, "The parties are the gamesters; but government keeps the table, and is sure to be the winner in the end."[4] But if you want a say on the ballot, you basically need to choose one of the two sides. So as with the legendary economist Milton Friedman, I am a libertarian with a "small *l*" and a Republican with a "capital *R*."[5] When I find someone running for office who is a Democrat but is closer to my libertarian philosophy than the Republican candidate, I have no problem throwing my full support behind her. Political philosophy should rise above political party affiliation.

MOTIVATED TO SPEAK UP

Why should I write down my thoughts? The most immediate answer is for pleasure. Literature and art are created often by those who simply enjoy it. Jazz legend Miles Davis once declared, "I'm always thinking about creating. My future starts when I wake up in the morning and see the light."[6] If it was good enough for Miles Davis, it is good enough for this aspiring writer.

Yet writing for enjoyment alone can be superficial. There can be a deeper, less superficial urge. Writing is often a painful, at times excruciating process. It has a steep opportunity cost by subtracting from or eliminating entirely other interests in life. This price I'm willing to pay because in a dark corner of my psyche I need to do it.

Another strong motivator I've had in authoring this book is the chance to stand up to the powerful. The same motivation inspired anti-socialist Friedrich Hayek to dedicate his book *Beyond Serfdom* to "socialists of all parties."[7] Actually, those in power already know the truth, making them the potential problem. So, I believe in not only speaking truth to power but informing others. Eventually, truth ends up being what we allow others to get away with, if we don't challenge those in power.[c] Continual civic engagement on vital issues is critical.

This is as American as life, liberty, and the pursuit of happiness. Thomas Jefferson wrote, "For here we are not afraid to follow truth wherever it may lead, nor to tolerate any error so long as reason is left free to combat it."[8] Football great (actually, the greatest ever) Jim Brown realized this when touchdowns weren't enough for him and he saw that hit records weren't enough for his friend, singer Sam Cooke.[9] Brown and Cooke were channeling Jefferson 150 years later and in the context of civil rights. If you don't speak truth to power in a way that allows citizens to take notice, eventually a society of individuals loses the ability to secure life, liberty, and the pursuit of happiness.

---

[c]   Here I took the liberty of paraphrasing the late philosopher, Richard Rorty, who said, "Truth is what your contemporaries let you get away with saying."

George Orwell summed it up well in the 1940s, "My starting point is always a feeling of partisanship, a sense of injustice. When I sit down to write a book, I do not say to myself, 'I am going to produce a work of art.' I write it because there is some lie that I want to expose, some fact to which I want to draw attention, and my initial concern is to get a hearing."[10] Today, there are certainly lies to be exposed and rebutted.

There are insidious segments of our society who are most interested in bleeding the rest of us to death. They have grown in influence and size so that today they are some of the most powerful voices in our country. Those who dare to challenge and question them face threats, attacks, and ridicule. This burgeoning class vilifies legitimate, earned success, while hypocritically appropriating its fruits.

Working for a public energy company, I saw it. Massive bureaucracies, at times heavily colluding with one another, feast on the efforts of honorable people and companies. You find it in government with the alphabet soup of agencies including the SEC, EPA, DOL, and FDA. You find it across academia. You can't miss it in broad segments of nonprofit groups and the media. This new power elite does not respect truth and threatens to kill current and future free enterprise.

Something has flipped in our society over the past few years; we've reached an inflection point. It used to be that the misfits, rebels, revolutionaries, and outsiders were the ones who hung out in coffee shops in big cities, smoking cigarettes (or maybe something else with a little more kick), had a few tattoos, spoke in the abstract, and didn't have obvious employable skills. The only way for these people to make it used to be the long shot of becoming a successful musician, an artist, or a poet. Outside of these few exceptions, all of them ended up living off the fruits of what the rest of us worked to build while contributing next to nothing tangible to society. They are what I call Leeches, or the Leech Class. We've never really paid enough attention to them because we were all busy toiling in the real world.

Oh, how the tables have turned! Today, those same individuals aren't on the outside looking in. Instead, they are running the show, displaying a confidence that smacks of arrogance and relentlessly driving all of us to alien places. For decades, while the rest of us have labored, the Leeches have been infesting government, academia, religious establishments, media, and the arts to program and bully an entire generation into their way of thinking. If you look across powerful segments of society, you see something frightening time and again.

Look at the professional politicians and bureaucrats who run the federal government—not too many of these people ever held a real job where they faced real accountability. Do you think their view of what their mission is has any semblance to the historical mission of our democratic government operating "of the people, by the people, for the people" as Abe Lincoln articulated in the Gettysburg Address?[11] Does a classic federalist view that as much decision-making power as possible should be vested with elected officials in towns, municipalities, and states closest to the people even stand a chance in today's federal government corridors? Washington, D.C. bureaucrats hold frightening sway over society.

Speaking of campuses, let's jump over to those ivory towers of academia, from public school teachers' unions to university administrators. Too few of these people are genuinely interested in the educational mission as parents or employers think of it. They have a mission in mind all right, but it sits in stark contrast to what a parent wants for her child or what a company wants for new hires. The mission is to politicize science, to indoctrinate students with closed-minded rhetoric, and to persecute views or research counter to the rhetoric. Give an apathetic individual a doctorate degree, provide an unlimited budget from government subsidy and inflated student tuition, create a zone where he has no real accountability to instruct (aka tenure), and watch out. But much more on that later.

How about journalism and the mainstream media? Journalism was once a proud profession that attracted talented people from every generation, such as a young Winston Churchill.[12] Healthy functioning societies depended on journalism to protect personal rights with transparency and to help spur advancements in the economy, science, and civics through open dialogue and debate. Today, we find the wholesale rejection of objective journalism and bias instead. Not hatched out of thin air, fake news has been a work in progress for decades, and our duty is to challenge it with truth and logic.

The futures of our kids and grandchildren need brightening. I've seen the damage done to people and communities around me, and it sickens me. The frustration wells up to where I feel like Golda Meir when she said, "I understand the Arabs wanting to wipe us out, but do they really expect us to cooperate?"[13] With stakes this high not to fall on the side of action would be an ethical failure.

Without pushback, the relentless attacks by our elites on my corner of the world will only continue. These intellectual elites display a thin veneer of altruistic paternalism toward the working class, yet just below that surface hides a deep-rooted disdain for everyday people. My region, call it western Pennsylvania or Pittsburgh or northern Appalachia, has been relentlessly vilified by such intellectuals who espouse myths. Our way of life and our values, which built this country into the envy of the world, have come under siege. Knowing there are so many out there in this great country feeling and seeing the same things makes me want to connect with them and offer support.

We have a saying in the energy industry in the context of employee safety and the responsibility to look out for not just yourself but your coworkers around you: "see something, say something, do something." If you can adopt this mentality in the way you think about, approach, and perform your daily job, it is amazing the positive impact it will have on avoiding accidents and becoming more efficient.

The philosophy of "see something, say something, do something" I've adopted in this book. It leads to a desire to stand up, not just for my little corner of the world, but also for the individuals who sustain society. Emotions triggered by what I see motivate me to dissent and to speak out. Plus, the corollary of "see something, say something, do something" is that if someone sees a fraud being perpetrated and does not speak out against it, that person is effectively guilty of aiding and abetting the fraud. I don't like the idea of being a fraud.

When I see the kinds of destructive things I'll discuss in this book occurring in our society, it frustrates me. The urban public school administrator who sends his kids to a suburban or private school drives me crazy. The church that preaches abstaining from sex to its flock and covers up thousands of sexual assaults by its priests over decades infuriates me. The urban housing government bureaucrat who has never had to spend a night in the decrepit buildings he manages riles me. We can only hope that the spirit behind "see something, say something" will encourage more people to "do something."

CONSEQUENCES

For years, I subscribed to a demeanor of political quietism, where I tended to keep opinions to myself and an inner circle of friends and confidants. Silence, though not ideal, was not self-betrayal, if I refused to compromise my principles. The best business leaders in today's anti-achievement environment sit silent, which is superior to empty bromides that so many business leaders cower behind.

Silence and bromides betray those languishing without a voice. The subjects in this book, which put an end to my political quietism, will produce consequences. John Ruskin quipped, "You may either win your peace or buy it: win it, by resistance to evil; buy it, by compromise with evil."[14] Silence, and certainly compromise, just don't work for me anymore. The only way to stand up to a bully is to take one on. It's the simple, seventh grade playground rule: when you see a bully, who creates a sham aura, there is a duty to counter it. I didn't learn everything I needed to know in kindergarten. Everything I needed to know in the real-life *Lord of the Flies*, I learned in middle school. Conjuring Midge Decter, "You have to join the side you're on."[15]

Throughout history, men better than I am, taking a bold step forward, felt intense pressure from the establishment and wilted. Everyone rightfully admires Galileo for daring to propose the certainty that the earth rotates around the sun. He stood up to the most powerful establishment at the time, the Catholic Church, and had the courage to challenge the flawed scientific consensus. But eventually, Galileo publicly recanted his theory once the Catholic Church's pressure took its toll on him, and the Catholic Church didn't officially clear Galileo's name until 1992.[16]

HIGH STAKES

The situation today threatens a core premise that our country was founded on; concentrated power is evil and must be contained to preserve individual freedoms. Because so much is at stake, we must remember Malcolm X when he said, "Usually when people are sad, they don't do anything. They just cry over their condition. But when they get angry, they bring about a change."[17] It is time to bring about change.

Is it too late? Perhaps. Yet engaging in this debate, even if resulting in defeat, fulfills the worthy purpose of staking the marker of truth so that future generations may pick up the cause and carry on.

THE AWESOMENESS OF CREATORS, ENABLERS, AND SERVERS AND HOW TO DEFINE THE LEECH

"One of these things is not like the others. One of these things just doesn't belong."

JAY ASHER, *THIRTEEN REASONS WHY*

"Only when the human spirit is allowed to invent and create, only when individuals are given a personal stake in deciding economic policies and benefitting from their success—only then can societies remain alive, dynamic, prosperous, progressive, and free."

RONALD REAGAN

THE FOUR BROAD CAREER DEMOGRAPHICS IN MODERN SOCIETY

There are so many career paths. Not everyone needs training in a highly technical field to be a success. Not everyone needs to earn a six-figure salary to have an impact. But society must recognize that certain professions are critical to sustaining and improving our enviable quality of life while other professions are increasingly hostile to it. Certain professions erode everyone's standards of living if they continue economically and culturally to function as a regressive tax on productivity. They present a creeping burden on free enterprise.

All professions and endeavors have a value footprint on society and impact economic utility. The footprint and impact can be large and positive, small, or negative. They might be direct and measurable or indirect and intangible. The footprint and impact could be immediate or take years to crystallize.

Boil it down and you see four categories of jobs, gigs, professions, organizations, or callings today. They are the Big Four, consisting of Creators, Enablers, Servers, and Leeches. The first three of these classes, in the words of Ayn Rand, "are the best of what there is on earth" while the fourth class fits an opposite description.[1] The first three view work as a value while the fourth often views work as nothing more than a means to feed off the efforts of others.

There can be no such thing as a failed Creator, Enabler, or Server; even when they fail at an endeavor the rest of society usually learns something. Conversely, when a Leech achieves its aim the rest of society suffers. The Creators, Enablers, and Servers were summarized well by President Calvin Coolidge when he said, "[T]he chief business of the American people is business. They are profoundly concerned with producing, buying, selling, investing, and prospering in the world."[2] The most important factor responsible for the unprecedented success of the United States over the past 250 years was not the oft-cited Protestant work ethic, large land mass, extensive river system, ocean borders, or luck. Although all of those factors were contributors to our success, the decisive factor was the principle of individual rights. Rights, which as a guiding principle unleashed the Creators, Enablers, and Servers without fear of a system, state, or collective stealing their value. The Creators, Enablers, and Servers of our society built and fuel a culture of making. The Leech stands in stark contrast to and in direct conflict with Creators, Enablers, and Servers.

People today often lament that America has become a nation of fault lines. Yet America since its start has always been a nation of fault lines. We experienced federal government versus states' rights, north versus south, blue-collar versus white-collar, Democrat versus Republican, East versus West, urban versus rural, black versus white, male versus female, populist versus elitist, and a host of other divisions that at times have wreaked havoc on our nation. In the end, the values underpinning what it means to be an American miraculously survived.

Today, we face a different fault line, one that threatens to change who we are as a nation along with the values that drove us to unprecedented heights. That fault line divides Creators, Enablers, and Servers on one side and the Leeches on the other side. Despite Creators, Enablers, and Servers having distinct characteristics that we will explore shortly, all three categories share one crucial trait: their product or effort furthers free enterprise and constitutes economic value. Society can't get enough of Creators, Enablers, and Servers if it wishes to thrive.

Conversely, despite encompassing different professions, organizations, and activities, the Leech is fundamentally a predatory tribe that understands to the extent it can coordinate actions to take from the rest of us, the more it will prosper and grow. This fault line separating the Leech and the rest of us makes a win-win scenario impossible for our country, since it is zero-sum. Whatever the Leech takes, consumes, or grows will come at the expense and to the detriment of the Creator, Enabler, and Server. Since Creators, Enablers, and Servers build, sustain, and grow this country, anything that diminishes their prominence and impedes their efforts will do the same to the country. The inflection point, where the Leech irreversibly and permanently tips the scales to its favor, may be at hand.

THREE THAT MAKE THE WORLD GO ROUND: CREATORS, ENABLERS, AND SERVERS

Let's take a tour of the Big Four, starting with the most crucial: Creators. Most important and the foundation of any modern free society are the engineers, scientists, surgeons, and computer programmers. You might call them techies and geeks, but a more apt label is the Creator class. Creators also include certain blue-collar professions found in construction, the building trades, and manufacturing. The Creator is the embodiment of competent man. Without Creators, we would never have exited the Dark Ages. They create the wealth to distribute and are a prerequisite to others' success.

What is unfortunate and disappointing is that today there is a cultural bias against the Creator class. Everyone, particularly younger people, is bombarded with constant images and messaging that say the Creator class is not cool. Instead, youngsters are exposed to a constant drumbeat of how they should be thinking about and emulating talent-less reality TV stars, morally bankrupt musicians, and professional athletes who mindlessly obsess over how well they can place a ball into some type of open space. To slot a child into the Creator career path today requires a parent or mentor to break the societal gravitational pull away from this path or to insulate the child from popular culture.

What's the litmus test to assess if a job falls into the category of Creator? Simple: does that job create, build, improve, or support something tangible? Something tangible can be a bridge, an airplane, or a power plant. In the tech world it includes the internet and artificial intelligence. Most importantly, it includes the human body. Tangible also includes the creation or development of innovative technologies or new scientific theories. It's the cumulative effort that led to the creations of Henry Ford, Marconi, the Wright brothers, and Jonas Salk. To be a Creator one does not need to be a Ph.D., a genius, or even a college graduate. Productivity alone defines Creators, not a piece of paper hanging on a wall.[a]

The second category is the support team to the Creators: The Enablers. Enablers include everything from accountants, nurses, data clerks, financiers, bus drivers, and clerical workers. The litmus test for the category is to ask if the position, job, or profession makes the job of the Creator and others possible, easier, or more efficient.

---

[a] The Creator class does not include the producers of artistic expression such as musicians, authors, and artists. Those fall within the Server class.

Don't underestimate the importance of this category because without them, the potential of the Creator category is throttled or lost altogether. How effective would surgeons be without the team of operating room nurses next to them? How would an inventor of an innovative technology be able to develop the technology and market it to the public without access to the necessary financing? The Enablers include high-powered financiers making millions of dollars a year for their skills and service, the CPAs and registered nurses making solid livings that allow them to live in pleasant bedroom communities, and clerks working in cubicle farms for yeomen's wages. Police and our armed forces are Enablers of society at large, giving security and maintaining the rule of law.

The third category is the Servers. Servers might seem easy to define, the waitress, fitness trainer, mechanic, landscaper, etc. There are other, more famous members of the Server class that may not at once pop into your mind: musicians, actors, and professional athletes.

The Servers class is much larger than most people think, because technology and advancements delivered by the Creator class keep expanding the type of services that are available to us. What Creators giveth to the Servers they also taketh via creative destruction. Think of Uber as a notable example of how technology and the Creators birthed a new Server profession of Uber driver. Today, the Uber driver is well on his way to destroying the traditional Server profession of taxi driver, notwithstanding New York City's politicians' attempts to protect the outdated system from modern-day reality (a topic we will discuss later).

Another reason the Server category is much larger than what we believe is that people in this category often want to redefine it as something else. Wrongly, certain people have a negative view of service providers and view employment in this category as less than desirable. Servers offer two vital things to society: an improved quality of life for individuals and increased efficiency for everyone. Two examples illustrate these two benefits of the Servers. First is the waitress at a restaurant who allows the rest of us to enjoy dinner out with friends in the evening. Second is the landscaper who takes on a necessary task of cutting the grass and frees up the available time of the homeowner to spend in areas where he is most productive. This second example is a classic illustration of the economic theory of utility. Note that this is different from what the Enablers provide alongside the efforts of the Creators. The Enablers are necessary to allow the Creator to function. Here, the Server is simply taking on a task that the customers could have done themselves and by doing so opens more time for the customers to do other things.

The essential components of society would function without Servers, but our quality of life would surely be diminished. In other words, without Servers our lives would be a lot duller, less efficient, and boring. But make no mistake: Servers rely on the earlier contributions to society of the Creator and Enabler classes. The Uber driver can't work without the automobile and the internet. The chef can't cook without the natural gas and the refrigeration. The musician can't perform in the arena without the trucks, the audio-visual digital equipment, and the electricity. Often, however, society inflates the status of certain Servers (including business executives) to outrageous heights.

SOCIETY'S CONFUSION WITH SERVERS

Servers often provide a luxury or a want, not a need. Today, society not only places certain segments of the Servers in high esteem, but society at times worships them by treating them as modern-day demigods; a distortion that leads to skewed priorities and an inflated importance. Roles quickly get reversed, and before you know it, instead of the Server being there for the benefit of the rest of us, the rest of us are there for the benefit of the Server.

You see this phenomenon with professional sports. Think of the star basketball player whom kids and many adults will follow and try to emulate every move he makes, whether on the court or off the court (just don't ask basketball stars to take a social justice stand against Chinese government oppression). In the end, having that athlete available to us for entertainment serves as nothing more than pleasant distraction from more stressful and important things in life. But if the athlete, the team, and the league disappeared tomorrow, life as we know it would march on.

In fact, things might improve if professional sports were to disappear. That's because society invests too many resources into these Servers via publicly financed stadiums and various other subsidies. The opportunity costs of not being able to put those resources to better use outweigh the purely entertainment and questionable economic benefits of these public subsidies for professional sports. Yet the pipeline of public subsidy continues to flow, often justified by misleading economic analyses using outrageous assumptions to project an image of financial justification. Throwing hundreds of millions of taxpayer dollars at billionaire owners so that they can build stadiums only used during part of the year and employ a small handful of non-resident multi-millionaire athletes, supported by an army of hourly workers making nothing close to a living wage should be thrown out as a sham.

Things are not much different in college athletics. Let's face it: major college athletics these days are no different than professional sports. Many people are shocked to learn that in thirty-nine of the fifty states the highest-paid state employee is either a university football coach or basketball coach.[3] In most of these thirty-nine states the difference between what the college coach is paid and what the governor is paid exceeds a factor of ten. Public university football and basketball coaches in these thirty-nine states have compensation levels that grossly exceed the pay packages for the heads of the state medical, law enforcement, and educational organizations. Taxpayers in these thirty-nine states are forced to pay excessive amounts of money for someone who can design a 3–4 defense or who can talk a seventeen-year-old into committing to the state school basketball program instead of those dollars being invested in efforts to provide improved cancer care, to keep the streets safe, or to improve math and reading proficiency in the public school systems.

Food for thought the next time you attend a sporting event: you are paying big bucks and wasting valuable free time to watch how well an adult or, in the case of college athletics, a kid, can kick, shoot, or throw a certain-sized circular-shaped orb into a defined space. Those shekels you shelled out for the tickets, parking, and concessions are on top of what you've already paid in income, sales, and property taxes that were used to pay for the stadium.

The skewed values when it comes to professional and big-time college sports have a negative impact beyond dollars and cents and act as a drag on our economy and society. Much more impactful and important are how astronomical salaries and media obsession on the select few athletes and coaches inspire countless kids and their parents to shoot for a career in professional sports. The odds of that occurring are excruciatingly long, to the point where they rival the odds of winning the Powerball lottery. For every 0.1% of student athletes that make it to the big money, 99.9% do not make it and are at increased risk of having no skills or career to fall back on. At least if a kid aspires and works to be the next Steve Jobs and fails, she is likely to have a fulfilling career and a rewarding life because of what she learned, developed, and earned educationally along the way.

A comparable situation is found with musicians and rock stars. Despite the common, often-repeated tagline out there about how rock and roll "changes the world" and inspires generations, the fact of the matter is that rock music is nothing more than a pleasant distraction from the day-to-day grind. Rock music and musicians change nothing substantial in this world; meaningful change only comes from the tenacious effort and accomplishment of individual drive. Music is nothing more than a luxury and mode of entertainment. If the music stops, life will march on with the same intensity it always has.

Looking to rock stars to figure out where you should stand on things like gun rights, free speech, and various areas of government policy is a form of self-inflicted ignorance. I'd rather go to a concert of an established artist and listen to an hour of the dreaded "new material" that no one wants to hear rather than listen to thirty seconds of their view on occupied Kashmir. Performer, please, focus on the next album or tour instead of lecturing us on how we should think or vote. The actual societal benefit you offer is a tiny fraction of what you think you provide.

The next time you are at a concert, look around at the audience. You will see scores of grown men and women acting like crazed children as they scream their adulation to the performer. As if the performer even gives a damn. The typical, romanticized formula for success applied by most of these artists is to continually self-indulge until divine inspiration transpires. Hopefully, they hit it big and make loads of money. Yet the performer might ultimately squander his fortune in hollow pursuits and poor decisions before he falls off the public radar to be replaced by another.

Then there are the select few, held in the highest esteem by the fawning media and ignorant fans, portrayed as true artistic demigods in the purest form. That's hogwash, too. Critically acclaimed musicians have been known to do commercials for clothing, promote alcohol brands, and appear in food commercials.[4,5,6] Acts across the musical spectrum promote websites pushing overpriced merchandise, while so many of these socially conscious charlatans have armed guards, live behind compound walls, and fly in private chartered jets with massive carbon footprints.

If you want to see a truly honest musician today, look no further than Gene Simmons of Kiss, who is unabashed about his willingness to endorse numerous products and market his image and act to its full revenue potential. Musicians, from Gene Simmons to Bob Dylan, provide a discretionary service to the rest of us for a fee, and they constantly look to gather more revenue to create a lifestyle for themselves.

Reinforcing the popular, self-important inflated image of rock and pop performers is a cadre of self-described journalists and critics who magnify the sound chamber of the profound messages from the artist. These individuals are not exactly the illuminati of our society. Stop asking them for insight into complex or meaningful issues. Remember, the performer is there for the audience and not the other way around. Freebird!

Since we are talking about rock stars and athletes who are entertainment Servers masquerading as thought-leaders and the conscience of society, it makes sense to discuss Hollywood. Movies and television are no longer about entertaining. They are all about programming thought and views. Hollywood has become a massive propaganda machine for a certain set of mores and issues. The overwhelming majority of entertainment delivers a favorable impression for certain views and an unfavorable impression for other views.

Film and TV writers, producers, and actors are classic Servers despite years of posing as a higher authority. I never understood how *The Mary Tyler Moore Show*, *Maude*, or *MASH* single-handedly changed society's views on a host of political and cultural issues. Thinking you've changed where America stands on an issue is different from having an actual impact. Film and TV elites in New York and Los Angeles, subsidized by the government using our money, want to believe they set the agenda and norms for the rest of us through their lecturing, glib scripts. People watch for entertainment—to laugh and pass the time. Unfortunately, the current roster of late-night hosts is so different from Johnny Carson and seem only capable of offering political and ideological jokes for half the country. Viewers typically do not want to and should not watch a late-night entertainment show to find out what their position should be on meaningful issues. The more late-night TV hosts, film directors, and TV writers try to lecture, the more people will turn off and tune out.

Although rock stars, Hollywood, and professional athletes perform a Server function, they find themselves often commandeered by the worst type of profession, one that we will soon explore. In certain instances, the athlete or music artist is a shill, unwittingly duped and exploited. Other times the pompous, self-important jock or singer is a willing accomplice whose actions are blatantly hypocritical to his words. In either instance, nothing will change until the rest of us re-establish the pecking order of who serves whom.

These narcissistic celebrities keep pushing new horizons to express their ignorance. Take a recent interview of an actor, who provided his views on subjects ranging from music he likes to shows he watches. In that article he bragged about solar panels on his house and how they allow him to power his home and drive his Tesla (shocking, I know) emission-free.[7]

Although the ideal of an emission free lifestyle may be desirable to this actor, someone should explain to him that there is no such thing as emission-free electricity generation. Mining rare earth materials for solar panels is an extremely carbon-intensive activity with heavy disturbance of the land, which requires carbon and fossil fuels. Once you have the materials, you then need to manufacture the solar panel and the electric vehicle, which requires even more carbon and fossil fuels. When the sun doesn't shine, guess what? You're sucking electricity off the grid, which is heavily dependent on natural gas, a carbon-based fossil fuel. These truths may disturb the actor's content view of his carbon footprint; reality has a habit of doing that to the best of us from time to time.

Without a proper pecking order, you end up with despicable behavior admired and noble actions deplored. The Vietnam era proved upside-down values distort reality. We should admire the average guy in the 1960s, who had his number pulled in the draft and answered the call in Vietnam, even when the war became a lost cause. That's a hero. Although I disdain violence, I empathize with the construction workers in New York City who, when provoked by anti-war demonstrators, delivered retribution in return. I look with disdain upon the film star who visited Hanoi for a photo-op, the hippie musician who dodged the draft and instead went to Woodstock to sing to a bunch of drug-numbed slackers lying in the mud, or the privileged class of college students throwing projectiles and spitting on police on the streets of Chicago in 1968 while avoiding the draft. Don't even get me started on anti-war leftists waving the North Vietnamese flag down the streets of our cities or the men who ran to Canada to hide under the false banner of political protest. Those individuals were not heroes; they were weak-minded, ignorant pawns used by those wishing to manipulate them for darker designs. They should walk the Vietnam Memorial in Washington, D.C., and then apologize for their pathetic actions to the vets there scanning the wall for the names of their buddies who didn't make it home.

The only anti-war protestors who deserve true respect were the veterans who legitimately served. They earned the right to protest and a hearing, even when they were throwing their medals over a barricade at the Capitol—except for John Kerry (regardless if he threw away or kept his medals), who in his infamous self-promoting speech to Congress accused American soldiers of acting dishonorably. As to the *Pentagon Papers* and how that generation learned to their horror that the government was less than truthful throughout the war, what is so shocking about that? Government lies to the people all the time. President Lincoln sugar-coated early Union military disasters suffered at the hands of the Confederacy. Prime Minister Churchill and Comrade Stalin took quite the poetic license when orating a rosier-than-actual situation in the early days of World War II. Those who continue to express dismay and shock that our government misled us during Vietnam should read a history book to understand that's what government does. To place blind trust in government is ignorant naivety and runs counter to Churchill's assertion that, "In wartime, truth is so precious that she should always be attended by a bodyguard of lies."[8]

Today, scores of baby boomers continue to canonize not those who answered the call but those who posed. The media, playing only one side of the incredibly complicated Vietnam saga, only confuses with misleading story lines. All this proves that a significant segment of that generation was the "*Leastest* Generation." Many went on to become celebrated career influencers in government, academia, and the arts. That is not by accident but by design, which is a good segue into our final category of job types.

THE LEECH AND ITS TELLTALE SIGNS: THE "LEECH WAY"
The fourth and final category of job type is the Leech. A fundamental differentiator from Creators, Enablers, and Servers is that the Leech and the professions it now dominates work and interact among one another as what political and social commentators often refer to as a tribe. Yet a more apt descriptor is the Leech as an organism, one with its own set of innate behaviors and instinctive tools. Whether labeled as a tribe or an organism, the Leech's growing burden on our society should sound

a call to action, for the Leech inherently is at best amoral and at worst immoral. As it prospers, Western civilization's core tenets of individual rights, free enterprise, and capitalism are at stake.

The Leech as an organism grows by controlling and feeding off Creators, Enablers, and Servers. A Leech is different from a liberal, progressive, or Democrat; for there are scores of all three who are Creators, Enablers, and Servers. True liberals focus on personal freedom for social issues, and traditional Democrats aligned their platforms with the needs of specific demographic segments of society.[b] Whether you agreed or disagreed, these well-established positions defined both groups year after year. That is not what governs the behavior of the Leech. Its DNA is wired to apply a menu of tactics that aids in its single-minded obsession with achieving relentless control and exclusively personal growth; I refer to its DNA as the "Leech way."

A crucial aspect of the Leech way is its ability to adopt convenient ideologies to cloak its singular intention of achieving control and its obsession with growth. That's why we find a high density of Leeches in modern liberal and Democratic-dominated bastions, both geographic and professional. The Leech injects itself into the ideology, agendas, and strategic direction of these liberal, progressive, and Democratic-dominated organizations and professions because it recognizes they serve as convenient hosts. The Leech converts one person and one organization at a time within these circles, slowly growing its critical mass of influence. At a certain point, the Leech assumes control of these entities and uses them to perform its future bidding. In the end, the original host is nothing more than a hollow shell with a familiar name. What we knew it once to be, it no longer is. What it officially stands for as espoused by its boilerplate mission statement is quite different from

---

b   When I state "true liberals" I reference the term as applied in the modern sense. Classic liberals are an altogether different, and far superior, animal than modern liberals. Classic liberals favored personal freedom and economic freedom while modern liberals are quite statist when it comes to economic freedom. That lack of economic freedom and support of state intervention usually makes the modern liberal an unwitting instrument of the Leech.

what it really stands for in its tangible actions. Ideology and mission end up being nothing more than a justification for its growth.

That means the Leech is free to morph what were once stalwart positions on critical issues into different or even polar-opposite positions. You see it frequently with politicians who switch views on core issues the moment the political winds change. The Leech way appropriates Lord Palmerston's statecraft observation that nations have no permanent allies, only permanent interests. Shapeshifting on ideology to serve the permanent interest of growing power and control is fundamental to the Leech way.[c]

This phenomenon is why throughout this book I correlate adjectives such as *apparent, self-described, so-called,* and *supposed* to the nouns *liberal, progressive,* and *Democrat.* The meaning of *liberal* has changed so substantially the past few decades that the label no longer correlates to what it once was. What it used to mean to be a Democrat no longer exists. Progressives, as we knew them, are gone. The genius of the Leech is that it managed unprecedented growth in its ranks and subsumed scores of professions, organizations, and movements without ever having to out itself as something altogether different and unique. Only the enormous success and prevalence of the Leech in our society makes it impossible for them to go unnoticed. Yet so many people who subscribe to liberalism, the Democratic Party, certain organizations, or movements don't realize with whom they are affiliating. The remaining few true liberals and Democrats out there must feel like a human left at the end of the *Invasion of the Body Snatchers.*[9]

Another aspect of the Leech way is a cunning ability to fuse religious and philosophical theory into a workable dogma, applied across a range of professions and situations. Just as extreme Islam applies dawah to

------

c   Leech ideological shapeshifting in action on a grand policy scale is evident with the environment. Jonah Goldberg of the *National Review* brilliantly points out how FDR's New Deal was based on the theory of war against nature while current Leechdom's Green New Deal is based on the theory of war to restore nature.

force sharia law on society, the Leech deftly applies its dogma so that it does the thinking and makes the decisions for the rest of us. Today, it might be climate change, equal outcomes, and identity politics; tomorrow it can shift to something different. Society's psychology shifts to align with the Leech dogma. This approach stands in contrast to its opposite: The Enlightenment.

The Enlightenment drove a seismic shift in Western civilization. The 1700s saw a shift away from religious and aristocratic institutions that thought for the individual and toward the ability and responsibility of people to think for themselves. Guiding lights, albeit somewhat flawed, like Immanuel Kant encouraged people to question authority and felt a meaningful life equated to the attitude of "dare to know."[d] One could argue the Enlightenment was the genesis of the Creator, Enabler, and Server; where the individual, not the collective or the entrenched elite, deserved the fruits of his own labor. The Enlightenment was a foundational step toward elevating reason above ignorance and created a duty of self-determination for the individual.

The Leech way of religion and philosophy is the antithesis of the Enlightenment and calls for a return to the subjugation of the Creator, Enabler, and Server. In truth, the Leech espouses a regression to ignorance, rational immaturity, and blind acceptance of doctrine set by self-described authorities. The Leech wishes society to reverse hundreds of years of progress, with the goal of blind acceptance of authority and thought akin to the way things were in the early 1700s. Attacking success and achievement from all directions, the Leech understands that making decisions and thinking for us can act like a drug. Slowly, more of us stop thinking, stop challenging, and blindly obey the higher authorities. Once everyone else tells you what to do, inertia and human nature help preserve the status

---

d   The "dare to know" line was Kant's preferred motto for the Enlightenment. To me, Kant is flawed due to his rejection of man's pursuit of happiness as a noble endeavor and his suspect views that demote reason. Nevertheless, Kant was a thought-leader who projected Western civilization into a higher, brighter era. For a great summary of what the Enlightenment was, read Kant's 1784 essay *What is Enlightenment?*

quo. As Kant wrote, "But on all sides I hear: 'Do not argue!' The officer says, 'Do not argue, drill!' The tax man says, 'Do not argue, pay!' The pastor says, 'Do not argue, believe!'"[10] The Leech believes that ordinary people must be broken-in and trained using both positive (for heeding) and negative (for resisting) reinforcement sparingly. The mechanism used to pull society back into the sphere of submission to higher authorities is government subsidy and paternalism. Individuals morph into a flock, with the flock blunted, bled, and harvested for Leech benefit.

The Leech way applies a view of win-lose between the Leech and Creators, Enablers, and Servers. The Leech knows it only grows and wins if the rest of us lose and shrink; it creates and operates within a state of conflict between those who make the rules and those who must comply with them. The economy, legal system, and government are increasingly rigged to institutionalize conflict and ensure outcomes that result in the value of the Creator, Enabler, and Server being appropriated and redistributed. Although the circumstances and times are different, the situation is eerily like the Cold War, where Communism stood in direct conflict with the economic and individual freedoms of the West; a classic win-lose situation. The Leech way, using the tactic of hiding within host entities, fights through various proxies like the Soviets used puppet intermediaries of Cuba, Vietnam, and East Germany to expand its influence.

The Leech way sees the value in scale to help achieve ambitions. Top-down, command-and-control, centralized authority is a tip-off of Leeches at work. This top-down, command-and-control centralized concentration of power employed under the Leech way is exactly what the Founding Fathers feared. Certain features of the Constitution looked to defuse such danger, from states' rights to the Bill of Rights for personal freedoms to the checks and balances of the three branches of government. The Leech has become quite adept at working around those liberties.

Propaganda is another core tactic of the Leech way and serves as an effective complement to the Leech's ability to hide within host entities while adopting prevailing ideologies. The Leech, like the Soviets (Lenin espoused seducing the public by secret operation and surprise), uses disinformation to wage its campaign upon society. Patiently pressed over years, the campaign delivers long-term returns. The United States came to realize the Soviet Union could never be appeased, only contained, or defeated. A similar realization for China is dawning on us. The Leech requires the same understanding.

The Leech way has the heart of a monopolist; for the Leech knows if it controls thought, ideas, and choices in a society, it controls everything. It decides who wins and who loses, and who suffers punishment. For the Leech, economic competition and individual freedom are extinguishable. The Leech behaves under the antithesis of President Calvin Coolidge's incantation of, "don't expect to build up the weak by pulling down the strong."[11] To the Leech, the strong must be bled dry to feed a growing nonproductive class.

The Leech way embraces the authoritarian playbook. Consider Russia's Vladimir Putin's rise to power. Putin coldly and clinically approaches Creators, Enablers, and Servers and offers them one of two choices: either hand over a substantial portion and control of their enterprises to him or face dire consequences. What is a consequence? Typically, for those who choose to resist, a public example can be made of them. This may include seizure of property, imprisonment, and an untimely, mysterious death. Putin does not allow simple things like borders to get in the way of making examples of those who resist; he is happy to impose deadly consequences anywhere. Once a horrific example happens, others are more likely to genuflect at his feet.

In the United States and Europe, Creators, Enablers, and Servers fall into the Leech's maw through similar unrelenting and aggressive muscling. That's why you see behavior across a host of industries that does not make sense. There are examples, including fossil fuel energy companies conspicuously shaming themselves and their products while swearing allegiance to inferior renewable energy sources. These companies saw what happened to the coal industry when it refused to toe the line, and they are rightfully fearful of a similar fate. Tech companies such as Facebook openly welcome government regulation of their businesses. Corporations curry favor with and appease the Leech, wrongly assuming their obeisance will help profitability. Nevertheless, vulnerable companies and industries are learning that appeasement only delays the inevitable. And when the battle finally arrives, appeasement has made the Leech stronger.

In comparing the Leech way with communism, socialism, and dictatorships, a distinction is necessary. A socialist or communist is obsessed with redistributing wealth from one group to another. Their scam is what Margaret Thatcher referred to as the endless shuffling of shekels around, with no wealth or value being created.[12] A Leech certainly wants to redistribute wealth, but not in the way a socialist or communist would desire. It goes further and wants not just to redistribute wealth but to consume it. Remaking society, the economy, and thought allows the Leech to eat.

The Leech way is not easygoing or lazy. One of the most important characteristics is it seeks ways constantly to expand its network so that it can feed, tax, and suck out more of the world around it. It adeptly plays the long game; thus, the Leech is much more dangerous than a run-of-the-mill looter looking for instant gratification. The Leech is obsessive and unrelenting, continually probing for prey further and deeper.

Those operating under the Leech way are adept marketers to the rest of society and mask their true intentions and portray themselves as something vital. The government bureaucrat looks after your safety. The environmental organization improves the air you breathe. The university administration and faculty broaden your horizons. The religious leader preaches selflessness as a virtue. Yet in each case their true intentions are to take more resources and decision-making away from us. Whereas the collectivist stifles the individual through wealth redistribution, the Leech left unchecked will destroy the individual by consuming him and his value. The Leech markets a lie to the point where the rest of us accept it as truth.

The Leech way demands strong and tight coordination across the varied professions. FDR summed up this aspect of the Leech way best when he said in one of his fireside chats, "[T]hose who cooperate in this program must know each other at a glance."[13] Dogma, religion, and philosophy are constantly propounded in the schools, reinforced by the media, funded by the government, and protected by the bureaucratic regulator. Homogeneity of thought through methodical destruction of alternative views is a prerequisite to a sustainable Leech ecosystem, reflecting a real, modern-day version of *Fahrenheit 451*.[e]

The extent of coordination under the Leech way across key professions and disciplines is impressive. Many decry the Iron Triangle of Washington, D.C., where three corners of politician, bureaucrat, and lobbyist coordinate to create an unvirtuous cycle of graft and redistribution.[14] The Leech has taken the Iron Triangle and applied it on a much grander scale, where the politician and government bureaucrat now work in continual concert not just with lobbyists but also with academia, the media, the plaintiffs' bar, environmental groups, and public sector unions.

Coordination across the Leech-dense spheres of academia, government, politicians, and the media changes the basic vocabulary and connotation of fundamental beliefs right under society's nose with few noticing. Language for eons has evolved freely, changing as individuals developed novel words or revised the meaning of old ones. No longer; the Leech understands the power of language and has methodically labored to control and regulate it, like it does commerce and personal decision-making.

You see a re-coding of vocabulary everywhere today that mirrors Big Brother's Newspeak.[f] The most fundamental yet nuanced change

---

e   The dystopian novel *Fahrenheit 451* by Ray Bradbury appeared in 1953. The story takes place in a then future society, where authorities outlaw books and selected firemen burn them. The temperature at which book paper burns is 451°. The lead character is one of the firemen who quits his job and joins a resistance group who preserve great literary and cultural works by memorizing them. There is hope for certain Leeches yet.

f   In the novel *1984*, Newspeak was the official language of Oceania used to further the aims of English Socialism. Newspeak served the dual purpose of reinforcing state doctrine and making free thought impossible.

in terminology is supplanting "the truth" with "my truth," "her truth," and "their truth." Once you dissolve the concept of objective truth, a world of opportunity exists to chisel away other core tenets of free enterprise and liberty. What was once "government spending" is now "investment." "Global warming" had a niggling problem of the globe not actually warming so it morphed into the broader "climate change." What we remember as "censorship" is now "tolerance." Core tenets of "equal rights" and "equal opportunity" slipped to "equal outcomes." And "freedom" has mutated to "fairness," with the Leech getting to decide what is fair. Certainly, the most distressing must be how "keeping what you have earned" has turned to "greed" and how "socialism" has evolved to "equity." When you change words and terminology central to a society's values, you change beliefs and society itself.

The Leech way encourages the manipulation of the distracted or less enlightened segments of Creators, Enablers, and Servers to tighten its grip. You see it every time a star athlete weighs in on a geopolitical issue as if he has wisdom beyond the rest of us. You see it when an actor suddenly feels the urge to preach her rhetoric to viewers at an awards show. You see it when a burnt-out rock star begins to speak out on a complicated economic issue as if it were simple, yet he can't function on his own without handlers. It is no coincidence that Fascists and socialists through history demanded that sports and entertainment culture conformed to the image and messages of the state and that the Leech way today appropriates sports, entertainment, and social media culture in the same way. To the extent that the Leech can dupe us into not only turning a dull eye from his actions but in many cases even helping him in his quest, we become those "useful idiots" attributed to Lenin or the more forgiving "useful innocents" Ludwig von Mises wrote about.[g]

If you think this an exaggeration, consider the views of a former President of the European Commission. Back in 1999, he famously

---

[g]   "Useful idiots" is a phrase often attributed to Lenin despite lack of a written record. "Useful innocents" can be found in Ludwig von Mises' 1947 book *Planned Chaos*.

stated in an interview how the EU bureaucracy deals with Creators, Enablers, and Servers: "We decide on something, leave it lying around, and wait and see what happens. If no one kicks up a fuss, because most people don't understand what has been decided, we continue step by step until there is no turning back."[15] Make no mistake, our ignorance is one of the most powerful weapons of the Leech.

Professions often infiltrated by the Leech are large and varied. The ties that bind these professions together become tactics of the Leech way. One could develop a formal, technical description of what defines a Leech profession. But let's define it by listing the things it is *not*, then by one thing it typically is, and finally, one thing that it *always* is. A Leech does *not* create something tangible. A Leech does *not* support building something of value. A Leech does *not* make life better or more enjoyable. A Leech will usually look to create unneeded rules, processes, and systems that require its existence and protects its activity or markets. And a Leech *always* skims an ever-growing part of the value created by someone else.

Leeches construct rules, tactics, or norms that protect their ability to live off and freeload on other people's sweat, creativity, talent, and effort. Growth is usually self-enabled: a new regulation issued by one bureaucrat births a new bureaucrat, while rhetoric drilled into students by college faculty creates the justification for more school administrators. State public utility commission bureaucrats gift monopoly utilities (heavily laden with their own bureaucracy) a guaranteed rate of return and at the same time force mandates for expensive wind and solar projects that get built on productive rate payers' backs. Think of the Leech class as an anti-innovation, rent-seeking tax on society. If this burden grows too large or takes too big a cut from the Creators, Enablers, and Servers, the entire system eventually collapses. Left unchecked, the Leech eventually sucks the life right out of the host organism.

Recognize that individuals can become unwitting components of the Leech machine. The individual's intentions may be pure, and he might put heart and soul into his work, believing that he's making a vital contribution to the betterment of society. This is completely understandable as many of us are fed propaganda and fables about how things work.

Cultivating unwitting individuals to work for the Leech is done through the unrelenting branding and messaging of society designed to lure talent and workers. In the 1950s, the coolest thing a kid would hope to be was a builder of things like bridges, cars, and buildings. The kid saw positive messages of those endeavors (think Tonka Toys™ and chemistry sets) and he aspired to do those things (picture building forts in woods and tree houses in yards). Then, in the 1960s and 1970s, the sexy jobs that you wanted when you grew up were where you got to manage, or boss, the people doing the work. You didn't necessarily want to be the engineer, you wanted to be the manager instead, in charge of engineers. Or the kid dreamed of becoming a doctor where he could supply a professional service that would be in demand. The good news for this aspiration was that if you fell short in your ambition you were likely to still have a productive career within whatever field you managed. Then, in the 1980s and 1990s, desirable career paths evolved into the types of endeavors that didn't do much building, serving, or managing at all but instead looked to insert itself into the middle of these things and demand a share of the economic rent. Law schools burst at the seams with enrollment, and everyone wanted to be an M&A banker on Wall Street or a partner for McKinsey. Adulated in movies, people associated those professions with power and money. We should not be shocked that today we find significant components of our economy and workforce engaged in activities that don't create, grow, or preserve anything. Too many individuals in these professions are as much a victim as the rest of us.

Yet we have a responsibility to wake up. First, an unwitting good-hearted person toiling competently for the Leech can have a damaging impact. Second, there is nothing worse than the individual who has neither the self-awareness nor the independence to think for himself. Martin Luther King Jr. said it best with, "Nothing in all the world is more dangerous than sincere ignorance."[16]

The knowing, scheming Leech is one thing—a worthy enemy who is fully aware of what he does. Disdain him, yes, but respect him too as someone who acts and takes control. But the unwitting supporter is altogether different—used by the knower and schemer. That is a sad way to wade through life and smacks of blindly following a religion. Once awoken from the religion that has lulled him into obedience, the unwitting must assume some responsibility to see things for what they are and change.

THE LEECH DRINKS SOCIETY'S WATER WHILE THE REST CARRY SOCIETY'S WATER

Simply being against something is rarely enough to inspire. To motivate people to act, one needs to fight for something. Yes, I am against the Leech and what it means for our country. But more fundamental than my antipathy to the Leech is my love and devotion to the Creators, Enablers, and Servers of our society. Society's focus should be on freeing talented individuals within these three classes to achieve and innovate, not on redistributing property and wealth to the nonproductive.

In a now-famous rant that has gone viral, CNBC's Rick Santelli astutely argued society should, "reward people that can carry the water instead of drink the water."[17] Santelli was expressing what Thomas Paine meant over 225 years ago when he separated society into two classes: those who pay taxes and those who received taxes.[18] Creators, Enablers, and Servers carry society's water while the Leech does nothing but drink the water. Unfortunately, the deck is stacked today disproportionally against those who carry the water. The top 50% of earners constitute 97% of total income tax.[19] That is the result of a methodical campaign waged for years across many fronts; a danger to a democracy where the majority votes for increased spending that the minority is forced to pay.

Franz Oppenheimer foresaw the current situation long ago when he assessed that humans have two basic methods to satisfy core needs: through one's own work and through the robbery of another's work.[20] One's own work comes via economic means in a free society; while robbery of another's work comes via legal, political means. Robbery and appropriation of others' work through political means is in Leech DNA.

The Leech has progressed from an external threat to society to an internal one. Liberal lawyer Howard Moore Jr. noted in the early 1970s that, "[T]here is no such thing as a legal revolution. All revolutions are illegal."[21] That statement was backed up by hundreds, if not thousands, of years of human experience. Today, that statement requires an asterisk beside it, because it no longer is an absolute. Through cunning, patience, and strategy the Leech has manufactured revolutionary change in the United States and across Western society. While the rest of us were distracted by life and not paying attention, the Leech methodically embarked on a fundamental re-engineering of the values, priorities, processes, and pecking order of our free society. This strategic long game was not only worked within the existing laws but it also evolved the laws so that they could be more accommodating tactical tools to help the campaign. I hold great disdain and contempt for the Leech and view him as society's enemy. But I must admit a certain degree of respect and admiration for what he has achieved, for he has delivered the first legal revolution in the history of mankind.

At the same time, politicians who embrace the Leech way and its ideology have performed one of the most impressive jiu-jitsu mind control moves ever. Bernie Sanders, Elizabeth Warren, and their ilk have convinced millions of legitimate Creators, Enablers, and Servers to vote against their own interests in elections. Smart people with college degrees working in fields that meet an array of vital needs of society willingly support politicians, laws, and policies that not only clearly harm free enterprise but also damage the individual's position in life; it's Stockholm Syndrome on an unbelievably grand scale.

America's global rivals understand the fundamental difference between Creators, Enablers, Servers, and the Leech. That is why China performs industrial espionage and pilfers technology from industries in key sectors of manufacturing, fossil fuel energy, defense, financial tech, IT, and data handling. You won't find the Chinese government, or its proxies, looking to steal or copy our legal profession, media, government bureaucracy, entertainment, environmental organizations, or urban planning anytime soon. Quite the contrary; the Chinese manipulate the latter groups to do their bidding and to transfer knowledge from the former. Our chief global rival strategically employs the Leech to hand over, buy, and steal competitive advantage from the Creators, Enablers, and Servers.

Which professions and industries are increasingly being held captive by the Leech? Certain ones are well-known, and they are quite large and powerful. While you've been busy creating, enabling, and serving, they have been evolving and growing.

THE LEECH MOTHERSHIP:

THE DEEP STATE

"Today it is not big business that we have to fear. It is big government."

WENDELL PHILLIPS

"Society in every state is a blessing, but government even in its best state is but a necessary evil; in its worst state an intolerable one."

THOMAS PAINE, *COMMON SENSE*

"[W]e have more machinery of government than is necessary, too many parasites living on the labor of the industrious."

THOMAS JEFFERSON

"There is nowhere to be found knaves more designing than at a legislature, where designing scoundrels lurk and with specious words and demure looks they calculate to entrap the unwary and like blood-suckers leech and suck the public."

EPHRAIM CUTLER

GOVERNMENT: EXPANSIVE, INTRUSIVE, AND ARCHAIC

A discussion of the Leech-dominated professions must start with the largest and most troubling: the government bureaucrats and the Deep

State. The descriptor *deep* is not describing something hidden or secret. Instead, *deep* is an apt descriptor of the reach of the tentacles of government everywhere. Today, a citizen may not own property, hunt, fly on a plane, get married, collect rainwater, sell a product, cut hair, drive a car, protest, grow food, move dirt, or open a lemonade stand without first obtaining permission from the government.[a] A startling 30% of workers in today's economy need some form of government permission to earn a living.[1] We like to believe we are a free society, yet we can't choose our profession or make everyday decisions without approval from the state.

For the behemoth state to survive, we must feed it. And since government creates laws and dominates law enforcement, it can regulate, control, and take whatever it pleases. You often read shocking examples of wasteful government spending. Everyone knows the stories of silly tax-funded research studies on, say, bridges (or, increasingly today, bike paths and commuter rail lines) to nowhere. What most of us fail to realize is that trillions in taxpayer dollars are not falling through the fiscal cracks by accident. Instead, the Deep State and its allies consume those dollars across certain professions and industries. There is an enormous difference between inept, wasteful spending and premeditated spending through wealth confiscation. Government is all about confiscation and spending; wasteful spending, while bad, is pocket change to the Deep State.

Consider the U.S. Postal Service. Once a shining example of American ingenuity, today's Postal Service is a digital age dinosaur that exists to consume. The demand for physical mail delivery continues to decline, posting a 25% drop since 2008 (over half of today's mail is junk mail).[2] The Post Office runs annual losses of nearly $4 billion, accumulated $78 billion in losses since 2007 and is saddled with $13 billion in debt.[3] Yet there are 600,000 employees at the U.S. Postal

---

a The government-induced economic shutdown in response to the pandemic took Americans' individual freedom to an all-time low. Walking in a park, going to work, and attending religious services became activities requiring government approval.

Service, with staffing levels and efficiency targets that ignore technology, competition, and innovation.[4] Mail carriers are represented by a public union, the American Postal Workers Union (APWU). The APWU successfully secured a clause in the labor contract that forces the Postal Service not to displace workers where technology, for example, could make operations more efficient.[5]

DEEP STATE ORIGINS AND EVOLUTION

The Deep State and its voracious bureaucrats are traceable back thousands of years to the ancient Egyptians. Nile River hieroglyphics show tax payment by ordinary Egyptians to tax collectors and enforcement personnel.[6] Back then, like now, Creators, Enablers, and Servers despised central government and bureaucrats, whose tax-and-spend model has been copied and refined by rulers for millennia.

The United States was supposed to be different, offering a fresh and disruptive break from the chains of oppressive central government. The Declaration of Independence proclaimed government exists to secure the rights of citizens. Thomas Jefferson, in his 1801 inaugural address, succinctly defined optimal government: "A wise and frugal government, which shall restrain men from injuring one another, shall leave them otherwise free to regulate their own pursuits of industry and improvement, and shall not take from the mouth of labor the bread it has earned."[7] Not coincidentally, the first words of the first section of the first article of the Constitution yield legislative powers to the Congress, an elected body and the branch of government that is most accountable to the people. The Framers were channeling the views of John Locke, who a century earlier articulated, "The legislative cannot transfer the power of making laws to any other hands: for it being but a delegated power from the people, they who have it cannot pass it over to others."[8]

How did the federal government evolve from what the Founding Fathers intended, a minimalist entity subject to clear constitutional checks, to the Deep State behemoth of today, where bureaucrats are free to make and adjudicate law on a whim? The short answer is that the Leech way succeeded in morphing the Constitution from a protector of Creators, Enablers, and Servers into a document that can be freely modified or reinterpreted anytime by the judiciary and bureaucracy. The legal profession's evolution from demanding that the Constitution be interpreted by what it plainly says (what is commonly referred to as the originalist view) into a belief that the Constitution is malleable and freely interpreted on a whim, has usurped the vital power to amend its meaning from the citizenry via constitutional amendments to the bureaucracy via self-enabling regulation.[b]

The long answer spans the past one hundred years of American history, starting around the time of the First World War. The concept of the Deep State began with President Woodrow Wilson and his naïvely progressive, globalist views. Wilson hatched the Federal Reserve, introduced the federal income tax, war-mongered the United States into the First World War, and championed the inept League of Nations. In addition, Wilson implemented racist segregation policies in the Post Office and armed forces and attacked free speech by imprisoning government critics under the Sedition Act of 1918.

This modern behemoth reached critical mass during the presidency of a Wilson protégé. Founder of the Deep State as we know it was the most over-rated president in United States history, Franklin Delano Roosevelt. Sure, FDR had a way with words that could connect with citizens during a time of economic and wartime upheaval.[c] Many of those words resonate today. There is no doubt that our longest serving president left an indelible legacy.

Yet there are distressing hard truths, often ignored, about FDR. He was an aristocrat; an elitist, who as a young man never had to put in

---

b   If you doubt this is so, ponder why there has not been a constitutional amendment since the early 1990s.

c   Ironically, so-called liberals who credit FDR with revolutionizing direct communication to the public with the use of radio also criticize Trump's disruptive application of social media to communicate directly to citizens.

a hard day's work at a job. He was suspicious and jealous evidently of self-made wealthy businessmen; he saw successful Creators, Enablers, and Servers as entities in need of controlling and commanding.

By today's standards, FDR was a racist. Americans are often shocked to learn that FDR refused to support anti-lynching legislation in Congress, which would have prevented the random murders of African Americans in the South. Trump bashers usually revere FDR if they are old enough, yet they obviously forget that while Trump built border walls to keep illegal immigrants out, FDR built walls within America to imprison Japanese American legal immigrants and citizens.

FDR showed little respect for the Constitution and the checks and balances between the federal branches of government. FDR's view of the Constitution was that he could do mostly anything he wanted if he rearranged things. When the Supreme Court didn't provide Roosevelt the decisions he wanted, he tried and failed to increase the number of justices and pack the Court with cronies.[9] Under FDR, that would have made the judicial branch a protégé of the executive branch. Although he lost the battle to pack the Supreme Court to a resistant Congress, FDR ultimately won the war in that a series of Supreme Court decisions through the late 1930s and early 1940s greatly expanded the power of government and the Deep State. The Supreme Court saw the real threat the popular FDR posed to its constitutional powers down the road, so it gave him what he wanted, validation of the New Deal's constitutionality.

FDR didn't stop ransacking the Constitution at the Supreme Court's doors; he also usurped certain foreign policy powers from Congress. When Congress passed the Neutrality Act, reflecting the wishes of the electorate to keep the United States out of the escalating global conflict, FDR ignored and bypassed it via the destroyers-for-bases deal with Great Britain and by imposing an oil embargo on Japan. Both actions were designed to drive the nation effectively to war.

The biggest fault of FDR was his placing of the community ahead of the individual. This flawed philosophy is un-American and led to justification of the New Deal, which fundamentally changed the

American economy and society. Leftist FDR supporters love to correlate the New Deal to ending the Great Depression. However, during FDR's second term, the country experienced yet another recession in 1937–1938, which drove unemployment to nearly 20% and which rivaled the most extreme depths of the Great Depression during the Hoover administration.[10] The U.S. economy did not rebound with vigor until after World War II.

The consequences of the New Deal were seismic. Using the common good as a shield, FDR grabbed control of the money supply when he exited the gold standard. Using the Great Depression's unemployment level as a convenient crisis, he trounced the Constitution's checks and balances system by, "treating the task [of getting people back to work] as we would treat the emergency of a war" and positing that, "an unprecedented demand and need for undelayed action may call for temporary departure from that normal balance of public procedure."[11] Roosevelt quickly created a massive alphabet soup of federal bureaucracies including the SEC, TVA, NLRB, and FDIC. He injected the societal drug that is the modern-day welfare state into our economy's veins. In short, FDR gave birth to the modern administrative state that is the entrenched conductor of Leech activity across society.

FDR's administrative state's offspring has grown over the past seventy-five years into a voracious Frankenstein monster. The power of the modern Deep State was often handed to it by the legislative and judicial branches of government, the very branches designed to keep it in check. The monster received a boost during the Truman administration with the passage of the Administrative Procedure Act (APA), which created the ability of executive branch agencies to effectively create law without the passage of a congressional statute.[12] The APA was a conscious decision by Congress to abdicate its constitutional authority to the administrative state, well past the crises of the Great Depression and World War II. The original 1946 law included a safety valve of a legislative veto, which allowed Congress to negate executive branch bureaucratic overreach. But the legislative veto option was eventually struck down as unconstitutional by the Supreme Court in the 1983 decision in *INS v. Chadha*, ironically for violating the separation of powers.[13] Without legislative veto protection, the APA took FDR's executive branch over-reach during times of economic and wartime emergency and gave it legitimacy during normal times, nullifying a congressional check on administrative state overreach.

It wasn't just Congress that lost the ability to check the Deep State. The judicial branch of the federal government does not have clean hands either. The judicial branch's ability to rein in the Deep State suffered a severe, self-inflicted blow with the Supreme Court's 1984 decision in *Chevron U.S.A., Inc. v. Natural Resources Defense Council, Inc.*[14] The *Chevron* precedent granted wide deference to administrative agencies in interpreting statutes, allowing bureaucrats to issue regulations at will without challenge from the courts if the actions are "not unreasonable" (versus wrong). The "not unreasonable" standard is crucial since it creates many actions/avenues for the bureaucrat to choose from, even when the statute created by Congress intended only one action. *Chevron* deference allows the bureaucracy to grow unfettered and free of judicial oversight and constitutional norms. What Congress willingly gave up in constitu-tional authority the Supreme Court officially sanctioned and widened.[d]

The judiciary also coordinates with the bureaucracy to play defense against attempts by a sitting president to throttle regulation. A key weapon in the defensive arsenal is the national injunction. If a president decides to roll back onerous regulation, anyone in opposition (including entrenched bureaucrats) can forum shop to identify a favorable judge in a federal dis-trict court and request an injunction. If granted, the injunction does not just apply to the entity bringing the request, but to everyone nationwide.

---

d   While the *Chevron* precedent pertains to agencies having wide discretion for administering statutes, a sister precedent (*Auer*) grants agencies wide leeway in interpreting its own regulations. There is hope that with the addition of Justices Kavanaugh and Coney-Barrett to the bench, the Supreme Court will overturn the *Chevron* and *Auer* precedents. Only time will tell.

Appeals often take years and can outlive the term of the sitting president. This tactic also evades the established role and erodes the importance of higher courts, which have the responsibility to resolve lower court disputes in a definitive manner. Fortunately, the Supreme Court of late has not looked kindly on lower court national injunctions.

As if judicial collaboration is not enough, the administrative state has also received protection from its own branch of government in the event that a sitting president desired to rein in the bureaucracy with the passage of the Ethics in Government Act (EGA) in 1978.[15] The EGA established the ability of the bureaucracy to create an independent counsel to investigate the president for alleged wrongdoing or abuse of power. So, if a drain-the-swamp minded president got elected, the Deep State could inject an independent counsel to investigate a fantastic fabrication such as, say, alleged Russian election interference.

The administrative state Frankenstein monster that President Roosevelt built in the New Deal was jolted to life during Lyndon Johnson's administration by his Great Society legislation.[e] With the federal government leading the charge, many like-minded state and local governments followed suit, creating a snowball effect. President Wilson conceptualized the Deep State, FDR fathered it, while Congress and the Supreme Court set the pathways to free it from constitutional constraints. Yet no one did more to grow the Deep State than LBJ, a man who spent his entire career in Washington, D.C.

The results of LBJ's Great Society have been devastating to America, both in dollars as well as culturally. Simply contrast the fiction and the reality of the much-ballyhooed War on Poverty, now over fifty years old. In 1964, LBJ laid out two key objectives of the War on Poverty: to reduce the poverty rate across the country and to enable poor Americans

---

e   It is no coincidence that Lyndon Johnson was a staunch FDR supporter who stood on the New Deal platform as a young politician running for Congress and later during his failed, first bid for the U.S. Senate.

to escape the clutches of poverty permanently by gaining their independence.[16] Yet the national poverty rate had already seen a substantial
reduction since World War II, dropping by half, down to about 15%
in the mid-1960s when the War on Poverty commenced.[17] In other
words, the vexing problem of the poverty rate was being solved on its
own, through good old economic growth fueled by Creators, Enablers,
and Servers, before the commencement of LBJ's war.

So, after fifty years and trillions of dollars of government intervention in the War on Poverty, what are the results? The poverty rate in
America still hovers around the mid-1960s 15% even though transfer
payments to low-income families exploded more than ten-fold in real
dollars.[18] According to government fiction, despite our best intentions
we've made no progress in the War on Poverty, and we need to keep
doubling down with more resources and programs.

The problem with this illusion is that the data, calculated and
reported by the U.S. Census Bureau, includes only transfer payments
defined as "money income" and excludes trillions of dollars of annual
government payments to low-income families such as food stamps,
Medicaid, and dozens of other programs. If one includes all the transfer
payments made to low-income families, the poverty rate in the United
States drops to under 3%.[19] By ignoring taxes paid by higher-income
households and not counting transfer payments to the lower income
households, the U.S. Census Bureau overstates income inequality by a
startling 300%. The trend of the declining poverty rate holds true for
minorities as well, with African American and Hispanic poverty rates
at the start of 2020 being the lowest on record.

The War on Poverty came with a heavy price. Instead of providing
focused, short-term support for those in need and letting the private
sector create job opportunity, the government designed aid programs to
be permanent and created a latent disincentive to work. This also creates
a culture of dependence on government that can jump across generations
of low-income families, perpetuating the cycle. The data back this up:
the labor participation rate of the lowest household income quartile of

prime-age workers is barely above 60%, and those workers are nearly twice as likely not to be working as their peers in the second-lowest quartile.[20]

Having been lied to, taxpaying Creators, Enablers, and Servers lose trillions of dollars of their hard-earned money. Meanwhile, children in low-income brackets face a life of government dependence and unfulfilled potential. The government bureaucracy and its affiliates gain by broadcasting a false narrative to justify more resources, staffing, and control.

Barack Obama closed out the presidential unholy trinity of Deep State growth by taking what FDR and Lyndon Johnson built and further embedding it within the lifeblood of our economy and society. The magnitude of eight years of President Obama is daunting: $122 billion in new annual regulatory costs thrown upon the economy.[21] Philosophically, Obama was more than willing to stomp over traditional checks and balances between the three branches of government by gloating, "We're not just going to be waiting for legislation . . . I've got a pen and I've got a phone and I can use that pen to sign executive orders and take executive actions and administrative actions."[22] Obama then aggressively proceeded to exert control across the three foundational segments of the economy: finance, healthcare, and energy. During the Obama administration, bureaucrats negotiated agreements such as the Paris Climate Agreement and the Iran nuclear deal and never brought them to Congress for approval.

Historians will not be able to overstate the cumulative impact of the Big Three Presidents, FDR, LBJ, and Obama. In the 1920s, total U.S. government spending was under 10% of GDP, post–World War II total government spending grew to over 20% of GDP, and in the 1970s it increased to 25–30% of GDP. Today, total government spending sits at an astonishing 35+ percent of GDP.[f] The Bureau of Labor Statistics shows that in 2018, Americans spent more on taxes than food, healthcare,

---

f   Government largesse expanded in 2020 with pandemic virus relief packages. Government spending is now projected at 50% of GDP, equivalent to World War II levels. That's over $70,000 per household, far above median household income.

clothing, and services combined.[23] Tax Freedom Day, the day in the calendar year when the nation as a whole has earned enough money to pay its total annual tax bill, fell on April 19 in 2019, meaning Americans work over 100 days into the year just to cover the nation's taxes.[24] Ponder whether the benefits of government come close to the costs of Americans spending more on taxes than food, clothing, and healthcare combined and working almost a third of the way into a year to cover the national tax bill. Today's Deep State is a very expensive colossus.

The colossus thrives even during periods of widespread crisis. When Congress passed the historic coronavirus relief package in March 2020, much media attention focused on highlighting the multi-trillion-dollar size of the package and misconstruing how corporations and industries were being bailed out à la the 2008 financial crisis redux. Only a select few stalwart outlets had the audacity to report the truth: that government was the biggest beneficiary of its own package, to the tune of $600+ billion. The list of handouts to the government was extensive, with much of the list having nothing to do with a pandemic: NASA was gifted $60 million, the National Archives got $8 million placed in its coffers, the Forest Service was awarded over $35 million, and the Kennedy Center had $25 million dropped into its lap.

The bureaucrat played the coronavirus crisis to perfection. Shuttering free enterprise caused economic pain, which the government then used to justify a multi-trillion-dollar relief package. Government was the largest beneficiary from the aid, allowing for rampant bureaucratic growth in the future.

Simple math highlights lack of Deep State accountability. The federal government has approximately two million full-time employees, excluding Postal Service workers. Somewhere between 80,000 and 100,000 new full-time employees are hired each year by the federal government.[25] Yet, the Government Accountability Office (GAO) reports that less than 4,000 employees are fired in a typical year for poor performance.[26] That equates to fewer than 0.2% of the workforce, demonstrating how a person, once employed by government, does not need to feel compelled to perform and serve the average citizen or taxpayer.

BEHEMOTH GOVERNMENT

No one really knows the true extent of the vastness of the administrative regulatory state. The numbers that we can measure for today's Deep State are huge: the American regulatory state consists of 300,000 bureaucrats with an annual budget in excess of $50 billion.[27] That is larger than the active armies of Mexico, Japan, France, Germany, or Israel. State and local governments employ over 19 million additional workers.[28] Growth has been staggering, to the point where today the combined 20-plus million army of federal, state, and local government workers exceeds workers in manufacturing by a 1.8 to 1 margin.[29]

Government workers don't come cheap. Federal workers enjoy wages that are 14% higher than private sector workers.[30] Total compensation packages that include overly generous healthcare, pension, and other benefits widen the gap to over 60% above the private sector. Policies and rules imposed on management make it painful, slow, or in some cases impossible to eliminate obsolete positions or to reassign workers to other areas. There is no sector in the Creator, Enabler, or Server classes that enjoys, on average, the fat pay-packages and job protections that government bureaucrats enjoy. Simply bringing federal worker compensation levels into line with compensation in the private sector would save taxpayers over $75 billion a year.[31]

Government bureaucracy is sucking the lifeblood out of the U.S. economy. Per capita federal spending, in real dollars, between fiscal 1941 and 2017 has increased seven-fold, from $1,718 to $12,239 (per capita federal spending jumped to a frightening $20,000 in 2020).[32] What's even more striking about this massive increase is that fiscal 1941 already experienced a huge run up in federal spending resulting from Roosevelt's New Deal programs. The largest share of the current federal spending falls into the lap of sizable government bureaucracies covering education, social services, training, social security, employment, and various other areas such as the VA. This part of the fiscal 2017 federal spend equates to over 15% of GDP.[33] The sevenfold increase in real per capita spend since fiscal 1941 has not resulted in anything close to a sevenfold improvement in government services. Sadly, none of us would be foolish enough to even expect such a thing.

Think for a moment about how much of the local, state, and federal workforce exists with no direct, tangible benefit to the taxpayers. Yet, these same bureaucrats make the rules that not only justify their current jobs but also expand their footprint to create even more bureaucrats. Congress slowly lost control of the purse strings through interagency collusion where one government agency procures funding through complex inter-agency agreements to feed another, completely unrelated agency. Oversight increasingly comes not from independent tribunals but instead from courts and judges that fall within the control of the bureaucrats themselves.

The burden government creates with fiscal largesse and the potential for government corruption are at critical levels. Most Americans sense this despite the bureaucracy's efforts to disguise and message around the dangerous reality. Chapman University conducts an annual survey that examines Americans' biggest fears.[34] Respondents can choose from wide categories that include crime, technology, geopolitics, environmental calamities, and personal health and safety categories. The top-ranked item for 2017, where the highest percentage of Americans reported being afraid or very afraid, was corrupt government officials. The same result was at the top of the list in 2016. Nothing else came close, with the second biggest fear of uncertainty on national healthcare legislation coming in at a much lower level than corrupt government. The American people sense the present danger that government bureaucracy poses.

A recent poll by Monmouth University reinforces where Americans' worries lie. The poll found a large and bipartisan majority of citizens are troubled that the Deep State of unelected bureaucrats drives policy in this country.[35] Concern cuts across political affiliation, with Democrats, Republicans, and Independents all showing worry regarding the power of government bureaucracy. Apprehension of the Deep State also unites Americans across a spectrum of interest groups from Latinos to gun-rights advocates to African Americans.

Do all government workers fall into the Leech category? Of course not, there is some level of government we need to protect air and water, to preserve law and order, and to provide basic services, including defense. But let's recognize that much of the current government complex consists of bureaucrats feeding off the taxpayer. They further their self-interests like everyone else, and if that means appropriating the wealth of others, so be it. The concept of altruism in government for the common good is an absurd myth. Every new regulation that creates a new job in the government necessarily takes away opportunity, jobs, or value from others. Governor Ronald Reagan in 1974 summed up how government was more about getting in the way of the American people instead of helping them when he said, "[B]usiness is more regulated in America by government than it is in any other country in the world where free enterprise is still permitted. If we had less regulation, we could have lower prices. Government has grown so big in these last four decades that not even the Office of Management and Budget in Washington knows how many boards, agencies, bureaus, and commissions there are." Six years before he was elected president, Reagan was lamenting the inexorable rise of the government bureaucrat.[9]

What has been the pace of new regulations in recent years? Unprecedented; a recent tally of the current Code of Federal Regulations fills over 175,000 pages. The *Federal Register* peaked out at over 95,000 pages in 2016 as the Obama era was ending. Each year, the private sector of Creators, Enablers, and Servers wastes over 11 billion hours complying with federal regulatory paperwork.[36] The rate of growth of

---

g   Reagan tended to view FDR and the New Deal favorably, believing the former created the latter as a patriotic duty from which Reagan himself received help. Reagan was not as favorable of Lyndon Johnson and the Great Society, which he viewed as government overreach into the economy and people's lives.

new regulations is increasing at a frightening clip.

Our government has reached a point where there are no longer three branches but now four: executive, legislative, judicial, and bureaucratic. Of the four, the two most powerful today are the executive and bureaucratic, with bureaucratic having assumed primacy since the administrative state is not subject to elections and term limits like the presidency is. There are over 300,000 federal crimes (no one, including the government, knows the exact number), many of them are strict-liability where guilt may be found without intent, and most are triggered by a violation of a bureaucrat-created regulation never passed by Congress. No individual or business is safe from the subjective whims of the federal bureaucracy.

Considerable blame for the fourth branch usurping power lies with Congress because it cedes constitutional authority to the bureaucracy when passing laws. Whenever you read words in a statute like *equitable, fair,* and *reasonable* they are a signal that Congress is providing wide discretion to the bureaucrats to decide how much power to wield. Over the years, there has been a massive shift of taxing and spending authority from Congress to the bureaucratic state.

This dereliction of duty by Congress is contrary to what the Constitution demands of the legislative body. The first thing the Founding Fathers articulated in the Constitution after the Preamble is found in Article I, Section 1: "All legislative Powers herein granted shall be vested in a Congress of the United States."

Why is Congress willingly handing over power to a Deep State staffed by unelected bureaucrats? For members of Congress, the top priority is re-election every two years or seeking other office. What better way to bolster re-election and advance political careers than to delegate via statute tough decisions to anonymous bureaucrats who are accountable only to other anonymous bureaucrats?

Give a bureaucrat authority and rest assured he will interpret it widely, liberally, aggressively, and issue opaque regulations. Rules that are black and white, are understood and easily followed. But the Leech is not interested in efficient, transparent, and decisive rules. To the contrary, a bureaucrat finds those traits in conflict with his ability to sponge off of the system. Instead, he wants lack of clarity, arbitrariness, uncertainty, and confusion in rules. Those are traits that create a rich and nurturing ecosystem in which the government bureaucrat thrives. Ronald Reagan said, "When you create a government bureaucracy, no matter how well intentioned it is, almost instantly its top priority becomes preservation of the bureaucracy."[37]

The Leech grows by hijacking our federal system of government with its prescribed checks and balances across three branches. The executive branch aggressively pushes administrative power to fill every nook and cranny of life. The legislative branch enables the aggressive administrative state by passing vague legislation. Lastly, the judicial branch, appointed by the executive branch and confirmed by the legislative branch, returns the favor by affirming administrative state dominance. While these checks and balances give the appearance of keeping each branch in check to serve the people, the reality is all three branches of government are so powerful that the people serve them. Alexander Hamilton understood well, "[A] power over a man's sustenance amounts to a power over his will."[38]

The worst-case scenario for the bureaucrat is a judge or elected officials telling him on the rare occasion to stand down on an issue. So, when in doubt, the bureaucrat errs on the side of more expansive power, not less. If the individual or company that stood up to the bureaucracy is unfortunate enough not to prevail, he or it should expect serious and long-term repercussions when the bureaucracy undoubtedly retaliates. Even if the wronged person (or company) is right and wins a battle, he is likely to lose future battles. Fighting and winning battles with government bureaucrats usually ends in Pyrrhic victories.

For decades, unelected, life-long bureaucrats have been issuing hundreds of binding regulations affecting lives and businesses with little oversight. Presidentially appointed FDA commissioners are a striking example. They have delegated to life-long bureaucrats buried in the bowels of the FDA the power over life and death. One such bureaucrat has issued close to 200 regulations in her FDA career. Her recent action was regulation of the vaping industry, ironically an industry that often aims to help people stop smoking.[39] If you want to know anything about how ridiculous the bureaucracy of the FDA has become, try saying the person's title without getting tongue-tied: Associate Commissioner for Policy and Director of the Office of Policy in the Office of the Commissioner at the Food and Drug Administration. Scores of bureaucrats keep writing rules that become law without ever having to face public accountability like a legislator. Yet the public is accountable for every rule issued by bureaucrats.

The framers of the Constitution saw the danger in delegation from elected and appointed officials to lifelong, unelected bureaucrats. That's why we have the Appointments Clause, which requires that binding regulations must be issued by executive-branch officers who are presidentially appointed and Senate-confirmed. The people vest the rule-making power in these officials through an elected president, whom they can remove every four years.

Federal law enforcement is another example of the Deep State immunity to checks and balances, oversight, and accountability. Evidence continued to mount in 2017 and 2018 that the Justice Department and the FBI had engaged in questionable and probably illegal behavior leading up to, during, and after the 2016 presidential election. We are all too familiar with the secret dossiers, intentional leaks, and biased text messages by now. Yet these federal law enforcement entities continue to ignore and resist all requests from their boss, the president, and Congress when it comes to looking into these actions on behalf of the American people. Subpoenas are cast aside, leaks to the press are used to sabotage the oversight process, Senate and House requests are ignored, and the limited information that is provided is so heavily redacted that it is useless to read.

The FBI and Justice Department exist to uphold the law. These federal bureaucrats now act with impunity and arrogance, knowing there will not be a consequence for blatant insubordination. They don't feel accountable to the president, Congress, or the people, knowing they can wait it out until the White House and Congress change over to more favored parties or sympathetic individuals. This is a lawless, slippery slope.

Avoiding accountability to voters, elected bosses, or Congress is not unique to the FDA, FBI, or Justice Department. Is there a more powerful and less trusted government agency than the Internal Revenue Service, or IRS? IRS power and authority are large; it was the IRS, not the FBI, who put Al Capone in the slammer.

IRS power comes from complexity manufactured by the bureaucracy over decades. Our tax code exceeds ten million words, reflecting a complicated and subjective maze of rules and regulations. *Money* magazine ran a now-famous experiment where it sent to forty-six tax preparers a hypothetical family's financial data and received back forty-six different answers as to what the family would have owed the government.[40] This mess has two major consequences to society.

The first consequence is that the IRS can use discretion to help favored institutions, industries, and groups and to punish others. The most recent example is the targeting of conservative nonprofit groups for auditing and denial of nonprofit status, but others exist. The complexity of the tax code allows the IRS to exercise subjectivity when targeting taxpayers.

The second consequence is close to $1 trillion in compliance costs.[41] These costs are not just accounting-related, although it should not be lost that Americans waste six billion hours a year on tax compliance. The $1 trillion levy also includes the costs of lobbying to secure favored tax treatment, tax policy negatively impacting work decisions across labor pools, and forgone economic growth. There are clear beneficiaries feeding off the $1 trillion cost: accountants, attorneys, government bureaucrats, and those lucky enough to find IRS favor.

The White House Office of Information and Regulatory Affairs (OIRA) is tasked with reviewing major regulations from executive-branch agencies before they are published. The idea behind the OIRA is a simple one: make sure the various executive branch agencies are coordinating in a coherent and logical manner on major regulations so that they are consistent with the law and have considered the true costs and benefits of regulations.

For years, the Treasury, along with its sub-agency the IRS, has shunned coordinating with the OIRA. The official, on-the-record reason cited by the Treasury is that its regulations are simply interpreting the laws and statutes, so there is no need for oversight. Yet all regulations and interpretive rules imposed on society by federal government agencies go back to congressional statute. If the IRS position is that the agency is exempt from economic impact reporting, then all government agencies would be exempt from this type of oversight by the public, Congress, and the president.

Creators, Enablers, and Servers face enormous risk in challenging the bureaucratic system. First, the arbiter of the dispute will most likely be another bureaucrat, either an administrative law judge or a sister agency. The arbiter is unlikely to be a Creator, Enabler, or Server let alone a traditional independent judge or jury. Second, challenging the bureaucrat can upset him or her and provoke increased oversight, attacks, and bring pain on anyone who doesn't roll over. The government bureaucratic system has become so powerful in America today that the most rational strategy for the rest of us when dealing with it is fall to your knees and submit.[h] In the 1930s, Leon Trotsky surmised that, "In a country where the sole employer is the State, opposition means death by slow starvation. The old principle: who does not work shall not eat, has been replaced by a new one: who does not obey shall not eat."[42]

Creators, Enablers, and Servers live in an altered state akin to Kafka's dystopian world in *The Trial*, where people find themselves charged with unnamed crimes by faceless bureaucrats from unknown agencies. In *The Trial* guilt is assumed from the start and the bureaucracy is opaque, complex, and inefficient. Hiring a lawyer, not surprisingly, only

---

h   A crucial part of President Trump's 2020 executive order on regulatory relief was a regulatory bill of rights that demands fairness in administrative actions, presumed innocence of the accused regarding alleged violations, neutral (not agency) judges, and prompt enforcement.

complicates matters and increases costs. The system ruins professions and businesses that fall within its tentacles. The main character, Josef K, succumbs to the bureaucrats and allows them to execute him. Kafka's fictional story, first published in the 1920s, serves as a chilling portrait of how today's Deep State works.

The numbers are troubling. The Mercatus Center recently published a study that quantified the cumulative impacts of government regulation. Quantitatively analyzing data across twenty-two industries over a period spanning from 1977 through 2012 showed that cumulative government regulation in the United States created a drag on the economy that equated to a reduction in annual GDP growth of 0.8%.[43] Now 0.8% of GDP may not sound like much. When you consider that a drag of 0.8% of GDP annually equates to an economy in 2012 that is smaller by $4 trillion than it would have been if regulation was simply held constant since 1980, you start to see how massive and distortive of an impact government regulation to sustain bureaucrats can be. To put it in personal terms, that $4 trillion of lost economy translates to $13,000 per capita in the United States—your money and mine—taken to feed government.

The annual *Ten Thousand Commandments* report from the Competitive Enterprise Institute (CEI) fires off striking statistics regarding the cost of regulatory compliance: $1.9 trillion annually and 10% of U.S. GDP.[44] If U.S. regulation were a country, it would be the world's eighth-largest economy, ahead of Italy and just behind India.[45] Regulation costs, measuring about half of the federal outlays and more than twice the annual budget deficit (pre-COVID virus), is a massive stealth tax that is increasingly utilized to fund ever-growing bureaucracies across government.

Creators, Enablers, and Servers, when faced with this negative compounding effect, start to change their decisions and behavior, which leads to less investment, employment, and growth. A quantitative analysis by Vogel and Hood shows that the average industry's regulatory risk has increased by close to 80% in five years (2010–2015).[46] This is especially true for industries in the manufacturing, energy, and transportation sectors. Guess what the study found went along with the explosion in bureaucratic regulation? Annual capital investment via capital expenditures dropped by $32 billion from 2010 to 2015. Layoffs and elimination of positions within companies totaled over one million in the same period. Unsurprisingly, companies that spent heavily on lobbying and trying to influence the bureaucrats outperformed those who did not. In other words, bureaucrats in government imposing these regulations on the Creators, Enablers, and Servers spawned new positions within companies who fed off the bureaucracy. This is classic behavior of the bureaucratic class; they're constantly looking to create avenues to develop and nurture offspring.

THE ENDGAME OF CONTROL

The federal government has a highly effective strategy to continue its inexorable growth and dominion over our country's economy. Although there are many sides to our modern economy, there are four pillars: energy, finance, healthcare, and (as we will discuss in the next chapter) a rising fourth sector, tech. Without these first three sectors, the wider economy doesn't work.

When the government directly controls critical parts of the economy, it has effectively nationalized it. The door is then open for Deep State central planning in the "public interest," which includes controlling how people think as a collective. As E. H. Carr stated, "It is significant that the nationalization of thought has proceeded everywhere *pari passu* with the nationalization of industry."[47]

Consider what the federal government bureaucracy and other Leech organizations have focused their efforts and attention on over the past decade. The three biggest splashes of the Deep State over the past decade have been Obamacare, the Dodd-Frank Act, and the Paris Agreement. One looks to have the government take over healthcare, one creates a bureaucratic stranglehold over banking, and one looks to allow the global bureaucracy to control the American energy industry. Support for all three moves by the federal bureaucracy came from a bevy of carnivorous organizations outside of the Deep State.

Efforts to take control of the U.S. economy experienced a step-up in intensity in early 2019 with socialist Congresswoman Alexandria Ocasio-Cortez's proposed Green New Deal. Ocasio-Cortez's draft resolution calls for eliminating the use of all fossil fuels within ten years, free government healthcare for everyone, and for the Federal Reserve and new "public banks" to finance it all. Climate change and pending global doom are the justifications for the Green New Deal, but the proposal goes far beyond carbon. The idiotic proposal focuses on energy, healthcare, and finance. That is not coincidental. Although Ocasio-Cortez understands nothing about free enterprise, she understands apparently that once the government controls those three sectors of the economy it controls all sectors. To accomplish the proposal's objectives, the government would run oil and natural gas companies out of business, ban the combustion engine, eliminate air travel, destroy private healthcare, eliminate beef from diets, and ruin the banking industry. While it was busy with that chaos, the federal government would be installing windmills, solar panels, charging stations, light rail transit systems, government banks, and hospitals all over the country. On a macro level, the Green New Deal envisions government forcing the financing of the politically favored, non-creditworthy industries (like renewables and subprime mortgages) and the denial of financing to the unfavored, creditworthy industries. Before you dispense with Ocasio-Cortez's proposal as a joke, keep in mind a cohort of established and powerful entities supported it, including co-sponsor and climate change alarmist Senator Markey (D-MA) as well as much of the mainstream media (Markey pathetically chose to vote "present" when his co-sponsored Green New Deal came to vote in the Senate).[48]

Indeed, the Deep State plays the long game and is not afraid to go for broke (or federal bankruptcy). The Leech understands how regulation can be used to manipulate competition; exploit the Creators, Enablers, and Servers; and help the Deep State.

The Deep State was at work when President Obama used the 2010 Dodd-Frank Act to create another federal government agency, the

Consumer Financial Protection Bureau (CFPB). The CFPB is no normal government bureaucracy. Instead, designed to be a Deep State version of a cyborg, the CFPB is akin to something out of *The Terminator*. The architects knew this entity would face accountability and reform sometime in future administrations. So it was created in such a way that its funding was locked in and not dependent on Congress, which is one of the classic checks and balances found in the Constitution to keep the executive and legislative branches in balance. The CFPB was also given Stalin-like police powers whereby it can demand companies turn over requested data and files without there being so much as a civil action pending against the company. That allows the CFPB to search for creative avenues to file spurious actions against private enterprise to bolster power.

Dodd-Frank also had a provision that allowed for the deputy director of the CFPB to serve as acting director if the director is absent or unavailable. In late 2017, this feature was used by then outgoing Director Richard Cordray to appoint his own replacement, then CFPB executive Leandra English. Both Cordray and English were past colleagues and favorites of Senator Elizabeth Warren (D-MA), a driving force behind Dodd-Frank and the CFPB. The aim was to make this entity self-appointing, empowered to determine its leadership, and unanswerable to the executive branch.

A problem quickly arose with this succession plan: The United States Constitution. The Constitution, specifically Article II, clearly gives the president control of the executive branch, which the CFPB falls under.[i] President Trump wanted Mick Mulvaney, not Ms. English, to be acting director when Cordray announced his plans to step down. The general counsel of the CFPB advised confused bureaucrats within the CFPB to treat Mulvaney as their boss since that was consistent with the law and the district court backed President Trump.[49] Nevertheless, Ms. English refused to stand down, continued to present herself as acting director, and

---

[i] Article II of the Constitution states that, "the executive Power shall be vested in a President of the United States of America."

sued President Trump. After considerable posturing, English resigned from the CFPB and dropped her lawsuit.

From the onset, the CFPB behaved like a bureaucratic predator stalking its prey. Dodd-Frank forbade the CFPB from overseeing auto dealers, despite that being one of Elizabeth Warren's desires from the get-go. Like a cunning animal, the CFPB found a way to indirectly achieve what it could not do up front. Instead of going directly at auto dealers, the Leech focused its hunt on banks and lending institutions that funded the auto dealers. Maniuplating buyers' market data and statistics, the CFPB attacked lenders with accusations of discrimination in lending practices. The lenders had one of two choices at that point: either pay whatever penalties the CFPB demanded and pressure their auto dealer clients to adjust policies and practices to fit CFPB demands, or fight the CFPB and have any other governmental approvals or reviews be held up until the CFPB dispute was settled. It's little wonder that lenders, who had no real choice in this matter, typically paid the shakedown money and forced the changes demanded by the CFPB upon their client auto dealers.[j]

The CFPB drama offers important lessons. First, the Leech class will robustly use the Deep State to expand its power over the rest of society. That's what Dodd-Frank and the creation of the new CFPB provided, and that's exactly what happened when the Obama-appointed team would famously whisper their intentions of the CFPB "pushing the envelope" to attack citizens, whom the government is supposed to serve.[k] The Deep State would never waste such an attractive opportunity to expand the reach of its oversight with the CFPB by letting free enterprise, individual rights, and the Constitution get in the way.

Lacking any civic principles other than power, a second lesson is

---

j   Similar behavior occurred with the CFPB attacks on the payday lending industry. Dodd-Frank gives no authority to the CFPB over payday loans yet the Obama-appointed Director Cordray did not let that stop him from having the bureau begin to run the industry out of business. One of the first items of business for Trump-appointed Director Mulvaney was to reassess the payday lending rule.

k   Politico originally reported the desires of CFPB bureaucrats to be "pushing the envelope."

that Leeches are more than willing to bend and break the checks and balances found in the Constitution. That's why the CFPB's purse strings under Dodd-Frank were not controlled by Congress but by a fee assessed on the Federal Reserve.[l] It is also why an outgoing CFPB director was arrogant enough to name his own successor and why his acting director-appointee refused to step down when the president named someone else as acting director.

The third lesson is that the bureaucracy will quickly fill any void left by Congress or other bodies normally accountable to the public. Shame on Congress for allowing the CFPB to cede congressional and executive branch authority to reckless, unaccountable bureaucrats. The Obama administration knew exactly what it was doing when signing the Dodd-Frank Act into law in 2010. All of this was done under the populist cloak of looking out for the little guy exploited by big, bad Wall Street.

Dodd-Frank didn't stop at the CFPB when creating a smorgasbord of feeding opportunities for the Deep State. The 2010 law also allowed the Securities and Exchange Commission (SEC) to pursue and seek penalties from defendants accused of wrongdoing in the financial services industry. The SEC can hire administrative court judges for processing CFPB cases. The SEC also argued that administrative judges would not need to be appointed by the president or approved by the SEC commissioner as required for administrative officers in the Constitution.[m] Instead, the SEC contends these administrative judges could be hired by the human resources department within the SEC, just like any other run-of-the-mill

---

l   The new Director of the CFPB, Mick Mulvaney, turned the CFPB funding mechanism on its head in early 2018 when he sent a letter to Fed Reserve Chair Janet Yellen informing her that the bureau was requesting "$0" for its quarterly funding. The director referenced a massive reserve already on the books at the bureau and the desire to be a prudent steward of taxpayers' money. Hallelujah!

m   The Appointments Clause of the Constitution requires executive branch "officers" who wield this type of power over citizens to be appointed by the president and confirmed by the Senate or in the case of "inferior officers" by the president or department heads alone. In both instances, accountability of these officers to the people still occurs via the ballot box.

employee. Since these judges are in-house and employed by the SEC, this hiring practice creates a conflict of interest. The judge, an employee of the agency bringing the case to the court, is deciding binding guilt or liability of the defendant. That would be akin to the judge in a homicide case being an employee of the police department that charged the defendant—not exactly the blind scales of justice for the accused, yet a wonderful set of circumstances to expand SEC dominion.

Not only is this a blatant conflict of interest, there is also something else at work. In this situation, you have a career bureaucrat buried within the SEC who is able to hire and fire at will scores of judges who will then exercise considerable authority to decide the fates of citizens and taxpayers caught in disputes with the SEC. The SEC bureaucrat and the judge in this scenario don't answer to the people in the way appointed officials do: if they screw up or run amuck, the president and Congress are powerless to remove them.

Fortunately, in 2018 the Supreme Court shut the door on this bureaucratic Trojan horse in the 7–2 decision in *Lucia v. SEC*.[50] The Court found that these judges wielded considerable power over citizens and thus needed to be appointed by the proper authorities and not career bureaucrats. If the judges and the SEC screw up, the people can oust the president in the next election along with the associated leaders, commissioners, and judges of the SEC. Although the Supreme Court has addressed this specific threat, do not think for a second that the bureaucracy is not scheming up new ways to expand its reach.

DEEP STATE LESSONS FROM EUROPE

One of my favorite paintings is *The Average Bureaucrat*, by the Surrealist great Salvador Dali.[51] The painting expresses Dali's disdain for bureaucrats by presenting a yellow, faceless bureaucrat. The bureaucrat has closed his eyes to everything around him; his head is down and he seems oblivious to his environment, he has no ears for listening, and his head is full of rocks and shells. Since the early 1930s, when Dali painted *The Average Bureaucrat*, the Deep State has evolved from a typically non-responsive, ineffective entity to become an all-encompassing, insatiable predatory monster.

We know where we are heading as a nation if the current, troubling trends of a growing Deep State continue. That direction points to what has already occurred in Europe, where both individuals and nations surrendered their right to self-determination without firing a shot. Both did so by placing decision-making authority into the hands of faceless, unelected career bureaucrats who subscribe to no principles or belief systems other than doing what is in the best interest of the bureaucratic machine they serve.

An initiative-taking and free-minded individual in Europe today must battle through endless bureaucracy built to sap the lifeblood from him, through layer upon layer of both national and European bureaucracy. The faceless agents in the European Commission decide what the individual thinks, how he works, and what he can and cannot do. The citizenry cannot remove those agents.

Which brings us to our second prominent European, EU antitrust chief Margrethe Vestager. When this uber-bureaucrat wants to go after the largest companies in the world, there is nothing that those companies, their employees, or their shareholders can do in the end other than acquiesce to what will hopefully be a bearable level of financial pain. Google and other U.S. tech firms are learning this lesson the hard way as Vestager takes it to Google by simply redefining the rules of the road when it comes to what antitrust regulation should aim to achieve. In Vestager's view, the primary principle of antitrust regulation is to impose a "special responsibility" on dominant companies to not abuse their power.[52] Of course, the bureaucrat gets to define unilaterally what that special responsibility and abuse of power are, much to the chagrin and demise of targeted companies.

The bureaucratic haul from U.S. tech firms in the name of antitrust protection, but really on behalf of EU bureaucrats, totals over $13 billion since 2004. The total is composed of over $9 billion from Google, $1.2 billion from Intel, $1 billion from Qualcomm, and over $2 billion from Microsoft.[53] In one year, 2018, Google was hit with a $5 billion fine by Vestager and the EU. This is just the start, as the numbers will keep growing over time. Vestager claims that these massive fines on companies will spur innovation and help society.[54]

In Europe, the bureaucrat has supplanted the individual when it comes to deciding what is best for the ordinary Italian, German, and other Europeans. Only through a turbulent breaking of chains such as Brexit and the resistance emanating from Eastern Europe can a country and individual hope to reacquire the lost freedoms once enjoyed.

That dynamic was at play with the *gilets jaunes* (Yellow Vests) revolt in France in 2019 when scores of Creators, Enablers, and Servers brought the country to a halt by saying, "enough is enough." Most Americans do not appreciate the irony of the movement using yellow vests in its name and on the backs of its members in the streets. First, government bureaucrats require by law that every motorist carry enough yellow vests for him and his passengers in case of an accident. The law helps justify the job of the technocrat, creates a windfall for the revenue-seeking vest manufacturers, and annoyingly taxes the drivers who must buy them. Second, political elites (the most notable being President Macron) forced higher fuel taxes on the population in the farcical pursuit of saving the planet. The fuel tax hit the non-urban working class that relied on cars hard while the tax had little to no impact on the urban wealthy. Although the Yellow Vests consists of disparate interests and lacks a cohesive plan, it stays uniform in its opposition to the bureaucrat and elitist.

Left unchallenged, the United States faces a similar or a worse fate than Europe at the hands of such schemers. The time when true liberals looked down on and criticized bureaucracy as much as conservatives do is long gone. Today, the Leech rules liberals and believes government and its bureaucracy are good and necessary parts of society. So-called liberals argue we need more government to cure a range of societal ailments. President Obama summed it up best when he said, "If you were successful, somebody along the line gave you some help. . . . If you've got a business, you didn't build that. Somebody else made that happen."[55] Obama beautifully articulated the arrogance of bureaucracies across the globe by believing nothing gets done without government and its allies. Anyone who has achieved anything meaningful outside of the bureaucratic class knows better and also realizes most accomplishment today is despite government.

LEECH-TARGETED CALLINGS

BEYOND THE GOVERNMENT

BUREAUCRAT

"Don't go into corporate America. You know, become teachers. Work for the community. Be social workers . . . make the choice as we did, to move out of the money-making industry into the helping industry."

MICHELLE OBAMA

THE LEECH TARGETS PROFESSIONS BEYOND GOVERNMENT
The government bureaucracy may hold the largest contingent of Leeches in society today, but it is far from alone. The economy and society have large hot pockets of Leech-targeted professions and constituents. Those pockets continue to rise in size and stature, compounding the burden on Creators, Enablers, and Servers. In certain instances, Leeches have commandeered entire professions, which now exist exclusively for them. In other instances, the profession keeps an essence of Creator, Enabler, or Server purpose, but it often is led by a Leech posing as the profession's protector and defender.

Often, government bureaucrats play a supporting role in the wars waged for control of the profession. Sometimes that support is direct, while at other times it is indirect. In all instances such support is by design. Left unchallenged, these segments of society and the economy will inevitably succumb and unite with government bureaucrats in a never-ending quest to pilfer others' value.

USING THE LAW AGAINST SOCIETY

Attorneys are one of the largest and oldest targets of the Leech, particularly the plaintiffs' bar. Don't misunderstand this as a hatred for attorneys; I'm one. More than a few of the greatest minds and best people I know are lawyers. Close to half of the signers of the Declaration of Independence and more than half of the attendees to the Constitutional Convention were attorneys. Attorneys were the first protectors of our republic.

The evolution of the legal profession from protector of the republic to what it is today tracked pari passu with the evolution of government from small and limited to today's voracious administrative state. Deep State creep through one hundred years of leadership spearheaded by Woodrow Wilson, FDR, LBJ, and Obama shifted the legal profession's focus from facilitating private transactions among Creators, Enablers, and Servers and protecting individual rights to working for the government. Today, the legal profession astutely correlates more regulation and higher complexity to more billable hours. The greater the regulatory universe, the greater the profit and power of the legal profession.

Consider how so many activities, transactions, and endeavors require a lawyer. The requirement of using a lawyer today is as pervasive as it has ever been in mankind's history. That is not by coincidence, but by design. Endless rules and laws sit on the books to create and protect a monopoly, one that attorneys continually feed from. Laws and codes are so complicated today that compliance requires droves of lawyers who do nothing but specialize in narrow areas of expertise. The legal system slows things down and often brings all activity and progress to a hard stop. Everyone, from the individual to the large corporation, is reliant on the lawyers to stay in compliance with an ever-growing volume of laws and regulations.

How far out of control it has become is clear in two ways. First, look at where the plaintiffs' bar always focuses their attention: where the money is, or to put it in Big Four parlance, the focus is where the Creators, Enablers, and Servers create value. Second, consider how many instances there are of the plaintiffs' bar working to drag an area that was outside of the Leech orbit into its gravitational pull. For example, scores of major law firms eagerly take legal stances that support the Left's positions in Supreme Court cases on executive powers and bureaucratic authority. Yet those same major law firms will vigorously avoid any public support of less-government-is-good positions on these issues. Three poignant examples illustrate the plaintiffs' bar at work.

The first example is Michael Mann, the Penn State academic who engaged in controversial climate change research. Mann sued the *National Review* for defamation after the publication criticized his data analysis.[1] The courts allowed Mann's suit to commence, and the plaintiffs' bar successfully penalized dissent via lawsuit. The results are alarming: free speech is chilled, scientific debate is stifled, science gets dragged into litigation, and the attorneys likely get paid no matter what the legal outcome.

A second illustration highlights a much larger nexus between the plaintiffs' bar and legal academia. Here the plaintiffs' bar hijacks what was traditionally a neutral entity whose mission was to interpret common law. That entity was the American Law Institute (ALI), which since the 1920s was a thought-leader on how attorneys and judges could clarify common-law areas to improve the administration of justice. The ALI restatements of the law served as de facto user's manuals for the legal profession. The contributors to the ALI that developed the restatements were historically nonpartisan.

That changed in 2009 when the ALI published *Restatement of the Law Third, Torts*. Of course, torts are the favorite stomping grounds of the plaintiffs' bar. As the ALI contributing authors to the restatements became stacked more toward plaintiffs' attorneys, it was not surprising to see the tort restatement attempt to rewrite the law to favor new ways for people to sue, through lawyers of course, along with ways to improve the plaintiff's chances for success. This trend appears in certain areas of the law, including consumer warranty, contract law, and liability law. Masking this effort as looking out for the little guy, the reality is that the ALI nakedly promotes new aspirations for what the law should be so that it spawns more lawsuits and litigation. The results are a more congested court system, more costs for businesses, more risk for property owners, and higher prices for consumers who eventually pay to cover the higher costs of all the litigation risk.

A third illustration is the plaintiffs' bar coordinating with federal regulators. Although we have a bevy of agencies to choose from, the Food and Drug Administration (FDA) shows how this works. The FDA, like a host of other government agencies, has adopted the habit of issuing warning letters to food and drug companies. These warning letters are not official rules or regulations. They are nonbinding and are presented to serve as nothing more than unofficial guidance. Often, they are unclear. The letters typically cover minutiae, nuanced technicalities like whether "all natural" and "low fat" can be used on certain food labels or if the volume of ice in a cold drink should be subtracted from the stated liquid volume on a drink container. A substantial majority of these warning letters is so mired in technicalities that average consumers would not see an impact on their choices or health.

What purpose do letters of warning serve, if they are unclear, mired in technical details, don't impact the health or choice of consumers, and are not binding? The answer is that such letters offer a target-rich environment for the plaintiffs' bar to launch hundreds of class action lawsuits on food and drug companies. Typically, these lawsuits never make it to trial but end up as multi-million-dollar settlements. Substantial majorities of the settlement dollars don't go to consumers but to attorneys' fees.

Today's regulatory legal system is a fixed game operating under a false cloak of respectability. The defense attorney hired by the individual or corporation, the plaintiff attorney or prosecutor bringing the action or charge, the judge sitting over the process, and the bureaucrat regulator drawing up the rules along the way are all beneficiaries of the system no matter what the outcome. Fighting, whether in court or out of court, is much more important to the well-being of lawyers, bureaucrats, and judges than winning or losing. The longer the process continues to play out, the more the system benefits, to the direct detriment of the client. Meanwhile, the individual, the taxpayer, and the corporation are the marks who continue to be worked by the system.

What's chilling about this rigged game is how it mimics what the criminal legal system has done when it comes to pressuring defendants, often from poor backgrounds and minorities, to plead guilty and forgo their right to a jury trial. The route of inducing those accused to cop a plea eases the administrative burden for the judges and the courts, allows the defense attorney to collect his fees, and notches another kill on the belt of the ambitious bureaucrat prosecutor. The accused is pressured with the specter of the prosecutor and judge instituting a much harsher sentence under a jury trial route versus a plea bargain, which is a big reason why over 90% of such defendants waive their right to a jury trial. The loser is the innocent defendant who follows the advice of his attorney and then pays the price with an admission of guilt, undeserved sentencing, and a criminal record that will hurt him for life. Today's rigged game across civil and regulatory legal disputes was copied from the criminal courts' playbook.

The role of the legal community in today's economy and society is the opposite of what we were taught. Historically, from Teddy Roosevelt's trust busting in the early 1900s through the liberal activism of the 1960s and 1970s, the legal system was viewed by many as an instrument of business owners to protect their economic interests. Voices in academia, government, public unions, and the media painted the legal system as being stacked in favor of wealthy individuals, corporations, Wall Street, and capitalism in general; that is, Creators, Enablers, and Servers. A focused, sustained, and steady campaign through the decades has transformed the legal system and has now reached the point where lawyers and judges have become part of the problem. Our legal system, not so long ago accused of only protecting commerce, was turned into an instrument of harvesting commerce to feed unproductive bodies.

The plaintiffs' bar stands at the center of a mass tort ecosystem. The ecosystem consists not just of the countless class action law firms, but also of marketing firms that identify and recruit potential clients for the class action suits, investors that fund law firms' suits, and a host of entities that look to creatively interpret data, science, and findings to link a product to harm. This ecosystem converges on Las Vegas twice a year for a giant conference, which describes itself as the largest gathering of mass torts entities in the world.[2] The focus of the conference is on refining techniques to perfect the ecosystem, including how to treat clients as commodities by packaging and trading them across lawsuits as well as how to cajole defendant companies to settle class action suits for a king's ransom.

Tobacco class action litigation set the precedent for how the plaintiffs' bar works with government and the judicial bureaucracy to procure hundreds of billions of dollars from the economy. The entire legal premise of this monumental effort rested on a dubious public nuisance theory, which allowed government and tort attorneys to pressure tobacco companies, supposedly on behalf of true victims, and then use the plunder to line bureaucrats' budgets and lawyers' pockets. Ex-smokers, the theoretical victims in the public nuisance charade, did not benefit from the litigation and only a fraction of the plunder ended up going toward smoking prevention efforts. The prices for tobacco products skyrocketed at the highest rate in history, providing a direct and regressive transfer payment conduit from the consumer (at the cash register) to attorneys (through fees). State governments ripped over $200 billion from private companies and consumers, which was quickly squandered on bureaucratic spending sprees. Attorneys pocketed $20 billion in fees, which doesn't include the handsome fees pocketed by attorneys defending the tobacco companies (another proof point that attorneys always seem to win, no matter which side they represent).[3] Bankers converged on inept state bureaucrats after the settlements, offering up-front cash in exchange for onerous terms and burdensome future payments, with the eventual costs being footed by taxpayers. Worst of all, a Pavlovian focus was established to search for the next fertile feeding ground where mass tort practitioners could shake down companies and consumers to enrich attorneys and government bureaucracies.

The next major opportunity for the plaintiffs' bar weaponizing public nuisance theory developed about twenty years ago, just after the ink dried on the tobacco settlements. This time the target was opioids. The parallels are obvious: victim props of smokers and addicts, shakedown marks of big tobacco and big pharm, and exactors of bureaucrats and attorneys spanning two professional generations. Expect the magnitude of the plunder from the opioid litigation to easily exceed that from the tobacco litigation, with attorneys and bureaucracies once again being the beneficiaries.[a] Do not expect the true victims of today's epidemic of opioid addiction to benefit any more than smokers did twenty years prior.

If you think the societal cost of mass tort litigation is an exaggeration or is limited to tobacco and opioids, contemplate the mass tort ecosystem in action by taking inventory of a growing tally of established, global corporations steeped with Creator, Enabler, and Server legacy that have succumbed to these predatory legal tactics. Johnson & Johnson (J&J), an iconic American company, now faces an existential threat stemming from tens of thousands of tort lawsuits filed across a range of the company's business lines, including surgical products, medications, and baby powder. Jury awards against J&J for a sole case can be in the hundreds of millions or even billions of dollars. These fantastic sums, when extrapolated to the full case load, spell financial ruin for a company that vastly improves quality of life for millions of people. Look at the nightmare facing chemical-agriculture giant Bayer: its 2018 acquisition of Monsanto and its popular weed killer product Roundup™ may destroy a proud company that markedly improved the human condition for 150 years. The pharmaceutical-agriculture company faced over 18,000 Roundup™ plaintiffs in July 2019 and

---

a   Many experts predict the opioid litigation bonanza could exceed an unfathomable trillion dollars.

then saw that number explode to over 42,000 plaintiffs three short months later (Bayer faced over 50,000 plaintiffs by April 2020).[4] That growth was largely catalyzed by over 650,000 Roundup™ lawsuit ads that appeared on TV in the first nine months of 2019 looking to recruit plaintiffs.[5] Bayer lost $30 billion in market value since the inception of the Roundup™ lawsuit feeding frenzy, and there looks to be no escape from suffocation by tort. J&J and Bayer are facing the same playbook used by tort attorneys in other industries, particularly manufacturing. It's a playbook that helped make asbestos attorneys rich, while scores of manufacturing and industrial companies making honest livings competing in the marketplace are bled.[b]

Even if the Creator, Enabler, or Server wins in court, they can still lose later. When five oil giants were sued by New York City, San Francisco, Seattle, and Oakland bureaucrats for future damages from climate change, everyone shrugged their shoulders. When the suit was brought by a plaintiffs' firm who went city to city trying to drum up additional plaintiffs, no one batted an eye. When the oil companies spent millions of dollars to defend themselves, shareholders accepted it. Thankfully, the oil companies prevailed in the suit, sort of. That's because more lawsuits are sure to follow, and no one is going to be surprised by it. The temptation for the companies to settle these suits will grow, earning the plaintiffs' firm a contingency fee and the city bureaucrat a windfall. The victors will be the plaintiffs' law firm, the big city bureaucrats, the court staff, and the oil companies' law firms and legal staff. The losers will be taxpayers who must pay for their government's legal escapades, people who use oil (everyone) who will wind up paying more for it due to this growing cost tied to producing it, and the shareholders of the oil companies who will realize lower profits due to this institutionalized tax.

---

b   Things have gotten so far out of control with the asbestos tort lawsuits frenzy that two key demographics are squaring off against one another: tort attorneys are suing universities on behalf of employees who worked in buildings that contained asbestos and later developed mesothelioma. Yet don't lament for the university; for even if it loses the lawsuit, the taxpayer and tuition-paying student will surely pick up the tab.

The plaintiffs' bar has defiled class action lawsuits to where they have become nothing more than revenue generators masquerading behind rhetorical showmanship. In 2010, Google had a class action lawsuit, representing millions of search engine users, filed against it for alleged fraud and invasion of privacy. Google settled the suit by agreeing to pay over $5 million into a fund to be distributed to nonprofits specializing in internet privacy issues. Google and the plaintiff attorneys selected the recipients. The plaintiff attorneys who brought the suit on behalf of the class charged upwards of over $1,000 an hour for their service and received over $2 million in legal fees.[6] Several of those nonprofits that ended up receiving settlement cash were already being funded by Google and were producing work product that supported Google's positions on various internet policy issues. Three recipients were plaintiff attorneys' alma maters.[7] In case you are waiting to read how much of the settlement the class received in the lawsuit: zero. The arrangement hatched by Google, the plaintiff attorneys, and the funding recipients was so blatant that in the summer of 2019 a federal appeals court had to strike down the settlement and send it back to the lower court for reconsideration.[8]

This stacked system of legal coordination affects everyone creating, enabling, or serving, not just large corporations. You are paying for it every time you go to the doctor. In just twenty one years, from 1969 to 1990, the number of medical malpractice lawsuits filed in the United States increased three hundred-fold.[9] The explosion in medical malpractice litigation exponentially increases medical malpractice insurance and overhead costs for medical providers, driving up healthcare costs for everyone.

Or consider landlords who rent houses or apartments to tenants. A sizable number of us would assume that if you rented from them and stopped paying rent, you'd face eviction. Most renters acknowledge this and typically waive the right to a jury trial in case of eviction with a clause included in standard lease agreements. It's a basic principle understood by landlords and their tenants.

Except that simple principle does not apply to the California residential rental market. In California, the confluence of the plaintiffs' bar, the courts, government bureaucrats, and big-city progressive politicians is methodically subsuming and ruining the residential rental market. This occurred over time and through a series of coordinated actions to stack the deck to favor certain stakeholders and to punish other stakeholders. The first move was back in 2005 when the California Supreme Court ruled that rental/lease agreement waivers of jury trials in eviction cases are unenforceable.[10] That led to a rush of new trials in eviction cases, creating more demand and job security for court bureaucrats. Then came the second move, which was the Sargent Shriver Civil Counsel Act enacted by California in 2011, which provided nearly $10 million in annual state funding for free legal counsel in civil cases.[11] Some of that money goes to setting up offices in court houses where free help in preparing for cases is given to eviction defendants, adding to the stack of civil eviction cases in the system. Then came the plaintiffs' bar now jumping over to the defendant's table, with lawyers coming out of the woodwork looking to defend clients facing eviction. Of course, the attorneys were signing up clients without much of a care whether the client was wrong or not. Instead, the lawyers were looking to use litigation to pressure landlords to settle, with the attorney pocketing a sizable part of the settlement. While all this is playing out over extended periods of time, the tenant who stopped paying rent does not have to leave the house or apartment and can continue to live there.

Going from bad to worse, in mid-2018 San Francisco passed Proposition F, which guarantees any renter facing eviction an attorney paid for by the city.[12] The California residential rental sector winners are: litigious attorneys with a new, target-rich environment of no-risk fees and clients; the court system with more lawsuits that will require more judges and higher budgets; the tenants who don't pay their rent and can remain in the residence indefinitely; and the government bureaucracy that will have to enlarge to administer all of this mess. The losers, unfortunately, are fairly obvious: law-abiding landlords who get fleeced in ever-increasing litigation and watch the value of their properties decline via effectively a government taking; tenants who pay their rents and will now pay higher rents to cover the litigation costs and eviction delays of their landlords; the taxpayers who will pay for the increased government and bureaucracy; middle-class to lower-income residents who are now facing even more expensive and more scarce affordable housing; and the homeless whose chances of finding rental housing to get off the streets just got lower. The biggest loser in this mess is the American sense of what is ethically right and wrong, for under the current reality of the California eviction process, the state is encouraging and rewarding tenants not to pay their rent.

Do all attorneys earn our disdain? As Florynce Kennedy once quipped, "The question arises whether all lawyers are the same. This is like asking whether everything that gets into a sewer is garbage."[13] A substantial segment of the current legal system is suspect, even though most attorneys are competent, ethical, and fair. Hate the legal game, not the individual attorney player (author included).

THE COMMON CRIMINAL: CLASSIC LEECH

Unfortunately, there are professional criminals. In fact, it is the oldest and purest Leech profession. The profession includes slick, educated white-collar convicts like Bernie Madoff to the physically brutal gang members. They all skim by hook, crook, or force what the rest of us produce. If we don't defend ourselves and fight off the criminal, we lose our wealth. Fending off criminals is costly to Creators, Enablers, and Servers, an illicit tax on their wealth.

TEACHERS' UNIONS VERSUS GOOD TEACHERS, STUDENTS, AND TAXPAYERS

Certain professions and entities are difficult to categorize into one of the Big Four. Sometimes the difficulty arises because a generic label of a single profession is used to describe what are many different professions. We jam them into one label. That is a mistake, especially when dealing with professions that have big impacts on society, which leads to inaccurate views on how to think about these roles and what we should expect from them.

The teaching profession serves as a case in point. The job category has many different jobs: kindergarten instructor, elementary school gym teacher, high school calculus teacher, public school administrator, college undergraduate philosophy professor, medical school professor-researcher, and so on. One size does not fit all.

What is expected of the teacher depends on knowing more about what type of teacher he is. The job of the kindergarten instructor is to offer young kids an environment where they start to develop social skills. The role of the elementary school gym teacher is to get kids moving, learning the value of physical fitness, and hopefully developing an appreciation for teamwork. The mission of the high school calculus teacher is to supply the student with math fundamentals, so the student is prepared for the next level, most likely college. The job of the college philosophy professor is to supply a basic understanding of theory and to guide the undergrad to a degree. The duty of the medical school researcher-professor is to teach graduate students how to perform research while at the same time aiming for medical breakthroughs, cures, or discoveries.

In terms of the Big Four, the kindergarten instructor and elementary school gym teacher are Servers; they satisfy a want of parents when it comes to developing their children. Life might not fundamentally change for the kids without gym class, although their wellness and social skills would suffer. The high school calculus teacher is somewhere between, or a combination of, an Enabler and Server. If the calculus student is eyeing a technical college degree, the teacher is providing the student intellectual capital that can be applied to succeed at the next level of college and to enter the workforce as a Creator. At the same time, the calculus teacher is also a Server, tasked with instructing how to calculate first derivatives. The medical school professor-researcher is a combination of Server, Enabler, and Creator. She is simultaneously providing facilities for, and instruction on, performing research to the grad student (Server), facilitating the grad student and research team to be all they can be in the lab or operating room (Enabler), all while driving toward a research breakthrough (Creator).

You hear talk about how a teacher's worth is measured by whether he inspired students. That's overblown; providing inspiration is not unique to teachers and can be found in all job categories. An engineer and her invention inspire new, later inventions from peers. A nurse inspires a surgeon to perform at a higher level or inspires a patient to recover sooner. A musical performer inspires the audience.

Instead, if you want to measure the effectiveness of a teacher, look to the skill level of the student at the end of the lesson, school year, or degree. Can the third grader add and subtract? Is the high school student able to write clearly and persuasively? Can the undergraduate civil engineering student perform the necessary structural calculations? Is the lawyer equipped to pass the bar exam? If the answer to these questions is no, then it doesn't matter how inspirational the teacher was, he simply has not done his job.

While we have been keeping it positive in our discussion of teachers, we need to also keep it real. Unfortunately, there are teachers who resist being measured, evaluated, and held accountable to tangible performance metrics. That type of teacher, and we have all dealt with that type as students or parents, runs counter to Douglas Lovelace Jr.'s observation that, "one of the hallmarks of a true profession is its ability to assess and regulate itself."[14]

Sadly, there are teachers today who happily wallow in mediocrity. Frustratingly, the system allows this, and in certain instances, encourages it. The bureaucracy and regulation that come with the Leech mindset grow in public education and start to overwhelm the more talented teachers out there working hard to have meaningful impacts. That drives the talent out of the profession and leaves students with inept, poor instructors.

Typically, teachers' unions and school administrators are in the middle of it all. Public unions, including teachers' unions, present a dilemma. Even Franklin Roosevelt, the creator of the government bureaucratic state via the New Deal, understood that collective bargaining and strikes by public unions should not be tolerated and instead should be viewed as insurrection since they harm the citizenry that the government worker has pledged to serve.[15] Although union representation constitutes only about 10% of all workers nation-wide, unions have thrived in the public sector and cover over a third of government workers.[16]

Public unions spent years and countless dollars solidifying their grip on taxpayers and students by successfully mandating collective bargaining in over thirty states.[17] Mandated collective bargaining in school districts has definitely benefited the union and the politicians who answer to them, probably improved marginal teacher's salaries and benefits, and absolutely harmed students. Public unions have also destroyed state budgets: states that force public workers, including teachers, to pay either dues or agency fees contribute a disproportionate share to this nation's $1.5 trillion-plus cumulative state pension deficit.[18] Destroyed state budgets wreck state services for all citizens, from kids to senior citizens.

Once created, a teachers' union enjoys close to eternal status, rarely having to face an election or decertification. Most parents, taxpayers, students, and even teachers fail to realize that teachers' unions exist without any current teacher ever having voted to form the union in the first place. Only one percent of teachers in Florida's ten largest school districts were on the job when those districts voted to unionize.[19] The New York City public school system teachers' union, the United Federation of Teachers, was created in 1960, meaning virtually no one out of the over 100,000 current teachers in the union ever voted to create it.[20] Ninety-nine percent of teachers in Florida's largest districts and all New York City public school teachers had a union forced on them from day one of their careers. This is institutionalized conscription of public schoolteachers, districts, and the students they serve in the form of a perpetual public union. Thankfully, much needed reform may be in store now that Florida and other states are starting to enact legislation requiring teachers' unions to stand periodically for recertification.[21]

After the public union inserts its hooks, it will clutch at anything and everything viewed as a potential food source. In 2018, the California legislature made an offer to the cash-strapped state public university system that would be hard to refuse: $120 million in cash to put toward the university system's woefully underfunded pension plan.[22] There was only one catch: the $120 million was contingent upon those universities agreeing to kill a plan to offer unionized workers a 401(k) plan instead of a defined benefit pension plan.[23] Why would the California legislature want to demand the elimination of a 401(k) plan that would improve the prospects of the already massively underfunded pension? The answer is simple: the public unions representing those university workers know that keeping workers in a perilous pension plan tied to future benefit promises is needed to continue to influence politicians in the legislature. For the public union and state politicians who answer to it, taxpayers, students, and public workers are pawns to be manipulated to achieve total control.

Teachers who view their job as a profession that carries enormous responsibility will hopefully think long and hard about the benefits of, and need for, a union they never chose but simply inherited. Instead, motivated teachers should rely on their ability, talent, and value to drive wages, job security, and advancement. The better you are and the more you outperform as a professional, the more money you make and the more your services are in demand. Unions historically have played a vital role in improving work conditions for a traditional blue-collar workforce, in industries that viewed labor as an exploitable commodity. Conversely, unions moving into the professional class of government workers typically spells trouble for professional standards.

Unionization of teaching has lowered the expectations and accountability of the profession. A culture has been created where high performers are not rewarded while underperformers, who are paid the same under a union contract, rarely face professional consequences. The union seniority system creates a workforce where younger, outstanding teachers receive lower compensation than older, underperforming teachers.

Until a recent U.S. Supreme Court decision, if you were a driven, motivated teacher and you didn't like what the system of union entitlement creates, in twenty-two states including California and New York, you had no choice but to continue to pay the union what is technically considered an agency fee.[c, 24] If you were a teacher in those same states and you didn't support a candidate that the union wanted to endorse and make campaign contributions to, you once again had to pay the agency fee to the union. If you were a high-performing educator in those states and the union wanted to fund climate change initiatives, sanctuary city advocacy, marijuana legalization pushes, or a host of other agenda items that you may not agree with, you yet again had no choice but to turn over a portion of your hard-earned salary to subsidize those union campaigns. If you were an impactful mentor-teacher in those states and you felt your paid agency fee being used to fund the union's positions violated your free speech rights, you needed to grin and bear it.

The argument espoused by public union bosses is that the teachers who don't want to pay union dues would be getting a free ride on the benefits of collective bargaining in the form of wages, job security, and time off. Applying this twisted logic results in forced conscription of teachers into the union, whether they want to be members or not. Teachers who don't want to take part and pay up aren't the free riders the union cast them as but instead are hostages whose free speech rights are hijacked.

Things came to a head concerning agency fees when a sixty-five-year-old Illinois state employee who opted out of the public union, Mark Janus, sued the union. Mr. Janus brought the suit because he felt paying the required agency fee, which was 78% of full union dues, funded union speech that ran against his personal views and thus violated his free speech rights. Thankfully, the Supreme Court in *Janus* decisively struck down the concept of public union agency fees not violating the free speech rights of employees wishing to opt out.[25] The decision also

---

c   Under federal law, unions cannot force a worker to join. But certain states have passed laws requiring employees at unionized locations who don't want to belong to the union to pay agency fees in lieu of union dues. The agency fee, or sometimes called a "fair share" fee, is typically slightly less than, but a sizable portion of, full union dues.

required the government to obtain proof that workers waived their free speech rights before deducting union dues from paychecks. The impact of *Janus* and the benefits to teachers have been immediate. A union can no longer force teachers who disagree with its political views into mandatory contributions. In the summer of 2018, Pennsylvania stopped collecting agency fees from 24,000 state workers, giving elementary school teachers an immediate effective pay raise of hundreds of dollars.[26]

Even though the Supreme Court sent a clear and resounding message to states and public unions with *Janus*, expect the more Leech-centric states (and cities) and the ever-probing public unions to search for and create methods to circumvent or frustrate the new law of the land. Post-*Janus*, a Pennsylvania local of the public union behemoth American Federation of State, County, and Municipal Employees (AFSCME) enforced resignation windows for employees who wanted to exit the union and stop paying dues or agency fees. Those resignation windows are open only for fifteen days once every three to five years (thankfully, several collective bargaining agreements for public unions in Pennsylvania are being amended to allow for employee opt-outs at any time).[27] Pennsylvanian public unions' *Janus* shenanigans are mild compared to what is going on in the Golden State. California's hatred for *Janus* runs so deep that it gladly tramples free speech rights to help suppress public workers' choice. A few days after the U.S. Supreme Court agreed to hear the *Janus* case, California passed a law that prohibits a public official/officer to "deter or discourage public employees" from remaining in, or joining, a public union.[28] Of course, the California state bureaucracy and the public union leadership are applying an expansive definition of what "deter" and "discourage" might constitute, and they use the threat of legal action to chill all speech that would explain the rights of public workers not to be part of a union. These types of tactics result in millions of government workers nationwide having their public union dues confiscated by union bosses. Despite *Janus*, self-motivated teachers wanting to escape the union doldrums may find themselves in a situation, where, once you're in, you're not getting out.

Besides hurting high-performing teachers, the union and collective bargaining arrangements hurt students over the entire course of their academic careers and working lives. The damage being done to our kids runs deep: studies found that compared to what employers require in the workforce, high school students on average are deficient when it comes to writing ability, math skills, reading comprehension, and work ethic.[29] According to the study of employers, less than 1% of high schoolers are deemed to be excellent in science and under 2% are excellent in math.[30] Students who matriculate the full twelve years through a school district with mandatory collective bargaining end up on average earning less, having jobs requiring lower skills, and being more likely to be unemployed than fellow students in school districts who did not have statutorily mandated collective bargaining.[31] The union's desire to kill a meritocracy culture within teacher ranks quickly morphs into a culture of mediocrity within student ranks.

Teachers' unions made sure the pandemic crisis exacted its heaviest toll on the demographic that faced the lowest health risk: kids. School administrators were easily manipulated by unions into shutdowns through the end of the 2019–2020 school year, the abandonment of grading, and the removal of student accountability.[d] The justification was the old standby of "equity," where students without access to the internet or the ability to speak English would be at an unfair disadvantage. The true motivation was to seize the opportunity of the crisis to shed teacher accountability by the measurement of student aptitude, grades, and test scores. Students paid the price, whether elementary or high school, rich or poor, black or white, or urban or rural.

Every time new data come out showing dropping or languishing test scores in math or reading, rest assured the teachers' union and its obedient politicians will amplify the constant drumbeat of needing more

---

d   A University of Washington study of remote learning across 477 school districts during the pandemic shutdown found only 27% of districts required tracking of student participation and only 42% of districts had homework count toward final grades.

"investment" in K–12 education.[e] This despite the fact that between school years 1999–2000 and 2014–2015, state spending on K–12 education went up an average of 18% (calculated using real, inflation adjusted, dollars) across the United States.[32] Since 1970, public school teacher employment ballooned by more than 50% while student enrollment increased only a few percentage points.[33] [34] Total public school employment grew even more when you consider the recent hiring booms in extended staff and administrative positions. Teachers' unions love to advocate for creating those non-teacher positions because it means more dues-paying members, even if there is little-to-no justification for the slots. In West Virginia, student enrollment fell 12% from 1992 to 2014 as non-teaching staff increased 10%, and in Kentucky over the same period non-teaching staff grew over six times as fast as student enrollment.[35]

Los Angeles is a more extreme case. The Los Angeles Unified School District (LAUSD) lost 245,000 students in the past fifteen years due to poor performance, such as a dismal 22% math proficiency rate for fourth graders, driving an exodus of students and families to charter schools and other districts.[36] But state-wide K–12 spending is up 70% since 2012.[37] What did all the money go toward? Not students; LAUSD teachers enjoy an average all-in compensation level of $110,000 per year and teachers can retire as early as age fifty-five and not have to pay a penny for healthcare until they are Medicare eligible.[38] The LAUSD is running a $500 million annual deficit that will drop it into bankruptcy within two years.[39] Despite the dire situation of the failing district, the LAUSD in early 2019 offered the teachers' union a 6% raise and a commitment to hire 13,000 more employees to avoid a walkout. Yet the teachers' union, representing 33,000 employees, went on strike demanding even more excessive increases in pay, pension, retiree

---

e   "Investment" in the context of K–12 education spending debates is typically code for higher taxes, pacifying powerful teachers' unions and feeding bureaucracy. Rarely is investment about more and better resources for the students.

healthcare, and bloated staffing that add up to $3 billion in additional costs and spells certain LAUSD bankruptcy.[40]

Instead of going to higher salaries for better performing teachers, money also poured into underfunded pension plans and excessive retiree healthcare benefits for retired teachers. The rate of increase is alarming: over 14% of education spending in 2018 was to cover pension costs, compared to only 7.5% in 2001.[41] Most of the West Virginia teachers who went on a state-wide strike for higher salaries in 2018 didn't realize that if taxpayer money poured into the state underfunded pension plan had instead been invested into teacher salaries, the average teacher salary would have jumped by over $10,000.[42] The troubled LAUSD is spending $350 million annually on retiree healthcare benefits, which is an amount sufficient to fund a $10,000 annual raise for active teachers.[43] LAUSD has seen pension costs more than double since 2014.[44]

Clearly, the troubling and pathetic performance of our public school systems cannot be attributed to lack of investment. The investment keeps growing. Because of union coercion, far too much of the investment goes to the ballooning non-teaching staff and the ever-growing pension and retiree healthcare liabilities for retirees far removed from the classrooms. A shrinking piece of the investment ends up in the salaries of solid teachers to serve and reward taxpayers, students, parents, and those high-performing teachers.

All the money and all the added positions have done little to improve student ability and have burdened taxpayers and government budgets greatly. Disappointingly, higher spending, in total dollars or on a dollars per pupil basis, does not correlate to higher pupil ability or rising standardized test scores. Often it is quite the opposite: several of the highest-spending states have the worst student competency scores in reading and math. They also boast highly entrenched and powerful teachers' unions that do not hesitate to skew data or abuse statistics to further gorge on the public taxpayer at the students' expense.[f] From the teachers' union perspective, poor performance and busted budgets are small prices to pay for burgeoning union rolls and dues levels.

The variation of the trusty Iron Triangle is employed by teachers' unions and other public unions, with devastating impacts on students, parents, and taxpayers. This variation of the triangle has the public union in one corner, which siphons millions of dollars every year into the election campaign coffers of legislators and appellate court judges (in states with elected benches). In some states, such as Texas and Pennsylvania, public union dues can be directly deducted from the paychecks of government workers straight into the pocket of the union. Once elected, the public union-bought legislatures and judges assume their positions in the two final corners of the Iron Triangle. The one corner (the legislature) makes the law that favors public unions and the other corner (the judiciary) interprets the law in a way to protect public unions when challenged. Politicians and elected judges then bend over backward for the public unions, granting unsustainable, out of market benefits that far outstrip state GDP growth and tax revenue.[9] Breaking this hold will require long, brutal campaigns on a state-by-state and school district-by-school district basis. Yet Creators, Enablers, and Servers would be hard-pressed to find a more worthy fight.

THE MEDIA: ONCE THE PROTECTOR OF DEMOCRACY NOW A PURVEYOR OF FAKE NEWS

No profession has experienced such a complete transition from the ranks of the Creators, Enablers, and Servers to the tribe of the Leech than journalism. The profession includes both traditional TV and print segments as

---

f   For a great summary of tactics teachers' unions apply to manipulate statistics, read "How to Lie with Statistics: Teachers Union Edition" by Allysia Finley in the Opinion section of the May 3, 2018, *Wall Street Journal*.

g   Check out the Wirepoints paper titled *Overpromising Has Crippled Public Pensions* at Wirepoints.com for a sobering, state-by-state comparison on public pension accrued liability and GDP.

well as digital and social media segments. Since the nation's earliest days, journalism and the media have played a unique role in public discourse and debate. That's why Thomas Jefferson wrote in 1789, "Were it left to me to decide whether we should have a government without newspapers, or newspapers without a government, I should not hesitate a moment to prefer the latter."[45] Sadly, what was the lifeblood of a strong, functioning democracy is today the public relations arm of the Leech.

The Society of Professional Journalism stipulates how critical information is to self-government and states, "It is the role of journalists to provide this information in an accurate, comprehensive, timely, and understandable manner."[46] Journalists were taught to report the news, which comprised the who, what, where, when, and why of the events reported. The opinions, ideology, and biases of the reporter had no place in the news, and it was the job of steadfast editors to guard against those things bleeding into the news stories. Abe Rosenthal, the legendary executive editor of the *New York Times*, would famously quip that his primary legacy would be that he, "kept the paper straight" and avoided political or personal biases from steering the paper to the left or right.[47]

What we have today is not that, for that is dead. Instead we have a large segment of journalists who either don't want to do the hard work that it takes to be a professional or who promote a biased philosophy and camouflage it as journalism. Through a toxic coalition of the lazy professionals and the dogmatic zealots, journalism today is ethical totalitarianism. It is far too common to hear a budding journalism student proudly proclaim he is entering the field to press for social justice and cultural change. A large segment of the American media manufactures facts and parades them as truth. Some of the most storied media entities in the land allow bias to supersede objectivity.[h] In the 1980s, Russians

---

[h] You can't even trust media today to self-report their political affiliation. A poll showed over half of all journalists were Independents while only 28% were Democrats. Something tells me that's incorrect. (http://archive.news.indiana.edu/releases/iu/2014/05/2013-american-journalist-key-findings.pdf)

knew *Pravda* was not the literal translation of "truth." Today, Americans know their media is a similar propaganda machine.[i]

The impact of a poisoned media is large. Malcolm X once stated, "[T]he media's the most powerful entity on Earth. They have the power to make the innocent guilty and to make the guilty innocent, and that's power. Because they control the mind of the masses."[48] A precursor to modern-day journalists' and the media's willingness to manufacture image and to suppress reality began in 1968 with the infamous coverage of the Vietnam War's Tet Offensive. Despite the offensive being a major tactical loss for the North Vietnamese communists by military standards, the media (most notably, Walter Cronkite) covered it in such a way that the American public viewed it as a communist victory. Ho Chi Minh's best ally and biggest weapon during the Vietnam War was not China, the Viet Cong, or even South Vietnamese ineptitude; it was the American media.

Scores of journalists today are guilty of both laziness and ideology. The editor of the *New York Times* proudly admits that the paper might embrace bias when covering a president it doesn't like.[49] This despite the *Times'* code of conduct stating, "No one may do anything that damages the *Times's* reputation for strict neutrality in reporting on politics and government."[50] Also concerning was the sacking of its editorial page editor and the subsequent resignation of Bari Weiss. The editor's offense was running an Op-Ed from a sitting Republican member of the U.S. Senate. Weiss's resignation letter lamented that Twitter has become the Times' ultimate editor and how she was bullied by staff because of her views. When you read that tagline of the *New York Times* front page that states "All the news that's fit to print," ask yourself what exactly that means to

---

i   Elon Musk knows there is a complete lack of respect for the media and journalism today. Musk laments the, "holier-than-thou hypocrisy of big media companies who lay claim to the truth, but publish only enough to sugarcoat the lie."

the modern-day journalist.[j] Abe Rosenthal is turning in his grave.

Remember the fiasco that was the Duke lacrosse rape controversy? There were many things wrong there, from not respecting due process to the behavior of government. But the most telling was how the media wanted to proffer a story instead of covering the facts. In a rare moment of transparency, the assistant editor of *Newsweek* shockingly lamented that, "The narrative was right, but the facts were wrong."[51] He was caught honestly stating what many mainstream media genuinely believe.

Even reporting on the weather can be fake news these days. When you turned on a news or weather channel to see the projected track of tropical storm Florence in September of 2018, you were greeted with a presentation that was more akin to a drama script and trailer for an action movie than a simple weather update. The reporters applied sensational, dramatic phraseology, including "monster," "crashes," "storm of a lifetime," "extreme threat," and of course the always dependable standby, "catastrophic." Video and photo images of tattered American flags being whipped at the beach were pasted everywhere to create symbolic imagery of how the climate was crumbling the Union. Those pathetic reporters assigned to cover the storm were planted in the middle of some beach or parking lot with a rain jacket emblazoned with the network logo, clutching a mic, and screaming above the wind about how windy it was. If it wasn't windy enough to make the point to the audience, a reporter would drop any remnant of journalistic integrity and act on camera as if he was being pushed back by an imaginary wind that didn't exist.[k] Coverage of Florence taught us that if you want to

---

[j] Recalls Christopher Hitchens in *Letters to a Young Contrarian:* "I myself check every day to make sure that bright, smug, pompous, idiotic claim is still there. Then I check to make sure it still irritates me."

[k] The standard for reporters faking weather conditions was provided during tropical storm Florence in 2018 when an out-of-breath reporter in a North Carolina parking lot was acting as if fierce winds were about to pick him up and carry him to sea. There were only two problems. First, the live video panned just behind him to show two people nonchalantly walking by with no problem as they leisurely took selfies. Second, the data on the screen showed actual measured winds far from hurricane force.

know what the weather is like, look outside, and if you want to be entertained by a fictional made-for-TV drama, tune in to fake weather news.

Today's media crisis is not liberal-conservative or Democrat-Republican. It is much deeper and more profound. Journalists have lost the respect and confidence of the American public. A 2017 study by the Pew Research Center found only 11% of Republicans, 15% of independents, and 34% of Democrats think national news organizations are "very trustworthy."[52] A 2019 Gallup poll indicated only 18% and 23% of Americans had a "great deal of" or "quite a lot of" confidence in TV news and newspapers, respectively (only Congress posted a lower confidence score).[53]

Elite journalists have little in common with the average reader. Is it really that surprising to see that half of the reporters at the *New York Times* and *Wall Street Journal* hail from elite colleges and universities?[54] A quick listen of the filth spewed at the 2018 White House Correspondents Dinner and a quick review watching well-known and supposedly professional journalists laughing and guffawing the night away tells you all you need to know about the current state of this profession.[i] What was once a noble mission to challenge government power has been reduced to defending an unaccountable bureaucracy.

We may very well have passed the point of no return. Today's mainstream media openly editorializes to the point of propaganda in alleged straight news stories. During the 2016 presidential election, certain media allowed favored campaigns to veto or edit story drafts before publication.[55] During the 2020 pandemic crisis, the media reported that during a press conference President Trump encouraged people to drink or inject home cleaning products as a remedy to the virus.[56] The press conference transcript shows he never said such a thing.[57] Yet it was relentlessly promoted until it became accepted truth. Mark Twain wrapped truth with humor when he said, "If you don't

---

[i]   Go to YouTube and search for "2018 White House Correspondents Dinner." Then watch the comedic train wreck and adulation from so-called professional journalists.

read the newspaper you are uninformed, if you do read the newspaper you are misinformed."[m]

The Leech understands the power of a controlled, aligned press and works to destroy a free press. The federal government already shovels over $440 million of our money each year to public broadcasting through the Corporation for Public Broadcasting, a Lyndon Johnson–hatched bureaucracy created in the 1960s.[58] But that is not enough; there is never enough when we are talking about government subsidy of the media and journalism. The state basket case of New Jersey in the summer of 2018 passed legislation to fund the Civic Information Consortium.[59] The Garden State's politicians, in concert with in-state academia and the media, appropriated $5 million of precious taxpayer money to funnel into subsidizing news coverage in under-served communities.[60] The money would be doled out by a bureaucratic board consisting of political appointees, academic appointees, and community groups.[61] New Jersey and its leadership have shown the rest of the country a novel way to subsidize journalists via government largesse. The media will undoubtedly return the favor by sending constant, biased, and misleading messages across a range of topics to promote and support its sponsors. What the rest of us should not expect is for Jersey journalists and reporters to criticize any of the key groups who feed them, including politicians and professors.

Yet even forced taxpayer subsidy will not save journalism from years of abuse of power and lack of integrity. Journalism is an endangered species heading for extinction. *Rolling Stone* magazine is a case in point. The supposed music magazine with the leftist rhetoric is facing tough times.[n] Circulation has dropped and newsstand sales are a fraction of

---

m   Evidence linking Twain to this quote is shaky at best. Nevertheless, whoever said it hit a chord that resonates more than ever.

n   To understand how ignorant *Rolling Stone* is when it comes to music, review its 100 Greatest Guitarists list. Eddie Van Halen sits at only #8, meaning seven guitarists were better? Randy Rhoads at a ridiculously low #36? Rush's Alex Lifeson at #98, far below an underwhelming Jerry Garcia and an overhyped Lou Reed? *Rolling Stone* would not know a guitar god if impaled by a Flying-V.

what they were.[62] The same trends are playing out across newspapers and magazines everywhere.

The demise of journalism is not from digital technology. Instead, journalism is dying because the audience no longer believes in media integrity. When the now infamous Mueller Report was issued in March of 2019, it showed Russian collusion was a hoax and exposed mainstream media's blatant bias and unethical behavior. Yet no one was surprised when the *New York Times* and *Washington Post* were awarded a 2018 Pulitzer Prize for, "deeply sourced, relentlessly reported coverage in the public interest that dramatically furthered the nation's understanding of Russian interference in the 2016 presidential election and its connections to the Trump campaign."[63] Those words are an epitaph rather than a salutation.

FOUNDATIONS AND NON-PROFITS: WOLVES PROWLING IN SHEEP CLOTHING

Charitable and nonprofit organizations are another group that spans a spectrum from those that Create, Enable, and Serve to Leeches. Where the charity falls on the spectrum is often determined by what income bracket its contributions come from: studies show the middle class donates mostly to religious institutions and basic-needs charities; while wealthy households concentrate their donations to universities, private schools, the arts, and medical foundations whose missions bleed into setting social culture and norms.

Then there are the charity world whales, prominent multi-billion-dollar foundations that provide the biggest and best examples of both ends of this spectrum. These large foundations are established and supplemented by ultra-wealthy sponsors using the U.S. tax code to inject mega-dollars into them without incurring capital gains or estate tax.

This compact has in certain instances spurred the most meaningful and impressive foundations on the globe. The Bill and Melinda Gates Foundation's ongoing work to eradicate polio and prevent malaria has tangible benefit to countless human beings. The Charles Koch

Foundation's work to protect free speech and entrepreneurship is on the front lines protecting free enterprise. Impactful foundations and charities like Gates and Koch attack societal problems much more effectively than inept government, which is why leftist believers in the omnipotent state often vilify these organizations as competitors. Laws and tax rules that allow wealthy individuals to create these types of foundations clearly have potential for a return on taxpayer investment.°

Despite shining examples set by exemplary foundations looking to do tangible good, there are other foundations out there that use these same tax laws to pursue something different. The aim of these entities is to use foundation tax rules to do two things. The first is to avoid tax payments on the donor's estate without losing control of his money. Once a foundation is set up, the founding donor can control his money for years as well as retain the ability to hire friends and family while paying them high salaries to manage the foundation. The second is to use foundation money to argue, push, lobby, and cajole government to adopt policies that favor Leech-friendly interests. Whenever you see a big-name foundation funding campaigns for things like carbon taxes and universal free college tuition (or, universal free anything, for that matter) look out for someone using the tax code to gain favorable treatment.

Often an established foundation created years ago by a founder who desired to promote the values of Creator, Enabler, and Server experiences a modern-day hijacking. Once hijacked, the foundation is weaponized to fund programs that clearly conflict with the intention and desire of the founder. The $1 billion Surdna Foundation serves as a cautionary tale. Founded by the great chemical industry capitalist John Andrus, the foundation focused for years on funding orphanages

---

°   Even the best foundations sometimes are not perfect when it comes to spending money where it is needed versus spending it on distractions. Foundations need constantly to review how their money is being spent to ensure the best bang for the buck is in their missions. Foundations that spend excessive amounts of endowment or income on overheard staff, shiny offices, lavish events, or glossy public relations do not deserve the favorable tax treatment that was granted with the understanding that the money would go toward the missions of the foundations.

and elderly homes to provide a fighting chance for the disadvantaged young and a comfortable life for the underprivileged old. John Andrus's views on people in between young and old was that they should look after themselves. Today, the Surdna Foundation exercises a mission far afield from the intention of its founder. Bureaucrats fund a range of programs that John Andrus would have found undesirable. When descendants of Andrus dare to challenge the current mission of the Surdna Foundation, its board, staff, and allies in the philanthropic community show little sign of changing course.[64] The original intent of a founder is thrown aside.

Deviating far afield from original, noble intention is not unique to foundations. One can find the same behavior with non-profit organizations whose history or name is one thing and current practices and actions another. What were once beacons and stalwart supporters of core values to the American way of life are now accomplices and vanguards in altogether different crusades. Two pertinent examples illustrate this trend.

The first example is the American Civil Liberties Union, or ACLU. Few individuals or organizations have done more historically than the ACLU to protect free speech in the United States. Whether the message was popular or unpopular, morally attractive, or reprehensible, the ACLU stood tall to preserve free speech as a fundamental constitutional right for all Americans. Consistency, principle, and predictability were ACLU attributes.

But today's ACLU is not the old ACLU. The current guidelines for determining which free speech cases the ACLU defends now include content or views. If the contested speech is contrary to the political views and beliefs of the ACLU, the group may simply refuse to assist the entity facing sanctions. Amazingly, the protection of free speech, which is the reason for the ACLU to exist, is placed second in line behind the political and social views of ACLU leadership.

The historic free speech tip of the spear, the ACLU, has changed. Instead of "I disapprove of what you say, but I will defend to the death your right to say it," the ACLU evolved into something along the lines of "I will defend to the death your right to say anything I agree with."[p]

The second illustration is the Southern Poverty Law Center (SPLC). The SPLC, founded in 1971, spent years successfully taking on the Ku Klux Klan and defending civil rights. But today, the SPLC has morphed into an entity that assigns hate labels. And assigning hate labels pays: the SPLC is fed by a $500 million endowment.[65] The SPLC has gone after people as diverse as a Jewish conservative thought leader (Dennis Prager) to a Somali-American woman who advocates for women's rights (Ayaan Hirsi Ali).[66] Nonprofit groups defending religious liberty have been branded as hate groups by the SPLC. The SPLC branding someone with the hate tag then gets reported and amplified across like-minded mainstream media and social media platforms. Major media treats the SPLC as an authority on hate, celebrities donate large sums of money to the SPLC, and corporations contribute millions of dollars to the organization.[67, 68] The SPLC's words, amplified by these powerful media allies, serve as a call to action for others.

Ironically, in 2019 the SPLC had to fire suddenly its cofounder and suffered the resignation of its president days later for unspecified reasons. Speculation swirled that the workplace culture left much to be desired.[69] A concerning situation for an organization that traces its lineage back to the civil rights movement.

There is another category of foundations and non-profits: ones that since their creation have been sold to the public as something different than what they truly are. Consider Planned Parenthood, which says it is a healthcare provider, but critics argue it is primarily an abortion provider. The debate centers around how many of its services versus clinical activities are abortions.[70, 71] Such nuance matters for image: Planned Parenthood comes across as much more sympathetic and positive when viewed as a healthcare provider for women versus

---

[p]   The line "I disapprove of what you say, but I will defend to the death your right to say it" is wrongly attributed to the Enlightenment thought-leader Voltaire. Instead, Beatrice Evelyn Hall wrote it in her biography titled *The Friends of Voltaire* to describe the great thinker's views.

an abortion clinic. It also matters for dollars: U.S. tax dollars cannot directly subsidize abortions; so, presenting a small percentage of clinical interactions as abortions preserves Planned Parenthood's $543 million in annual federal funding.[72]

Abortion is legal in the United States and Americans mostly support a woman's right to choose. Those facts are not in dispute or up for debate in this book. What needs revealing is Planned Parenthood's playbook. Planned Parenthood aggressively uses its funding to market, advocate, and lobby a range of positions far afield from providing healthcare to women, such as advocating positions on federal judge appointments, climate change, immigration, or federal appointments to the UN and various NGO positions. Planned Parenthood is not only a healthcare provider or more narrowly an abortion provider but sits at the center of the advocacy universe on a host of issues.[q]

Certain foundations and nonprofits are not as subtle as Planned Parenthood and brazenly buy access to government. Consider the interesting case of Bloomberg Philanthropies granting $6 million to New York University (NYU) Law School's State Energy and Environmental Impact Center. That donation alone is not a concern: Bloomberg is free to waste as much of his foundation's money on climate change posturing as he likes. What is of concern is that the NYU entity took the money and used it to entice the New York State Attorney General's office to hire attorney bureaucrats, dubbed "special assistant attorneys general," whose salaries the center would pay for over a two-year tenure.[73] The caveats the center insisted on were that the individuals would work on progressive climate change positions and provide quarterly progress reports back to the center.[74] The New York State Attorney General's office was happy to accept the offer.[75]

Sure enough, two special assistant attorneys general were placed in the New York AG's office and they went about doing what attorneys do:

---

q   The 2016–2017 Planned Parenthood Annual Report touts environmental justice, immigration policy, and a host of other causes as core to its effort.

the AG brought suit against Exxon, supported New York City's lawsuit against oil companies, and sued the Trump administration EPA. And New York is not alone: Maryland, certain other states, and Washington, D.C., are following suit. The template has been set where foundations and nonprofits openly plan with government bureaucrats to rent state police powers as a weapon to assault Creators, Enablers, and Servers.

WALL STREET: HOW TO DIFFERENTIATE

Wall Street is a mosaic of many different professions, each playing separate roles and falling into various categories of the Big Four. Think of the varied responsibilities and roles of stockbrokers, mergers and acquisition bankers, money managers (hedge funds, mutual funds, etc.), private equity bankers, and financial advisors. It is misguided to throw all these professions into one bucket.

Stockbrokers for years were the classic Wall Street profession. Stockbrokers are the conduit for investors who want to buy and sell stocks. That conduit is not free, and brokers typically charge a fee for each transaction and might also take a percentage of profits resulting from the transaction.

Conceptually, stockbrokers fall in the Servers of the Big Four. They provide a service to the rest of us that allows their expertise and network to be applied on our behalf, so we are freed from spending time and money figuring out how to buy 100 shares of Amazon ourselves. They make our life easier and turn us loose to spend time on other things thereby increasing our utility.

However, there is another face to stockbrokers. Certain rules and barriers to entry for investors buying and selling securities are designed to preserve the need for stockbrokers. It wasn't too long ago when, if you wanted to buy or sell a stock, you had to go through a broker. That's a classic Leech characteristic: rules constructed to protect the profession and a fee charged for the service that feeds off a stream of activity (investing) of others (investors).

We discussed how technology can create new categories of Server professions and make other Server professions obsolete via creative destruction. That is the case for stockbrokers with the advent of the internet, online trading, and exchange traded funds (ETFs). Today, the stockbrokers' protected market has been overrun by these innovative technologies breaking down the barriers to entry and undercutting the classic broker route by offering much quicker and cheaper alternatives.

Financial advisors are a classic Server profession, especially when one views the role as someone who designs and executes your financial plans as opposed to the shot-caller on investment decisions. They make our lives easier by helping with our financial plans and portfolios. They offer services to file our tax returns and to open and manage various accounts.

Some people are comfortable with financial advisors taking on a wider role, where the planner makes actual investment decisions on behalf of the client. Under this expanded mandate, financial advisors morph from exclusively Server to Server and Enabler, moving them closer to money managers.[r]

Hedge funds, one of the best-known money managers, are investment partnerships where the general partner invests the pooled capital of the limited partners to get returns in both up and down markets. Hedge funds are quite varied and employ a range of different strategies to maximize returns. Money managers, especially hedge fund managers, often receive unpopular press and publicity as greedy, arrogant, and elitist. That's unfortunate because money managers, including hedge fund managers, play a vital role in our economy. They are classic Enablers or Servers, depending on who the client is. The biggest clients and investors in hedge funds are pension plans, insurance companies, universities, and charities. So if the hedge fund performs and delivers a good return on the client's investment, that client will have the resources

---

[r]   A note of caution should be applied to financial advisors when compensation incentives motivate the advisor to direct client money into certain investment vehicles. That's a potential conflict of interest that clients should be on the lookout for. Always understand how your advisor is paid for his service.

(i.e., money) to enable it to further its mission or allow it to provide better service to its customers (for example, lower insurance premiums to rate payers or better pension benefits to retirees). Hedge funds, due to their wide mandate to invest virtually anywhere, help equilibrate capital pools. They can invest directionally, counter to peak and trough cycles, which helps smooth cycles. Hedge funds supply capital at critical times to businesses looking to access financial markets.

The criticism of hedge funds hovers around the fee structure and compensation levels for the general partner. The infamous 2-and-20 rule where the general manager receives 2% of assets no matter what the fund performance is each year and 20% of the profits above a certain threshold can certainly lead to some stunning fees and compensation levels, even in poor performing periods. But fees and performance have a way of working themselves out in the hedge fund industry. There is accountability, almost too much at times, where if a hedge fund doesn't deliver, either because of out-of-market fees, poor returns, or both, clients can simply place redemption calls on their money and invest with other money managers and funds. Survival of the fittest is alive and well in the hedge fund world. If Mr. Market supports a 2-and-20 fee structure, then so be it.

Private equity bankers suffer the same criticisms and misunderstandings that dog hedge fund managers. They also share many of the same traits of the hedge fund manager when it comes to offering needed support, opportunity, and service to the Creators, Enablers, and Servers out there. The résumé of private equity as an Enabler and Server is extensive and impressive when you consider all the Creator, Enabler, and Server businesses that were seeded, grown, or liberated by private equity over the years.

Then there is the mergers and acquisitions (M&A) banker. An M&A banker might be less interested in whether there are good deals for the client than he is interested in just getting a deal done. The M&A banker structures the deal to take a percentage. Whether in the end the deal was good or bad for the client is not a factor in determining if or how much the banker is paid. You will see some very effective M&A bankers convince a client one year to over-pay to acquire a business and then turn around in a couple of years and convince that same client to sell the same business at a loss. The cash register rings twice for the M&A banker in this situation, regardless if the deals made money for the client. If M&A bankers ceased to exist, deals would still happen. Sometimes M&A bankers have tell-tale signs of the Leech way.

WHERE LEECHES TEND TO CONCENTRATE

As with real estate, location matters when it comes to the Big Four. Since the nature of the Leech is to explore ways to create new Leeches and to propagate its control over others, you might expect to see them concentrated in certain geographical locations. Like any organism, it will look to settle where the ecosystem is most favorable.

Those favorable ecosystems are on the two coasts, particularly in urban areas. New York City, Los Angeles, San Francisco, Boston, and, of course, Washington, D.C., are metropolitan areas that pulse intense red on the Leech heat index. Coastal California and downstate New York are long-established incubators for Leech activity. Leech culture has become so entrenched in these areas over time that the design of the rules, regulations, and systems support the Leech way of life.

Once critical mass happens, the city or region transitions from an exporter of value (derived from the efforts of the Creators, Enablers, and Servers) to an exporter of need. Creators, Enablers, and Servers across the nation pay for and subsidize the need. Sometimes the price paid is direct and in the form of higher taxes, excessive regulatory fees, and low to no accountability in public services/servants.

For example, the pre-Trump federal tax code allowing complete deduction of state and local taxes on federal income tax calculations rewards financially out-of-control states and cities while it differentially penalizes regions of the nation where fiscal discipline and lower taxation are exercised. The Leech centers stay on the path of irresponsibility and unsustainable spending while allowing residents to pay less federal tax.

The reduced federal tax revenue from these states and cities was paid for by everyone else who filled the gap, either through direct taxes or through more of the federal budget having to go toward interest expense to service a growing federal budget deficit.

All of that changed suddenly with federal tax reform in 2017, when this ill-advised perk was reduced and capped in exchange for much-needed lower tax rates on personal and corporate incomes. Suddenly, states and cities drunk with high government spending could no longer shield their income-earning citizens from high state and local tax rates. Expect mass migrations of top earners out of economically repressive places like California, New York City, and New Jersey and into states and localities that allow producers to keep more of their hard-earned wealth. In the past ten years, millions of Americans have migrated from high tax states to low tax states, and that trend will only accelerate.[s] Don't expect the bureaucrats and policy makers in regions experiencing the exodus to change their spending or their extreme rhetoric, at least not until things reach a fiscal breaking point. It is no accident that California Governor Jerry Brown referred to the Trump tax plan as "evil in the extreme" and described Senators as "acting like a bunch of Mafia thugs" when they voted to pass the law.[76] Governor Moonbeam knows a threat to his food source when he sees it. For the first time in a long time, an action came out of Washington that favored Creators, Enablers, and Servers to the detriment of the Leeches. Time will tell how much of it is undone by President Biden and Congress.

The price paid by Creators, Enablers, and Servers is hidden sometimes. Federal subsidies for roads, schools, entitlement programs, and housing disproportionally favor the large coastal urban areas at the expense of flyover states. The same is true for tax dollars to subsidize the arts: Open the Books data show that federal agencies in 2016 poured over $200 million, or nearly half of the total $440 million of

---

[s]   For an excellent, interactive tool that ranks states by their tax policy and resulting economic competitiveness, check out "Rich States/Poor States" at *http://www.richstatespoorstates.org/* .

spend, into only ten states.[77] Would you be surprised to find out that those ten lucky states included some of the most left-leaning areas of our country, including New York and California? Would you find it shocking that these tax dollars were often used to create a plethora of leftist propaganda parading as art?

Coastal urban elites also enjoy a hidden subsidy from the rest of the nation and middle class in the form of electric vehicles. Politicians and environmental groups use climate change alarmism to shove electric vehicle mandates down the throats of the citizenry. Automakers can't make money producing electric vehicles. So bureaucrats and lobbyist proceed to throw federal and state subsidies on the shoulders of the same citizenry to help narrow the losses of, and provide false hope to, the automakers as they manufacture electric vehicles at a loss to satisfy the mandates. The starting prices for the electric vehicles are considerably higher than those for the average gasoline-powered car. That's why only 1% of electric vehicle buyers made less than $50,000 a year and why nearly 80% of the federal tax credits for electric vehicle purchase were claimed by households with adjusted gross income greater than $100,000 a year. Despite all the subsidization and mandates, the electric vehicle segment accounts for only 0.5% of total vehicle sales, automakers continue to lose money manufacturing the vehicles, and the impact of electric vehicles on climate is somewhere between minuscule to negative. The net wealth transfer flows of this sequential scheme are billions pumped from flyover states to the coasts, billions siphoned from the middle-class taxpayer to high-income earners, and billions pulled from the shareholders of automakers to rent seekers. Think about that the next time you see an overpriced electric vehicle on the road.[t]

---

t   Proponents of electric vehicles love to obfuscate these vexing issues by pointing to Norway as the standard of success. Electric vehicles in Norway post an impressive 50% market share of new vehicle sales. Impressive until you realize the massive subsidization the government applies to electric vehicles, to the point where there is no free market for new car sales. Where does the government get the money to pay for all those subsidies? Oil revenues from the burgeoning Norwegian fossil fuel industry. Without oil revenue, there would be no subsidy and no discernible electric vehicle market share in Norway.

Think about how much of our federal tax dollars get continually poured into Washington, D.C., a city created for and dedicated to the bureaucratic class, to build and support an extensive range of amenities and services beyond what the rest of us enjoy in our hometowns. Everything in the District of Columbia, from the city, to the jobs, to the infrastructure, is paid for by the rest of the country. Five of the six wealthiest counties in the United States are Washington, D.C., ring counties in Virginia and Maryland, filled with people making exceptional livings off the bureaucracy and at the expense of the taxpayer.[78] The next time you are in our nation's capital and you see one of those District license plates with "taxation without representation" stamped on them, realize what it should really say is "paid for by the rest of us."

What of tangible substance is built, extracted, or manufactured by Creators in New York City, Washington, D.C., or Los Angeles? Those economies may have been started by Enablers and Servers but now answer to the Leeches. The rules of the game are set so that taxpayers subsidize these regions, which have become epicenters of economic rent-seeking, financial speculation, and favor-swapping. Their elite are also protected from the negative impacts of the myriad rules, regulations, and bureaucracies they nurture and impose on everyone else.

While it may be a small consolation, the United States is not the only nation experiencing Leech geographic oppression. Just look to our friendly neighbor to the north. Alberta Province in western Canada embraces a strong work ethic that values the individual. Alberta has abundant reserves of fossil fuel energy, including oil, natural gas, and coal. Increasingly, bureaucrats and politicians across Canada impose stringent regulations, taxes, and requirements on Alberta and its booming energy sector to hinder and stop energy extraction.[u] The

---

u   Prime Minister Trudeau and the Left in Canada during the pandemic unleashed more punishment on Albertan free enterprise when they made federal emergency funding contingent on recipient commitment to the Paris Climate Agreement and zero net carbon emissions by 2050. In the middle of the pandemic, the Trudeau administration also announced plans to double the national carbon tax. That's the thanks the Leech provides to value creating industries like oil and gas, which provided about $8 billion annually in government payments.

increasing burden placed on the Creators, Enablers, and Servers in Alberta is used to siphon money from the province to locales including Vancouver on the west coast, Quebec Province in the east, and the bureaucratic heaven, Ottawa.

The Leech understands its locational demographics well and constantly probes for ways to strengthen its influence. Progressives and the Left clamor for abolishing the Electoral College for presidential elections. The argument goes that the popular vote should determine the president in a democracy. Yet the Electoral College was designed by the Framers of the Constitution to protect against regionalism and supermajorities in certain states from dictating who will be the president. Scrapping the Electoral College and replacing it with the nationwide popular vote strengthens the hand of urban areas, magnifies the influence of populous states such as California, and gives complete election oversight to the federal government. It should surprise no one that as to who would benefit from abandoning the Electoral College.

THE TECH INDUSTRY'S DEAL WITH THE DEVIL

If you can find industries, fields, or careers that are ahead of government bureaucrats, you have a precious window of opportunity to do important things. Think of the fantastic, disruptive achievements of John D. Rockefeller in oil and Walt Disney in entertainment, where these great men did not wait for or need a bureaucrat's support or approval to create empires out of nothing. Yet once an exceptional entity is created, you can be sure that the Leech will soon be sucking precious resources from it.

Microsoft is a modern-day warning shot. When it first arrived, it was free to disrupt and change the world. Great progress and wealth were created. But once the regulators and bureaucrats caught up, Microsoft increasingly became just another food source for the Leech mob to devour. The attention regulators placed on Microsoft precluded it from eventually acquiring upstarts such as Google. Ironically, the origins of Microsoft trace back to an opening created by the government bureaucracy meddling with another successful tech company, IBM. Company names and disruptive technologies change over time, yet Leech stalking of success stays constant.

The single biggest reason Facebook, Google, Tesla, Uber, and Amazon have grown exponentially is not technology, strategy, a visionary CEO, or changing consumer trends. As important as those drivers have been, the single most important driver was that these enterprises were created and grew at a time when government and its allies didn't know they existed, didn't understand what they did, or often both. Fixated bureaucrats corral, control, and feed off the three big, proven pillars of our economy and society: energy, finance, and healthcare. Meanwhile, technology companies were growing exponentially, virtually free from government interference.[v] The tech giants Google, Microsoft, Amazon, Apple, and Facebook acquired over 400 companies in ten years without regulators challenging any on antitrust or other grounds. But government and a host of affiliated Leech acolytes have woken when it comes to the new economy, particularly the tech industry.

These tech Creator, Enabler, and Server companies have been so wildly successful that "tech" today stands as an equal, fourth pillar of our economy alongside energy, finance, and healthcare. Alas, we should not be surprised to see an array of interests across government, the legal profession, the media, academia, and elsewhere fixating on ways to pry control of the data economy away from the ones who built it and into the lap of the Leech. The prying will be in the forms of shareholder activist campaigns that have nothing to do with shareholder value and government bureaucrats pushing to regulate internet platforms as heavily as utilities, which have nothing to do with net neutrality. Politicians in cities that were put on the map by the tech industry, such as Seattle, Cupertino, and Mountain Valley, look increasingly to tax the hometown companies to the point where leaving may be the most viable

---

v   As renowned tech investor Peter Thiel puts it, innovation today is concentrated in digital
     industries because bits are lightly regulated while atoms are heavily regulated.

option. [w] Inevitably, certain presidential contenders will publicly call for the breakup of large tech companies. Taking cues from the Leech nest that is the EU, American regulators will soon use the Trojan horses of data protection and privacy as blunt instruments to break down and prey on the tech industry. [x] The activists, regulators, and politicians will be aided and abetted by academia, the legal profession, and the media. Ultimately, the goal is to corral the tech industry, like the energy, financial, and healthcare industries, to the point where it becomes an indentured servant that exists to feed others.

Expect a delicious irony coming down the pike for Silicon Valley tech firms. For years, the tech industry has subscribed to a host of leftist, misguided views on everything from identity politics to climate change. Now those same tech titans are thinking twice about their positions. Suddenly Amazon wonders aloud if Seattle, with its various tax schemes (head tax, new hire tax, and highly paid worker tax) aimed at large corporations to pay for affordable housing and the homeless epidemic, is the right place for a new corporate headquarters. And just when the online retail giant thought it had New York City eating out of its hand for its much-coveted second headquarters, the hand was bitten by state politicians, regulators, and activists to the point where Amazon embarrassingly announced it was canceling plans for the Queens complex. Uber woke up one morning in 2018 to discover its largest market, New York City, had banned it from hiring newly licensed drivers to meet the growing demand from New York City residents. It's déjà vu all over again in late 2019, when the ride-hailing firm wakes up to news that London is pulling its license to work. Pinterest, who confidently censors topics, such as anti-vaccination, that it deems to be "polluted thought" finds the tables turned on it when it's labeled as

---

w Politicians in Leech-centric areas also advocate for a tax on data, akin to a carbon tax. Proponents include the governor of California and local/state politicians from New York City.

x A Capgemini survey found that U.S. firms already spend 4% of their global revenue preparing for the EU's General Data Protection Regulation (GDPR). Touted as serving to protect consumers' data and privacy, in truth, GDPR's broad reach is a tax on free enterprise, whether in the tech industry or a host of other impacted industries.

an oppressor of speech. Facebook and Twitter suddenly find their business models in decline with earnings eroding in Europe as the new EU regulations on data privacy and protection take effect. The tech industry today faces a concerted and coordinated array of attorneys, bureaucratic regulators, and politicians launching attack after attack in the forms of class action lawsuits, multi-state investigations, and multi-layered probes consisting of states, the federal government, and supra-national entities such as the EU. Conjuring up Malcolm X, the tech industry's chickens are coming home to roost.

Google's recent troubles prove how external advocacy of leftist positions correlates to oppressive internal company culture. Although the search engine giant presents itself as the supporter of an open internet and a neutral provider of information, the internal culture is far from unbiased and balanced. Concerned and conservatively minded ex-employees filed a class action suit in California against Google for abuse and discrimination they received from company employees and management. The lawsuit points to internal emails, the in-house chat system, and seminars that continually shunned and bullied those employees who dared to express political views that differed from what most of America outside of humanities departments at universities would consider extremely leftist and socialist positions on a variety of issues. A sobering inside look at a provider allegedly committed to neutral and open content betrays something to the contrary.

Yet Google, which has eagerly aided the Leech platform to help catapult itself to great heights, now finds itself subjected to the legal tactics it embraced. Those same bureaucrats, politicians, academics, and journalists the company worked to placate now base their rallying cries for heavy regulation on Google's market share, its draconian internal culture, and its heavy-handed imposition of various social policy aims via its search engine coding. What the search giant thought were California social justice admirers have now turned to tech industry haters, as they vandalize company commuter buses in fits of leftist gratuitous mob violence. The weapons Google deployed to win favor in the past have turned and are now squarely pointed at the company, and they are being aimed at the company by the very stakeholders Google thought of as friends.

You can't help but admire Google as one of the great innovators in the tech sector and at the same time feel it is getting what it deserves. There is a populist intolerance for differing conservative political views at large tech firms as there is in Hollywood. That intolerance exerts itself internally on employees and externally on users. The brutal imposition of political cultural conformity aligned the tech industry within the Leech-heavy communities of academia, the media, and government. Tech assumed that adopting stances in line with these communities would earn favor with them, bolstering tech's social license to run and enlarge its competitive standing in business. Tech assumed its support for the Leech cause would create a defensive moat that would keep its business models safe.

The whiz kids of Silicon Valley missed a crucial element. The Leech cares nothing for ideology other than using it as a tool to extract resources from producers. Once the ideology has served its purpose, it is discarded. If the adoption of a different, even opposing, ideology from a prior one offers the opportunity to feed off someone else or something new, the Leech will not hesitate to flip. Leeches are agnostic to beliefs and values. They adjust and deploy them to gather more power, control, and resources. That's the evil genius of the Leech way.

Tech leaders would do themselves a favor by reviewing "inductivist turkey" theory. A turkey grew accustomed to the farmer feeding him every morning. The turkey wrongly reasoned there was nothing to fear when the farmer approached him on Christmas Eve morning. When the turkey walked up to the farmer, the farmer promptly slit the turkey's throat to prep the gobbler for Christmas dinner. The lesson, of course, is that things that occur in the past do not guarantee they will occur in the future. A farmer nurturing a turkey to grow before the slaughter is akin to a Leech aiding the growth of a tech firm before the inevitable devouring. The only difference is the tech firm is naïve and obedient enough to appease the Leech along the way.

The bigger and more successful the company or industry, the bigger the Leech prize. Ideology that may have been aligned with or supportive of the tech industry will quickly be dropped and replaced with an ideology that will call for more industry manipulation, control, and taxing. That's what is happening to the tech industry today. Apple is being muscled by activist shareholders and lawyers through lawsuits that claim the company's smartphones are damaging American youth. When Amazon wants to adopt innovative technology like drone delivery to become more efficient, a host of regulators tell them, "Not so fast" and exert control. As soon as there is an accident tied to a Tesla car operating on autopilot, federal bureaucrats from the National Transportation Safety Board become judge and jury in the accident investigation and slap down Elon Musk the minute he dares to speak up about his views on the accident's cause. Suddenly, government oversight must scrutinize Google and Facebook to make sure they are not purveyors of fake news and influencing elections. In 2018, Google found itself being shaken down by EU bureaucrats for a whopping $5 billion fine along with the specter of a $15 million a day running penalty if it doesn't revamp its business model to the bureaucrats' liking.[79] The 2018 shakedown is bookended by a 2017 hit of almost $3 billion and a 2019 slap of over $1.5 billion.[80] Germany's social media law may impose a 50 million euro fine on platforms that fail to take down fake news or hate speech postings within 24 hours of a complaint. No one even gives any of this a thought, for everyone recognizes what it all is: a legally-sanctioned tax pretending to be in the best interest of consumers.

What's even more troubling for the tech industry is that those looking to gorge on it are rapidly evolving their stalking tactics. Government bureaucrats, the plaintiffs' bar, and academia are justifying grabbing and strengthening their grip on the tech industry. The shifting of logic is across three fronts. All three arenas are instructive because they shine a light on the Leech's tactics and its ability to play the long game.

The first, and what will probably prove to be the most challenging arena where applied logic is changing, is antitrust theory. Historically, large companies like Standard Oil or AT&T were forced to break them-selves up by the government because their dominance in an industry, product, or service pushed out competition, limited choice for con-sumers, and raised prices. Government justified the ordered break-ups to protect the consumer's best interests by reintroducing competition, increasing choice, and lowering prices.

Today, tech companies such as Amazon confidently tout how they are reducing, not increasing, prices for consumers. Even though Amazon controls a large part of the digital book market, it feels it has nothing to fear from traditional antitrust exposure. Google gives its product away for free; thus, even though Google controls almost all internet searches, it does not fear antitrust action. For as long as these companies have been around, they were not concerned with the threat of antitrust break ups by government even though these companies were demolishing competitors left and right and gaining growing market shares. The companies viewed the threat through the lens of past historical inter-pretations of antitrust.

However, a host of government bureaucrats, lawyers, and profes-sors are arguing that even though these tech companies are not hurting consumers today, they are going to hurt consumers tomorrow. The reasoning is that killed-off competitors would have innovated new products, offered more choice, and even lowered prices if left alone and able to continue functioning. Emblematic of this reasoning is the European Union, led by its antitrust chief Margrethe Vestager, who has been advocating the theory that dominant companies have a "special responsibility" not to abuse power.[81] As to what that special responsi-bility might include, Vestager is conferring with academics to define. Many expect regulators to start to equate data to market power as an antitrust route to start heavily regulating or breaking up entities like Facebook. Expect this EU-centric view of tech companies and regula-tion to take root in the U.S.

Antitrust theory is also posing another substantial risk to tech titans by shifting focus from monopoly power to monopsony power. While monopoly is the ability of an entity to fix consumer and product prices, monopsony is the ability of an entity to control worker wages and supplier prices. A monopoly is a dominant seller while a monopsony is a dominant buyer. Assessing the need for antitrust regulation under a monopsony filter fundamentally changes the risk profile for large tech companies. Suddenly it doesn't matter if Amazon is reducing prices for consumers today or in the future. Instead, the key question under monopsony theory changes to whether Amazon has become so large it effectively controls and reduces its workers' wages or suppliers' revenues (which in turn precipitates a reduction in the suppliers' workers' wages). This new strain of antitrust theory is already spreading virulently across academic and bureaucratic circles.

The new antitrust theory pathways of future customer harm, special responsibility, and monopsony are already posing tangible threats to big tech. What makes this so effective is that antitrust theory is based on subjective interpretations of corporate behavior. Justice Scalia opined that, "the mere possession of monopoly power . . . is not only not unlawful; it is an important element of the free market system."[82] Companies typically do not fall under the antitrust grip of government for being big but instead for being big and conducting themselves in bad ways. Bad conduct is in the eye of the beholder, or in this case, of the government bureaucrat. As tech titans grew into enormous pools of potential resources to feed from, cohorts across academia, the legal profession, and the government bureaucracy suddenly decided the actions of these corporations were not in the public interest. The Leech gets to replace the free market system referenced by Scalia with a planned economy where resources are reallocated to lawyers and bureaucrats.

Compounding the problem is that the tech industry is not doing itself any favors by boorish, unethical behavior that subjects it to legitimate, traditional antitrust exposure. If a social media giant decides to ban a media outlet because the media outlet's beliefs run counter to leftist views, it is not impossible to find the platform is planning with traditional, leftist media outlets to run the targeted outlet out of business. This type of anticompetitive behavior was a problem for John D. Rockefeller and Standard Oil, and it will soon be a problem for YouTube and Facebook. It is also the type of problem that does not require any evolution or change in existing antitrust legislation to become real. Today, there are countless law firms and attorneys working for the Silicon Valley giants who are brushing up on the nuances of antitrust law and preparing battle plans. They should expect a long, drawn-out war.

A second arena of shifting logic posing risk for the tech industry is in something as simple as a definition or name. A name can make a massive difference when it comes to the degree of regulation, control, and oppression the government can exert. Are Google (via YouTube) and Facebook platforms and conduits for information or are they publishers? This nuanced detail is becoming a critical factor that may impact the futures of the biggest tech giants in the world.

As a platform or conduit (sometimes referred to as a public forum), a network provider, social media engine, or search algorithm is not subject to onerous government oversight. If considered a platform or conduit where people spread thoughts and opinions, it has the added advantage of not being legally responsible for content on its sites. The disadvantage of acting as a platform or conduit is that you must keep the space open to everyone, whether you agree or disagree with their politics and social views.

Google, YouTube, and Facebook now face a self-inflicted, legitimate risk because they want to have it both ways. They want the lax regulation and shield from legal liability of a platform or conduit, and they want the ability to control what material and messages are placed on their spaces of a publisher. For years, Google was considered nothing more than a search engine and Facebook nothing more than an app, both were basically platforms and conduits. That set them free to hunt down and suffocate traditional news providers such as print media and cable news. That also allowed them to push favored political and social views while suppressing conservative views without fear of libel or slander charges. Ironically, tech firms controlling content to favor Leech-favored views is what the Leech is now using to create leverage and control over the tech industry. Today, widening legal and academic circles are postulating that the Googles (because of their ability to impact search results), the Facebooks (because of more than half of young people getting their news from apps), and the Amazons (because of the ability to promote or not promote selected books) are news and content publishers. That would subject these tech titans to the same standards as newspapers and news stations. It would also open them up to legal liability tied to the content on their sites, which would be a boon to lawyers. Others in the same academic and legal circles are arguing these entities need to be regulated to force them to be open to everyone. The intolerant ideological cultures of the tech firms and their suppression of opposing viewpoints are their undoing. Acting like they were the thought police and propaganda machines for the Leech has also made them a Leech food source.

A third rail of risk is also growing. While redefining tech titans from platforms to publishers is real, the days of social media and search firms being shielded from liability arising from the actions of their users are coming to an end. Section 230 of the Communications Decency Act of 1996 is a critical piece of internet legislation.[83] That's because the section provides immunity for internet providers and social media platforms when publishing information provided by users.[y] Basically, Facebook and Google don't need to worry about legal liability if a user is posting or using the platforms for something illegal or that harms others.

But once Google and Facebook started to impose content guidelines for advertising services, they went from disinterested platforms open for all to editorial influencers of content. In response, Congress is considering whether that broad shielding from liability needs narrowing.[z]

---

y   The critical part of section 230 of the statute reads, "No provider or user of an interactive computer service shall be treated as the publisher or speaker of any information provided by another information content provider."

z   Unfortunately, President Trump was another proponent of repealing or watering down section 230.

In March 2018, the Senate passed legislation that allows plaintiffs' attorneys and regulators, two of Leechdom's founding members, to sue or charge internet companies whose platforms were used by sex traffickers. The legal argument is that the platforms aided and abetted trafficking. Expect further internet and social media company liability for user activities beyond sex trafficking and more feeding opportunities for lawyers and bureaucrats.

CAREER ADVICE TO YOUNG PEOPLE
IN THE AGE OF THE LEECH

How often have you read, heard, or watched someone of experience offering advice to younger people about career and life paths? You hear the old standbys of, "picking a path you are passionate about" or "making a difference in the world." Through the years, when I gave such advice, I tended to fall back to the old standbys as well. Then I changed my career advice.

First, I advise talented people under no circumstances to engage in a profession or endeavor where the Leech dominates. You won't create value and your talent will be wasted. It's along the lines of what Churchill said of the, "profound significance of human choice, and the sublime responsibility of men."[84] Besides, no one should want to go through his professional life being the person who, in the words of Adam Carolla, adds to the beach sign things you are not allowed to do.[85] Life is short, why waste it impeding others?

Second, I counsel talented individuals to seek out industries and careers that are to a large extent unregulated by government. Government bureaucrats are the single biggest threat to Creators, Enablers, and Servers. Government bureaucracy and intervention also stifle technology advancement by impeding innovation. Technology and opportunity may move quickly, but so does the Leech. Young people wishing to build and achieve are well advised to get in front of the Leech, not behind it.

TRAINING GROUNDS PART 1:

WHO RUNS ACADEMIA

"Education is a system of imposed ignorance."

NOAM CHOMSKY

"Universities are becoming laughing stocks of intolerance."

STEVEN PINKER

"I should sooner live in a society governed by the first two thousand names in the Boston telephone directory than in a society governed by the first two thousand faculty members of Harvard."

WILLIAM F. BUCKLEY

"Our Nation is deeply committed to safeguarding academic freedom, which is of transcendent value to all of us and not merely to the teachers concerned. That freedom is therefore a special concern of the First Amendment, which does not tolerate laws that cast a pall of orthodoxy over the classroom. . . . The classroom is peculiarly the 'marketplace of ideas.' The Nation's future depends upon leaders trained through wide exposure to that robust exchange of ideas which discovers truth 'out of a multitude of tongues, [rather] than through any kind of authoritative selection.'"

SUPREME COURT JUSTICE WILLIAM BRENNAN

THE ROMANTIC PERCEPTION OF COLLEGE
VERSUS THE TROUBLING REALITY

College is a time in life when one learns how to think through a bumpy, trial-and-error, and, at times, turbulent process. It's a place where young minds become exposed to different thoughts, viewpoints, and experiences and eventually evolve into well-rounded, independent-thinking, and open-minded people.

The mottos of the country's most esteemed colleges (with a quick conversion from sophisticated Latin to plain English) convey a consistent theme. There is Harvard with simply "truth" (*veritas*), Yale with the one-upper "light and truth" (*lux et veritas*), Columbia with "in thy light shall we see light" (*in lumine tuo videbimus lumen*), and the California Institute of Technology with "the truth shall make you free" (CIT shuns the Latin and goes with straight English).

Wikipedia defines academic integrity as, "The moral code or ethical policy of academia . . . This includes values such as avoidance of cheating or plagiarism; maintenance of academic standards; honesty and rigor in research and academic publishing."[1] The key words in that definition: *standards, honesty,* and *rigor.* Descriptors with which everyone wants to be associated.

Yet these mottos and definition could not be further from the reality of today's campuses. The lofty words and distinguished buildings mask an intellectual rot. Academia embraces a culture of aggressive intellectual intolerance that tracks and destroys diversity of thought, while disingenuously wrapping this naked effort at censorship in the cause of social justice. In a sad regression to less enlightened times, the most crucial form of diversity is eradicated. Free thought on campus is dead and buried.

In his 1941 State of the Union address, Franklin Roosevelt spoke of four essential human freedoms: freedom of speech, freedom of religion, freedom from want, and freedom from fear.[2] Today, colleges and universities deny students all four of Roosevelt's freedoms. Speech is not free but censored. Religion is not free because campus leftists restrict it. Students want and need skill sets colleges deny to them, and fear suppresses freedom.

Oppression on campus is superficially about the desire to control but more fundamentally about imposing rigid ideology. This pays dividends for Leeches as more of their beliefs invade and conquer campuses. Control society's thoughts and eventually you control the economy, which can then be turned loose to serve its new master.

CRAZED PROFESSORS, SHATTERABLE STUDENTS, AND UNIVERSITY ADMINISTRATORS: WORKING IN HARMONY

What is a crazed professor? The typical profile is a tenured, or desperately trying to become a tenured, professor in the humanities, social sciences, or liberal arts, embracing of a political ideology somewhere to the left of Bernie Sanders, who has never worked successfully in the private sector. The crazed professor constantly seeks opportunities to nail down job security by expanding sympathetic curricula and gaining tenure for himself and other crazed professors.

Although crazed professors constitute a minority of faculty, they enjoy an outsized impact on academia. He loves to make a scene that will elevate his profile within the school and beyond. Unfortunately, university governance plays right into the crazed professor's lust for the spotlight. That's because even the most obvious of decisions at a university must go through an excruciating consensus-building process that requires approval from staff, faculty, students, trustees, and alumni. A single dedicated crazed professor can bring a necessary and logical decision-making process to an abrupt halt. When the president of Ryder University in New Jersey wanted to cut low-demand and languishing majors like French and Philosophy to balance the school's budget, a group of professors called for and secured a no-confidence vote in their president that made national news.[3] As the current challenges of higher education mount and some leaders look to make necessary changes, the nuclear button of a no-confidence vote is being pushed by professors more than ever.

The crazed professor, while looking out for his own selfish interest in the short term, is also adept at playing the long game. He can afford to be patient, since most professors today spend only a fraction of the time teaching classes that their predecessors did decades ago.[a] Tenured professors enjoy generous full-time pay packages for part-time work that demands less than eight hours a day of effort for only six months a year. At most liberal arts colleges these days, the bulk of the instructional workload for core introductory classes is left to part-time faculty, temporary faculty, or grad students (all of whom, ironically while working at institutions that grandstand on income inequality, are paid next to nothing and typically do not enjoy job security, healthcare, or retirement benefits). That leaves more time for the crazed professor to invest into his strategic, long-term goal: taking a captive and gullible student body, and over the course of years beating into them a steady stream of propaganda that tattoos a Leech value system on what will become graduates. Those graduates, properly indoctrinated into the fold, will add to the ranks of the Leech across society and the economy.

What are crazed professors rarely? Those who toil in areas of study that the market covets and demands. You typically won't find such a professor in the engineering, medical, or core science fields. Those professors are busy being Creators, Enablers, and Servers.

Crazed professors are the residual product of a methodical eradication across academia of anything not extreme leftist. A recent study shows that left-leaning faculty of American higher education has a ten-to-one advantage to right-leaning faculty in the areas of journalism, law, economics, history, and psychology.[4] It's not unreasonable to expect the same, or even higher, ratios to be found across the humanities and outside of STEM fields. The study also found elitist, private, and non-religious universities have far less political diversity than state schools. A centrist professor in a political science department is an endangered species while a right-of-center professor doesn't exist. The killing-off of everyone not left-of-center

---

[a]   And good luck finding these underworked individuals in their offices or on campus outside of class times.

creates an unhinged, out of touch, and extremist faculty. Yet universities with a one-sided bent on ideology have the audacity to feel competent in offering a well-rounded education. And these intellectual prisons keep accreditation by alleged objective bodies.[b]

Anytime you see *administrator* in the title of someone on campus, the safe bet would be to assume he is a root cause of this epidemic. An administrator within a modern university system is code for bureaucrat. These administrators create and perpetrate endless causes of action, red tape, drama, and victimization to create justification for their jobs. The more outrageous and absurd the claims, the better, so long as the bureaucracy's power and budget grow. The ranks of the university bureaucrats continue to expand at an alarming rate: in 1990 the ratio of faculty and staff positions to administrator positions was 3.3 and by 2012 the ratio plummeted to 2.2.[5] From 1987 to 2012, over half a million administrators were added in higher education. And there is little reason to believe this trend will stall. When you strip out staff positions, too many colleges employ more non-teaching administrators than full professors. The faculty and students who go along with the bureaucrats are either useful idiots or willing accomplices to perpetuate the waste ecosystem.

The true power base in today's higher education system no longer sits with students or faculty but instead lies with the administrative bureaucracy. The tone is set at the earliest stages of a student's academic journey: most newbies to the higher education game are astonished to learn that admissions are typically run exclusively by the administrative bureaucracy, with little-to-no influence wielded by teaching faculty. The administrative bureaucrat is the puppet master pulling the strings so that the faculty and student body perform the required dance and adopt the sanctioned ideologies. The administrators' control spans the student's journey from admissions to graduation and the professor's career from

---

b   California's state university system is one of the most politically biased in the nation. Ironically, Section 9 of the California State Constitution declares that the University of California "shall be entirely independent of all political or sectarian influence and kept free therefrom."

grad assistant to tenured professor. Wasteful, excessive bureaucracy results in higher tuition, more distraction of student and faculty time, and lower rates of return on students' investment in higher education.

What is meant by the shatterable student? The good news is the shatterable student constitutes only a small minority of the student body. But the bad news is he mastered how to work the system to commandeer and disrupt the educational process. The shatterable student, although constituting a small portion of the student body, enjoys outsized influence on today's academic quads.

Foremost, the shatterable student is underworked. The quick math of fewer than thirty hours of studying and class time per week times just over thirty weeks of school a year yields an annual academic investment of time for a college student that is less than that for a typical eighth-grader. College students today invest significantly less time and effort into their studies than prior generations.

If you recently took a recruiting tour for high school students at a college campus, the shatterable student becomes blatantly clear. Student tour guides brag about organic-only selections in the dining halls for those picky palates, the countless social clubs for every imaginable demographic a person might identify with, dorm room suites that surpass the quality of kids' rooms at home, and pedestrian-only campus streets and walkways so as to not require the students to have to look up from their smartphones for vehicles while walking on campus.[c] The school will be sure to mention the low student-to-faculty ratio to ensure the personal touch as well as the extensive study abroad programs that serve as glorified vacations to exotic locales.

The presentation section of the campus tour will undoubtedly

---

c   My favorite experience on a campus tour was a student guide who wanted to emphasize how personal the support staff at that school were. She told the story of how when she returned from her study abroad semester in Italy the worker at the student union coffee bar remembered the student liked her espresso with sugar. Not having to even ask for the sugar was a great example of how that school's community was a cut above the norm. That's a stark collision of coddled rich students' requests for their espresso with blue-collar workers grinding for minimum wage.

emphasize those nice euphemisms of sustainability, diversity, inclusiveness, and equity. If you are touring a Jesuit, Catholic, or other Christian school, the presentation section of the tour will make multiple mentions of students not needing to subscribe to the school's religious affiliation, to the point where the strong impression is left that the school is embarrassed by, even apologetic for, its religious identity. By the time the tour concludes, the parent and prospective student both realize the college experience is not going to be a challenging opportunity requiring focus and hard work but instead will be a customized, catered four-year vacation of fun and relaxation.

Shatterable students are not born this way; they are formed and cured in the cultural environment that surrounds them. More specifically, shatterable students act like the most insulated and coddled humans in the history of the world, because that was how some of them were raised. College students today were born around 2000. For some, their entire lives have consisted of tightly supervised sports and activities, gluten-free food, constant parental attention, and limited social interaction with other kids that did not involve a smartphone. This has culminated in a segment of a generation unable to deal with run-of-the-mill issues and conflicts. When these kids who have experienced nothing but life in a bubble get to college, they demand an environment that the rest of us, or their fellow classmates, laugh at. If ideas are expressed that the shatterable students disagree with, they demand safe spaces to shield them from the speaker of the ideas, they push to disinvite speakers with whom they disagree to prevent them from stepping foot on campus, and they insist that the university administration handle the stressor in question in its entirety just like their parents would have done for them before they headed off to college.

Not long ago, the expectation of a student entering college was to go in a bit naïve, soft, and narrow-thinking and to exit after four years as well-rounded and focused. The graduate would be ready for battle in the world, armed with discrete skill sets. College threw you into the fire and for the first time in your life you had to adapt and, in the process, improve while learning how to think. Today, college is designed to do the exact opposite: students exit narrower minded than when they went in, clueless as to how the world works, and with a sense of entitlement that only a four-year immersion in a nanny state can create.

A small but powerful cadre of college students has become expert at creating self-victimhood, to the point where it is a virtue on campuses. If a student desires to be a celebrity and admired on campus, the student needs to find a way to stake a claim to being a victim. One does not need to be a low-income student to claim victim status: outrageous student behavior is found at the most elite of institutions and with the most privileged of students. Sometimes, the more coddled and richer the shatterable students are, the more likely they are to embrace self-victimization and oppression at the slightest affront.

An analysis of the subject of student learning disability vibrantly illustrates victimhood at work on campus. Certainly, there are select students who have true learning disabilities and require reasonable accommodation during their collegiate experience. But most people are surprised to learn that today almost one in four students at select colleges and over two million college students nationwide are considered disabled.[6] Disability rates have skyrocketed in a few short years and will likely continue to rise.[d] Many of the disabilities relate to mental and learning issues that can be challenging to assess such as depression, anxiety, attention deficit, and stress. Students' self-diagnosis leads to self-actuating behavior such as simply not getting out of bed in the morning. A Harvard study in 2014 found that, on average, student attendance at lectures falls from 79% at the start of a semester to 43% at the end of it.[7]

Indications are a portion of the growing ranks of allegedly learning-disabled students are gaming the system. Statistics and the numbers tell you that. The barriers to getting tagged disabled are low and the benefits gained are many. Legally all that is needed to be designated disabled is

---

d   By way of example, Pomona posted 22% of students as disabled in 2018, up from just 5% in 2014.

a note from a doctor. Once the student has the note, he is entitled to a range of accommodations during his four years on campus: extra time for exams, being allowed to walk around during class, and, my favorite, bringing a comfort animal to a lecture or exam.

The fact that the student who doesn't get those perks is disadvantaged in the same class is irrelevant to the shatterable student. That fabricated disabilities are an insult to students who suffer from legitimate disabilities is meaningless to the university bureaucrat administrator (no doubt carrying a wonky title that includes some combination of *associate dean, excellence, wellness, and personal success*). Thus, it comes as no surprise that suddenly we may be facing a manufactured epidemic of student disability across American colleges and universities.[e]

Ideas inconsistent with the shatterable student's fragile way of thinking trigger emotional injury. A recent poll showed that two-thirds of graduating Harvard seniors at some point during their four years decided not to express a view or opinion for fear of offending others.[8] A duty to prevent the perceived emotional injury is being projected by infantile students onto college administrations. Administrators are eager to accept the duty and project it back to students because it swells staff ranks and budgets. We are seeing a completely new form of tort injury take root in society and ground zero is the quad, dorm, and dining hall of your favorite institution of higher learning. A perusal of recent events across academia sums it up best. Unfortunately, there is much to choose from.

Harvard in 2017 decided the library would no longer charge a fifty-cents-per-day fee for overdue books. The reason, according to Harvard's Associate Director for Access Services Administrative Operations and Special Projects (indeed, that's his title, providing yet another example of

---

[e]   The epidemic is rapidly trickling down to high schools. Disability claims are skyrocketing for high school students nationally, especially in wealthier districts and private schools. Students and parents clamoring for the disability designation enjoy added test times and separate testing locations, including for the all-important SAT and ACT standardized college admissions exams. SAT and ACT administrators refuse to name which students enjoyed the special testing privileges when reporting scores to college admissions offices.

why tuition is out of control across colleges everywhere), was witnessing firsthand the stress that overdue fines cause students.[9] Harvard, the preeminent university in the land, has decided that its high-achieving student body cannot handle the pressure of returning books to the library on time. The obvious solution is to end the responsibility.

Student protestors at Seattle University demanded the humanities curriculum be modified to eliminate works such as Mark Twain's *The Adventures of Huckleberry Finn* because such works, "traumatized, othered, tokenized, and pathologized."[10] The dean of the college and the president of the university immediately bowed to the demands, promising to listen and to hire consultants to study the extent of the damage done.

Students' concerns about how unbearable life is at Ivy League Brown led to the administration instituting "safe spaces." Safe spaces are defined in different ways by high-priced experts who are more than happy to spend copious amounts of taxpayers' and parents' money. Suffice to say safe spaces are areas where a student does not need to stress. At Brown, the safe space was a room where students could eat cookies, watch a video of puppies playing, handle Play-Doh™, and rest on pillows and blankets.[11]

Scripps College in California had a labor problem when a strike ensued on campus. The strike involved students who were resident advisors (RAs) and admissions ambassadors. You know, the students who make sure there isn't drinking in the dorms, and who are the tour guides for high school students considering attending.

What were the striking Scripps students' gripes? As if coached by a public union, there was the obligatory argument that the RA's labor was not appropriately respected. Which means that the RAs felt the $16,000 a year of free room and board was not enough for enduring noise complaints, messy laundry facilities, and lost security cards.

To up the ante, the admissions ambassadors at Scripps decided to jump into the fray by threatening to bad-mouth the school to visiting high school students unless the college agreed to the strikers' terms. Despite the college president capitulating to many of the demands, the RAs continued to strike as well as encourage the tour guide ambassadors to tell prospective students how unbearable life was at Scripps. What were the lessons learned at Scripps? Find creative ways to become a victim, threaten, and wait for the system to bow to your demands. Then repeat, making bigger excessive claims and insisting on exceedingly gross ransoms.

A speaker on campus can trigger shatterable students into a frenzy. When conservative speaker Heather Mac Donald tried to speak at Claremont McKenna College (CMC) in California (an affiliate of Scripps College), student protestors devolved into disruptive behavior, suppressed free expression, and threatened violence. Mac Donald could not enter the auditorium for the scheduled event. She had to be sequestered in a secret location to livestream her talk, the audience was blocked from entering the auditorium, and the lecture could not be heard because the student protestors were banging on the windows of the auditorium and screaming.[12] Police were ineffective from the get-go; as soon as the protestors challenged the security perimeter, the police immediately backed away. Before you knew it, the mob controlled the event. Taking a tally of the CMC score, we have free expression, law and order, and accountability in the loser column. In the winner column are mob hysteria, bureaucratic administrators who will have even more job justification, and intolerance.

The University of Arizona published guidelines for classroom interaction titled *Diversity and Inclusiveness in the Classroom*.[13] The policy encourages students to refrain from debate and from directly pointing out facts that counter another student's positions because it might prove hurtful to feelings or egos. At UA, dialogue with no outcome is far superior to debate where students search for the superior position. The policy offers a fall back if a rogue student refuses to ignore facts and dares to counter a flawed argument from another student. In such a case, the offended student should simply respond with an "ouch." The offending student should respond with an "oops" to close the loop. The policy was issued by the vice provost for inclusive excellence.

The tab for attending Bucknell University full-time clocks in at over

$70,000 per year. Much of that cost is attributed to nursing shatterable students with a bloated administrative bureaucracy. Both the shatterable student and administrative bloat were on full display when conservative speaker Heather Mac Donald also spoke on campus in November 2019 (Mrs. Mac Donald can't catch a break on today's leftist campuses). Some students were so freaked out by the specter of a lecture from a conservative that Bucknell leadership decided to convene concurrent to Mac Donald's event a "moderated scholars panel" consisting of a professor, the interpersonal violence prevention coordinator, the director of the Women's Resource Center, and the interim associate provost for diversity, equity, and inclusion.[14] This potpourri of administrative bureaucrats and professors covered topics of rape culture, racism, and trauma. The event concluded with faculty and students invited to take part in self-care by painting rocks.

The California State University System, the largest higher education institution in the United States, shows how administrations in academia worsen the shatterable student mentality. As expected, students wishing to be accepted to University of California (UC) campuses need to meet a number of requirements, including hitting minimum college entrance exam scores (before UC announced in 2020 its intention to abandon that requirement), meeting high school grade point average requirements, and meeting deadlines for submitting applications and supporting materials. Most of us believe that the responsibility for these requirements falls on the prospective student. Not if the student is applying to UC Irvine: the UC administration decided students who applied for admission, and then missed the posted deadlines for submitting application materials, faced an unjust and inequitable result if their admissions offers were rescinded.

It all started when students who had admissions rescinded due to not submitting timely application materials, such as transcripts, threw a tantrum heard from San Diego to Eureka. Student tantrums, even those from kids who aren't even students yet, are noticed and placated quickly by campus administrators these days. Any doubt as to how the UC administration viewed the responsibility of the prospective student when it came to the application process ended when the chancellor weighed in. The chancellor agreed to readmit any student who was late on paperwork deadlines but met the other criteria for admission. He said the decision to rescind admissions, "rocked us to our core because it is fundamentally misaligned with our values," and offered his "sincerest apologies."[15]

The UC chancellor could not have delivered a clearer message to incoming students: you are not accountable for your own actions, if you don't like an outcome simply throw a fit, deadlines really don't matter, and there is someone else always readily available to blame for your own failures. No need for a formal campus orientation for incoming freshmen when you have this lesson delivered by UC leadership.

To make the college journey complete, shattcrable students will need official, quantitative metrics to prove that they are special. What better metrics than GPA and honors designation upon graduation? Alas, grade inflation has raged like an out-of-control wildfire across American universities for years. The average GPA in the 1960s was 2.5 while today it is north of a 3.0; it is safe to surmise the GPA inflation is not because students today are smarter.[16] More students at colleges and universities are graduating with honors than ever before. Almost half of the students graduating in 2018 from Lehigh, Princeton, and Southern Cal did so with honors, while over half of the graduating students did so from Harvard and Johns Hopkins.[17] Now that everyone needs to be recognized as special, what used to be truly distinguished is now truly average.[f]

Students entering college begin indoctrination during high school. Increasingly, high schools serve as four-year incubators to map the minds of young people to the proper ideology. Identity politics is infused in impressionable minds within public school systems. Environmental radicalism can be found not just in high school textbooks and curricula

---

f   Not all colleges and universities are moving in this ill-advised direction. Georgetown University in 2017 began to award honors designations based on a student's relative class rank instead of a minimum GPA threshold. Kudos to the Hoyas!

but also in preschool and elementary school coloring books. Good old peer pressure and blind adherence to the crowd forces high schoolers to advocate for positions no matter what the student thinks. After the Florida school shootings in March 2018, schools across the nation staged walkouts and protests to advocate gun control. No matter what your views are on gun violence and gun control, most observers found it odd that these self-described protests and walkouts were approved, supported, and often coerced by school administrators. The renegade was the kid who didn't walk out, not the kid who was following the lead of teachers and administrators. By the time kids graduate from high school they are prepared for the college culture.

High school students are also prepared for non-accountability before the first day of freshman year. That's because the college admissions process sends prospective students a message that standardized admissions tests such as the SAT and ACT have little meaning in consideration for acceptance. In 2018, the elite University of Chicago announced it was dropping the requirement to submit SAT or ACT scores in admission applications. The dean of admissions didn't camouflage the logic behind dropping the requirement of submitting standardized test scores when he unabashedly stated, "We want to remove any policy or program that we have that advantages one group of students over the other."[18, g]

This despite compelling research that indicates higher incoming students' standardized test scores correlate to better college grades and more challenging college coursework.[19] Don't expect the push toward erasing all forms of measured accountability to stop with standardized tests or admissions. Increasingly in academia as well as in high school, educators are now lobbying to end high school grades and cumulative high school GPAs in the college admissions process. There are also advocates calling for standardized test scores to end not only for admissions

---

g   The University of Chicago is not alone. The University of California released a plan to cease using the ACT and SAT in admissions, despite its own faculty senate concluding in a study that standardized tests help predict student success and do not increase racial disparities.

consideration, but also for evaluation of merit scholarships.

Removing quantifiable, measurable metrics from the admissions process makes it easier for administrators to impose their will without having to explain why a less academically accomplished student was admitted over a more accomplished one. Making submission of standardized test scores optional also ensures only students scoring well on their tests will submit scores, which will result in a higher average standardized test score for the university, making it look better on paper and in rankings. Also, marginal students who bombed the SAT or ACT will be more likely to apply to a college if they don't have to send their scores. More applicants increase demand and lower the college's acceptance rate, creating the illusion of a more selective, and thus more desirable, choice for parents and students. The process punishes hardworking, accomplished students; while transparency in the college admissions process is torpedoed and merit is abandoned.

We discussed earlier how the federal government's Iron Triangle is part of the Leech way, where bureaucrats work in concert with politicians and special interests to exert control. An Iron Triangle variation is part of academia: the administrator takes the place of the bureaucrat, the crazed professor subs for the politician, and the shatterable student replaces the special interest.

We save the best example of the Iron Triangle at work in academia for last. When President Trump nominated Judge Kavanaugh for the Supreme Court, the Judge's alma mater, Yale Law School, went into Iron Triangle overdrive. A petition was filed with the school administration with signatures of students and faculty stating that the Kavanaugh nomination created an "emergency . . . for our safety."[20] Dozens of Yale professors called off classes so that their students could protest in Washington, D.C. School administrative bureaucrats put out plates of cookies for the students during the trying time to help ease their stress. Judge Kavanaugh taught at Harvard for ten years. Not to be outdone by their rivals at Yale, Harvard students filed a Title IX lawsuit, claiming the Judge's presence on campus represented a hostile environment.[21]

The Judge's 2019 scheduled class was abruptly canceled by Harvard, and he was removed from the school's website. There you have it: the perfect example of how academia uses the Iron Triangle, combining the power of feckless bureaucrats, crazed professors, and shatterable students.

THE CAMPUS POLICE STATE

Institutions of higher learning employ modern-day thought police with expansive powers that can selectively run a noncompliant student or professor off campus. A recent study reported over 200 American colleges and universities currently employ bias response teams and systems.[22] Big or small, private or public, East or West Coast, millions of students at higher education institutions across the land are policed by a new reign of terror. The culture of micro-aggression and victimhood has been weaponized to assault thought, speech, and belief. No one is safe.

At the University of Florida students are encouraged to report one another to the Bias Education and Response Team for certain reprimand, indoctrination training, and follow-up tracking. The team consists of nearly a dozen individuals who are at the ready to dispense everything from soothing alleged victims to reprogramming alleged offenders.[23] Florida has a full-fledged and growing bureaucracy to oversee these teams, all of it paid for with tuition and tax dollars. Florida is far from alone.

The University of Michigan's since-disbanded Bias Response Team consisted of an impressive array of well-paid administrative bureaucrats ranging from the Office of Institutional Equity to the Office of the Vice Provost for Diversity, Equity, and Inclusion. A recent analysis indicated Michigan spends $11 million annually in salaries and benefits for over ninety bureaucrats assigned roles in equity and diversity activities.[24] This all-star cast of tuition-busting bureaucrats deems both intentional and unintentional acts worthy of potential bias prosecution. The Bias Response Team initially advised students that the most important indicator of whether bias occurred is the offended student's feelings.[25, h] That meant the standards for what constitutes bias and subsequent discipline resulting from the alleged bias were grossly subjective and were set by the thinnest-skinned student on campus. The University of Michigan standard of the listener's feelings also violated the First Amendment of the Constitution since the speech content does not matter; instead, the listener's reaction was what matters. We can happily apply the past tense to the Michigan Bias Response Team, because the university disbanded it under duress when it suffered a 2019 defeat in court, which found the Bias Response Team punishing and intimidating free speech. Nevertheless, we should remain vigilant and not rest easy, for the Michigan bureaucracy swiftly created a new entity, the Campus Climate Support team, to take the place of the Bias Response Team. The Campus Climate Support team is deployed to, "focus on addressing concerns that may create harm to members of the University community."[26] It would not take a giant leap for the administrative bureaucracy to weaponize such a vague purpose into something that tangibly suppresses free speech.

Iowa State harms free speech with its Campus Climate Reporting System, which encourages students to report to campus police, administrators, and attorneys everything and anything that might offend the most sensitive ears, including what is discussed in classroom lectures and debate.[27] Don't care for a professor's views? Want to character assassinate a rival student? Disgruntled about a grade? The Iowa State Campus Climate Reporting System can settle all those scores, and more, with the simple completion of an online form and the click of a mouse.

The NYU campus is populated with posters that advertise a bias reporting hotline where students can report "experience of bias, discrimination, or harassment" to the morality cops.[28] The University of

---

h   After a lawsuit was filed by the speech advocacy group Speech First against Michigan for its assault on free speech, the university removed the "own feelings" guideline from their website and updated its student code to be consistent with established Michigan law.

California at Santa Cruz and at Berkeley offer smart apps, thought up by psychology professors and administrators, to report micro-aggressions and perceived instances of bias.[29, 30] The spirits of the USSR's NKVD and George Orwell's Big Brother are alive at our universities.

Villanova is a well-known Catholic university with a proud legacy. That legacy is under attack because Villanova has revised its student course evaluation template to include questions regarding the professor's cultural awareness, whether the class environment was free of bias, and if the instructor was sensitive to identity traits of students.[31] There is a spectrum of issues where Catholic doctrine and leftist ideology directly conflict with one another. Inevitably, that conflict will manifest when an instructor discusses a sensitive topic and a course evaluation complains of bias or insensitivity. Expect bureaucrats in the administrative offices of Villanova to sacrifice over 150 years of academic integrity at the altar of the thought police and academic mob. Also expect the professional reputations of instructors to crumble the instant hyper-sensitive students rat them out for upholding Catholic teaching.

The University of Florida, NYU, Berkeley, and Villanova are light-weights compared to the situation at Evergreen State College in Olympia, Washington. In 2015, Evergreen's president decided to change the educational approach of the college. The heart of his fundamental change centered on the Equity Council, which had the power to align all decisions and curricula in the college under an equity agenda of equal outcomes. This effectively placed the power of the college into the hands of the humanities and social sciences faculty, administrative bureaucrats, and leftist students at the expense of nonpolitical students and faculty in STEM disciplines.

Once these interests had control, a chaotic downward spiral ensued. In early 2017, student groups began to promote and push for a Day of Absence where white students and faculty were pressured to leave campus on the prescribed date of April 12.[32] The concept was not to boycott something but to pressure a group, based on race, to be barred from stepping foot on campus.

As things were devolving at Evergreen, a biology professor by the name of Bret Weinstein sent an email to the administration questioning the wisdom of the concept. The student newspaper published the professor's email, the Day of Absence happened, and the situation turned dark and ominous for both Evergreen and Professor Weinstein. Protestors turned violent, radical students roamed campus armed with baseball bats, the president's office was overrun, he was held hostage, and the campus police believed protestors were stopping and searching vehicles looking for our intrepid biology professor to, one would guess, do him physical harm. Professor Weinstein was barred entry to his classroom to teach. The graduation ceremony had to be moved nearly forty miles from campus because of security concerns. The results at Evergreen were sobering: intimidation is the de-facto culture, reasoned logic takes a back seat to radical ideology, and dissenters who dare to voice views trigger public and physical attacks.

The academic mob mentality at Evergreen took its toll. Professor Weinstein won a sizeable legal settlement from the school and resigned.[33] Full-time enrollment declined in the fall of 2018 compared to 2017 as prospective students and tuition-paying parents observed what happened and said "no thanks."[34] The school's emergency reserve fund had to be tapped to cover costs associated with the Day of Absence debacle. The incurred costs, plummeting projected enrollment, and crumbling finances claimed a new dormitory project as a casualty and will likely require significant reductions in faculty and staff. Evergreen administration, not because of competency and common sense but because of necessity, canceled the Day of Absence for 2018.

Even statues and buildings are not immune to the gaze of academia's police state. Yale created the Committee to Establish Principles on Renaming along with a byzantine maze of bureaucratic churn.[35] The committee doesn't exist to cure cancer, discover a new planet, or advance the state of the art in nanotechnology. Instead, the committee, consisting of faculty, alumni, and students, is tasked with addressing the epic problem of how to figure out which campus buildings or structures need to be renamed. This must not be an easy task, for the committee consists of over ten Ivy League-caliber individuals who publish extensive reports and research to the university president and hold numerous "drop-in" sessions across various stakeholder groups. No historical figure's name is safe, with the committee bent on institutionalizing a process that will systematically erase Yale's legacy, one building at a time.

Most of us don't understand how extreme the police state has become across this country's academic institutions. Ironically, Americans tend to view developments abroad to be inconsistent with the mores of an open society, yet when we see the very same behavior occurring domestically at our universities, we think nothing of it. Consider the brutish tactics applied in the Turkish and Hong Kongese education systems. These tactics, loudly condemned in the United States, closely mirror what is occurring openly at American colleges.

First, let's explore the current situation in Turkey. The year 2016 brought seismic shifts to the nation of Turkey, with the failed attempted coup in July 2016 catalyzing unprecedented overhauls of the military and judiciary. "Purge" describes what occurred in Turkey as President Erdoğan tightened his grip on all aspects of Turkish society. Of course, "purge" does not conjure up positive impressions in open societies.

Academia and higher education have not escaped President Erdoğan's response to the failed coup and his clampdown. The government, through the Council of Higher Education, required all deans across Turkish universities to resign. To be reinstated, each dean had to show he was not tied to the attempted coup. Every university had to reveal faculty members who had ties to President Erdoğan's rival, Imam Gülen, who was believed to have been behind the attempted coup.

If you are a professor who is in favor of a secular society in Turkey, you are out. If you supported peace talks with Kurdish separatists, you are out. If you are a supporter of Imam Gülen, you are most definitely out. Academic qualifications take a back seat to where you sit on the political spectrum. It is much better from the government perspective to have a civil engineering professor who is mediocre in technical acumen but who subscribes to government-sanctioned political views than it is to have one who is the best and brightest in technical acumen but does not share the government's views on Islam or the Kurds.

The Turkish government is also putting its money where its ideological mouth is. Thus, areas of study and departments within the universities that are important to the rhetoric of the government get the funding. Funding has exploded for Islamic studies, Ottoman history, and related areas. There is also a strong presence of "ideological nepotism," as Professor Ali Alpar puts it, where the government stacks the ranks of the deans and faculty with members of the ruling party or its religious affiliates.[36] Determine what content is consistent with the party's rhetoric and hire the right people to run the show and lecture from the podium. The rest will follow.

Consider the situation in Hong Kong and mainland China. The metropolis's sovereignty was transferred from Great Britain to China in 1997 under the Handover Agreement. As part of Handover, it was agreed that Hong Kong's economic and political systems would not be changed for fifty years, or until 2047.[37] China decided unilaterally to accelerate that timeline, and the squeezing out of views differing from those of the Communist Party is underway across various segments of Hong Kong society.

One of the most visible areas where China has clamped down is the education system. President Xi envisions transformation of Chinese society through education and openly expresses his goal of converting campuses into "strongholds that adhere to party leadership."[38] Hong Kong's education system is no exception. Secondary school teachers in Hong Kong who promote any form of support for Hong Kong's independence or self-determination face teaching license revocation. Since this is Communist China, the risk of not toeing the Party line likely extends beyond losing a teaching license and threatens loss of freedom. When serving as Hong Kong's Chief Executive, Mr. Leung Chun-ying stated that views on Hong Kong independence are, "not a matter of freedom of speech" but of, "right and wrong" and that, "schools have a responsibility to guide students in the right direction."[39] On top of these statements, the former chief executive compared students' open discussion of Hong Kong independence or self-rule as similar to the sort of conduct that could "harm their lives and bodies" and that teachers have a duty to steer the students away from that type of behavior.[40]

The Chinese government is also seeking to institutionalize pro-communist and anti-democracy ideology into the official curriculum of Hong Kong schools with the proposed Moral and National Education (MNE) coursework.[41] Although the MNE coursework was delayed from official implementation due to public backlash in Hong Kong, government pressure to adopt it in Hong Kong schools will only grow.[i] The goal is systemic indoctrination of Hong Kong's young into communist doctrine as they matriculate through the education system.

Hong Kong shows that the world's most populous country understands the importance of the education system and academia when it comes to injecting and enforcing ideology across the population. China also recognizes the effectiveness of pushing its agenda and views under the duty of doing what is right, just, and ethical. The government dispatches armies of observers across thousands of universities to watch what is said and taught in the classroom. If an instructor is not sufficiently espousing the communist ideology, he can expect to suffer negative repercussions, from censure to imprisonment.

What is occurring in Hong Kong is quite mild compared to what the Chinese government is doing to Muslim Uighurs in Xinjiang region. The minority group is forced by the government to attend reeducation camps. Tuition, room, and board are free. Unfortunately, attendance is mandatory, with no certainty on time or credit hours required to reach graduation (release). The government has gone to great lengths to define the camps as campuses, vocational training centers, and boarding schools.[42] The government puts on a good show when foreign visitors arrive; reporters touring the camps witnessed students (inmates) singing

---

i   Now that the Hong Kong education system is subject to the Chinese national security law, MNE-infused coursework is a certainty.

in English "If You're Happy and You Know It, Clap Your Hands."[43] Estimates project up to one million Uighurs have been accepted (incarcerated) into the reeducation camps (prisons).

Most Americans see the situations in Turkey and China and think that is not the situation in this country, but there are several startling similarities. The Foundation for Individual Rights in Education (FIRE) estimates that over 90% of American campuses employ policies and practices that suppress and prohibit constitutionally protected free speech.[44] China removes pro-democracy books from Hong Kong libraries while American humanities departments remove *Huckleberry Finn* from reading lists. Attacks on due process across American campuses are also evident through Title IX enforcement guidelines, whereby amateur judges may determine the accused's guilt for sexual assault with a less demanding preponderance of the evidence standard.[j] One of the most prestigious and liberal universities in China, Fudan University, recently modified its charter by removing freedom of thought and adding dedication to patriotism and serving the Communist Party.[45] Meanwhile, one of the most prestigious and supposedly-liberal universities in the United States, UC Berkeley, now requires faculty candidates to complete diversity, equity, and inclusion statements whereby a job will be landed only if the candidate subscribes to or mimics the sanctioned views; job candidates with nonconforming views likely stand little chance to land the positions.[46] Berkeley systemically eradicates from its ranks the most crucial forms of diversity: diversity of thought, ideological leaning, and political affiliation.

---

j   The preponderance of the evidence standard was the guideline instituted by the Education Department under President Obama for colleges to adjudicate sexual assault charges on campus. That burden of proof is easy to meet, applying a "more likely than not" standard used in civil cases. The impact was that an accused student could face expulsion and a permanent staining of reputation and record without proper due process or demonstrating that his alleged act violated the higher burden of proof standards applied in criminal cases. Education Secretary DeVos, under President Trump, allowed universities to choose between the two levels for burden of proof.

HOW GOVERNMENT AND ACADEMIA
COOPERATE TO GROW POWER

Fundamental to the current state of U.S. higher education is the relationship between government and university leadership. Through regulation and policy, government creates and supports avenues for sending resources through other Leech conduits. Ronald Reagan noted that government aid is followed by government control.[47] One of the biggest conduits that government feeds is higher education. It is difficult to show whether government controls academia or the other way around, because there is such a high degree of ideological alignment that blurs the lines. Not coincidentally, four of the top nine organizations contributing to President Obama's 2012 campaign were universities (Berkeley #1, Harvard #5, Stanford #8, and Columbia #9) while two of the top nine were parts of the federal government.[48] The government-university nexus is critical to the institutionalization of the Leech class across Western society.

One of the vital methods for Leeches to achieve a growing footprint over the economy is to establish conduits that not only allow for housing, indoctrinating, and feeding but that also espouse a philosophy and ideology that fabricates the need for the Leech. One of the most crucial conduits is the university system. Colleges and universities speak often of diversity, but only physical diversity, such as race, gender, and ethnic background, is desired. Diversity of thought is threatening to the modern university's primary purpose as incubator.

Faculty and administration do their best to coddle and nurture the shatterable student. The provost at Evergreen, where the Day of Absence started, urged professors across campus to exercise discretion when assigning grades to students who had diverted their time and energy from academics to disrupt and protest on campus. The provost wasn't encouraging faculty to penalize these students; instead he was encouraging faculty to boost these students' grades.[49] The provost saw these disruptions as inherently good for the school and as a bizarre form of extra credit outside of the classroom.

Yale is one of the most selective universities in the world. High school students obsess over activities, grades, and standardized test scores to try to build a résumé that will deliver a ticket of admission. Yale's admissions office runs a blog that prospective students constantly comb over for clues that might provide the slightest edge in this effort.[50] In 2018, the admissions office let it be known on the blog that prospective students needed to be versed and active in social justice issues.[51] In other words, when writing that essay you better come across as an active proponent of a host of sanctioned causes. If not, expect rejection no matter what your SAT score and high school GPA are. One wonders how many bright, accomplished students applying to Yale simply manufacture stances on select issues simply to level the playing field where decisions will be made on merit and not bias.

The next time you see a high GPA from a college graduate, think about whether the credentials reflect a strong work ethic in a competitive academic environment or instead reflect something quite different. College administrations pressuring students to think a certain way and pressing faculty to inflate grades for radical students who disrupt life for the rest of the student body is the new normal.

A favored tactic of college administrators is to suppress speech by preventing guest speakers with dissenting views from lecturing by expressing concerns over student safety from campus protests. Yet outside of the appearance on campus of speakers with dissenting views, whenever student safety is at risk, college administrators go to extremes to protect students. Think of all the hotlines, reporting mechanisms, and tribunals that are in place across American universities to deal with sexual assault and discrimination. College campuses deploy emergency phones, strategically placed and backed by twenty-four-hour campus police. Don't forget the popular policy of having therapists on staff to help triage students from hurtful comments. Administrations are fully capable of using student safety concerns, real to imagined, as a pretext for increasing staffing, budgets, and power. But, if allowing and protecting freedom of expression are at issue, and that speech or speaker is not favored, administrations are quick to point to the threat of violent opposition as a convenient excuse to suppress the speech.

Government not only protects academia from accountability, it also supplies cover for it by instituting regulations and policies, such as Title IX, that suppress individual rights and promote bureaucratic power. Obama's Education Department pushed colleges to apply a preponderance-of-the-evidence standard when dealing with, and judging, cases of alleged campus sexual misconduct.[52] Many refer to this as the more-likely-than-not standard, which is a much lower evidentiary threshold than the clear-and-convincing and beyond-a-reasonable-doubt standards applied in habeaus corpus and criminal cases. The preponderance-of-the-evidence standard only requires a 50.01% likelihood of guilt.

Lowering the required standard of evidence for alleged sexual misconduct cases has serious implications. First, lowering the proof greatly increases claims of sexual assault brought to campus administrators and tribunals. A Title IX action can be brought against the accused for something said years, or even decades, ago.[53] The duopoly of a lower burden of proof and the ability to go back years means that situations that under normal criminal law standards would never rise to the level of formal charges get filed in a Title IX case and often result in a finding of the accused's guilt. The backlog of cases rises, offering a convenient opportunity for the university bureaucracy to expand to manage the growing caseload.

Lowering the evidentiary threshold creates wide discretion for the academic bureaucracy to rule on and cast subjective judgment. Title IX also presents opaque and wide definitions as to what is assault and harassment, yielding yet further subjective leeway. Wide bureaucratic discretion, coupled with the potential loss of one's reputation, job, or income creates an atmosphere of intimidation within academia. Faculty are less willing to engage in open dialogue with students and other faculty for fear of the Title IX sword coming down on their necks.

Since the lowering of evidence standards for sexual assault claims on campus, the Title IX bureaucracy has swollen into a maze of kangaroo courts and Star Chambers. For many universities, the standard Title IX sexual misconduct process includes investigators, judging panels, closed sessions, open sessions, and scores of witnesses' testimony.

Lowering the burden of proof to a preponderance-of-the-evidence standard increases the probability of the accused's guilt with serious, life-altering consequences. Being found guilty of sexual assault under Title IX can result in school expulsion. After expulsion, the accused carries a label of sex offender, which impairs the accused's ability to complete studies anywhere, let alone graduate and find a job.

The most elite universities in the world are not immune to the devastating impact Title IX has on the rights of students and faculty. Yale's official policy definitions of sexual harassment and sexual misconduct include verbal statements that might have the effect of creating an intimidating environment.[54] A marginally creative investigator, or one who is motivated to show how important his job is, could drive a bus through that definition.

Even when the accused prevails in a Title IX battle, he loses the war. Title IX questioning may consist of dozens of queries that put the accused under tremendous stress. Often the accused does not have the benefit of legal counsel. It is allowable under the Obama-era rules to forbid the accused from questioning or cross-examining witnesses. Adjudicators in Title IX cases are often amateurs with no formal legal training and can be fellow students, faculty, retired faculty, or university bureaucrats. An individual's entire future is not guarded by the constitutional protections that exist just beyond the campus gate.

The questions and answers in a Title IX process create a permanent record like an academic transcript. The rolls are growing of individuals who were accused of sexual misconduct under Title IX under dubious-at-best accusations, who then prevailed in their Title IX defense, only to face new charges or threats from other entities, laws, or policies that use the Title IX record for new attacks. Examples include using Title IX records to launch denial of tenure or unpaid leave for tenured professors. There is also a disturbing trend where, as in the case of the University of North Carolina, the media pressures and sues colleges to publish the names of those found guilty under Title IX proceedings. This would have a devastating, potentially permanent, adverse effect on the unjustly accused student who falls prey to a rigged system applying a flawed standard that denies due process.

The tribulation of a humanities professor at the University of Michigan illustrates how university bureaucrats and entitled students with an axe to grind coordinate to weaponize Title IX proceedings. The instructor was an acclaimed twenty-plus-year veteran professor with a clean professional record who focused her work on gender issues. But in 2016, she made the mistake of questioning one of her graduate students as to whether the student had plagiarized part of a paper.[55] Before she knew it, the professor's office was raided by police, and she was formally accused of harassment by the student under a Title IX investigation.[56]

Leading the investigation was the university's Office for Institutional Equity. The Office cleared the accused professor of the Title IX charge. But wait: the Office also concluded her behavior was inappropriate. That warning allowed her boss, the dean of the College of Literature, Science, and the Arts, to punish the professor publicly. Her pay was frozen, her sabbatical option was removed, and she was barred from serving as a primary advisor to doctoral students.[57] The Office refused to state what policy the professor violated or what behavior was inappropriate. She did not return to work and sued Michigan for violation of her due process and free speech rights. The accused professor's plight shows that everyone on campus is at risk of Title IX attack. It's good to see a professor with a newly discovered appreciation for constitutional rights, even under these less-than-ideal circumstances.

Those who dare to speak up in defense of the accused under Title IX and testify in their support face retaliation in the form of separate Title IX investigations being launched on them.[58] Simply questioning the chilling impact of Title IX on academic freedom can trigger a complaint. Defenders of those accused of Title IX violations should expect everything from social shunning to bullying from professors, fellow students, investigators, and staff.

Thankfully, in 2018 then-Education Secretary DeVos scaled back Title IX's assault on student due process by allowing schools to exercise discretion on whether they apply the preponderance-of-the-evidence or clear-and-convincing standard in instances of sexual misconduct. DeVos also proposed regulations that mandate live hearings and cross-examination. Don't expect a groundswell of schools to shift to the higher standard of evidence though, because doing so would reverse all the gains, power, and control gifted to the bureaucracy by the Obama administration's interpretation of Title IX guidelines. Once the bureaucracy develops a taste for the fruits of others' labors and rights, it will resist givebacks any way it can.

The federal government also supports entrenched academia by going to great lengths to harass, oppress, and kill-off any competition of traditional higher education. This is classic Leech behavior where an outside entity poses a threat of competition or accountability and the Leech cohorts close ranks and attack. Under the Obama administration, the federal government dished a massive assist to traditional universities by running for-profit colleges out of business. How? By holding for-profit schools to standards that the federal government would never hold traditional universities to. If a for-profit school could not meet financial metrics such as debt-to-earnings ratios for graduates, it faced penalties and oversight that would wreck it. The threshold for landing a school an effective death sentence was higher than an 8% debt-to-earnings ratio. That's what killed Corinthian Colleges in 2015 and ITT Technical Institute in 2016. More followed, in a premeditated eradication of for-profit schools.

A change in administration in 2016 paused the systematic government annihilation of for-profit schools. Of course, public, and nonprofit schools were exempt from these rules, and the Obama administration refused to release their debt-to-earnings data. Holding such schools to the same standards, the estimate is 40% of private nonprofits would fail.

Imagine telling a liberal arts college that if graduates didn't meet specified debt-to-income ratios it would face fines that would cripple it within a certain number of semesters. Or think about the response if the government imposed stifling regulatory penalties on a humanities program at a state university because the program persuaded students that there would be decent jobs waiting for them after graduation. A cataclysmic meltdown would follow on college campuses like during the Vietnam War era. At least consistent and transparent earnings and debt data across higher education institutions and degree programs were made available to the public when the Department of Education revamped its College Scorecard website in 2019.

Government doesn't stop feeding academia by just undercutting due process rights of students or by killing off for-profit competition. Government also makes sure it is pouring money into the academic bureaucracy. Until 2018, government contributed more toward tuition at public colleges and universities than students did in over half of the states in the Union. Governments siphon tremendous amounts of tax dollars into universities.

Part of that money is siphoned directly to the institutions and part is indirect via subsidization of students and parents so they can keep paying tuition to schools. The latter is in the form of low-interest federal student loans, allowing deduction of student loan interest expense from personal income taxes, student loan forgiveness programs, tuition waivers and tax exemptions for graduate students, and various tax credits, including the American Opportunity Credit and the Lifetime Learning Credit.[k]

The federal government under the Obama administration ran up a $1.4 trillion student loan portfolio that covers loans made to over 40 million undergrads, graduate students, and their families.[59] The Education Department during that period had the audacity to claim with a straight face that taxpayers would be making a return on this

---

k   For a sense of how out of control and prominent federal tax policy plays into the subsidization of academia, check out IRS Publication 970 titled *Tax Benefits for Education* at www.irs.gov. Close to 100 pages of complexity that surely keeps legions of bureaucrats, attorneys, and staffers justified and on the taxpayer tab.

portfolio because interest payments and principal repayments would more than cover expenses and upfront investment. Each year the Education Department publishes a financial report that includes expectations on how the student loan portfolio will perform. As recently as 2015 the official government view was billions of dollars of surplus for taxpayers. That shifted to an $8 billion-plus shortfall in 2016, which ballooned to a $36 billion shortfall in the 2017 report.[60] These critical data and details are buried in the report's footnotes.

Dig a little deeper, and you quickly understand how the government was applying flawed and misleading assumptions to overstate surpluses and understate the deficits of the loan program. Default rates are low-balled despite close to five million borrowers having defaulted or failed to make payments in over a year. Income-driven repayment plans, which are effectively restructured debt to avoid default, were also understated despite constituting 23% of all federal student loans in 2016 and having over six million Americans in the portfolio. The GAO and Department of Education now estimate a $74 billion subsidy cost for income-driven repayment plans alone, far exceeding prior estimates.[61] The Congressional Budget Office (CBO) paints a much starker picture, estimating that taxpayers will be on the hook for over $200 billion in student loan forgiveness under the income-driven repayment program over the next ten years.[62] As 2020 came to a close, the Education Department and its consultants estimated taxpayer losses on the federal government student loan portfolio will exceed $400 billion.[63]

Add to these numbers a litany of dubious assumptions, such as longer-term interest rates not rising from historic lows, and you end up with the bureaucrats systemically misleading taxpayers. The GAO concluded the Department of Education can't even audit or sanity-check its own internal projections, leaving a massive, growing entitlement program running blind.[64] The changing story from the government over a few short years tells the tale. Not long ago, the government was saying all was well, with the student loan portfolio running surpluses. Yet the portfolio was running deficits. Then the government was saying it was a mild deficit when they knew it was really a gargantuan deficit.[1] Finally, in 2020 we hear from the CBO that student loan forgiveness will present over a $200 billion hit to taxpayers in the coming decade. Apparently, it also takes more bureaucrats to manage the student loan portfolio than originally warranted: the annual administrative cost of overseeing the toxic portfolio has gone from $800 million in 2010 to $2.9 billion in 2019, more than a 300% increase.[65]

While federal bureaucrats busily obfuscate about student loan default rates, universities engage in manipulation of federal rules for determining whether schools fall under regulatory oversight if excessive levels of student loan defaults occur. If default rates of graduates exceed certain thresholds three years from graduation or dropping out, those schools face sanctions from the government. Sanctions carry grave consequences, including the inability to take part in federal student aid programs. But forbearance, which is a fancy term for stopping payment on student loans for up to eighteen months, doesn't count as a default under the government rules, and defaults beyond three years do not count as a default under the rules either. So, as more of a school's graduates or dropouts holding student loans are in forbearance and stretched beyond three years, the lower the default rate score for the school.

Manipulation of the system wasn't far behind. Intrepid colleges and universities now hire "default management consultants" who call and email graduates all day long, encouraging them to postpone payments on their loans for up to eighteen months, extending them beyond the three-year window under the federal rules and reducing the official number of defaults going into the government formula. This scheme has reached epidemic proportions, with over two-thirds of student loan borrowers who started repaying in 2013 choosing forbearance within three years.[66] In fiscal year 2016, a laughable ten schools were

---

[1]   To put the $36 billion deficit reported by the Education Department in 2017 for the student loan program in perspective, remember that the TARP during the 2008 financial crisis to bail out banks and the auto industry totaled only $33 billion.

subject to sanction by the government, with ultimately only two actually sanctioned.[m] This gaming of the system occurs despite colleges and consultants knowing that delaying payments on loans increases the interest expense of the loan materially to the graduate or dropout, hurting financially over the long term. Sacrificing the best interests of the graduate and the taxpayer happens to allow the university administrators to escape sanction from their cohorts in the federal bureaucracy.

The subsidization and chicanery don't stop there. Current federal tax law exempts from taxation investment income from university endowments. So, whatever return Harvard, Yale, Princeton, and Stanford make on their multi-billion dollar endowments they get to keep tax-free, whether they put that return to use to offset rising tuition costs (never) or simply sock it away to make an already huge endowment larger (always). In late 2017, Congress, as part of tax reform legislation, imposed a small excise tax on endowment income from private universities that had at least $500,000 of endowment per student. The impact of such a modest tax might motivate elitist ivory tower institutions to invest endowments and endowment income into worthy areas like STEM research, STEM programs, and student tuition relief. Such a tax would also help reduce endowment asset managers speculating in the risky vehicles that currently dominate such portfolios. The proposal was met with vocal and intense opposition from elite universities, who decried the 1.4% investment income tax as an attack on education and lobbied to appeal it since inception.

The richer the institution, the higher the degree of government subsidy. Over the past few years, eight Ivy League schools received over $40 billion in federal support, ranging from favorable tax treatment to direct payments.[67] In fiscal year 2016, the federal government provided over $38 billion to universities and colleges for research and development,

---

m   Figure 8 in GAO report 18-163, *Federal Student Loans: Actions Needed to Improve Oversight of Schools' Default Rate*, shows that out of the ten schools subject to sanction in 2016, nine appealed and eight of the nine were successful in their appeal.

with a disproportionate share going to elite institutions.[68] A substantial portion of the $38 billion in R&D spend, often half, goes not toward the experiment in the lab but instead toward subsidizing massive overhead tied to faculty, administration, and facilities maintenance.

Universities produce a return on all that government support by indoctrinating students into ideologies favored by government. After four years of programming, graduates not only have the right mindset but are also ready to throw themselves into careers in government and related organizations. This allows the future generation of leadership to keep the cycle going, a virtual manufacturing facility for bureaucrats and affiliated professions.

Government, using policy, has rigged a system to help it and the universities at the expense of students and taxpayers. The cost of a college education is the rare service that has not become cheaper over time. To the contrary, the cost of a college education has risen at alarming rates over recent decades and has nearly tripled the rate of inflation and escalation of other service baskets. Tuition rose 46% between 2001 and 2012 (in constant 2012 dollars) while the cost of many other services dropped significantly. Since 1990, college tuition has increased nearly 400%, while all consumer prices rose less than 100% and medical care costs rose just over 200%.[69]

There is a reason why college tuition cost increases outpace everything else: government aid and financial assistance are designed and injected at levels that drive up the demand for college, allowing colleges to raise tuition costs without fear of consequence. It's a self-inflicted and intentional pricing bubble for the asset of college education. Universities can accept more marginal students and don't need to worry about whether graduates land jobs that justify the tuition incurred. Colleges don't even need to worry about whether students pay back their loan balances as paying tuition is up front. It's the government, and eventually the taxpayers, who are at risk if the student defaults on the loan.

The thought that government student loan programs inflate the cost of tuition has been around for decades and is often tagged as the

Bennett Hypothesis after former Reagan administration Education Secretary Bill Bennett.[70] The correlation has become so severe that today even the New York Federal Reserve has found that 60 cents of every increased dollar of student aid results in increased tuition.[71] This premeditated non-virtuous cycle of government using taxpayer dollars to provide subsidy, which is then used to bloat university enrollments and tuition levels, benefits the university bureaucracy to the detriment of everyone. Congresswoman Virginia Foxx did a great job summarizing the Bennett Hypothesis in action when she said, "We know that having allowed students to basically have unlimited borrowing with unlimited forgiveness has driven the cost of college [upward] . . . the more money the federal government was putting into higher education, the higher the cost of going. It should have been the opposite."[72]

Endorsement of the government-academia nexus is plentiful. Prior Federal Reserve Chairwoman Janet Yellen consistently argued during her tenure that economic and jobs data show how important it is to have a college degree. She is famous for citing how the unemployment rate for college grads is lower than that for those without a college degree and how college grads make more money on average than workers with only a high school degree.

Those views may be true in a vacuum, but the situation is not that simple. A student who takes on hundreds of thousands of dollars in student debt to obtain a liberal arts degree will be unlikely to find a job anytime soon that produces a rate of return on the tuition investment, even though he may make marginally more money than if he hadn't attended college. And, barring an advanced degree in areas such as medicine or law, the jobs he is likely to land will most likely be in professions where the student would have been better off saving that tuition or using that money to start up a business or develop a skilled trade. The story is different for someone graduating with a degree in engineering, science, or IT, but those are classic Creator, Enabler, or Server jobs. The last Federal Reserve chair warranted to naïve students that simplistic, flawed macro data tells you to give all your money (present and future) to a college for a liberal arts degree and a future return on investment that will likely never materialize. Dr. Yellen knows better. But the federal government needs a vibrant university system to foster policies that favor big government, and the university system needs to keep the money flowing in to support its ever-growing appetite. So, the ruse continues.

INTIMIDATION AND SUPPRESSION: BULLIES ON CAMPUS

The leftist rulers of universities work relentlessly to make certain opposing viewpoints never get heard on campus. The drumbeat of identity politics, victimhood, and censorship sounds across curricula.

Students eagerly join the fray, from shouting down opposing views to far worse. A recent survey shows that one in five students feel in certain situations violence is acceptable to stop a speaker.[73] Civil societies call this censorship and assault, but universities call this being "culturally sensitive." Aggressive censorship exercised by those in control quickly intimidates others. A 2010 report by the Association of American Colleges and Universities found that only 40% of college freshmen "strongly agreed that it is safe to hold unpopular positions on campus" and that by senior year it's down to 30%.[74] A national survey by FIRE and YouGov indicated over half of college students admitted to stopping themselves from stating or sharing a thought in class.[75] The students get the message loud and clear over their four years, from the first day they step foot on campus to graduation day.

A lecture on crime prevention by former New York City Police Commissioner Ray Kelly was canceled after Brown University students booed him off the stage.[76] Scripps College in California invited and then disinvited *Washington Post* columnist George Will because he criticized ever-expanding definitions of assault.[77] A February 2017 planned appearance by right-wing speaker Milo Yiannopoulos at Berkeley resulted in a riot, volleys of Molotov cocktails, and property destruction.[78] After the debacle, the student newspaper at Berkeley promptly ran an Orwellian op-ed titled, "Violence Helped Ensure Safety of Students."[79]

Planned commencement addresses by former Secretary of State Condoleezza Rice (Rutgers University), human-rights activist Ayaan Hirsi Ali (Brandeis University), and International Monetary Fund head Christine Lagarde (Smith College) were scuttled by faculty and student protesters, who cited Dr. Rice's role in the Iraq War, Ms. Ali's criticism of radical Islam, and the IMF's rules for lending money.[n] The most hypocritical of the group was Ms. Ali's treatment at Brandeis since she was speaking out against radical Islam in defense of women's rights.

A film studies professor at various New York colleges, is revising his syllabus of classic films for classroom analysis, perhaps to avoid offending students and the repercussions. Films like *Birth of a Nation* due to racism, a W.C. Fields film due to handicap issues, and that dangerously offensive film *Tootsie* due to gender views have all hit the cutting room floor in his class syllabus. It is easy to criticize the instructor's decisions, since a twenty-year-old adult student should be able to handle the gender issues presented in *Tootsie*. But you commiserate once you factor in the bureaucratic monster, academic mob, and harsh treatment the professor would face if a leftist-minded, hyper-sensitive student decided to pick a fight.

Speaker Charles Murray, who espouses conservative views, was to lecture at Middlebury College. A petition, instigated originally by faculty, was taken up by students calling to disinvite Murray because some students felt his views were offensive. When Murray showed up to speak at the event, a mob drowned him out by screaming chants laced with extreme profanity. When the event organizer moved Murray and the moderator to a remote location where they could broadcast their discussion to the audience without intrusions, the radicals pulled fire alarms and continued their screaming. When the event ended, Murray and the professor who served as moderator were confronted outside of the

---

n   For a running tally of speakers who have been disinvited from events at college campuses, review Fire's (Foundation for Individual Rights in Education) online resources section at: https://www. thefire.org/resources/disinvitation-database/.

broadcast building and the female moderator was physically assaulted and injured. In total, the college disciplined over sixty students, with the most severe punishments being letters sent to students' files.

There seems to be a strong correlation that shows the more esteemed the institution, the more egregious the behavior. In 2015, the Yale administration, hyper-sensitive to the moods of its student body, set a policy that banned any Halloween costume that could be viewed as offensive. No fewer than thirteen university administrators and bureaucrats developed this impressive policy in excruciating detail.[80]

One of the university administrators responsible for student life, Erika Christakis, made a fatal mistake. She had the audacity to voice reason on a college campus by suggesting in an email that instead of a costume ban, a better approach might be for students to ignore costumes of other students they found offensive. When introducing logic and reason onto an elitist campus, expect a storm to ensue.

The storm hit both Mrs. and Mr. Christakis, both of whom served as administrators for student life at Yale. The Christakis duo made a second fatal mistake when Nicholas Christakis tried civilly to engage students who were upset over his wife's email. Students surrounded Mr. Christakis in the quad, hurling insults and profanities. Eventually, Mrs. Christakis succumbed to the relentless pressure; with zero support from the administration and no other faculty speaking up in her defense, she resigned. The Yale administration decided after this ugly debacle to award Yale's Nakanishi Prize to two seniors who led the charge in vilifying Mr. and Mrs. Christakis.[81]

Another consequence of the Yale incident was leadership using Christaki's email as justification for the addition of a deputy secretary for diversity, equity, and inclusion along with a group of diversity specialists.[82] These new bureaucrat slots bolstered the existing army of diversity bureaucrats spread across the New Haven campus.° Yale also provided

---

° For a sobering, itemized list of the diversity-related bureaucrat positions currently staffed at Yale, give a read to Heather Mac Donald's "At Yale, 'Diversity' Means More of the Same," in the opinion section of the April 24, 2019, *Wall Street Journal*.

more funding for the Yale Center for the Study of Race, Indigeneity, and Transnational Migration.[83] The Yale bureaucrats weaponized their own ridiculous policy and a benign faculty email to force more funding of the campus administrative state and to justify more bureaucrats on the administrative rolls.

A close second to the cultural sensitivity dogma found across universities is the adoption of the Church of Climate Change as the officially sanctioned religion of academia. As evidence, check out these gems:

The University of California, Irvine, offered a workshop to find and assist faculty who were interested in voluntarily injecting climate change rhetoric into their courses.[84] Subjects and courses having nothing to do with climate change were of special interest. Faculty attending the workshop were paid $1,000 upon completion and an additional $200 for attending a follow up networking event.

From MIT we have a lecture from Ghassan Hage titled, "Is ISLAMOPHOBIA Accelerating Global Warming?" Professor Hage is the Future Generation Professor in the School of Philosophy, Anthropology, and Social Inquiry, University of Melbourne.[85] The professor examines the relation between Islamophobia as the dominant form of racism today and climate change. Hage is rumored to be working on a book covering the same topic.

Like any fanatical religious culture, you best not question the doctrines of climate change religion. For the online course, "Medical Humanities in the Digital Age" at the University of Colorado–Colorado Springs, three instructors emailed enrolled students informing them that any debate about climate change was not going to be tolerated in their course. They stated, "The point of departure for this course is based on the scientific premise that human-induced climate change is valid and occurring. We will not, at any time, debate the science of climate change, nor will the 'other side' of the climate change debate be taught or discussed in this course."[86] When a few of the students who enrolled became uncomfortable about the one-sidedness of the first lecture, the instructors let the students know that eviction from the course due to the professors' intolerance would allow for other options.[87] This assumes that the remaining course menu is not subjected to the same thought police censorship.

Campuses punish the sin of "cultural appropriation." What is cultural appropriation? Academics wax poetic defining it, including law school professors such as Susan Scafidi, who authored the book, *Who Owns Culture? Appropriation and Authenticity in American Law.*[88] Although specific definitions vary, cultural appropriation can be as simple as using another culture's fashion, music, language, or food. With such a wide definition and low threshold defining the sin of cultural appropriation, campuses run rife with cultural police marking sinners.

At Bowdoin College in 2016, a group of female students wanted to hold a birthday party for a friend and sent invites out to others to come to a tequila party. Taken at the party were photos of students wearing miniature sombreros on their heads. That started a massive controversy and reactionary backlash from Bowdoin leadership. The college's administration started an investigation into the possible "act of ethnic stereotyping."[89] The *Bowdoin Orient*, Bowdoin's student paper, published an editorial calling the party a violation of empathy and evidence that those students are ignorant about the feelings of others.[90] The student government general assembly convened, and with an arrogance and altered reality that only the United Nations could rival, issued a statement of solidarity with any students who were scarred by the photos and by the cultural appropriation.[91] The resolution passed included a laundry list of demands to the administration, including the setting up of safe spaces across campus for those who might be hurt from the photos. After reviewing all these statements, one has a hard time discerning if the issues were with the tequila, the sombreros, or both.

ASSAULT ON ACADEMIC FREE SPEECH
AND FREEDOM OF EXPRESSION

Cold War–era Soviet dissidents like Andrei Sakharov were able to change the world because of the support of Western academia despite being under house arrest in the Soviet Union for years. Imagine today a university allowing, let alone supporting, someone challenging the science of climate change or disagreeing that socialism is virtuous? Today, the last place such a dissident would look for support is a Western university.

From coast to coast, anyone expressing views not in line with the consensus is attacked physically and verbally outside and inside the lecture hall. Making matters worse is that dissenting conservatives on faculties nationwide have plummeted to small minorities when compared to so-called liberal faculty. Research cited by the Heterodox Academy shows the ratio of left-to-right professors has increased from 2-to-1 in 1995 up to 10-to-1 today.[92] There is an intellectual cleansing of faculty ranks.

The persecution of dissenters hurts the very people the university exists to serve, the students. The American Association of University Professors' (AAUP) mission statement starts off with the desire, "to advance academic freedom and shared governance."[93] Yet, the AAUP has a problem with student journalists shining a light on the behavior and actions of faculty in the classroom and on campus, especially when the transparency is applied to professors who are espousing sanctioned political ideology in forums and classes while quashing dissent and balanced discussion. When student-contributing and student-run organizations like College Fix, Professor Watchlist, and Campus Reform report what is being said and done on campus, the AAUP posits that the professors are victims being persecuted.[94] Victims like the music professor who spent class time telling students on election eve to vote for Hillary Clinton because of her stance on a range of social issues.[95] Or victims like the duo of history and sociology instructors who spent time in their course spewing profanities and forcing alternative American history fictions on students.[96] This twisted definition of *victims* by AAUP and others cannot be appreciated until you witness the zeal of these victims in attacking their customers, the students.

Objective analysis of the facts shows a systemic attack on free speech across higher education. A recent report from FIRE shows nearly 40% of U.S. colleges currently enforce severely restrictive on-campus speech codes that prohibit constitutionally protected speech.[97] Amazingly, the startling 40% is a significant decrease from the nearly 50% tally of schools in years prior. When you include schools that employ cloudy policies that could be manipulated to suppress legally protected speech or that are clear, narrower suppressions of free speech, that percentage grows to nearly 93% and includes a who's who of our most esteemed and largest higher education institutions. Only about six percent of the nearly 450 schools assessed pass muster as clear protectors of free speech on campus.[98] By the way, private universities are almost twice as likely to embrace codes severely prohibiting free speech as public universities.[99] That's in part because previous Chairman Bob Goodlatte of the House Judiciary Committee pressured public universities that employed severe speech restriction policies.[100] Congressman Goodlatte's laudable effort reminds public universities of their constitutional obligation to protect freedom of speech.

Students aren't the only victims in this environment. Professors are also fair game in this turn-on-thy-neighbor world, as shown by the troubling tale of Professor McAdams at Marquette University. McAdams, a tenured political science professor, criticized in a blog a Marquette graduate instructor who told a student in her ethics course that she would not tolerate opinions opposed to same-sex marriage in class.[101] The university administration suspended him without pay, arguing his view and comment made him unfit to teach. One niggling detail Marquette seemed to ignore was that McAdams had an employment contract with the university expressly protecting his right to practicing academic freedom along with his constitutional rights (not that one needs a contract to protect one's constitutional rights). Off to court the parties went, with the Supreme Court of Wisconsin ultimately vindicating Professor McAdams.[102] Marquette, before, during, and even after the Supreme Court decision, stubbornly defended the suspension, despite being forced to pay and fully reinstate the good professor.[103] The school justifies its sour grapes by hiding behind concern for the safety of the graduate instructor who shut down freedom of expression and academic debate in her class.[104]

Even Jesuit higher education institutions these days will choose to defend the free speech-oppressive academic over the students subjected to her oppression, the professor brave enough to call her out, academic freedom, the sanctity of contract, and freedom of thought.

Beyond official codes and reporting systems are the more informal but just as chilling "language matters" campaigns found at many universities. This campaign finds words or phrases that are unacceptable on campus. Inoffensive stuff like "man up," "lame," "crazy," and the ever-sinister "hey, guys" have been placed on campus speech police hit lists.[105] Banning words is the first step in banning thought.

Cases heard by these reporting systems and censorship campaigns show how absurd things have become in the altered reality of universities. At Rutgers, questioning someone's blood type is offensive.[106] At Oregon, the head of the reporting system did not feel bound to respect freedom of the press protections and found that the school paper did not dedicate enough coverage to students falling within certain physical demographics.[107] Students at Penn demanded that a portrait of Shakespeare be removed from the English Department because the bard was suppressing students' voices and abilities to learn.[108] Not to be outdone by its Ivy League rival, Princeton's human resources department banned use of gender pronouns, including *he* and *his*.[109] Tennessee and Stanford issue detailed policies on the proper use of the pronouns *ze, zirs,* and *hirs* to replace the likes of *he* and *hers*.[110]

The level of duress placed upon freedom of expression on U.S. campuses is analogous to free speech suppression in China. In China, students can be questioned by police and, in some instances, detained for a text or social media post that is critical or questioning of Chairman Xi or local government. On certain American campuses, students can be investigated and punished, up to and including expulsion, for questioning or criticizing climate change science or the legitimacy of socialism. In China, the state monitors and encourages fellow citizens to report on individuals who express or harbor views counter to the party line. On American college quads, school administrators pride themselves on setting up various forms of hotlines to allow students and faculty to rat on their classmates or colleagues for a host of micro-aggressions. In China, the most censored phrases on social media platforms like WeChat include "human rights," "corruption," and "rule of law" while at American universities phrases that have the potential to precipitate official rebuke are "Christian" (non-desirable), "he" (sexist), and "capitalism" (evil).[111]

HIGHER EDUCATION YIELDS FAILURE AND BUYER'S REMORSE

Measurable standards prove that universities are punishing students, employers, and society. Students exit university more closed-minded than when they entered. That is a far cry from the view of Malcolm Forbes, where "education's purpose is to replace an empty mind with an open one."[112] Employers hire graduates who have been programmed since freshman year what to believe. Graduates lack critical thinking skill sets because more credit hours are devoted to political indoctrination and propaganda coursework than to traditional core curricula. Students and parents pay higher levels of tuition, inflated by the added costs of the on-campus police state and intolerant bureaucracy, and get less of a return on investment of time and money. Polling shows over half of three key demographics, men, eighteen-to-thirty-four-year-olds, and those describing themselves as white working class, think college is not worth the cost.[113]

College Learning Assessment Plus, or CLA+, administers tests across hundreds of colleges and universities to measure improvement in critical thinking skills of college students from freshman to senior years.[114] The CLA+ test evaluates not only critical thinking but also problem solving and analytical reasoning. Students must analyze data for the exam using spreadsheets, research papers, and other information to develop positions or views. The test looks to mirror workplace situations.

One would think that most universities would demonstrate substantial gains in critical reasoning scores for students after four years of study. Instead, CLA+ data show disturbing results. At over half of the schools analyzed by the *Wall Street Journal*, many of them public institutions subject to Freedom of Information Act disclosures, at least a third of senior students could not perform rudimentary functions such as: interpret data from a table, evaluate the quality of evidence in a document, or develop a coherent position.[115] These abysmal results for many institutions of higher learning show many college seniors can't filter fact from fiction.[p]

Gaining from this mess are certain university faculty, bureaucrats in college administration, and the government. Beneficiaries are many, whose salaries are paid by a combination of student tuition and taxpayer subsidization of the school budget. The university bureaucrats keep collecting paychecks and watch their power base grow. The government, or at least the parts of the government that are ideologically aligned with academia's philosophy and intolerance, keep feeding the machine with funding and regulations that favor the continuation of the cycle.

None of this comes cheap. Student loan debt is a massively growing crisis in America, currently sitting at around $1.7 trillion and increasing by roughly $100 billion per year.[116] Over 40 million Americans carry student loan debt, averaging over $38,000 per person.[117] The current level of student loan debt in the U.S. exceeds credit card debt. The debt is highly concentrated among students who don't land a meaningful job with an undergraduate degree, often in the liberal arts. That's why four out of ten college graduates these days end up in jobs that don't require a degree.[118] That's also why 60% of the national student loan portfolio is in some form of default or arrears (10% is 30 or more days past due, 20% is in forbearance, and 30% is in income-based repayment plans).[119]

---

p   The CLA+ findings are reinforced by a report from the American Council of Trustees and Alumni (ACTA) that highlights embarrassing knowledge levels of college graduates of American civics: half of graduates did not understand term differences between senators and representatives, 40% didn't know Congress had the sole power to declare war, less than 20% understood the Emancipation Proclamation, and 10% thought Judge Judy was on the U.S. Supreme Court. These abysmal results are from a multiple-choice question format, indicating actual knowledge is worse.

Facing poor-to-no job prospects with an unmarketable four-year degree, humanities and liberal arts majors opt for graduate school, throwing good money after bad and going deeper into debt. A disproportionate share of liberal arts and humanities graduate students are women. That's why graduate students hold more than a third of all student loan debt and women hold two-thirds of the total student loan debt.[120]

Rising college debt default rates corroborate the trend of growing ranks of college graduates lacking marketable skills or doing work that does not require a college degree. Not surprisingly, the more underemployed a graduate, the more likely a loan default will occur. The Federal Reserve estimates 40% of recent college graduates fall into the underemployed category.[121]

If student loan default rates are too high, accountability would demand that either the universities lower their tuition (via belt tightening) or change their curricula to teaching skill sets more in demand (via retooling faculty and focus). We know academia suffers from severe phobias of accountability and change, and its trusty cohorts, left-leaning administrations and bureaucrats in Washington, D.C., share the same fears. In 2017, the Education Department released a memo admitting it overstated student loan repayment rates across hundreds of colleges and trade schools.[122] The new, correct data showed a skyrocketing rate of default for student loans across the nation. The *Wall Street Journal* determined that 99.8% of all trade schools and colleges in the nation overstated repayment rates for student loans using the faulty data.[123] The new, correct data indicate at least half of the students at over 1,000 colleges and trade schools have defaulted or failed to pay down any of their debt within seven years.[124]

Since so many college graduates march straight from the commencement line to the bank line to apply for a credit card, mortgage, or car loan, there is a potential cascading set of defaults that student loans trigger. In what should be obvious to government Ph.D. economists, the Federal Reserve Bank of New York sees college graduates who are burdened with high levels of student loan debt (or defaulting on student loans) having problems securing mortgages to buy houses.[125] Rising default rates on student loans may be the canary in the coal mine for mortgage and other debt defaults to come.

Why were the student loan repayment data corrupted and the phony results reported? The Education Department blamed coding errors.[126] Government bureaucrats watching the performance of academic bureaucrats assures failure. The correct, new data clearly show that higher education is woefully failing the stakeholder students, employers, and taxpayers.

It may be difficult to feel empathy when hearing how today's students are getting duped by the higher education system. However, doing so misses a critical detail in this scam: it's not just the student who is on the hook and paying the price for a useless degree. In 2017, students had $86 billion in loan debt owed by people sixty-years-old or older, a 161% increase since 2010.[127] Many of those individuals took on the debt to underwrite their kids' or grandkids' college education. If student loan forgiveness becomes law, taxpayers stand to foot a bill more than $1 trillion.

Being on the hook as parents and taxpayers for the higher education boondoggle is exemplified by the Parent Plus program run by the Education Department. Parent Plus is the ultimate example of the nexus of federal government bureaucracy and the university system in action. As is often the case, the Leech class introduces a new Trojan horse to stalk us under the banner of altruistic, good-for-society reasons. With Parent Plus, those reasons were the desire to allow prospective students to attend their school of choice even if they were unable to afford it under normal means. Who could be against that?

What the Trojan horse unleashed was a program that has the federal government making loans to parents and grandparents of students to pay for college tuition. At the start of 2017, 3.5 million families borrowed more than $77 billion from Parent Plus.[128] What type of credit score would you need to be eligible for Parent Plus? Effectively, all you need is a social security number and the government is more than willing to loan you the money. Creditworthiness, assets, debt, and ability to repay are largely ignored. If anyone complains that these financial metrics should be considered when making loans, the administrators at colleges benefitting from the loans argue any implementation of ability-to-repay standards would result in low income students being unable to attend college.

So how is Parent Plus performing when it comes to the families of these students and taxpayers at large? In a word: *horribly*. As is to be expected when you make millions of loans to people who can't afford to repay the loans and to families where their kids have unmarketable skills after graduation. According to the GAO, as of September 2015, 10% of borrowers in Parent Plus, or 330,000 borrowers, had gone at least a year without making a payment on the loan.[129] That exceeds the default rate on home mortgages during the worst of the housing crisis. The Education Department's own data shows an added 180,000 loans in the program as of May 2016 that were at least a month delinquent.[130]

Realize that federal law doesn't allow Parent Plus loans to end if the borrower goes bankrupt. Instead, the borrower faces the specter of having tax refunds and social security checks garnished to help pay off his debts. That often means students' parents are putting off retirement, avoiding necessary healthcare expenditures, and living below the poverty line while their child graduate is living in the basement looking for meaningful work. Any unpaid amount left after bankruptcy and garnishing is picked up by taxpayers. Parent Plus is an effective means for universities to suck money not just from naïve students but also from parents, families, and taxpayers.

Colleges and universities are adept at obfuscating to students and parents what the true, net cost would be to attend a school. At the root of the deception of true cost is that there is no standard method to report the cost of attending a university to a prospective student in financial aid award letters.[q] Colleges and universities are free to use any terminology, format, and metrics they choose in these letters. Often the institution

---

q   The typical, standard progression for a prospective student who gains admittance to a university is to first receive a congratulatory acceptance letter followed afterwards by a financial aid award letter.

takes the liberty of playing word games and manipulating numbers to dupe the recipient into thinking the cost of attending will be much lower than what it is. Common deceptive tactics employed include treating loans the same as outright grants, as if the loans will never have to be repaid, misusing an "unmet need" metric as if it were the same as "net cost," and failing to state the total cost of attending the school so that it could be compared to the aid level quoted in the letter.[131]

Although the size of this crisis is in the trillions of dollars in student debt and skyrocketing default rates, an accurate view of the full extent of this crisis requires going beyond the financial numbers. Gallup conducted a poll for the Strada Educational Network to gauge how college graduates felt about their educational experience and investment decisions in hindsight. The poll found over half of Americans would change at least one educational decision if they could do it all over again.[132] Over a third would choose a different major.[133] People who had certification in a technical, vocational, or trade program had less buyer's remorse than those with a four-year bachelor's degree. The poll also found unsurprisingly that STEM graduates were the least likely to express regrets with their educational and investment decisions while those in liberal arts fields were most likely to say they would change their area of study if they had a do-over. Gallup and Strada performed a scientific analysis to tell us what we already know: this country is facing an epic and growing case of buyer's remorse with the higher education system.

HIGHER EDUCATION'S CRISIS WILL WORSEN WITHOUT ACCOUNTABILITY

After World War II, General Eisenhower served as President of Columbia University. Recognizing the importance of fostering a culture of free thought and open debate that is the lifeblood of a vibrant university, he vowed that under his tenure there would be, "no intellectual Iron Curtain" at Columbia.[134] Ike's view of what constitutes a favorable culture at a university sits in stark contrast to the culture prevalent across today's campuses.

Higher education is in deep denial. Business leaders, everyday Americans, and college students recognize there is a major problem. In a recent Gallup poll, only 11% of business leaders strongly agreed that universities graduate students with skills needed to succeed in the workplace.[135] Another Gallup poll showed only 13% of Americans strongly agree that college graduates in this country are well-prepared for success in the workplace.[136] A third Gallup poll taught us only 34% of students strongly agree that they will graduate with the skills and knowledge needed to be successful in the job market and just over half believe their major will lead to a good job.[137] Compare these stark views with the survey of chief academic officers that returned a laughable 96% self-assessed view of "doing a good job."[138] Denial is not an Egyptian river when it comes to education leaders.

Today's young adults graduating college represent a Generation Zero: devoid of necessary skills required in the market, burdened with student loan debt, and resigned to living at home while working non-permanent jobs in the gig economy that never required wasted years of college.[r] Many of Generation Zero don't attain a degree: less than half of Americans between the ages of twenty-five and thirty-four have an associate degree or higher.[139] A far lower percentage ends up with a degree and a job that justifies the cost of tuition.

Yet most tailoring of high school curriculum is for college. The slanted curriculum, bolstered by government policy, helps colleges and universities to lure families into willingly throwing life savings and future earnings toward a dubious degree. The false premise that higher education is working for everyone guides the entire system, collective psyche, and decision-making.

What's puzzling about the obsession this nation has with shoving kids into the gears of a broken college education system is that traditional

---

r   The documentary *Generation Zero* by Steve Bannon paints a sobering picture for many young adults coming out of college in today's economy. This problem is not unique to the United States: the Japanese refer to the trend of young adults who don't leave their parents' home due to the poor economy as "parasite singles."

blue-collar workers have never been happier. A 2018 poll of blue-collar workers found 91% are proud of their work, 86% are satisfied with their jobs, 85% feel their life is headed in the right direction, and 80% believe their job provides a good living.[140] Those are numbers that a politician would lie, cheat, and steal to secure. This reality is masked by a relentless campaign of obfuscation by academia, government, and the media to paint blue-collar careers as dead-ends and college degrees as the only real future for young adults.

Yet universities keep raising, at triple the rate of inflation the past decade, their already unconscionable tuition rates to feed a bloated administrative bureaucracy and to sustain an obsolete and non-practical spectrum of departments in the humanities, social sciences, and arts that have little demand in today's marketplace.

The more elite and the more private the school, the more egregious the situation. Columbia, the University of Chicago, Duke, Penn, and Yale all have sticker cost levels for tuition, room and board, and other expenses that exceed $68,000 per year. Yet their endowments range anywhere from about $7 billion to $25 billion each. The Ivy League in total controls a cumulative endowment of $120 billion, which comes out to about $2 million per undergraduate student.[141] The five largest endowments at the end of fiscal year 2016 are a who's who of elite institutions: Harvard ($35.7 billion), Yale ($25.4 billion), Stanford ($22.4 billion), Princeton ($21.7 billion), and MIT ($13.2 billion).[142] In 2018, Harvard, Stanford, and Columbia all received over $1 billion in gifts while community colleges received on average $2 million in gifts.[143] Despite these ridiculous endowment levels and gross inequality between the Ivy League haves and community college have-nots, the federal government shoveled over $40 billion of taxpayer money to Ivy League schools from fiscal year 2010 through 2015.[144]

Notwithstanding massive financial resources, acceptance rates for these elite private schools sit well below 10% of applicants, and that is by design. These universities coordinate to restrict choice, timing, and decisions of potential students by dictating the terms of every step of the application process. Worse yet, elite universities work with the College Board, owner of the SAT, to acquire (i.e., purchase) student SAT scores and other personal information so that schools can tempt targeted students into applying, only to be promptly rejected. That allows the university to post a higher number of applicants and a lower acceptance rate, creating an artificial boost to its coveted image of exclusivity. It also creates a tidy revenue stream for the College Board. Unfortunately, the benefits to the universities and the College Board come at the expense of the unsuspecting students who have their personal information applied against their self-interest, resulting in false hope along with wasted time and money spent on applying to schools that have no intention of accepting the applicant. If the tactics and practices of elite universities were applied to businesses, those businesses would be accused of cartel-like collusion, predatory marketing, and anticompetitive behavior.[s]

An elite academic institution with vast financial resources facing these realities should find a way to invest the endowment to create capacity for more deserving students to attend the institution or to use the endowment to lower tuition for existing students. Perhaps they might employ a combination of both while ceasing anti-student behaviors. Math underscores the point. Harvard enjoys a $40 billion endowment.[145] Using Harvard's undergraduate enrollment of just over 6,700 students, the endowment works out to almost $6 million per student. Tuition, room, board, and fees total about $63,000 per year, which would require a paltry 1.2% annual return on investment for the endowment principal. In other words, Harvard could waive 100% of tuition, room, board, and fees for all undergraduate students if it simply used the first 1.2% of annual return on investment from its endowment in lieu of tuition. Or consider that in 2018 Harvard received gifts

s   The Department of Justice under the Trump administration assessed the National Association for College Admission Counseling's ethics code. The DOJ may suspect the ethics code is used by colleges to limit competition among themselves for students, in violation of antitrust law. Of course, avoiding competition and corresponding accountability are part of academia's DNA.

totaling $1.42 billion.[146] That works out to over $200,000 per student, enough to fully fund annual tuition, room, and board multiple times over without ever having to touch the $40 billion endowment's principal or investment income.

The United States is a free enterprise, capitalistic society burdened with a leftist higher education system. Until taxpayers, customers, and citizens hold this system accountable, things will only worsen. Yes, it is sobering that, as time goes on, more of us coming out of college and into society will be trained in a culture that preaches intolerance of dissent, shirking of personal accountability, and waiting for others to get things done. But we can take solace in knowing that the failure of academia to produce graduates armed with the skill sets demanded by the market will force a reckoning of the entire higher educational system. We might be seeing the start of such a reckoning: National Student Clearinghouse data shows declining national higher education enrollments throughout the past decade.[147] May that reckoning come soon.

TRAINING GROUNDS PART 2:

HIJACKING STEM

"Suicide is probably more frequent than murder as the end phase of a civilization."

JAMES BURNHAM, *SUICIDE OF THE WEST*

STEM EDUCATION: NATIONAL STRATEGIC IMPORTANCE

Recall that Leech instinct pulls it toward value-creators to eat. A recent trend in education has proved to be fertile ground for Leeches and has seriously degraded the quality of crucial technical fields society relies on. That trend has been the viral transformation of STEM education into STEAM education. One little letter added to the mix can make an enormous difference in a bad way.

STEM stands for science, technology, engineering, and math. Society ceases to function without technology and technically competent professionals. In contrast, the humanities, represented by the "A" (for arts) in STEAM, are a want not a need. Although the humanities have a proud legacy, the country can't run on them.

Of course, we sit today at the most technologically advanced time in history. The rate of change is fast and dizzying. Technological advancements don't just make life better, they make it possible. Today, more than ever, society and our nation require more technically trained professionals. Most children in grade school today who go on to technical professions will be working in fields as adults that don't currently exist.

Through the decades, the United States has been the gold standard when it comes to developing talent in the science and engineering fields. That is changing. *U.S. News & World Report*'s global ranking of top engineering universities has three Chinese universities in the top ten, including number one overall, while the United States scored only two in the top ten.[1] Chinese STEM graduates exceed U.S. STEM graduates by more than an eight-to-one margin, and that ratio is expected to nearly double by 2030. In 2015 the United States produced 100,000 engineering undergraduate degrees while China boasts engineering and science students in the millions. China opened nearly 2,000 new universities in fewer than fifteen years, many of them focused on technical fields, demonstrating a doubling down on STEM investment. China scores at the top of the global list for math proficiency of fifteen-year-olds while the United States scores in the bottom half.[2]

Rival nations view STEM education as a critical, national strategic resource. Russia and China view technology of such strategic importance that they eagerly steal vital information from other nations. The Chinese and Russians use technology and professionals trained in that technology to pilfer more technology. China employs its Thousand Talents Program to recruit/lure talented professors at U.S. universities to come to China to lecture and share their research. The stated official purpose of the program is to celebrate innovation and elevate Chinese competitiveness, yet the essence of the program is blatant industrial espionage and technology snatching. The communist state focuses the program on the fields of medicine, industrial technology, computer science, aviation, agricultural science, physics, and chemistry. The program operates legally and illegally, as we saw in 2020 when noted Harvard nanotechnology professor Charles Lieber was charged with lying to the U.S. government about his involvement with the Thousand Talents Program—involvement that included $1.5 million in lab funding, $50,000 in monthly salary, and

$150,000 for annual living expenses.[3] You will not find the Thousand Talents Program poaching many professors in the fields of the social sciences, humanities, arts, music, philosophy, government, or religious studies. Disappointingly, certain passive U.S. universities allow the adroit Thousand Talents Program to steal our technology, technology funded by billions of U.S. taxpayer dollars.[a]

The Organization for Economic Cooperation and Development (OECD) expects China to soon surpass the United States in research and development investment.[4] One driver of the gap closing is the importance our rivals place on technical professions. Of course, the fact that many of our rivals do not hesitate illegally to "borrow" what we have developed doesn't bolster U.S. competitiveness.

In China, children at a young age are selected for STEM tracks that provide special attention, support, and opportunity during their lives. Families in India and China push their children to become the next star coder, engineer, mathematician, or scientist. Kids in the United States who are attracted to these fields are ridiculed and ostracized as geeks and social outcasts. Culture assists India and China to improve their competitiveness while culture hampers and erodes U.S. competitiveness.

Another key reason the STEM gap between the United States and other nations is closing is that the United States consciously waters down STEM content across technical fields. The methodical dumbing-down is led by liberal arts academia and government bureaucrats who see an opportunity to freeload off the demand and need for critical STEM fields.

There is another insidious factor at work that pushes erosion, weakening, and supplanting of STEM. Throughout history, the scientific community has been the most consistent, steadfast bulwark to protect against and resist tyranny, especially tyranny of thought. The more closed-minded academia becomes, the more ideologically rigid the campus

---

a   Texas A&M learned that over 100 faculty members were secretly recruited by the Chinese, despite only five disclosing their participation. (*Wall Street Journal*, January 31, 2020)

culture becomes, the less tolerant students and faculty are of free thought, and the less likely leaders in STEM fields will speak up and rebut unenlightened oppression. What better way to eradicate the greatest threat to suppression of free thinking than to hinder STEM? Instead of science checking politics, politics checks science.

MANUFACTURING A HUMANITIES CRISIS

A way to undermine freedom in STEM education is to demand political correctness, as in the humanities. Everywhere you turn in academia, you hear about the "humanities crisis." But many of us outside academia have little understanding of what humanities professors teach or what that crisis is.

Humanities are no longer traditional English literature, art, or philosophy as we might remember fondly. Today, they are quite different. What was once four years of immersion into the classics is now four years of surgical, ideological programming of students. Humanities curricula across the higher education system have been dramatically revamped by a cadre of students and faculty thought police to reflect identity politics and victimhood ideologies.

The manufactured humanities crisis is used to invade and conquer the social sciences, such as economics or sociology. The social sciences play a pivotal role in undermining STEM curricula and disciplines. The days when the social sciences sat between a quantitative/qualitative spectrum bookended by STEM on one side and the humanities on the other side are long gone. Elements incubated in the humanities have consumed the social sciences and now wage war on STEM disciplines.

Signs of drastic change in traditional humanities and social sciences curricula are everywhere. English literature used to be about reading Shakespeare, while today it is about teaching how great authors' works, including the famous bard's, were oppressive. Shockingly, students today can obtain an English degree from Yale without ever having to study Shakespeare. Similarly, university history majors will hear how Great Britain and the United States were tyrannical empires rather than how they saved the world on numerous occasions from the threats of fascism, communism, and socialism.

What most people consider obscene is quite acceptable within current humanities programs. Carnegie Mellon University's humanities department threw Karl Marx a 200th birthday celebration. The festivities included a speech from the Dean of the College of Humanities and Social Sciences referring to Marx as a great man with vision.[b] This was the Dean of Humanities at a top-notch STEM university, named after two great capitalists, talking about how awesome a guy was who founded a movement that resulted in the murder of over 100 million people.

Advocates for the humanities define this manufactured crisis differently, depending on their ideologies and self-interests. But they agree on one thing: the critical need for more funding for humanities faculty, more tenured humanities professors, more buildings dedicated to the humanities, more humanities classes, more humanities degrees, and ending the humanities crisis. All of this "more" must come at the expense of something else since most students only need and can afford so many credits, campuses have only so much space for more buildings, and college budgets have theoretical limits. Addressing the critical crisis in the humanities would have to come at the expense of STEM programs and budgets.

Academia's charlatans pounding the message of the manufactured humanities crisis to coerce more resources does come with a stark exception. Chapman University recently announced over $15 million in gifts from donors to establish an institute that would challenge tensions between economics, or the concept of resource scarcity, and the humanities.[5] This is truly great news for a humanities critic such as me to get excited about.

There was a problem with the Chapman announcement, however:

---

b   Dean Scheines went so far as to state at the kickoff speech that students can't be unwilling to celebrate Karl Marx. For a full video of the speech go to YouTube and search "Why Karl Marx Now: 200 Years Later."

part of the gift came from the Koch Foundation. The Koch Foundation is a noble organization fighting constantly to protect values that aid and nurture Creators, Enablers, and Servers. The Koch Foundation contributing to the institute precipitated criticism that rained down on the university, its leadership, and faculty for having the audacity to accept a gift from the evil Kochs.[6] Chapman serves as proof that campus extremists seek to consume non-humanities areas, such as economics, not to better integrate with them, even to the point of quashing highly sought-after private donor funding.

Vocal humanities advocates tout how companies and recruiters place heavy importance on communication skills, teamwork, and problem solving when looking to hire college graduates. Such chatter serves as justification for inserting more "A" into STEM or STEAM. Sorry, but I don't see how one can argue that an art major is better equipped at problem solving than a computer science engineer. Using the argument of the value of a well-rounded education to justify jamming the humanities curricula into STEM fields is a smoke screen. Forcing humanities coursework upon STEM programs has nothing to do with rounding out a student's education. The real rationale is to allow liberal arts and humanities departments across academia to avoid necessary reforms and downsizing to match the current economy's demands. By peeling off dollars from in-demand STEM fields, the liberal arts and humanities departments stay funded. Humanities departments can then dictate to the STEM disciplines how to operate. You see this in hybridized STEM course titles such as "The Ethics of Coding" or other nonsensical course titles. The last place on earth an engineer, programmer, or scientist should look for moral guidance in preparing for the competitive world is the humanities department across the quad.

Some of the places where the manufactured crisis in humanities is having an impact are startling. Stanford University President Marc Tessier-Lavigne is an accomplished neuroscientist and presides over one of the most respected educational institutions in the engineering and technology fields. As president, Dr. Tessier-Lavigne has all kinds of things to worry about, including keeping Stanford at the top of its academic game and managing the inevitable crises that will pop up on any large campus. But the president instead is obsessing over whether Stanford is too focused on the engineering and technology fields and is not spending enough time and money on the humanities. Much of the recent Stanford campus spending has been on new art museums, theaters, and humanities degrees. Where that places engineering and technology in the president's priorities and how that keeps Stanford's STEM programs best-in-class are troubling questions to ponder.

Stanford's top-tier Computer Science Department is about as STEM-heavy as it gets, attracting brilliant students from all over the world. Instead of focusing the time and attention of faculty, lecturers, and students on all things computer and information technology related, the administration at Stanford has apparently other, more pressing matters to waste the department's valuable time and money on. A document was distributed to the department's faculty that laid out a series of guidelines designed to nurture an inclusive culture, which lecturers were encouraged to follow.[7] The guidelines instructed them to praise students who did their homework, to regularly tell the students how the instructor was appreciative of their effort, and to coddle students who were failing at mid-term by telling them there was still a chance for a good grade in the course. This wastes precious faculty and student time.

THE DILUTION OF STEM ACROSS SOCIETY

Government, academia, and foundations are unabashed supporters of watering down and diluting STEM education by their continual and methodical promotion of the humanities and arts over STEM. That's even true for institutions that trace their lineage back to STEM-centric legacies. A quick look around at the most prestigious awards out there paints a striking picture.

The MacArthur Foundation has been around since the early 1970s and currently sits on over $6 billion in assets. The foundation is renowned for their Fellowship program, referred to in the media as "genius grants," where each year about two dozen fellows are awarded five-year grants of $625,000 to pursue their areas of interest. The mission of the foundation is "building a more just, verdant, and peaceful world."[8] Since the foundation's creation decades ago, the mission and what it means has evolved significantly, to the point where one wonders what the MacArthurs themselves would think of the foundation today. A look at recent past years' geniuses is shocking. You might assume a majority came from STEM disciplines, considering how science and technology are vital to life today, but you'd be wrong.

Seventeen of the twenty-three 2016 recipients, or 73%, have nothing to do with STEM disciplines. They include career descriptions of lawyer, linguist, theater artist, sculptor, playwright, art historian, cultural historian, writer, financial services professional, poet, another artist/writer, video artist, jewelry maker, long form journalist, composer, and a graphic novelist. Only six of the twenty-three 2016 grant recipients were in STEM fields.

The same concentration of the genius grants in non-STEM fields appears in the 2017 recipients, which included these so-called geniuses: a guy who wants to improve everyone's understanding of the migrant experience between the United States and Mexico; a landscape architect who wants to design urban areas to better integrate with their ecosystems; a musician who wants to focus on the history of lesser-known musicians; and an opera director who stages performances dealing with immigration issues on train platforms.

In 2018, this MacArthur Foundation trend continued. Of the twenty-five genius recipients, less than a quarter were in STEM fields. Nineteen of the twenty-five recipients consisted of a mosaic of lawyers, community organizers, artists, journalists, sociologists, playwrights, and various other non-STEM luminaries. The class of 2018 proved once again the MacArthur Award today is not about scientific genius but instead about elevating non-STEM, politically correct rhetoric.

It only gets worse. As non-STEM as the 2016 through 2018 genius classes were, 2019 proved to be the most anti-STEM. Over 70% of the twenty-six recipients in 2019 consisted of individuals from the legal profession, the arts (including a graphic novelist, a landscape artist, an urban designer, a choreographer, and a guitarist), and humanities fields. Only seven of the twenty-six recipients were in STEM fields, and five of those seven focused on climate change or social justice areas. That left two out of the twenty-six geniuses, only a neuroscientist and a cognitive scientist, with legitimate STEM focus.

What types of professions do we see in these geniuses from the 2016 through 2019 classes? A Creator or two, a few Enablers, and some Servers.

One can only wonder what discovery or breakthrough would occur if the foundation chose all the recipients from STEM fields. Every non-profit that chooses to fund the arts and humanities over STEM fields is imposing an opportunity cost on society—the cost of not gaining from whatever advancement the STEM funding would have provided. Depending on the field and project, that opportunity cost is conceivably measured in millions of lives.

The same anti-STEM behavior is shown by government when making awards. The Presidential Medal of Freedom is important—it's the highest attainable civilian honor. In 2015, President Obama awarded the medal to seventeen recipients. Out of the lucky seventeen, only one had any direct STEM-centric achievements (Katharine Johnson, a NASA mathematician). The other sixteen recipients included four pop music singers (Barbara Streisand, Gloria Estefan, Emilio Estefan, and James Taylor), two baseball players (Yogi Berra and Willie Mays), a Hollywood director (Steven Spielberg), a Broadway composer (Stephen Sondheim), a federal government bureaucrat (EPA Administrator William Ruckelshaus), and three politicians. Keep in mind the Medal of Freedom is for "individuals who have made especially meritorious contributions to the security or national interests of the United States, to world peace, or to cultural or other significant public or private endeavors."[9] This award is supposed to be given in recognition of the best of the best of our nation. Now, I admit I indulge in some Miami

Sound Machine from time to time. Sure, Willie Mays could flat-out play. Yogi Berra might be deserving of the honor if for nothing else he'd earned a Purple Heart in World War II combat. But of the seventeen most deserving citizens out of the 328 million of us in this great country, do you mean to tell me only one is out there with a STEM-related set of accomplishments that is deserving of this honor? But four pop singers and two baseball players make the cut? Clearly, a message was being sent loud and clear: this country values and elevates the fluff, the spectacle, the distraction, and the pomp much more than the Creators and Enablers who toil tirelessly, and usually anonymously, to get things done for the substantive betterment of all society.

How the government decides to use our tax dollars to fund science research also betrays an anti-STEM bias. The National Science Foundation (NSF) is the premier national funder of basic research and has an annual budget of $7.5 billion. Created in 1950 by Congress, the NSF today has drifted far from its original mission to promote the progress of science and to advance the national health, prosperity, and welfare. Instead, today the NSF has been commandeered by a troika of the federal bureaucracy, academia, and various so-called liberal and self-described environmental groups to allocate taxpayer money to projects that have nothing to do with the furtherance of science or technology.

What types of projects? All kinds of weird stuff that defies how it would further our national health, prosperity, or welfare: things like studying the veil-making industry in Turkey, the impact of animal photos in *National Geographic*, whether selfies make you happier, how hunger can make couples fight more, shrimp running on a treadmill, and the social impacts of tourism in northern Norway, just to name a few. But nothing beats the NSF spending nearly $700,000 to fund a climate change musical.[10] That's right: the NSF spent almost $700,000 of our money not on climate change research but instead on a musical about climate change.

The NSF can become obsessed with well-intended, subjective desires, potentially demoting science behind other considerations. The fixation is evident internally, with the NSF diversity mission statement declaring diversity as a prerequisite to progress in science.[11] The fixation is also evident externally, with the NSF awarding $1 million of taxpayer money to the University of New Hampshire for a "bias awareness intervention tool" and another $2 million to Texas A&M's Department of Aeronautical Engineering to "remediate microaggressions and implicit biases" in engineering classes.[12]

How does this happen? Simple answer: by design. The NSF has a powerful position within its bureaucracy known as the Directorate for Social, Behavioral, and Economic Sciences, or SBE. You can imagine how wide of a discretionary game board the SBE has to play with if a flexible reading is applied to what constitutes social, behavioral, and economic sciences. This allows the SBE to funnel whatever monies it sees fit to projects that have nothing to do with scientific research but that instead feed various non-STEM recipients. The same type of twist occurs at other government research entities, including the National Institutes of Health (NIH). Lost is deserving research that could potentially improve all our lives, while our tax dollars are squandered, and our STEM competitiveness is hamstrung—all while bureaucrats, humanities academics, and various special interest groups having nothing to do with STEM benefit.

The dumbing down of STEM is not just prevalent in the esteemed awards and funding communities, but across academia. Colleges have entrance requirements, such as grade point average, standardized test scores, and readiness exams, for high school students wishing to earn admission. Typically, if a student fails a readiness exam in math or a related subject, the student must enroll in a non-credit remedial class.

Despite the logic of this approach, colleges and universities are taking aim at remedial courses. State university systems in Colorado, West Virginia, Indiana, Tennessee, and California decided to dump remedial courses for freshmen who are deficient in math and other basic areas. The excuse was that remedial coursework excludes deficient students from the main student body. Another approach by state universities is limiting material covered in remedial courses to what will be needed in expected majors. So, if the student wants to major in English literature but failed the math proficiency exam, his remedial math class would only cover what was needed for English literature coursework.

Making matters worse is the reality that many high school students are woefully unprepared for even the most basic STEM-related demands of college. The ACT's 2018 annual report showed yet another national decline in math and science college readiness for high school graduates. Only 40% of 2018 high school graduates who took the ACT exam scored a benchmark indicating they could pass a first-year college algebra class.[13] Science readiness was even more pathetic, clocking in at an embarrassing 36% readiness. Not enough time, focus, attention, and accountability are being invested into STEM disciplines at the high school level, which only exacerbates the growing problem at the college level.

These are results of a fundamental problem in primary and secondary school education. Public schools are often led by administrative bureaucrats, and politicians, and influenced by teachers' unions that are much more concerned about optics than the substantive education and proficiency levels of students. The worst exemplar is New York City's public schools, where just about every student across dozens of schools in grades three through eight are given passing grades on report cards and are allowed to advance to the next grade, yet less than 20% of those students are able to pass state-wide proficiency exams in math and English (one school granted every student passing grades and posted a 7% passing rate on the state's English proficiency exam).[14] New York and other major school districts across the nation are passing thousands of students on to the next grade, knowing the students are woefully unprepared. Pass rates and graduation levels supply convenient optics for the school district leadership while students suffer the life consequences.

All this corner-cutting for students who are ill-prepared for the rigors of a college curriculum takes a toll on the STEM capabilities of all graduates. The popular woke argument that dropping remedial courses is a fair and equitable approach for struggling students considers it is better to lower the standards and quality of the degree than it is to provide tools for the ill-equipped student. The only beneficiary is the university because students graduate with minimum (if any) STEM skills, while tuition rolls and graduation rates remain high by admitting and giving diplomas to ill-prepared students.

Contrast the conscious dumbing down of STEM in the U.S. system with the ruthless, unappealing Chinese system. In China, if you don't succeed academically you are left behind, it doesn't matter who you know or what crutch of an excuse you lean on. Only the best, defined by effort and scores, get to move to the good schools and graduate in the STEM fields. We may have reached a time when a new Chinese engineer is predictably more competent than a new American engineer.

WHILE ACADEMIA AND COHORTS ATTACK STEM, THE MARKET REWARDS STEM

While the federal government bureaucracy and foundations are busy siphoning precious tax dollars away from STEM research and into the arts and humanities, you'd think academia would worry about student employability after graduation. The job market should be the key driver of where we invest our educational tax dollars. Outside of a handful of elite schools, what you major in is more important today than what school you graduated from.

The job market has driven a steady decline in demand for degrees in the humanities and liberal arts. The American Academy of Arts and Sciences, one of the biggest advocates of the humanities, reports that humanities degrees continue to drop, year after year, and the humanities' share of total bachelor's degrees has declined for over a decade.[15] Their website amusingly admits that, "the role of humanities in the economic life of the United States may not be as readily apparent as that of engineering."[16]

When you look at the share of liberal arts majors as a percentage of all degrees, we are sitting at an all-time low, off by two-thirds from the peak in the 1960s. Studies from Federal Reserve economists show a much higher level of underemployment in liberal arts grads when compared to grads in STEM-heavy fields as well as much better rates of return on tuition investment for STEM fields versus the liberal arts.[17] Managing student debt load is a relative breeze for STEM graduates compared to their humanities colleagues; a typical professional with a degree in engineering is burdened with roughly half the debt-to-income ratio of a typical psychology major.

PayScale is a firm that collects salary data across a range of college degrees. PayScale looks at both early-career pay (0–5 years of experience) and mid-career pay (10+ years of experience). Top ten majors for mid-career pay the past few years have included petroleum engineering, nuclear engineering, actuarial mathematics, chemical engineering, electronics and communications engineering, computer science and engineering, electrical and computer engineering, systems engineering, geophysics, and aeronautical engineering.[18] You don't see a single humanities or social science major in the top twenty. The highest ranking non-STEM related major is "government," ranked fifty-one, which is frightening in its own right, as the bureaucracy continues to spread its tentacles. The traditional humanities majors of history, film, music, theater, art, philosophy, and theology populate the bottom of the rankings. These data are screaming for more investment into STEM-related classes and degrees and less investment in humanities curricula.

If you think head-to-head comparisons with STEM fields unfair, consider what happens when you compare liberal arts and humanities degrees to blue-collar jobs. A range of degrees in the liberal arts, humanities, and the social sciences can't hold their own against jobs not requiring a college degree. A farmer makes more than a degreed community organizer, a mechanic earns more than a drama major, and a plumber enjoys a larger income than an ethnic studies graduate. Many people are surprised to learn truckers make more money, on average, than the median income of college grads with a master's degree in the humanities.

Only 26% of adults with college experience strongly agree that the education they received is relevant to their work and life.[19] That is a pretty damning finding from the customer base, and it would send shudders through any accountable business concerned about customer satisfaction. Any guess as to which field of study had the highest level of adults with college experience feeling their education was relevant? You guessed it: STEM. The field of study with the lowest registered level of relevance: liberal arts.

While students, employers, and parents are waking up to the contrasting economic realities of the STEM and humanities fields, what do you suppose our friends in academia are doing? If you answered with obfuscating, avoiding, or resisting efforts to improve transparency, then you deserve a star. For years, higher education administrators and lobbyists have fought successfully against the requirement for data disclosure to show prospective students and taxpayers which majors produce strong economic and professional outcomes, and which failed.

In 2018, the Education Department unveiled proposed rules requiring all higher education institutions to report more detailed financial information on graduates across different degrees. While this would be a win for truth, students, and taxpayers, expect major and prolonged resistance from non-STEM areas of academia and its administrators.

REINFORCING THE GLASS CEILING

One of the troubling consequences of forcing arts and humanities down the throats of students across the public high school and university systems is that it reinforces the gender wage gap. Federal government data show that nationally women comprise over half of the college student body yet are only about a fifth of graduates in STEM-heavy fields of engineering and computer science.[20] STEM-related degrees are where the best-paying jobs are for graduates. Moreover, using data from a recent Georgetown study, one sees that four of the five highest-paying degrees/majors are predominantly male: petroleum engineering at 87%, math/computer science at 67%, aerospace engineering at 88%, and chemical engineering at 72%.[21] These are all classic, hard-core, old-school STEM disciplines. Even the fifth, pharmaceutical sciences, with just over 50%

of the graduates being female, is a classic STEM discipline.

Conversely, four of the five lowest-paid degrees/majors are heavy on the liberal arts/humanities and are predominantly female: counseling/ psychology at 74%, early childhood education at 97%, human services/ community organizing at 81%, and social work at 88%.[22] The only one of the bottom five paying majors that had more males than females was theology/religion. Think of how we could eliminate the gender wage gap overnight and at the same time produce more Creators, Enablers, and Servers by simply de-emphasizing the bottom five paying degrees/ majors and reinvesting those resources into the top five paying degrees/ majors. If that redeployment of resources could be correlated with a shift in female students from the bottom five majors into the top five, it would erase the gender wage gap.

To parents of daughters out there, that sounds good. Just don't expect any of this to happen without triggering cunning maneuvering from academia and leftists. Instead, expect profuse lip service about the need for getting more female students in STEM fields coupled with tactics that will further degrade an already troubling level of STEM readiness.

The reality on the ground at campuses across the United States is quite different from the talk in the media and in college brochures. All students, but particularly female students, receive a constant and steady message from humanities and social science professors about how demoralizing a career in a STEM field would be. Anyone in a STEM field knows the type of innuendo coming from those outside of STEM: STEM disciplines lack creativity, everything in STEM is blind and dull robotic process, a career in STEM will pigeon-hole you into a narrow professional path moving forward, and, finally, STEM fields are inherently sexist. Despite this being utter nonsense coming from people with zero STEM experience, don't underestimate the impact this messaging has on impressionable young adults.

Besides the steady harangue of STEM put-downs by the humanities that you find at universities, another tactic you see with numerous colleges and universities is to use the lack of female STEM students as a convenient excuse to expand an already bloated administrative bureaucracy. Engineering programs across the land, from Ohio State to UCLA, now boast more bureaucrats on the rolls, carrying some title that includes "dean," "chief," "equity," "diversity," or the like.[c] Few of these bureaucrats meaningfully improve the state of STEM or female representation in STEM. All of them drain resources from the true STEM curricula, faculty, programs, and facilities.

The plight of women in STEM is exploited by the administrative bureaucracy when it wants to grab more influence and power, but that can quickly change if the female student is Asian American. That is because Asian Americans, male and female, are doing quite well when it comes to higher education and STEM fields. So well that top-tier universities turn away the best performing and most deserving Asian American students using highly questionable tactics.

Harvard University was sued by Asian Americans and put under Justice Department investigation for potential violation of Title VI of the Civil Rights Act, which prohibits race discrimination by federally funded organizations. Harvard is accused of assigning lower "personal" ratings to Asian applicants compared to other applicants in its admissions process.[23] Asian Americans scored disproportionately high on academic and extra-curricular ratings yet scored disproportionally low on the subjective personal ratings for qualities of "kindness" and "attractive to be with."[24] The concern is that the admissions formula was manipulated by Harvard to stack the deck against this ethnic group. Harvard's own internal study from 2013 shows that Asian Americans would have comprised 43% of the freshman class if academic achievement alone were considered but the actual admitted-student population was only 19% Asian American.[25]

Not surprisingly, the Justice Department did not start this

---

c   UCLA's College of Engineering boasts an Associate Dean for Diversity and Inclusion while Ohio State's College of Engineering upped the title inflation with a Chief Diversity Officer for Diversity, Outreach, and Inclusion.

investigation until the Trump administration took office despite complaints filed by dozens of Asian American associations in 2015. Harvard denies that it knowingly discriminates against Asian American applicants and has to date prevailed in court.

While deserving Asian American applicants are taking it on the chin from the biased Harvard process, legacy applicants who were born into a family where a parent went to Harvard enjoy a more than 33% admission rate, offspring of donors clock in at an over 40% admission rate, and kids of Harvard faculty and staff enjoy almost a 50–50 chance of admission.[26] By the way, it would be remiss to not mention that Yale was also under investigation by the Justice Department for bias against Asian American applicants.

This is another example of the Leech practice of using a label or rule when it suits a need and then dropping it or switching it when convenience calls for it. You saw that practice in action in 2019 with the infamous celebrity college admissions cheating scandal. When corporate executives and celebrities like Lori Loughlin (aka Aunt Becky from *Full House*) cheated the system and paid to get their undeserving kids into elite schools, a firestorm of outrage erupted. Some of the loudest voices criticizing the accused came from elite academia. Yet Aunt Becky shared a similar goal that Harvard has, she just used different tactics. Aunt Becky and her ilk worked the system using the tactics of bribing coaches and cheating on standardized tests so that they could artificially elevate their child's standing relative to the competition. Harvard finagles its own system using the tactic of lowering composite scores of deserving Asian American students to lower that student's standing relative to the less-deserving, less well-prepared competition. One tactic is cheating by elevating the desired target while the other tactic manipulates by lowering the competition. Despite different tactics, Harvard and Aunt Becky shared the same goal.

HOW THE RELIGION OF SUSTAINABILITY BLEEDS STEM
Pick up any college magazine, annual report, or strategic plan and you

will inevitably come to the point where the word *sustainability* arises. But what is sustainability, exactly? The truth is that no one really knows. You can't measure it. It is a state of mind, a vague concept that when applied broadly envelops everything around it. Even definitions developed by self-described experts leave the reader confused as to what sustainability and sustainable development are. The United Nations offers the most widely quoted definition with, "Sustainable development is development that meets the needs of the present without compromising the ability of future generations to meet their own needs."[27]

How are we supposed to figure out what the needs of those future generations will be and what tools and technologies they might have at their disposal to meet these needs? The UN definition of sustainable development compactly fits within a single sentence, but when you study it for thirty seconds you realize sustainable development defies definition.

That is by cold, calculating design. The thought-police spread across academia, government bureaucracies, and environmental groups invented the religion of sustainability.[d] The religion and associated ideology are then applied across society, first and most notably within academia, to increase control and dominion over Creators, Enablers, and Servers.

Sustainability has become the ultimate liberal art and the official religion of higher education, and it is applied across academia.[e] That's why a couple of years ago, when Yale rolled out their Sustainability Strategic Plan, President Peter Salovey had the moxie to tell students to "fake it till you make it" to present an image and mirage of sustainability behaviors.[28] That's right, the Yale president publicly encouraged students to pretend their way through sustainability theater. Is it any

---

d   Rajendra Pachauri, the former chair of the United Nations Intergovernmental Panel on Climate Change, stated in his resignation letter, "The protection of planet earth, the survival of all species and sustainability of our ecosystems is more than a mission. It is my religion and my dharma." Pachauri resigned in 2015, accused of sexual misconduct.

e   Sustainability as the "ultimate liberal art" is borrowed from an outstanding report on the sustainability scam titled *Sustainability; Higher Education's New Fundamentalism*, from the National Association of Scholars.

wonder to learn that President Salovey holds degrees in psychology and sits within the Psychology and Sociology Departments? He is a humanities and social sciences lifer, now running Yale for the benefit of the liberal arts and to the detriment of STEM.

So much of this sustainability nonsense enters the realm of the absurd and mirrors brainwashing by thought police. Emory University asks students to study in populated public areas at night to conserve electricity and to take some time for "stillness" each week.[29] The University of Virginia has incoming students recite, "I pledge to consider the social, economic, and environmental impacts of my habits and to explore ways to live more sustainably during my time here at U.Va. and beyond."[30] Students are then asked to repeat the pledge at graduation. Our Orwellian future has arrived.

Being a devout believer in sustainability and purging carbon use are expensive propositions, measured in money, time, and other resources that should go to efforts consistent with the true purpose of higher education institutions. A recent report by the National Association of Scholars (NAS) offered the case study of Middlebury College to demonstrate just how much all this costs.[31]

Middlebury is a small college with about 2,500 students and is not a cheap place to obtain a degree, with annual tuition and room and board exceeding $60,000. Although Middlebury is no bargain, rest assured that tuition goes toward sustainability. The college boasts a sleek, carbon-neutral biomass plant that provides the campus's electricity and heat, had an upfront cost of $19 million, and costs almost $4 million more a year to operate than the old fuel oil plant it replaced. It's these types of foolish economic decisions that ensure college tuition skyrockets as educational quality plummets.

Yet the foolishness continues. Middlebury boasts a robust bureaucracy of sustainability administrators with titles that include a Dean of Environmental Affairs, a Director of Sustainability Integration Office, and various other directors, associate directors, and staff all tied to the sustainability quest. Total annual compensation for these bureaucrats comes in over $1 million per year. When you add in compensation for faculty in sustainability, interns, and other staff, the total exceeds $2.5 million annually.

Then there are the various other activities and endeavors done in the name of sustainability at Middlebury that add even more cost. These include insistence on buying locally grown organic food instead of food from cheaper, out-of-state sources, composting and recycling instead of cheaper landfilling, and a host of professional development seminars for faculty and staff on how to be better sustainability warriors. There are dozens of other activities that fall under sustainability efforts, ballooning costs even further.

Increasingly, STEM-focused departments are being sucked dry of resources that are being assigned, distributed, or commandeered to the on-campus cult of sustainability. The Association for the Advancement of Sustainability in Higher Education counts over 1,500 sustainability programs littered across academia globally.[32] These range from simple certificate programs to doctorate degree programs. Cornell boasts over 700 courses deemed to be sustainability-focused or sustainability-related.[33] The Big Red of the Ivy League offers dozens of major and minor degrees focused on sustainability and asserts more than 96% of its departments have faculty that conduct sustainability research.[34] The sustainability academic complex is spewing out thousands of useless degrees annually, consuming thousands of faculty, and spending billions of taxpayer and tuition dollars continuously. That means less traditional STEM curricula, fewer and lower-quality STEM faculty, diluted quality of graduates in STEM disciplines, and older STEM facilities. Adding this to the ever-increasing tuition required to pay for all this sustainability largesse transforms a bleak situation into a dire one.

EXAMPLES OF ACADEMIC ASSAULT ON STEM

Examples of the hijacking of STEM disciplines and curricula are everywhere one looks these days. The rhetoric and doctrine used in each case are that of a religion. Adherents in the administration, faculty, and student body function as cultural police to enforce norms. STEM and science fields fall squarely within their gaze.

One of the primary channels commandeered to enforce ideology is the peer-reviewed academic journal. Professors and researchers are mostly evaluated by measuring how often they publish and in which prestigious journals. The "publish-or-perish" culture is not new to academia and has always played a significant role in driving academic career paths, including tenure. What is new is how STEM and social science journals have been conscripted to serve as propaganda vehicles.

The quality of published articles in these journals has suffered greatly as a result, and the peer-review process has been diluted to the point of being a joke, literally. Back in 1996, a physics professor successfully published a hoax paper in a prestigious journal to demonstrate that absurd, made-up scientific blabber will get published if the blabber reinforces rhetoric and political views favored by the reviewers and academic culture.[f] More recently, another hoax paper, this time the ridiculous 3,000 word paper titled "The Conceptual Penis as a Social Construct," breezed through peer review and was published in *Cogent Social Sciences*.[35] The authors argued that climate change was caused in part by the male penis. Leech ideology has taken over serious journals and peer review.

Peter Boghossian, a professor at Portland State University, concocted a series of fake academic research papers across a range of grievance study areas. Boghossian successfully had seven of these ridiculous papers accepted for publication and four published in peer-reviewed academic journals. Why did Boghossian go through the extensive ruse? As he put it, "It had to be done. We saw what was happening in these fields, and we were horrified at the faulty epistemology that these people were using to credential themselves and teach others."[36] Boghossian is a humanities professor who cares about academic integrity and is willing to act to expose threats to it.

----

f   Physics professor Alan Sokal published the hoax paper titled, "Transgressing the Boundaries: Towards a Transformative Hermeneutics of Quantum Gravity" in *Social Text*, a top cultural studies journal. Give it a read online for a laugh.

Predictably, academia threw everything it had at Boghossian when his embarrassing ruse was unveiled. A fellow professor at Portland State who was an editor of one of the duped academic journals, along with scores of other professors, attacked him. The university formed a committee that recommended Boghossian be investigated for research misconduct and, to top things off, sanctioned him for violating Institutional Review Board research criteria.[37] Instead of thanking Boghossian for shedding light on a broken culture, the system lashed out at him in typical Leech way fashion.

Although hoax research papers being accepted by and published in academic journals exposes the broken ethos of academia, legitimate papers in academic journals highlight the same issue. Take geography, while often categorized as a social science, it uses many STEM-based competencies. A 2017 paper in *Gender, Place, and Culture: A Journal of Feminist Geography* coauthored by two geography professors had little to say about geography.[38] Instead, the coauthors posited that citing white males in geography papers impedes inclusiveness in the field of geography and should be avoided. The implication is that quality of research is secondary to the demographics of those cited.

Progress in Human Geography is a peer-reviewed journal, meaning nothing is published in the journal until it is reviewed by a group of doctorates in geography and related fields. The journal published a paper titled "Glaciers, Gender and Science" that advocated merging feminist studies with the study of glaciers so that society can approach "human-ice interactions" in a more equitable manner.[39]

The authors are from the University of Oregon. Knowing that certain geography expert peers reviewed and sanctioned it for publication within an academic journal is alarming. The paper "Glaciers, Gender and Science" is a lot of things; science is not one of them.

Chemistry, about as STEM-centric as it gets, is not immune to attack. The University of California–Berkeley, engages its non-STEM doctorate students and faculty to re-design the undergraduate general chemistry course to, "dismantle racialized, gendered, and classed hierarchies of competence in chemistry."[40] That's code for less chemistry fundamentals and more social justice rhetoric in Chem 101.

Botany, another STEM field, is no longer about crop science or cell biology. Our friends at Evergreen State College in Washington state offer a course titled "Botany: Plants and People," where students learn about how they can enjoy more socially just and sustainable relations with plants. With curriculum like this, Evergreen isn't equipping the student for the private sector.

Mathematics is the foundation of all STEM fields and thus is a prime target for assault. A Smith College mathematics professor developed the course "Inequalities: Numbers and Justice," which aims to show how mathematics and statistics are used to promote racial capitalism, climate change, and a portfolio of other evils.[41] The course implies that mathematics is biased and unreliable.

How about what the esteemed, STEM-heavy, Carnegie Mellon University is doing with its engineering curricula? CMU is marketing engineering programs to prospective students by bragging that you don't need to take too much math, computer, science, and engineering classes to obtain the degree. Administrators tout dual degree and minor degree programs for engineers where the second, minor degree is in the humanities. That allows a student to graduate as an engineer with less than half of his coursework in science, engineering, or math. CMU is marketing its engineering program to students by convincing the student he doesn't have to take much engineering.

STEM-centric Cal Tech announced a two-year moratorium on using standardized test scores for admissions, citing the pandemic and equity concerns. Now admissions will be decided on a trio of qualitative considerations: the student's high school coursework, a math teacher recommendation, and the ability of the student to use math "naturally" in life.[42] An objective and quantitative meritocracy has been supplanted by subjectivity in the Cal Tech admissions process.

Medical schools are not immune to STEM dilution. Alarmingly, that translates to less STEM and scientific method and more distraction.

The trend is evident with the American College of Physicians (ACP), an organization of medical educators and students touting the noble mission, "to enhance the quality and effectiveness of health care."[43] Yet a perusal of the ACP website finds extensive position papers on a range of non-medical topics, including gun control and climate change. Those position papers are coupled with the ACP lobbying medical schools to incorporate these non-medical topics and positions into the curricula. With only so many hours of instruction, simple math dictates more ideology in the curricula results in less scientific instruction.

Increasingly, actions to bleed and dilute STEM resources are morphing into outright attacks on science. Evergreen State College offers another example. A combination of student and faculty extremists, most of them not in STEM departments or degree programs, went on record in May 2017 demanding of the college administration that STEM faculty be targeted and singled out for anti-bias training.[44] The college president quickly obliged and promised to bring in faculty for the training and committed that if they didn't get on board with the dogma that they would face sanctioning. Keep in mind that anti-bias training is one of the most popular blunt instruments of intimidation that the radical Left applies to bludgeon those who have the moxie to dissent or resist.

Academia's erosion of objective science extends beyond college, dogging STEM professionals throughout their careers. As a registered Professional Chemical Engineer in the Commonwealth of Pennsylvania, I have completed dozens of hours of continuing education coursework. This is not cheap or quick, running into the thousands of dollars. Many courses have large portions dedicated not to engineering, science, or technology but to subjects such as sustainability, triple bottom line, social impacts, ethics, and the like. These courses are attempts to program your mind to conform. Engineers must consent to the programming or have their professional licenses revoked.

IF THE LEECH APPROPRIATES STEM
EDUCATION, SOCIETY WILL SUFFER

The infusion of Leech ideology onto STEM must end. The situation is beyond self-correcting. The federal government must switch from aiding the dilution of STEM to reinforcing it. The most effective way is through the purse strings. The federal government shovels $40 billion a year to universities for research. That money goes to cover costs well beyond the work in the lab, from administrative costs to general maintenance.

A powerful message to academia would be making government research funding contingent on the university's support of free speech, open scientific inquiry, and opposing views. Faculty and students in STEM fields would also be less fearful to speak up against tyrannical thought police on campuses. A requirement to defend free thought is consistent with longstanding federal government policies. In 1945, Director Vannevar Bush of the Office of Scientific Research and Development said, "Freedom of inquiry must be preserved under any plan for Government support of science."[45]

To see a troubling reality today, compare two quotes from political bellwethers:

"Think of an economy where people could be an artist or a photographer or a writer without worrying about keeping their day job in order to have health insurance."

NANCY PELOSI

"I must study politics and war, that our sons may have liberty to study mathematics and philosophy. Our sons ought to study mathematics and philosophy, geography, natural history and naval architecture, navigation, commerce and agriculture in order to give their children a right to study painting, poetry, music, architecture, statuary, tapestry and porcelain."

JOHN ADAMS

What Adams understood a long time ago and Pelosi is ignorant of today is society's capacity to dabble in the arts rests on a requisite foundation of STEM skills and workers. John Adams understood the country's strengths, Nancy Pelosi only diminishes them.

FUNDING SOURCES PART 1:

THE FED

"Money is much too serious a matter to be left to the central bankers."

"Watch money. Money is the barometer of a society's virtue."

THE FED: MASSIVE MANIPULATION OF CAPITAL MARKETS

Historically, the Fed was as an independent entity focused on monetary policy and keeping inflation in check. Today, the Fed takes orders from select politicians and bureaucrats and has a charter employing aggressive, hands-on management of every market imaginable. The Fed is the biggest, and increasingly the only, market-mover that matters when it comes to the stock market, the bond market, commodity prices, and currency exchange rates. If you want a read on markets, you simply need to know where the Fed is. The Fed often takes its cue from what the Deep State federal government desires for the quarter or calendar year.

The numbers are striking. The Fed has reduced interest rates, using the Federal Funds Rate as a proxy, from about 5% back in 2007, down to sub-0.5% in early 2010 until 2016. Only after undeniable and overwhelming evidence of an economy firing on all cylinders during the Trump presidency did the Fed start modestly to tighten (and the tightening didn't survive 2019). Domestic securities held on the Federal Reserve balance sheet exploded from under $1 trillion in 2006, to over $4 trillion by 2015, to a mind-blowing $7 trillion by 2020, which drove interest rates even lower and asset bubbles ever larger. Banks now hold more in Fed-induced excess reserves than in industrial and commercial loans. The United States never experienced a more aggressive and larger Fed in its history. While unprecedented Fed action occurred in the United States, central banks in Japan, the EU, and the United Kingdom also adopted aggressive monetary policies. The big four central banks amassed a staggering $11 trillion of financial assets on their balance sheets (before pandemic-justified central bank measures).

Between 2008 through 2016, over half of the rise in the S&P 500 index came from Federal Open Market Commission (FOMC) decision days.[1] Between 1995 and 2016, the S&P index did ten times better on FOMC trading days than on non-FOMC days.[2] Although only 3% of the trading days from 1995 to 2016 have been FOMC days, 35% of the S&P's total return over that period came from those days.[3] Statistically, the correlation between Fed actions and stock market performance is not a coincidence.

The Fed also supplies a stock market floor, making investors more speculative and willing to take on risk. Since the epic ten-year bull market began (pre-pandemic), the S&P 500 averages significant gains in the weeks following a day when the index sold off materially. These rebound levels within a week or month after selloffs are unprecedented.[a] What's different? Investors have grown addicted to the Fed swooping in after selloffs to support the market and to re-inflate valuations. Fed support comes via words and actions. If there is no risk attached to a selloff, then buying the dips is free money or so the market has come to believe.

---

[a]   The Fed's massive, pandemic-justified intervention into the free market in 2020 set new levels of "unprecedented." Car rental giant Hertz was prepared to issue stock in the summer of 2020 to raise capital to finance its bankruptcy. Investors were eager to pony-up money for an equity stake in a bankrupt company carrying $19 billion in debt because the Fed's actions encourage wild market speculation. SEC concerns ultimately paused the Hertz plan.

HOW THE FED STRETCHED ORIGINAL
CONGRESSIONAL INTENT INTO EPIC POWER

The Federal Reserve states, "The Federal Reserve System is the central bank of the United States. It was founded by Congress in 1913 to provide the nation with a safer, more flexible, and more stable monetary and financial system."[4] As to goals, "the Federal Reserve sets the nation's monetary policy to promote the objectives of maximum employment, stable prices, and moderate long-term interest rates."[5]

Think about the words *safer, flexible, stable,* and *moderate.* The Fed's charge has always been to stay in the background, let Mr. Market do his thing, and serve as a governor to help smooth the peaks and valleys of inevitable economic cycles. "Nice-and-easy" or "steady-as-she-goes" would be good mottos for the Fed when it comes to its historical mission.

Today, the Fed is anything but a steady-as-she-goes institution. The Fed is found across multiple areas of our economy. The Federal Reserve no longer serves as a passive governor of the economy. Instead, it is an active, and at times, the largest participant in key market sectors. Today, the Federal Reserve drives the economy to the point where it is the economy.

Whatever happened to the goal of moderate long-term interest rates? Even that definition has changed radically. John Williams served as President of the San Francisco Fed and is now the President of the New York Fed and is viewed as an important Fed policy voice. Williams for years has been an advocate of the Fed developing and deploying new, aggressive monetary tools along with a corresponding overhaul of Fed policies to allow the institution to exercise more power and discretion. What was really interesting was the cause Mr. Williams identified that required the changes to policy: lower peak interest rates in the future compared to the past. Mr. Williams pegs the long-term spread between interest rates and steady-state inflation at just 0.5%, absolute.[6] Couple that with the Fed's long-term inflation target of 2.0% and one comes up with a long-term interest rate projection of 2.5% or lower. That is far below historical interest rates when the economy is humming on all cylinders. The new expectation of 2.5% is lower than historical because of both the drop in the assumed spread and the drop in the assumed target inflation rate. The Fed has adopted a self-fulfilling lower-for-longer view on interest rates, reflected in every capital market imaginable, from Treasuries to the S&P 500.

Don't let recent rate hikes when the Trump administration first took office fool you. Sure, in absolute terms the Fed was finally getting around to a series of long overdue rate hikes. The Fed was, that is, until late 2018, when market skittishness forced the Fed to halt rate hikes and then start cutting rates in mid-2019. But when you assess where the real Fed fund rate, defined as the difference, or spread, between the absolute Fed fund rate less inflation, sits, you realize we have been living with real negative interest rates for the balance of the past ten years. The post-election period of modest rate hikes in late 2016 and early 2017 resulted in a more negative real Fed fund rate than before the hikes due to higher inflation. Just like pre-tax returns and pre-tax income not mattering as much as after-tax returns and after-tax income, don't let these small token absolute rate hikes mislead in an era of significant economic expansion brought on by Trump administration policies. The meager rate hikes did not signal a change of the Fed's policy or agenda. To the contrary, they affirmed the existing policy and agenda, just as much as the 2019 rate cuts did.

The Fed was created by Congress to be independent, historically the fear was politics, and politicians, usurping Fed responsibility. That fear today is the opposite: the Fed is increasingly overstepping its scope of responsibility and entering into the arenas of what traditionally are, per the Constitution, the domain of the executive and legislative branches. Sometimes this Fed mission creep was at the encouragement of the executive and legislative branches, such as when the Fed Chair lobbied Congress, the capital markets, and the taxpayer to support the bailout after the 2008 crisis, or when the Fed gained more power through Dodd-Frank. Other instances of mission creep are found by the Fed driving allocation of capital across wide segments of the economy, including housing, on a massive scale via quantitative easing.

Today, the Fed directly intervenes in not just monetary policy but also fiscal and regulatory policy. Too many accept this as normal. Not too long ago, it would have been viewed as usurping congressional and executive branch authority. The Fed was granted independence, but only in conjunction with limited monetary policy authority. Meddling in fiscal and regulatory affairs, whether in collaboration with or in conflict with Congress and the president, betrays the 1913 Fed independence mandate.

As if Fed creep into fiscal and regulatory policy was not enough cause for concern, former leaders of the Fed advocate for its expeditionary probing in politics. Bill Dudley, one year removed from the president of the influential Federal Reserve Bank of New York, publicly called for the Fed to resist the Trump administration. Dudley brazenly quipped that the Fed, "could state explicitly that the central bank won't bail out an administration that keeps making bad choices on trade policy, making it abundantly clear that Trump will own the consequences of his actions."[7] Dudley didn't stop there, adding, "There's even an argument that the election itself falls within the Fed's purview. After all, Trump's reelection arguably presents a threat to the U.S. and global economy, to the Fed's independence, and its ability to achieve its employment and inflation objectives. If the goal of monetary policy is to achieve the best long-term economic outcome, then Fed officials should consider how their decisions will affect the political outcome in 2020."[8]

THE FED USES THE DUAL MANDATE TO RUN WILD
Expanding the mission of the Fed is nothing new, and originally it was driven by presidents and Congress. Today, we speak of the dual mandate of the Fed, to maximize employment and control inflation, as its core mission. That was not always the case. Maximizing employment was not part of the Fed's mandate upon its creation. Then in the late 1940s, at the end of World War II, Congress began to grapple with the concept of maximizing employment. The concern was millions of

soldiers returning home without jobs while industry reset and reduced output to peacetime levels would drive unemployment up and increase the chances for a recession, or even depression. In the 1970s, during a period of economic upheaval, President Ford raised the need for the Fed to address through monetary policy both inflation (price stability) and employment. In 1975, Congress adopted a resolution that instructed the Fed to adopt policy to maximize employment and control inflation. This dual mandate, originally captured in a resolution, eventually became law when Congress amended the Federal Reserve Act in 1977.[9]

A simple reading of the Federal Reserve Reform Act of 1977 shows that "dual mandate" is a misnomer. The statute mentions three, not two, Fed mandates: maximum employment, stable prices, and *moderate long-term interest rates*. You won't find mention of the third mandate of moderate long-term interest rates in the Wikipedia summary of the 1977 Reform Act or from defenders of the Fed.[10] That's because a mandate of moderate long-term interest rates contradicts the spectrum of ideology, policies, and tactics the Fed and its supporters have employed for the past decade. Since a mandate of moderate long-term interest rates frustrates the Fed's ambitions, the Fed has simply decided to ignore it. Thus, the "dual mandate" fabrication becomes fact.

An obvious problem with the dual mandate is that economists can't agree on anything. That includes what the desired, best level of inflation should be. There's truth to the adage that if you put ten economists in a room you will have (at least) eleven opinions. A recent study by Anthony Diercks proves it: a survey of over 100 studies from economists that stated a quantitative optimal inflation rate displayed a range of a high of 6% to a low of negative 8%.[11]

A bigger problem with the dual mandate is maximizing employment through monetary policy. Austrian Nobel Prize-winning economist Friedrich Hayek argued for decades that such an approach will fail, and that the broad power found in the dual Fed mandate runs the risk of despotism in a democracy. Rapid technological change and globalism have only reinforced Hayek's long ago fears.

Over time, free markets distribute capital and workers to the new growth areas of the economy. In the long term, employment and productivity improve. If the Fed alters monetary policy to bolster short-term employment, it deters economic evolution and hinders the market's ability to allocate capital and workers to newer, more productive, growth areas. In fact, with a virtual army of disagreeing Fed economists and board members, monetary policy designed to reduce unemployment is a shot in the dark. One can easily predict a situation where the Fed picks winners and losers in the capital markets by the way it develops policies.

While Fed competence beyond supporting the money supply is dubious, it hasn't stopped officials from weighing in on other issues. In April 2019, Fed Chair Powell was penning letters to Congress assuring that the Fed stood at the ready to manipulate the financial system in response to the ever-pending Armageddon of climate change.[12] Not to be outdone, the San Francisco Fed held a climate change conference later in the year, with President Mary Daly proclaiming that holding the conference was, "essential to achieving our mission."[13] As if the dual mandate of inflation and employment is not enough, we now have a third (fourth, actually) Fed mandate of "weather."[b]

In the summer of 2019, despite record employment and tame inflation, the Fed decided to cut rates, using trade tensions between the United States and China as justification. The president of the Atlanta Fed penned an essay during the chaotic summer of 2020 advocating that the Fed construct monetary policy to pursue the worthy, yet unmandated, objectives of reducing racial inequality and creating a more inclusive economy (President Biden promised the same for Fed policy on the campaign trail).[14] You also have Fed leadership convening with a range of special interest groups to "hear them out," much like

---

b   European central banks have been using climate change alarmism to manipulate capital allocation for a while. The governor of the French Central Bank argues the ECB has a mandate to save the environment and openly lobbies the ECB to discriminate with its quantitative easing by favoring the purchases of green bonds.

a congressman or president will meet with special interest lobbyists. Surely, this is not what Congress had in mind when creating the Fed.

The Fed took to the podium in the summer of 2019, lobbying to justify the Fed's entry into the payment system for U.S. banks, which would directly compete with the existing private banking system.[15] The populist justification offered was taking on the big banks and protecting the public interest.

When it comes to singing the praises of an uninhibited Fed, the biggest advocate is naturally the Fed. That has not always been the case. Historically, the chair of the Fed and board members would narrowly limit public comments to monetary policy. What was tagged as "Fed-speak" was a conscious effort by the Fed to be as vague and non-transparent as possible when speaking publicly. Legendary Fed Chairman Alan Greenspan had the audacity on camera to call it, "purposeful obfuscation," which most of us would equate to lying.[16] Urban legend is that Greenspan, after appearing on Capitol Hill, once told a congressman that if he understood him, he must have misspoken. The goal of the Fed was to say little, bore, and be vague.

Today, whenever the leadership of the Fed speaks publicly, it would be hard to differentiate the transcript from that of a politician running for office. The Fed leadership openly advocates and campaigns for preserving its vast powers, much of it willingly surrendered by Congress via laws such as Dodd-Frank. Fed-speak has evolved from mush-mouthed garble designed not to move markets to blatant advocacy intended to change them. Money is now made off Fed-speak unlike under Greenspan. The Fed also advocates in its communications effort, of course, for greater discretion, power, and scope.

One of the trusty ways to see when the Fed is getting on its soapbox is whenever it references the perils and dangers of the 2008 financial crisis. The battle cry started back during the financial crisis when Chairman Bernanke justified extreme monetary policy with the need to inflate equities and housing prices, which would make households more willing to spend to strengthen the economy.[c] The campaigning continues. Consider these recent examples:

Chair Yellen on Capitol Hill stated in 2017, "The events of the crisis demanded action, needed reforms were implemented, and these reforms have made the system safer," adding, "Already, for some, memories of this experience may be fading—memories of just how costly the financial crisis was and of why certain steps were taken in response."[17]

Fed Vice Chair Stanley Fischer stated to the *Financial Times* in 2017, "After 10 years, everybody wants to go back to a status quo before the great financial crisis, and I find that really, extremely dangerous and extremely short-sighted."[18]

And former Chair Ben Bernanke heralded in the new decade by saying in January 2020, "QE and forward guidance, and possibly other new tools, should be part of the standard monetary toolkit moving forward."[19]

One of the new tools that central banks use today, which began during the 2008 financial crisis, is negative interest rates—in other words, a world where you pay the bank to hold your savings, not the other way around. The concept is simple: set rates negative to induce savers holding cash to spend it and stimulate the economy. The ultimate use-it-or-lose-it scenario.

However, one of the unintended consequences of negative interest rates is that savers and holders of capital may simply withdraw their savings from banks and hold it themselves, thus avoiding the carrying cost, or tax, of negative interest rates. To blunt that avenue of escape from the saver's Hobson's choice of a tax on savings in the bank or spending beyond what you desire, central banks would love to take away the ability to withdraw cash in large denomination bills. The saver would be faced with three options: spend the savings (which the central bank would want in this scenario), pay the effective tax of negative rates on

---

[c]   I describe the Fed monetary policy as extreme while Chairman Bernanke at the time applied the understated "unconventional" as the adjective.

the savings (the Fed's intended behavior from the saver to spend is not realized but at least the government gets more indirect revenue), or buy lots of suitcases along with a lot of land to bury all the $10 bills when he withdraws his money from the bank. If you think this is paranoia and fantasy, consider that European central banks, the negative interest rate champions, stopped printing € 500 notes in 2019.

USING CRISES TO ELIMINATE CHECKS ON FED POWER

François Villeroy de Galhau, the Governor of the Bank of France, brilliantly summed up four uncertainties all central banks face: they don't know where they are; they don't know where they are going; they are impacted by what others do yet don't know what others will do; and they know there are structural changes yet don't know what they are or what impacts they will have.[20] These four challenges would motivate a Creator, Enabler, or Server to tread carefully and to be humble. Not so for the Fed, because despite these uncertainties, the Fed and other central banks are unaccountable for the impact of their decisions, and they play with others' money.

The 2008 financial crisis was music to the Fed bureaucracy's ears. Head count at the Fed boomed during and after the crisis to over 22,000 bureaucrats and hundreds of Ph.D. economists. Not accidently, much of the hiring explosion was justified by having to manage the Dodd-Frank Act. The Iron Triangle of Congress, the federal bureaucracy including the Fed, and Leech-dominated special interests was flourishing.

The Fed used the economic distress of the pandemic to grow. Chair Powell summarized the Fed's opportunity to the Senate Banking Committee in June 2020 with: "What we're thinking about now is providing the accommodation this economy needs for as long as we need it."[21] Under the pretense of saving the economy from a government-induced shutdown, the Fed increased power in three massive stages. The first stage was cutting interest rates to historical lows; the second stage was purchasing Treasury bills, buying mortgage bonds, and lending to banks at unprecedented levels; and the third stage was unprecedented emergency power lending to money markets, municipal governments, businesses, and corporations. Economists project the Fed balance sheet to double and equal nearly half of annual U.S. economic output.

One of the most important documents the Fed holds is what is called the *Doomsday Book*, which lays out views on what the Fed can do within its powers during extraordinary times or crises. Who decides what powers are enumerated within the book? The army of Fed lawyers decides, the same bureaucrats who over the years muscled increasing authority for the Fed and chipped away at shrinking oversight from elected officials. The Fed's internal lawyers refuse to release the contents of the *Doomsday Book*. No one knows what the Fed believes is within its powers and what limits, if any, it accepts.

If the Fed is unlikely to stop itself, then who keeps it in check? The obvious choice would be Congress since it created the Fed and the Constitution grants Congress power, "to coin money and regulate the value thereof." But Congress is more likely to politicize the Fed further. That may make the Fed more aggressive in expanding its mission beyond the boundaries of today, and light-years away from boundaries set a hundred years ago at its creation.

THE INSULATED COCOON OF FED LEADERSHIP

Fed leadership is critically lacking in important diversity. What is glaringly absent is not the superficial diversity of skin color or gender but the more meaningful diversity of background, education, and professional experience. Advocates of the Fed fawn over how nonpartisan it is, routinely applying that argument to rebut legitimate concerns cited by Fed critics. Fed leadership is neither non-partisan nor bipartisan. Instead, Fed leadership is uni- or monopartisan, with everyone thinking the same in both policy and ideology.

Consider the prior Chair, Janet Yellen, as a prime example of what Fed leadership typically represents. Dr. Yellen may be the object of mythical hero-worship across the Deep State, but she has little to no private sector experience and has spent her entire career in elite academia and government. Her bio tells the story since the mid-1960s: undergrad from Brown, Ph.D. from Yale, professor at Harvard and Berkeley, and various jobs at the Fed culminating in Chair in 2013.[22] She spent fifty years embedded in an ecosystem where accountability, results, and consequences either didn't matter or were marginalized. She is clearly a brilliant economist; yet she has never had to run a large business, make a payroll, or compete in the market. She's only read about those things in textbooks and opined on them in sophisticated academic policy papers. As Fed Chair, she suddenly managed trillions of dollars and made epic decisions that affected every man, woman, and child in the United States. With Yellen's background being typical across the Fed leadership team for decades, is it shocking to see lack of clear strategy, mission creep, and political forays displayed across Fed actions on a regular basis?

Lacking a well-rounded background is a perennial Fed problem. At the end of the Obama era, for example, ten of the seventeen Fed governors and regional bank presidents held Ph.Ds. in economics. As of September 2018, only three out of the twelve Federal Reserve regional bank presidents held degrees that were not in economics or law. Most also hail from insulated and elite universities. Although the names and faces may change, the lack of diversity in education, backgrounds, and experience is a Fed weakness.

The makeup and backgrounds of the individuals forming the Fed Board of Governors after four years of Trump has not changed much. Current Fed Chair Jerome Powell is a lawyer, although he did spend some time in private equity. Vice Chair Richard Clarida holds a doctorate in economics and has spent his career in academia and government. Governor Randal Quarles is a lawyer. Governor Lael Brainard, another Ph.D. economist, spent nearly her entire career in government, academia, and Washington, D.C., think-tanks.[23] Nellie Liang, a Ph.D. economist, was nominated for the Board of Governors by President Trump in 2018 and spent over three decades as a Fed staffer. Another Trump nominee, Michelle Bowman, is a lawyer who, despite decent experience in banking and small business, spent years working within an array of federal and state bureaucracies. What you don't see with the Fed Board of Governors is what you would expect and hope to see: an abundance of wide-ranging experience in banking, business, industry, and other components of the private sector.

President Trump looked to inject more pragmatic, real-world talent into the Fed leadership. The perfect exemplar was the consideration of Herman Cain for the Fed Board, a non-academic, honest-to-goodness successful businessman with tangible private sector experience. President Trump then attempted to inject diversity of thought into the Fed by nominating Judy Shelton, a critic of currency exchange rate manipulation and massive central bank-driven capital allocation, for a seat on the board of governors in 2020. The economics establishment, mainstream media, and academia behaved as if Ms. Shelton was an insane heretic for questioning these Fed-favored weapons of mass value destruction, despite both failing to deliver sufficient GDP- or productivity-growth.

As the Fed promotes various forms of physical diversity, it ignores the type that should matter most for a central bank: diversity of thought. In 2018, the president of the San Francisco Fed position was filled by its research director, Mary Daly, who is an inspiring story of a high school dropout who earned a doctorate in economics. But there are two concerns regarding Mrs. Daly's promotion. First, she is more of the same, spending her career inside academia and government bureaucracy and apparently having limited exposure to competitive business environments. Second, the buzz around Mrs. Daly was not about her views on monetary policy but more on aspects of her personal life and how they improve the diversity of the Fed. The search firm used by the Fed to find the best candidate was Diversity Search.[24] The Fed should also employ a search firm entitled Professional Diversity Search, which in addition to physical diversity would also focus on finding individuals with the strongest grasp of monetary policy, market realities, and broad real-world experience.

The Federal Reserve is managed by a forecasting team, who have spent most of their careers as unaccountable academics and bureaucrats. Such concentration leads to groupthink on important issues.[d] Groupthink based on Ivory Tower theories or bureaucratic stratagems has been wrong more often than right: the Fed grossly undershot projected GDP growth during the start of the Trump administration and refused to update GDP growth to higher levels until it was mugged with unequivocal data. John Kenneth Galbraith once quipped that the purpose of economic forecasts is to make astrology look respectable.[25] The most powerful central bank in the universe is led by a team who have built careers on little more than pontification without any ramification for being wrong.

In early 2019, former Chair Yellen said she did not believe that President Trump had a grasp of economic policy.[26] She shouldn't call Trump an economic illiterate. Yellen presided over a Fed that continued to pump trillions of dollars of stimulus via asset purchases and suppressed interest rates over the course of years. The epic, unprecedented manipulation of markets by bureaucrat/economist Ph.Ds. from elite universities delivered meager GDP growth and historically elevated levels of nonparticipation in labor markets, year after year. Once Yellen exited the Fed and the Trump administration cut tax rates and reduced burdensome regulation, GDP instantly jumped up, and unemployment plummeted. Both improvements occurred despite interest rates raised by the Fed during the same period.

FED POLICY: WINNERS AND LOSERS

The Federal Reserve, acting as the primary active driver of the U.S. economy, has been fixated on exceptionally low interest rates for years. Fed policy redistributes trillions of dollars in value across segments of society, with those profiting from the policy becoming addicted to it. Who gains from the Fed-delivered low-to-zero interest rates? Follow the money.

Monetary policy that delivers low-to-zero interest rates benefits debtors and penalizes creditors. Another name for debtors is borrowers

---

d   What Herman Cain coined as the "professor standard."

and another name for creditors is savers. Creditors include the millions of retirees who receive a pension check and active workers who contribute to a pension or retirement plan, since they hold a financial interest with hopes it pays out in the future.

If you owe money, or better yet, if you want to borrow more money, you love exceptionally low interest rates since it keeps your interest expense down. If the interest rate drops to the inflation rate, you have free money. If the interest rate is lower than the inflation rate, fundamentals unravel, and behaviors become unpredictable. Free money motivates the borrower to borrow more.

Compounding this behavior are banks willing to lend to risky borrowers in an exceptionally low-interest-rate environment. Banks begin to chase yields like everyone else in a low-rate world and take on significantly more risk for ever-shrinking rewards. If the economy hits the smallest of bumps, these shaky borrowers begin to default on loans, which will place substantial stress on the banking sector. We know from 2008 that stresses on the banking and financial sectors of the United States or the EU can quickly spread to other sectors of the global economy.

If you lend money or have a savings account, you are not a fan of low interest rates because it provides little-to-no income or return for your hard-earned nest egg or for the risk you took on as a lender. Free money removes the benefits and motivation to save. Zero or negative interest rates destroy the value of savings.

Savers most affected by low yields in savings and money market accounts are the Main Street, mom-and-pop variety. Ironically, previous Fed Chair Yellen famously promised to set policy and interest rates, "to help Main Street not Wall Street."[27] While Main Street savers are getting hammered by the Fed, Wall Street's big boys are loving it.

While the big guys park their net worth in equities, hedge funds, and a range of exotic investment vehicles that benefit from exceptionally low interest rates, the little guy is stuck getting next to nothing for his hard-earned savings. The government then has the audacity to tax the meager interest earned as income, taking returns from paltry to effectively zero.

There is an interesting exception to how low interest rates discourage saving: exceptionally low interest rates may have an unintended consequence of encouraging savers to save more. The saver believes he will need an even bigger nest egg to make up for lost interest income. Increased saving and reduced consumer spending are the unintended consequences of zero interest rate policy. This phenomenon is prevalent in Japan, which was afflicted for years with threat of deflation despite negative interest rates. Data also show net household savings ratios have not budged in the United States, Germany, and a host of other European countries over seven years of ultra-low or negative interest rates.[28] That's not exactly what the Ph.D. economists at the Fed and other central banks had in mind when they drove interest rates to zero or negative to catalyze consumer spending.

Free money erodes the cultural values of saving and economic responsibility. Living beyond your means used to be a cultural scarlet letter. Increasingly, living beyond means is rational behavior due to Fed policies. Today, millennials with zero savings can secure a bank mortgage to purchase a home priced in the hundreds of thousands of dollars if their parents pledge investment assets as collateral, through a startup company if the buyer agrees to solicit the house on Airbnb and share the proceeds with the startup company, or through a pension fund via an equity contract where a portion of the home's future value is pledged to the fund. All of these creative, non-traditional avenues drive up demand for homes, drive up the price of homes, and create a risk that the millennial homeowner will simply walk away from his mortgage commitment if and when the housing bubble pops.

The biggest debtor is the U.S. federal government. The current national debt stands at over $27 trillion, over $80,000 per citizen, and over $220,000 per taxpayer.[29] That is over 100% of the nation's annual gross domestic product (GDP). And the $27+ trillion in debt excludes the massive, debt-like entitlement liabilities of Medicare and Social Security. Worse yet, the national debt continues to grow, with the federal government posting massive deficits each fiscal year.[e]

Those numbers are from the government and should be viewed with skepticism due to bias. Reality is worse. For a sobering view of the financial shape of the U.S. federal government, listen to Professor Laurence Kotlikoff of Boston University. Professor Kotlikoff has been sounding the alarm for years about the federal government's financial situation. Back in 2010, he estimated the true fiscal gap to be over $200 trillion, about ten times the official number from the government and an astounding 1,025% of GDP.[30] The difference is that the government doesn't count as debt the ever-growing liabilities of Social Security, Medicare, and other entitlements. Social Security, which is projected to run annual deficits and exhaust its reserves by 2034, adds over $34 trillion to the federal debt load (representing the present value of projected future benefits less projected future taxes less the current trust fund).[31] Include these types of entitlement outlays, and suddenly you come to the same conclusion that Professor Kotlikoff does: the United States is a gigantic debtor and may already be bankrupt without substantive fiscal reform and sustained accommodative monetary policy. To remain solvent, the federal government's only hope is to be able to borrow massive amounts of money in the future.

Rising interest rates may accelerate the time to default. Ultra-low interest rates may delay but will not prevent default. Only entitlement reform, higher taxes, or a combination of the two will avoid default. Even higher economic growth, although powerful, only delays eventual default if we don't fix entitlements.

All that government debt and continued borrowing has interest payments attached to it. Thus, the federal government is a huge beneficiary of low interest rates. Interest payments on the debt, currently over $300 billion a year, are the fastest-growing area of federal spending. That is saying something since federal government spending includes

---

e   The federal government's 2020 orgy of spending in response to the self-inflicted economic
     shutdown from the pandemic will dramatically increase both national debt and annual deficits.

out-of-control components such as Medicare and Social Security. Ultra-low interest rates allowed the Obama administration (and, yes, the Trump administration) to binge on debt, with government debt increasing over 50% as a percentage of GDP from 2008 to 2015. Yet interest servicing costs dropped from 1.7% of GDP down to 1.2% of GDP during the same period.[32] The Fed created an environment where government debt levels exploded and close to zero interest rates created the mirage of a free lunch by reducing the burden of the interest cost on our economy.

This is indeed a mirage since interest rates can't and won't stay ultra-low forever.[f] But the debt level remains and grows with each annual budget deficit. When interest rates increase, and they will, the amount the government spends on interest will increase with it. Prior to the 2020 pandemic, the Congressional Budget Office was projecting that the interest rate on ten-year Treasury bonds would climb to 4% by 2029. Such moderating interest rates coupled with growing national debt level would nearly triple interest payments, from $325 billion in 2018 to more than $900 billion in 2029.[33] By 2029, interest will represent over 13% of the federal budget, climbing faster than any other budget line item.[34] This is dead money that cannot be spent on other government priorities of education, national defense, research, or infrastructure. The nation's interest expense is extremely sensitive to interest rates: a one percentage point increase in interest rates costs the country an added $1.9 trillion over a decade (using pre-pandemic debt level).[35]

Looking at the United States, Japan, and the EU, we see both an illogical and an unprecedented situation. The cost of borrowing for governments has dropped precipitously and in some cases to negative. At the same time, national finances have degraded from sickly economic growth and structural inefficiencies like entitlement programs. The unprecedented nature of this situation is summed up by Jim Grant

---

f   Despite what academics and leftist ideologies tout with the fiction of modern monetary theory (MMT).

and Richard Sylla, who find no evidence that the current situation of zero-to-negative interest rates has ever existed before.[36]

This unprecedented situation is also highly immoral. Governments and central banks collaborate, by design and through fiscal and monetary policies, to set interest rates and control inflation. Governments all over the world currently sell debt to their citizens at interest rates well below inflation. Governments are imposing money-losing investments on its citizenry to allow the state bureaucracy to keep growing and spending. Governments, including the United States with Treasury bonds, often tax citizens on the meager interest they earn from the principal. That digs the citizen investor into a deeper hole yet supplies more revenue for the bureaucracy. The U.S. government and Federal Reserve commit state-sanctioned, monopolistic wealth redistribution on the scale of trillions of dollars.[g]

FED POLICY: WINNERS AND LOSERS PART II

The federal government's partners in bingeing on easy money and deficit spending are state and local governments. Total state debt is over $1.2 trillion.[37] Many states deserve credit ratings worse than third world countries. Illinois has the lowest rating of any state at Baa3 (Moody's), which is barely above junk status. That is the same rating as the not-so shining examples of Azerbaijan, Costa Rica, Namibia, Tunisia, and Uruguay.[38]

The same is true for certain municipalities. Total local government debt in the United States sits at $2.1 trillion, and many local governments are in dire straits.[39] The best known is Detroit, which experienced bankruptcy, but there is a slew of others in unsustainable financial shape even at current ultra-low interest rates. The top-ten American cities with the highest debt per capita include Denver, Washington, D.C., San Francisco, New York, Atlanta, Detroit, and Chicago.[40]

---

g   President Reagan made this point decades ago. Check out on YouTube then candidate Reagan with William F. Buckley (*Firing Line*, January 14, 1980, episode S0401).

For too many states and local municipalities, to stay afloat without meaningfully raising taxes and cutting spending requires borrowing money at ultra-low interest rates. If state and local governments were to face rising interest rates, the status quo becomes unsustainable virtually overnight. That most states and cities with the highest debt burdens and in the worst shape are heavily Democratic is no coincidence. The Fed's policies are designed and administered in lockstep with leftist economic doctrine commanded by the Democratic Party's extreme wing.

If you are the leadership in a state that can't seem to get its financial house in order and habitually spends more than it takes in, have no fear because the Fed is here! With a policy of very low-to-zero interest rates, the Fed helps financially remedial states two ways.

The first way is obvious. The interest expense burden for high debt states in a low interest rate environment looks a whole lot better than the burden at higher rates. So much better, that in basket case states of Illinois and Connecticut and dysfunctional cities of New York and San Francisco, it is the difference between being on fiscal life support and being insolvent.

Even with this gift from the Fed, states that are fiscal messes see borrowing costs for general obligation municipal bonds significantly higher than bonds from better rated states. Investors worry that states in a financial mess may default on their debt, leaving creditors high and dry. That's where a partner steps in to join the Fed in bailing out states that can't or won't get their spending and financial house in order: credit rating agencies.

Credit rating agencies enjoy discretion to choose winners and losers across industries by granting higher or lower credit ratings than what quantifiable metrics alone should allow. Coal companies are viewed by credit rating agencies as non-investment grade no matter how strong their financial metrics while municipal governments' debt might get the benefit of the doubt in the form of ratings well above their means. Sometimes states and local governments facing looming budget woes enjoy ratings as if they are Berkshire Hathaway.

This situation was underscored in 2010 when credit rating agencies "recalibrated" their credit ratings for state and local government municipal bonds. Recalibration resulted in upgrades in ratings to tens of thousands of municipal bond issuers spread across state and local governments. California and Puerto Rico were two of the biggest beneficiaries, receiving not just a single notch, but a three-notch upgrade in their ratings from Moody's. These agencies stated the new higher ratings did not reflect any change in the issuer's credit worthiness. Yet the upgrades resulted in significantly lower borrowing costs for the issuers and lower yields for the investors.

When Connecticut, Illinois, and Chicago see borrowing costs increasing above those of disciplined states and cities, the undisciplined governments work with the credit rating agencies to pull a quick one on the investing public. A creative investment banker is called in to perform a deft financial engineering to create bodies that give the appearance of greater security than a city or state warrants financially, usually a new corporate entity that issues bonds to investors secured by sales tax revenues backed by legislation. The credit rating agency turns around and issues a high credit rating on those borrowings, saying they are more secure than standard general obligation bonds. The high credit rating reduces the yield of the debt, reducing government borrowing costs. Incorrectly, investors think they are placing their money in a safe bet.

This parlay has its origins in 1970s New York City and more recently was applied by Puerto Rico. In Puerto Rico, over $15 billion in these types of sales tax-backed bonds were issued at excellent credit ratings to lower the island's borrowing costs. When Puerto Rico went into default, those imagined secure bonds traded at a fraction of their issue price with the original investors losing money.

The city of Chicago recently secured the top AAA bond rating on these types of sales tax-backed borrowings; even though it is far from clear that an investor in these bonds would be protected in a future Windy City bankruptcy or default. Once the Windy City had the gold-plated credit rating printed, it proceeded to issue billions in sales tax bonds at low interest rates that belie the true risk to investors. Financially wrecked states like Connecticut are sure to follow suit. Investors see these AAA ratings ascribed by what they assume to be objective and smart credit rating firms, erroneously assume credit rating agencies have investors' best interests at heart, and foolishly think nothing can go wrong with their hard-earned dollars.

The Fed, with low to zero real interest rates, helps financially remedial states a second way: by reducing the returns of competing investment products, such as savings accounts. With no other places to go with savings, investors are more likely to chase low yields from municipal bonds issued by financially sick states, since there is no viable competition or alternative to attract investors. In a world where the retiree wants to invest her savings for interest income, she faces two choices. She can deposit her cash in a savings account and get next to zero, or she can invest in a state or local municipal bond, get 1% or 2%, and hope that the state or municipality does not default. Recall value investor Ray DeVoe's adage that, "more money has been lost reaching for yield than at the point of a gun."[41]

Another group with much to gain by very low interest rates are homebuilders, car companies, and various other businesses looking to sell to buyers who normally could not afford it (or should not buy it) but will do so with the lure of free money. There are too many major sectors of the U.S. economy today where profitability directly correlates to current Fed policy. Take commercial real estate, where investors demand a yield on their investment at a spread over long-term bonds. Ultra-low interest rates set by the Fed distort and lower the yield on commercial real estate securities, creating inflated valuations and distorted asset bubbles. When rates increase, expect the profitability and valuation of the real estate sector to swiftly decline.

Not by coincidence, certain industries where growth is predicated on exceptionally low interest rates are also industries that the federal government has taken ownership interests in, directly or indirectly. With General Motors, for example, exceptionally low interest rates encouraged consumers to borrow to buy more cars. That makes GM stock worth more, resulting in government financial and political gains.

Beyond GM, an even larger situation looms in housing, where the federal government has effectively assumed control of the two largest mortgage companies in the country, Fannie Mae and Freddie Mac. Fannie and Freddie, coupled with the Federal Housing Administration, form an astounding 80% of home purchase mortgage guarantees.[42] The economy may be experiencing yet another housing bubble. Air in this bubble-pumping effort is the Fed instituting exceptionally low interest rates, making home financing through a conventional thirty-year mortgage not just affordable, but the cheapest on record. More attractive mortgages help pump up home values, creating a pleasant mirage of healthy Freddie Mac and Fannie Mae balance sheets.

Housing price inflation doesn't stop with exceptionally low Federal Reserve interest rates. Today, the government requires only 3% as a mortgage down payment, while delinquent unpaid taxes no longer count against a home borrower's credit score, and loans are guaranteed for vacation homes and rental units. Signs of an overheated housing market are evident: since mid-2012 housing prices are up nearly 30% without a corresponding rise in income.[43] When the housing market turns, and it surely will one day, expect massive mortgage defaults reminiscent of earlier housing bubble pops with taxpayers left holding the bag again.

How about people and institutions who invest in the stock market? They include the wealthy one-percenters as well as the financial industry. What impacts has Fed policy produced? Because exceptionally low interest rates create little to no return for cash and bond portions of investment portfolios, investors become more willing to chase return in equities by placing higher percentages of portfolios in equities and by paying more for them.[h] That behavior drives valuations of stocks

---

h Gullible investors are tempted by even riskier financially engineered instruments to chase yield, including leveraged exchange traded notes (ETNs). When the pandemic economic calamity hit commodity and financial markets in early 2020, many mom and pop investors in these instruments were wiped out in a matter of days.

higher, manifesting in high price-to-earnings ratios for the S&P 500 index compared to historical norms (note that even though stock prices may not increase, if they stay stable while earnings are struggling, P/E ratios still rise and drive bubble valuations). Before the volatility of late 2018 hit, the P/E of the S&P 500 sat at 25, materially higher than its historic average (it sat at 23 in mid-2020). You can count on one hand how many years in the twentieth century had higher P/E ratios, and none of those years were prior to 1998. The stock market rises on a massive, unprecedented bubble.

One compelling confluence created by ultra-low interest rates is that of large employers, whether they are private corporations or government, and the individual retiree and worker. As interest rates drop and stay low, the unfunded gap between pension assets and future payment obligations balloons. That's because low interest rates dampen expected returns on the invested pension assets and at the same time lowers the discount rate, which increases the unfunded liability of the pension. Low interest rates over a lengthy period create a double whammy for the health of pension plans, both public and private.

That double whammy has two risks. The first risk is to the retiree or worker who is expecting a future pension. As the return on assets drops and the unfunded liability of the pension grows, the chance of a pension default or cut in benefits grows. The second risk is to the company or government entity that funds and supports the pension. The widening unfunded liability of the pension will require more money injected to shore it up. The growing demands of funding the pension results in less money invested into other critical areas, larger debt loads, and potential loss of confidence in the entity by the capital markets. Eventually, the pension strain can bankrupt any company or government.

This dynamic is already unfolding for government entities across the nation, including Detroit, Stockton and San Bernardino in California, and Central Falls in Rhode Island. Massive, growing unfunded pension liabilities for stalwart corporations such as GE, AT&T, and Delta are already affecting share prices and borrowing costs. Expect these trends to continue as Fed interest rates stay abnormally low. This may catalyze a pension crisis that could quickly morph into a market/financial crisis.

AN UNACCOUNTABLE FED FLIRTS WITH DISASTER

Since the creation of the Fed in 1913, the value of the dollar has declined by more than 95%. The devaluation of the dollar was not by accident and demonstrates the fundamental difference between the Fed's view of money and the Creator's, Enabler's, and Server's views of money. For the Fed, the purpose of money is to effectuate social change. For the individual, the purpose of money is to keep his hard-earned value through a stable and reliable currency. Not only are these purposes different, today they are opposites and mutually exclusive.

The financial meltdown in 2008 created a crisis of opportunity for the Fed to accelerate its aims and vastly expand its powers. The Fed did not let a good crisis go to waste and used the panic to embark on an unprecedented orgy of stimulus via near-zero interest rates and trillions of dollars in quantitative easing (more money created), spanning years. Over the past ten years, the Fed has focused its attention on supporting the stock market and other asset valuation bubbles as much as it has on the traditional metrics of inflation and employment. The mantra of "you can't fight the Fed" justified blind and frenzied speculation in capital markets. Ultra-low interest rates were the medication prescribed to the economy, and we've become addicted to it over the past two decades.

Milton Friedman taught us that inflation and inevitable asset bubbles come from monetary growth and excess money.[44] Only the federal government controls the money printing press, thus government must bear full responsibility for inflation. We still live in an era of extreme monetary policy despite GDP growth ramping up and the unemployment rate dropping before the pandemic. Not surprisingly, the stock market, bond market, real estate, and other asset bubbles expand ever larger, making the inevitable concussive burst more dramatic. The longer the Fed delays returning to higher, normal interest rates and a smaller, normal balance sheet, the greater is the chance that the next downturn will occur when interest rates are so low that the Fed loses any meaningful ability to stimulate. Isaac Newton proved that what goes up must come down.

The Fed, which is wielding unparalleled authority, has a spotty track record. The Fed's policies doubled prices during the First World War, converted a recession in the late 1920s into the Great Depression, doubled prices in the Second World War, and catalyzed inflation in the 1970s. The Fed places enormous emphasis on inflation levels as part of its dual mandate and then miscalculates it at the worst possible times.[45] The Fed's poor performance history may have an unfortunate new chapter added when the lasting impacts of its handling of the 2008–2009 financial and 2020 pandemic crises become apparent.

FUNDING SOURCES PART 2:

UNWITTING RETIREES

(AKA "OTHER PEOPLE'S MONEY")

"Left-wing shareholder activists seek to leverage the mass economic power of institutional investors such as pension funds, whose managers are supposed to focus strictly on their fiduciary responsibilities to retirees."

ELAINE CHAO

PUBLIC PENSIONS FACE SERIOUS CHALLENGES

The job of managing a public pension fund is an important one. The larger the pension fund, the bigger the responsibility. The financial viability of companies, cities, municipalities, states, and the federal government relies on these fund managers to be prudent, transparent, and steady in their duties. Enormous financial resources are poured into public pensions, with state and local public pensions' annual benefit payments to beneficiaries comprising about 1.5% of U.S. GDP.[1] Taxpayers are the funding source, so our money is on the line too.

Despite the essential role of public pension fund managers, the news today is rife with how certain managers of some of the largest pension funds have lost their way on fiduciary duty. Managers pursue interests far beyond the traditional scope of the pension fund, diluting attention, undermining fund performance, and reducing security. While the funds pursue distracting campaigns far from their charters, managers from the largest pension funds, from California to New York, engage in unethical and illegal activities. Fund beneficiaries suffer as a result.

Public pension funds in the United States face insurmountable financial hurdles brought on by lax stewardship. Public pension funds across the United States carry a $4 trillion shortfall, equivalent to the economy of Germany.[2] State pension funds post a $1.3 trillion funding deficit between assets and future liabilities.[3] Since 2007, liabilities of public pensions increased 64% while assets grew only 30%, driving funding gaps wider.[a] Liabilities continue to balloon as politicians and bureaucrats agree to above-market concessions to their public union bosses, while fund managers chase ideology over returns. All these sad public pension stories arise by allowing billions of dollars of taxpayer and worker money to fall under the control of government bureaucrats and politicians. When you place hundreds of billions of dollars of Creators', Enablers', and Servers' hard-earned money into the laps of the distracted, terrible things invariably happen.

REMAKING THE JOB OF PENSION FUND MANAGER

The Employee Retirement Income Security Act (ERISA) is quite direct as to the role and responsibility of pension fund managers. ERISA states that the responsibility of fiduciaries of pension funds is to manage the plan solely in the interest of participants and beneficiaries and for the exclusive purpose of providing benefits and paying plan expenses.[4] One facet of this responsibility is to diversify the plan's investments to minimize the risk of large losses. Managers must avoid conflicts of interest, meaning the pension fund manager may not engage in transactions on behalf of the plan that solely benefit the manager or parties related to the plan, such as the plan sponsor.

A growing number of pension fund managers of states and cities have gone rogue when it comes to their responsibilities. Misguided

---

[a] Results are for 109 public pension plans that reported 2018 results as of April 2019, as reported by the Boston College Center for Retirement Research.

managers use the funds' influence to advocate for, and force change on, a range of politically correct issues.

A convenient vehicle for such ambitions is found in the oft-cited environmental, social, and governance bucket, or ESG for short. ESG investing is reflected most obviously by that popular tag line, "doing well by doing good." ESG investing is found in terms such as *impact investing* and *ethical investing*. ESG funds are growing at an explosive rate, reaching $12 trillion in assets under management in the United States at the start of 2018, a 38% increase from the prior year.[5] Wall Street is more than happy to jump on the ESG bandwagon since it means higher fees and commissions, and it has been creating new ESG funds and products at a dizzying rate. These funds invest in or shun certain companies or industries depending on a host of ideological filters.

ESG filters driving pension fund managers is exemplified by climate change zealotry. Too many public pension fund managers are obsessed with climate change, distracting them from their fiduciary duty and harming fund performance. Vocal fund managers lecture about how they won't invest in fossil fuel companies and demand carbon disclosures from them. Other pensions and retirement plans dive head-first into ESG-focused funds even though the fees are higher than, and the performance is subpar to, standard investment routes. A booming industry of middlemen looks to shove high-fee, low-performing ESG-focused funds down the throats of pensions and 401(k) retirement plans, sacrificing higher fund returns, lower fees, and healthier financials for retirees and workers. The beneficiaries of the pensions are harmed.

Excluding an investment class from consideration in a portfolio because of purely subjective criteria hurts returns, increases risk, or both. Data show average annual returns in states applying politically correct divestment programs were 0.4 percentage points lower than states that were not handcuffed with divestment requirements.[6] Public companies in the energy and tech sectors show no correlation of company share price performance to ESG weighting, whether over- or under-weighted, while on average, ESG funds underperformed the S&P 500 for significant periods of time.[7] Data debase the fiction of ESG fund performance besting funds not hobbled by such limitations, with even simple indices like the S&P 500 posting superior performance.

Confusion is added to the mix since what is ethical is relative. ESG investors claim one can objectively and quantitatively evaluate companies on ESG performance. It's not that simple. In such instances, what is socially worthy or moral is not a universal formula. That's why some ESG funds rank Tesla as the top rated ESG car company and other ESG funds rank Tesla at the bottom of the industry.[b] ESG machinations are often redundant on a practical level since investors realize that companies that can't operate in a safe, environmentally sound manner will be run out of business in a short period of time due to decreased productivity and increased costs. Savvy investors don't need a subjective, opaque filter to tell them what the Darwinian market already tells them.

The demise of Pacific Gas and Electric (PG&E) exemplifies the stark contrast between investing reality and ESG fantasy. First, the fantasy: for years, the California utility racked up ESG accolades from self-proclaimed governance experts. Sustainalytics.com deemed PG&E an ESG outperformer, *Corporate Responsibility* magazine's 100 Best Corporate Citizens ranked PG&E as the top utility in the nation, and *Newsweek*'s Green Rankings also placed PG&E at the top of the utility heap. The company boasted that over a third of its power came from renewables, which helped deliver a string of best-possible governance ratings from Institutional Shareholder Services (ISS). PG&E was the belle of the ESG ball.

Nevertheless, the ESG fantasy was in stark contrast to the reality that was amassing for years. PG&E was a severely dysfunctional organization in the arenas of governance, safety performance, and environmental stewardship. The utility's rap sheet over the past twenty years includes convictions for over 700 misdemeanors that took the court clerk over

---

b   Two of the best known ESG rating firms are MSCI and FTSE. In 2018 MSCI ranked Tesla at the top of the ESG heap while FTSE ranked the electric car manufacturer at the bottom.

an hour to read aloud (1997) and felony convictions stemming from misleading regulators and the public about the state of a gas pipeline that ruptured and killed eight people (2010). PG&E made attorney Erin Brockovich a household name and Hollywood movie sensation when she represented clients who were eventually awarded over $600 million from PG&E in court cases stemming from contaminated drinking water. From 2012 to 2016 PG&E supervisors looked the other way as employees fabricated thousands of on-time results to hit internal targets for responding to excavation work around buried power and gas lines, accumulating over 170,000 violations of state law. And when managers complained that a higher-level manager was pressuring employees to falsify results, the utility decided to punish the whistleblowers and promote the accused wrongdoer. Clearly, this was not a best in class track record for E, S, or G.

Then, in 2017 and 2018, wildfires raged across California and it was determined that over 1,500 fires, several of them catastrophic, were caused by PG&E's poor maintenance practices, deferred safety upgrades, slow responsiveness, and obsolete equipment. The death toll exceeded 100 and 22,000 buildings were destroyed across 350,000 scorched acres. A company audit months after the fires reported nearly 10,000 problems with power lines throughout its system.[8] Before you knew it, the utility was facing tens of billions of dollars in liability. PG&E filed for bankruptcy in early 2019, bringing home the reality of wiped-out investors despite all those shiny yet hollow ESG credentials.[c]

Moving forward, PG&E customers can expect the largest intentional blackouts in history, exemplified when two million Californians had power cut for days in October 2019, during fire-prone windy periods as the utility post-bankruptcy looks to pass on risk to the rate payers.

---

c   The reputational bankruptcy of PG&E quickly followed its 2019 financial bankruptcy. In 2020, the utility pled guilty to 84 felony counts of involuntary manslaughter stemming from the Camp Fire disaster. It took over half an hour in court for the judge to recite each criminal count and victim name and for the PG&E CEO to answer 84 times with, "Guilty, Your Honor."

The CEO went on record that same month lamenting that it might be a decade before the self-inflicted blackouts end.[9] Of course, the jettisoning of risk to those the utility exists to serve will be justified on the ever-accommodating excuse of addressing climate change and serving corporate greed; California Governor Newsom's assessment of the root cause of the intentional blackouts was found in his quip that, "It's about corporate greed meeting climate change."[10]

What won't be named are the true root causes of the crisis by the governor. First, for years government bureaucrats, environmental groups, and politicians forced the regulated utility to divert billions of dollars from necessary line maintenance and equipment upgrades to various climate change and renewable energy adventures.[d] The consequences were dire: a failed 100-year old metal hook designed to suspend high voltage transmission lines started the deadly 2018 Camp Fire. A second root cause was those same bureaucrats and environmental groups prohibiting the utility and other businesses from practicing effective vegetation clearing practices, making the wildfires more intense and faster moving. Governor-appointed leadership of the inept state public utility commission may have set the stage for the catastrophes by prioritizing renewable energy and climate change mandates ahead of electricity grid safety and reliability oversight.[e]

Intentional blackouts by a government-controlled utility have serious negative consequences, spanning from macro GDP to the individual. Each blackout event imposes $2.5 billion in costs for residents and businesses in the state.[11] Intentional blackouts mean health risks

---

d   Consider PG&E squandered $500 million in electric car subsidies and $150 million in battery storage projects in 2018, in addition to $130 million in a three-year electric vehicle charging station buildout (as reported by the *Wall Street Journal*, 10/25/19). All to pursue the utility's climate change agenda.

e   With a lack of urgency typical of government bureaucracy, the state public utility commission in 2015 opened an inquiry into PG&E's safety culture. That inquiry muddles on year after year, including through the period of devastating fires.

for the elderly who won't be able to use medical devices that require electricity as well as lost revenues and increased expenses for businesses such as restaurants and grocery stores when they can't serve customers in the dark and lose refrigerated inventory. Expect broken laws when the lights go out as looting, panic, and criminal endeavors proliferate. Homeowners and businesses are now buying carbon-fueled generators in droves because everyone knows the utility cannot be trusted to supply safe, reliable electricity.[f] Adding insult to injury is that intentionally turning California into a third world electricity grid does not prevent the inept utility's decrepit infrastructure from starting more fires: PG&E disclosed in late 2019 that one of its transmission lines failed in the area of a Sonoma County fire that destroyed hundreds of buildings. This was not exactly the ESG dharma PG&E promised to investors.

Certain companies are more than adept at applying ESG marketing tactics to hook gullible investors on an epic scale. The case of WeWork offers such a cautionary lesson. The office space tech darling (at least for a period of time) boasted a $47 billion valuation in early 2019 and possessed one of the savviest investment firms on the planet as a major owner: SoftBank. WeWork was as ESG friendly as it gets, at least on the surface. The company's founder and initial CEO, Adam Neumann, constantly spouted a potpourri of ESG missives including how WeWork "advances inclusion and equity in the global economy," wanted "to build a world where no one feels alone," and existed "to elevate the world's consciousness."[12] When the company was deciding which stock exchange to list its shares on before its planned IPO, Neumann sat the CEOs of NYSE and NASDAQ down to ask which one would ban meat and plastic in the exchanges' cafeterias. Such a ban would curry favor with WeWork and land the exchange the coveted stock

---

[f]   Even the anti-carbon California PUC was forced to allow PG&E to purchase $94 million of
diesel generators to provide 450 MW of local power during preventative outages in the summer
of 2020. PG&E wanted to utilize cleaner natural gas turbines, but environmental groups
opposed it; thus, dirtier diesel generation was the only viable remaining option.

listing. NASDAQ practiced one-upmanship by committing to create a We50 index of companies practicing sustainability. Not before long, NASDAQ, SoftBank, and scores of others looked foolish as WeWork's substantial financial woes and its CEO's problematic public behavior peeled away the glossy ESG veneer to expose a stark reality. Valuation plummeted from $47 billion to less than $8 billion, Neumann was ousted as CEO, the IPO was canceled, the company had to be bailed out by SoftBank to avoid ruin, and a reorganization to cut costs could not be effectuated because the company was in such dire financial straits it could not afford to pay severance.

Accurate and effective ESG screening can provide an investing edge, but it requires painstaking analysis of individual companies on a continuous basis. Instead, many ESG investment products and investors rely on static, one-size-fits-all methodologies that look good on paper but fail miserably in reality. When the latter approach is embraced with ESG investing, common sense tells you a portfolio of high-fee ESG investment options will not keep pace with the performance of a lower-cost portfolio without ESG constraints. Yet segments of the financial services industry, media, and academia continue to tell investors the opposite. Capital markets constantly adjust views on valuation and companies are continually delivering varying levels of true ESG performance. Investors should look to the tangible performance and actions of individual companies across health, safety, environmental, and governance metrics to assess investment worthiness and to decide which companies pass ESG muster.

As ESG popularity explodes, there is growing risk of questionable marketing and presentation of ESG products by the financial services industry. As the array of funds titled with key terms like *responsible, sustainable, green, ethical,* and *environment* continues to grow rapidly, a large group of these supposed-ESG funds are simply run-of-the-mill mutual funds. They either changed names without a serious change in portfolio holdings or are new funds that optimize returns like traditional funds with no meaningful exclusion of companies or industries. Just as unscrupulous companies look to mislead investors by adopting currently popular bitcoin or block-chain phraseology in their investment materials with no intention to pursue or current presence in these technologies, a host of financial services companies are rolling out ESG-friendly titled funds with no meaningful difference in their holdings compared to non-ESG mutual funds. Numb investors who feel some guilt-ridden urge to pursue doing well by doing good are being conned in a multi-billion dollar charade of wordsmithing.

Even corners of government have raised warnings to retirement plan managers. The Labor Department has issued bulletins for 401(k) plan administrators warning that ESG factors are not necessarily relevant economically and that just because a company or fund is ESG-focused does not mean it will be a good performer on investment return. The Labor Department instructs managers and administrators not to place social beliefs and goals ahead of the monetary interests of the savers and participants in the plans.

Not long ago, the SEC shared the Labor Department's suspicion of the ESG fad, with SEC Commissioner Hester Pierce fearing that ESG might stand for "enabling stakeholder graft."[13] In 2019, Mrs. Pierce continued to express concern regarding the ESG movement's motives and stated, "We ought to be wary of shrill cries from a crowd of self-appointed, self-righteous authorities even when all they're crying for is a label."[14] Later that year, it was reported that the SEC sent examination letters to investment firms asking for details on ESG filters used when making investment decisions as well as how shareholder proxy voting is decided for ESG issues.

Fund managers vote shares not owned by them. That carries a duty for the manager to vote to maximize the financial performance of the company, not in a way that aligns with subscribed-to political or ideological beliefs. The Labor Department is simply reiterating what ERISA already says in statute, but to hear the federal government bureaucracy restate this position shows how bad the situation is with pension, index fund, and 401(k) plan managers and administrators.

Before leaving the ESG investing world, lets dispense with the unwarranted conclusion that younger investors including millennials are more than willing to take a lower rate of return in exchange for investing in only ESG-worthy companies and funds. Such logic is a non-sequitur. First, most young investors, like those before them, are new to investing, so just because they are willing to do it now does not make it smart later. Second, don't be surprised if lip service paid to ESG investing is overtaken by actual investments where younger investors see best return prospects, ESG-focused or not. Most likely, experience will reverse engineer the minds of young investors into ones that are capitalist and rational. When that happens, blindly chasing what others deem to be ESG investing will be considered something quite different from "doing well by doing good." Fortunately, data so far show ESG-focused ETFs comprise a small fraction of the total ETF industry favored by individual, small investors.

California runs two of the largest public pension funds in the world, CalPERS and CalSTRS. CalPERS covers a wide spectrum of state and local government workers while CalSTRS is dedicated to teachers and school district workers. CalPERS boasts nearly two million members. As of June 30, 2017, CalPERS had over $435 billion in liability obligation that, when compared to its assets, yields an unfunded liability of over $100 billion and less than 70% of the money needed to meet future commitments.[15] The largest public pension in the land is facing an enormous financial challenge.

Yet you would not know it reading the CalPERS annual report. CalPERS dedicates substantial portions of its annual reports along with significant amounts of manager time and money on a range of issues far afield from the fiduciary duty of making sure the pension can meet its obligations to beneficiaries. CalPERS' reports and press releases celebrate signing the Paris Pledge for Action so that the pension could participate in climate change activities. The pension applauded its CEO for addressing the United Nations on climate change. CalPERS spent considerable time and dollars reviewing the carbon footprint of companies held in the fund's investments. They launched the Global Real Estate Sustainability Benchmark for assessing and evaluating social and environmental factors in real estate. The fund directly engaged in a range of politically-charged proxy battles at various public companies that had nothing to do with those companies' performance or results. Prominent in the glossy strategic plan reports was how much water CalPERS saved, how far its carbon footprint shrank, how much landfill space was avoided from CalPERS trash, and how all those CalPERS buildings are now LEED-certified.

Four of the nine worst-performing funds within the CalPERS portfolio of over 230 funds in the 2016–2017 fiscal period focused on renewable energy and other environmental plays.[16] None of the top-25 best-performing funds in the CalPERS portfolio were ESG-focused. The distorted approach to investing over time helped take CalPERS from a surplus position of almost $3 billion in 2007 to an underfunded position of over $100 billion in 2017, which is an impressive feat when you consider the stock market nearly tripled between 2010 and 2017.

The President of the CalPERS Board of Administrators finally paid the price for placing personal politics and ideology ahead of the fiduciary duty to protect and improve the financial health of the plan. In 2018, California government workers and retirees voted to oust the sitting board president Priya Mathur and put in her place Jason Perez. A key differentiator in the election was Perez taking Mathur to task for placing political ideology ahead of fund returns when she steered investment decisions. Independent studies show CalPERS lost billions in investment returns over the years just from deciding to shun tobacco stocks.[17] As the fund went from shunning not just tobacco stocks but also fossil fuels and firearms stocks, the nearly two million workers and retirees represented by CalPERS had had enough and removed Mathur.

CalPERS is not alone. The New York State Common Retirement Fund is another whale pension fund, managing over one million workers' assets. In early 2018, the state comptroller announced the fund was going to pour $4 billion into a low emission index fund that invested in already bubble-inflated stocks and purposely reduce investment options that could yield returns in companies like Exxon and Chevron.

Goldman Sachs helped develop the low emission index in return for a tidy fee of $600,000, which comes out of the employee and retiree asset base.[18]

The New York State Common Retirement Fund chasing low carbon emission nirvana pales next to the approach of the New York City Pension Funds (City Funds). The dynamic duo of Mayor Bill de Blasio and City Comptroller Scott Stringer direct the City Funds, which covers cops, firefighters, teachers, and city workers. Although their duties to city residents as elected officials are serious, the dynamic duo spends time on a host of distractions that have nothing to do with the well-being of constituents.

Comptroller Stringer is quite an eco-warrior, leading anti-natural gas and "keep-it-in-ground" anti-fossil fuel campaigns across New York.[19] He is also a regular on the speaking and panel circuit for everything and anything related to environmental activism. In 2017, Stringer publicly appeared or spoke at hundreds of events, with only a handful of those events related to investing or finance.[20] Comptroller Stringer is also busy with activist campaigns against public corporations. In fiscal 2017, he filed over 90 separate shareholder proposals to almost the same number of companies.

In January of 2018, Comptroller Stringer announced the City Funds were divesting all fossil fuel assets and investments. At the same time, Mayor de Blasio proudly announced he was going to sue energy companies, including Exxon, because of alleged harm the city suffered from climate change. The media, academia, and environmental groups were quick to voice support for these moves. The divestment action and lawsuit announcement are silly on their faces and most reasonable people tend to ignore them. What gets more serious and should not be ignored is considering these public displays for attention in relation to the performance and health of the City Funds, for which both men share responsibility.

The City Funds are facing a gaping hole of unfunded liabilities. New York City admitted City Funds were $65 billion in the hole in fiscal 2016, but the bureaucrats used questionable assumptions for discount rate that substantially reduced the size of the hole.[21] When more reasonable and market-based assumptions are applied for discount rate, the deficit of the City Funds balloons to over $142 billion.[22] Annual cash contributions by city taxpayers to shore up the City Funds have exploded by over 600% in just fifteen years, totaling over $9 billion in fiscal 2017.[23] Experts project that 80 cents of every dollar of income tax collected in New York City will need to be allocated to the City Funds to cover the unfunded liability deficit.[24] That means no money left for schools, infrastructure, and public safety.

City Funds performance has been poor, worsening the unfunded liability hole. For the ten years between 2006 and 2016, the City Funds average performance was a 6.2% return, well below the self-established target of 7%.[25] A big driver of the underperformance has been the concentration of 12% of the City Funds' assets into the "Developed Environmental Activist" class. This asset class has underperformed by a whopping 600 basis points over three years. The divestment of, and refusal to invest in, fossil fuel companies are projected to cost the City Funds up to $120 million annually and $1.5 trillion over the next fifty years, making the gaping unfunded liability hole wider and deeper.[26]

WHAT HAPPENS TO PENSIONS WHEN MANAGERS LOSE TRUE NORTH?

Public pension fund managers who are distracted from their fiduciary duty run risks beyond poor returns and weak balance sheets. Sometimes those risks manifest in malfeasance and criminal behavior of key employees within the fund. Unfortunately, prominent examples exist.

Back in 2014, the New York State Common Retirement Fund hired money manager Navnoor Kang to be responsible for its $50+ billion bond portfolio. While the Fund was busy with external activism, it wasn't minding what was going on under its own roof. Turns out Mr. Kang was fired a year earlier from his previous job on Wall Street with Guggenheim Partners for a host of unethical practices tied to not reporting entertainment and gifts he received, in violation of Guggenheim's internal policies.[27] Kang was taking concert tickets and other gifts from brokers at other firms who were receiving commissions for trades that Kang sent their way; that's classic pay-to-play in the investment world. Guggenheim showed Kang the door.

Apparently, the New York comptroller and the New York State Common Retirement Fund did not spend five minutes to call Guggenheim as part of the hiring due diligence of Kang. If the Fund or the comptroller had simply done what any company would have done when hiring Kang, the $50+ billion bond portfolio would never have had the risk Mr. Kang presented.

Care to guess what Mr. Kang did when he assumed control of the $50+ billion bond portfolio at the New York State Common Retirement Fund? According to his eventual indictment on charges of securities fraud, Mr. Kang continued his ways perfected at Guggenheim, just on a grander scale. The indictment states Mr. Kang added certain investment brokers to the list doing business with the state pension fund, and those brokers proceeded to bribe Mr. Kang with expensive watches, vacations, drugs, and prostitutes in exchange for trading business and associated commissions.[28] The damage done to the pension fund and the retirees is incalculable and unknowable.

A private investment firm discovered Kang's wrongdoing when Stifel Financial uncovered fraudulent expense accounts for one of its brokers. The requested expense account reimbursements were to pay for the gifts and trips used to bribe Kang. Stifel informed the SEC.

Kang pled guilty in 2017 to taking bribes. Despite his egregious actions and alleged obstruction of justice along the way, Kang's sentence was less than two years in prison. Furthermore, Kang did not admit to all of the allegations leveled against him in his pleading of guilt and the omissions were not challenged by the prosecution. Why the prosecution allowed such a lenient outcome for a slam dunk case and the financial scale of the risk created is unclear. Handling criminals like Kang gently further perpetuates a culture of non-accountability, even in criminal instances, where the pensions of thousands of people are jeopardized.

This is not the only time this happened at the New York State Common Retirement Fund. Back in 2010, the comptroller, Alan Hevesi, pled guilty to accepting almost $1 million in bribes a few years earlier from money managers in exchange for investment of $250 million of the Fund's assets.[29] What followed was typical political fallout, with lots of posturing about how the state was going to clean up the mess.

Starting in 2013 and through much of 2016, while Mr. Kang was taking bribes under his state employer's nose, the New York State Comptroller Thomas DiNapoli was publicly bragging about the great governance of the New York State Common Retirement Fund. Funston Advisory Services was hired in 2013, after the Hevesi scandal hit, to perform an independent review of the pension fund. The report praised DiNapoli and the Fund's governance as industry-leading and developed dozens of recommendations to improve the controls. Funston then issued a final report in June 2016, which rained glowing accolades down upon the comptroller and the New York State Common Retirement Fund. Quotes from the executive summary of the final report provide a flavor for the degree of admiration Funston had for the Fund: "the level of transparency compares well with other large peer funds," "take[s] ethics and conflict of interest standards seriously," "are to be commended for their progress in the implementation of the recommendations from the initial fiduciary and conflict of interest review," "the vast majority of . . . recommendations have been addressed," and "stable and competent leadership."[30] Worse, Funston expressed as its biggest concern the need for the public pension to hire more bureaucrats and to pay the management team higher compensation.

The ability of Mr. Kang to do what he did highlights severe governance inadequacies at the New York State Common Retirement Fund. Kang was able to add eight new investment firms to the list of approved firms that the pension would do business with, including the two firms named in the indictment. Either there were no controls in place at the pension to review and vet such additions or the controls lacked teeth, were ignored, or easily avoided.

CalPERS is not immune to wrongdoing within its pension leadership, experiencing both its CEO and a member of its oversight board of directors indicted for a pay-to-play ruse. Federico Buenrostro was the CEO of CalPERS from 2002 until he was fired in 2008. Alfred Villalobos was a former board member of CalPERS and at one time was also Deputy Mayor of Los Angeles. Both men worked out a scam that suckered private equity firm Apollo into paying millions of dollars in commission fees in exchange for CalPERS directing $3 billion of its assets to Apollo for investment. The commissions were paid to a shell company controlled by Villalobos, with cash proceeds delivered to Buenrostro in shoe boxes and paper bags.[31] The handoffs occurred at a hotel across the street from the state capitol building. The CEO used the money to buy all sorts of nice things and to pay for his wedding, which was held at Villalobos's mansion.[32] Later it came to light the CEO used some of the stolen money to pay for his eventual divorce. The CEO pled guilty to the charges and Villalobos committed suicide before he could stand for trial.

After this disaster, California committed to hire the "best" possible leadership it could find to run CalPERS, eventually hiring Marcie Frost as CEO in 2016. Mrs. Frost does not have a résumé that you would expect for someone to be CEO of a massive pension plan holding over $350 billion in assets (as of 2018) and facing a severe funding deficit impacting future benefit payments to millions of plan participants. Mrs. Frost came from the much smaller Washington state retirement system and does not have a college degree.[33] But CalPERS stated upon the hiring that she was actively enrolled in a dual degree program from Evergreen State College (the same Evergreen discussed in earlier chapters). But there were problems. First, Frost had completed only one course, back in 2010, and had not completed any courses since.[34] Second, the course she took, in experiential creative writing, was as a non-admitted student.[35] Third, Evergreen State did not offer dual degree programs.[36] Compounding the troubling situation is the departures of seasoned executives within CalPERS. CalPERS steadfastly stands by the CEO. [37]

PUBLIC PENSIONS AND THE DEVIL IN THE DETAIL

Actuarial credibility and public pension fund manager objectiveness are critical to a fund. While projecting pension health using assumptions for the future is a complicated task, there are two critical assumptions: discount rate and return on assets. The discount rate is the method used to express all the future liability of the fund, in the form of checks to retirees and beneficiaries, to a current year present-value. Discount rate sets the present-value, cumulative amount owed by the fund; the lower the discount rate the larger the present value of the liability, all other things being equal. Return on assets is what the fund assumes, on average, the assets will earn into the future. The lower the return on assets, the larger a fund's deficit will be.

Asset assumed returns used to be noncontroversial. That's because for decades pensions could meet their funding obligations at a return on assets level of 7–9%, which was close to the risk-free rate that thirty-year Treasury bonds delivered. That was an era of pension Valhalla: juicy return on asset levels that funded obligations without the need to take on risky investments, coupled with reasonable ratios of active workers contributing plan funding to retired workers withdrawing plan payments.

Starting in the 1990s, pensions experienced a one-two punch to the gut. The first punch was an unfavorable demographic shift in the ratio of active workers injecting assets into plans versus retired workers pulling out assets. An aging and shrinking workforce alone were not moving this ratio in the wrong direction. The unfavorable shift in the ratio of active-to-retired workers was accelerated and worsened by politicians and bureaucrats, seeking short-sighted votes and influence through political giveaways. These giveaways included reduction in early retirement age, reduction in required years of service, and the addition of overtime into pension formulas that inflated benefit levels significantly. Cumulatively, these giveaways pushed certain public pension plans into cash flow negative territory in the 1990s, setting the stage for unsustainable funding models over the long haul.

The second gut punch was the Federal Reserve pounding interest rates toward zero. The policy of ultra-low interest rates dropped yields on bonds dramatically, including the pensions' old standby, the low-risk thirty-year Treasury bond. Once the Fed had its way on interest rates, there was no longer a minimal risk option like Treasuries to help deliver a 7–9% return on assets as in the past. That meant a much lower return on assets, which pressured an already unsustainable funding model. As of mid-2017, ten-year annualized median returns for public pensions were under 5.6%, quite different from the 7–9% annualized returns assumed over that same period (and still blindly applied today by numerous public pensions).[9]

In reaction, pension fund managers took on more risk in the investment portfolios to try to boost return on assets. Pensions grabbed equities, with public pensions holding on average 60% of plan assets in equities at year-end 2018, a thirteen year high.[38] Worse yet, public pensions dove headfirst into real estate and a host of less-liquid and higher-risk alternative investments to chase returns. The 150 largest pension funds posted a startling 25%-plus of 2016 assets in alternative investments, triple the level from just a decade earlier.[39] Unfortunately, ultra-low interest rates also pushed up valuations on equities and alternative investments of real estate, commodities, and private equity to all-time high, bubble levels. That creates dual risk of lower future returns on these assets as well as higher likelihood of corrections or crashes that create major, short-term hits to assets. Facing public pension funds are an unholy trinity of short-term negative cash flows, long-term unsustainable funding models, and riskier investment of fund assets into overpriced, illiquid vehicles.

---

[9]   The past ten-year median annualized return for public pensions is from the Wilshire Trust Universal Comparison Service. By way of comparison, the nation's two largest public pensions, California's CalSTRS and CalPERS, were assuming over 7% annualized return on assets for several years and in 2018 finally announced plans to drop assumed future returns to 7% or lower.

This dynamic has worsened over the past two decades. Both public and private pension plans across the United States, the EU, and Japan are facing the same, dire quandary. The Hoover Institute projects a $3.8 trillion deficit in U.S. state and city public pension plans.[40] That deficit widened in the first quarter of 2020 as the economic shutdown precipitated by the pandemic spooked markets and pummeled public pension returns with an average loss of 13.2%.[41] The World Economic Forum says that by 2050 the six largest global pension systems, the United States, the UK, Japan, the Netherlands, Canada, and Australia, will have a combined $224 trillion shortfall.[42] The bleak situation is driven by the deadly combo of ultra-low interest rates hurting plan asset returns and declining active worker-to-retiree ratios. The six countries currently have eight active workers per retiree, but in 2050 that ratio will likely drop to only four.[43]

You might expect this situation would prompt fund managers to raise a public alarm about the sorry state of public pension finances, and what must be done to reverse it. Unfortunately, public pension funds' staffs are often bureaucrats led by politicians, and the pressure to down-play the crisis might exceed the likelihood of dealing with the crisis.[h]

A study by two noted finance professors at Erasmus Rotterdam and Stanford highlights the issue. The study combed through over 230 public pensions disclosures. The research found the average assumed future return on assets was 7.6% annually, for anywhere from ten to thirty years.[44] The 7.6% return on assets annually is composed of assumed returns across asset classes that the pension funds invest in.

To gauge how reasonable a 7.6% return is, the finance professors

---

h   CalPERS is a good example of aggressive assumed return on assets and taking on high risk. Its recent chief investment officer (since departed in a cloud of controversy) defends its aggressive 7% assumed risk-adjusted rate of return on assets by promoting "better" and "more" assets. The "better" is the pension's heavier emphasis on private equity/credit investments despite their illiquid and difficult to mark-to-market nature. The "more" is higher portfolio debt leverage, which amplifies risk and volatility. What CalPERS labels "better" and "more," retirees and workers should consider risky and desperate.

drilled down to the portfolio weightings of cash, bonds, stocks, and alternative investments. The research found cash was projected to return 3.2% annually and bonds 4.9% annually.[45] Both of these assumptions are absurd under current economic conditions and the Fed's low interest rate environment. The best money markets yield around 1% while lower-risk, investment grade corporate bonds yield nowhere near 4.9%. This means for the pensions to hit their 7.6% overall return on assets assumption, the returns on equity would need to be much higher than what is assumed currently by the pensions. Yet equity markets are hovering at historically high price-to-earnings ratios, indicating expected future equity returns of only 4% (along with a heightened risk of correction).[46] As Peter Bernstein noted, "capital markets are not accommodating machines that crank out wealth for everyone on demand."[47] So, the alternative is public pensions investing in much riskier assets to try to boost returns, from corporate junk bonds to a host of illiquid alternative investments subject to write-down exposure when conditions deteriorate.

Why are public pension fund managers so reluctant to get realistic when it comes to projecting return on assets over time? Because getting real with lower return on asset levels will show the pension plan is in dire financial health, unable to meet its future promised obligations to retirees and current workers. Using fiscal 2016 data, dropping the median 7.6% return on assets to 6.5% would increase total liability for state pension plans to $4.4 trillion and the funding gap would jump to $1.7 trillion.[48] Already woefully underfunded plans in New Jersey, Illinois, and Connecticut would drop to funding levels that would stir panic. Anger would quickly move toward the rogues' gallery of pension plan bureaucrats, politicians, and public union bosses.

Instead, expect these bureaucrats and their politician bosses to take superficial, incremental steps closer to realistic return on asset assumptions to stall, obfuscate, and avoid the crisis management desperately needed. By the time the pension has a realistic assumption on asset returns, the fund may be in default. Except, of course, in New Jersey, where the nation's most underfunded state pension system recently had the gall to raise the return on assets assumption from 7% to 7.5%.[49] Demonstrating how ridiculously far state bureaucrats will go to avoid blame.

The second critical assumption when calculating pension plan health is the discount rate. Public pension plans are not required to follow the same rules for this assumption that private pension plans are required to follow. Private pension plans must apply a risk-free rate based on U.S. Treasuries. With the thirty-year Treasury bond yielding far below 3% for significant periods of time the past number of years and then plummeting to all-time lows with the outbreak of the 2020 virus, private pension plans are subjected to steep increases in liability. But state public pension funds used an average discount rate of 7.11% as of 2017.[50] A perusal of data on public versus corporate pension plan assumptions for assumed discount rate shows the striking contrast. A recent study of the one hundred largest corporate pension plans showed an average discount rate of 3.49% for fiscal year 2017.[51] As an example, General Electric assumed 4.34% at the end of 2018.[52] By comparison, CalPERS utilized a 7.375% discount rate for fiscal year 2018–2019.[53]

That gap in discount rates makes an enormous difference in the perceived health of a pension. For public pensions in the United States, the difference in funding shortfall that is projected between these two discount rates is over $2 trillion.[54] A mere 1%-point reduction in discount rate for CalPERS results in a $30 billion increase in funding gap, equivalent to $2,600 per California household.[55] In more blunt terms, the difference between these two discount rate assumptions goes from a view of pension plans being in serious trouble to one of being fundamentally broke. The 7.6% discount rate reflects an altered reality that doesn't exist today while the second assumed discount rate reflects the Fed reality on interest rates that exists for everyone. Private pensions are living on planet Earth while public pensions are living in a galaxy far, far away.

Stakeholders of public pensions rely on actuaries to supply fair and balanced assessments of financial health. Troubling cracks are appearing in actuaries' objectiveness. There are two major clubs in the actuary world, the American Academy of Actuaries, and the Society of Actuaries. Usually, actuaries are boring, but recent discussion within these groups has been salty.

Members of these two groups who comprised a Pension Finance Task Force were ready to publish a paper critical of the way many public pension funds assumed the future rates of return on plan assets.[56] When actuary organizations leaders found out, they shut down the studies and disbanded the task force. The report was never published, sending the authors into a tizzy, calling the decision censorship.[57] As retribution, the organizations forbade the authors to publish the paper independently, hinting at potential legal action.[58] The situation creates a concern that actuaries face pressure not to speak up from the pension funds and governments that hire them.

What public pension managers perpetrate by muscling actuaries should come as no surprise. Compare what government bureaucrats and politicians reveal in municipal bond prospectuses with what they claim in lawsuits. Municipal bonds are issued by governments to raise money for a range of things, including keeping the public pension plan afloat. In these prospectuses, investors are told about the expected risks of investing in the municipal bond. California and New York prospectuses show, at best, vague and uncertain views on whether climate change poses a threat to the city, municipality, or state issuing the bonds. The coastal climate-alarmist bastions of San Francisco, Los Angeles, and San Diego make little mention of climate change or rising sea levels in bond risks, for two particularly good reasons.[59]

The first reason is that the typical vague view expressed in these prospectuses is true; predicting climate change or its impact is like predicting who will be president in 2100. The top meteorologists in the world can't consistently and accurately predict the next winter's severity, let alone climate fifty years from now. Computer models from climate scientists are of little value and nearly everyone knows it.

The second reason is that saying climate change poses a present, real, and substantial threat to a city or state will significantly increase the risk associated with, and thus the cost of, the municipal bond. That means the government will pay a higher interest rate on that debt, which will add stress to already stressed budgets in steep deficits. By conveniently downplaying climate doom risk in municipal bond prospectuses, bureaucrats and politicians enjoy the easy money that low interest rate municipal bonds provide. Ignoring or obfuscating supposed climate change peril when a city borrows money pays off: a study that compared the interest rates on municipal bonds from twenty cities that were on coasts or faced flooding risk to twenty cities that were inland and did not face such risks showed no statistical difference in the cost of the debt.[60]

Yet these very same local and state government bureaucrats and politicians behave in direct conflict with their statements in the bond prospectuses when they shake down energy companies by suing. New York City Mayor de Blasio in early 2018 smugly announced he was suing Exxon and other energy companies for the damage climate change has reaped and continues to reap on his city.[61] New York State Attorney General Eric Schneiderman went after Exxon in 2015, culminating in charges for violating a state securities law and defrauding investors by not properly disclosing climate change risks; in 2019, the state's supreme court dismissed the suit, chided the attorney general's office for bringing it, and stated the claims were "hyperbolic."[62] In California, the cities of San Francisco and Oakland chose a similar tactic in 2017 when they sued a number of oil companies for their contribution to climate change, which the cities argued would raise sea levels to the point where the Bay Area floods and suffers massive damage. In 2018, Judge Alsup threw out the lawsuit brought by Oakland and San Francisco.[63] One of the key points in the Judge's decision was language used by San Francisco in their general obligation bond offering that admitted the city could not predict damage from climate change.[64] The judge recognizes what we all know: climate change can't be accurately predicted, let alone potential damage from it.

Securities filings and lawsuits carry serious responsibilities, the most prominent being an expectation of document and filing veracity. Knowingly falsifying or hiding material facts in either situation is unethical and illegal. Might the nation be experiencing deceit on an epic scale across many public pension plans and state and local governments? From cooking the books with rosy asset returns and discount rate assumptions to not disclosing expected climate change risks in municipal bond prospectuses while suing energy companies for that risk, politicians and bureaucrats apply a double standard.

MANY LOSERS AND ONE WINNER

There has always been a conflict between elected officials negotiating future retirement pension benefits to government workers in contract negotiations while garnering the same workers' votes for reelection. The politician grants richer future retirement benefits through new labor contracts in return for government workers' votes and endorsements from the public unions representing these workers.

Outside of this Faustian bargain is the taxpayer and savers who fund and lend to the local and state governments in the form of income tax, sales tax, property tax, and municipal bonds. This is occurring across many cities, municipalities, and states where a bigger share of government budgets is consumed by pension plans whose gap between assets and obligations continually widens.

Recall New York City facing four out of every five dollars of collected income tax having to go toward shoring up its gaping pension deficit. The same scenario is playing out in California with CalPERS and CalSTRS. Both pensions present enormous funding voids, requiring local governments in California to give more to CalPERS and CalSTRS to close the funding gap. Over the past ten years, California taxpayers through local governments increased contributions to CalPERS from $7.2 billion to $12.3 billion.[65] That results in higher taxes, services cut for parks, police, and libraries, and shakier local government finances.

California schools are particularly fleeced. Pension costs assessed to California school districts for both CalPERS and CalSTRS are projected to reach just under $1,500 per student by 2024, which is a nearly $1,000 per student increase compared to 2013–2014.[66] A big driver of that costs increase is a pension formula that grants extremely generous retirement benefits to public workers: typically a teacher with just twenty-five years of service will be awarded a pension benefit of 50% of their final compensation before retirement.

The state assesses school districts across California massive bills to plug the rising pension costs and pension funding gaps, with no way to increase revenue since state law caps property taxes at 1% of the home's value. Faced with skyrocketing expenses for pensions and no way to increase revenues proportionally, a school district has two avenues. One avenue is to cut payroll in areas that don't fall under the union contracts: support staff, secretaries, and school nurses. The second avenue is to circumvent the 1% of a home's value cap on property tax with special, flat parcel taxes. The result for the taxpayer in that school district is the double whammy of a lower quality of education due to the staff and program cuts coupled with higher taxes.

Another stakeholder is in a similar, unenviable situation with the taxpayer: the saver who invested in a municipal bond issued by the state or local government. If the public pension fund falls into such a financial mess that a reasonable tax increase can't cover the shortfalls, there is a significant chance that lenders to the local government will not get their money back. Defaults on its debt obligations is what happened in Harrisburg (Pennsylvania), Detroit (Michigan), Jefferson County (Alabama), San Bernardino (California), and Puerto Rico.

Municipalities in Illinois are also on a road to default in such Chicago suburbs as Harvey, which has defaulted on eight debt interest payments in two years. The road begins with politicians subservient to public union bosses granting exceedingly generous retirement benefits to police, firefighters, teachers, sanitation workers, and bureaucrats. The pension cash outflows to pay for these benefits soon outpaces cash funding inflows, creating poorly funded pensions (Harvey's police pension plan has only 33 cents on hand for every dollar of benefit promised while its firefighters pension plan holds only 17 cents for every dollar of promised benefits).[67] Lawmakers allow troubled pension plans to skip or reduce legally-mandated funding catch-ups so that the government can keep on spending in other areas, placing the pension in even worse condition. The Illinois Supreme Court, at the behest of public sector unions, determines that pensions are constitutionally protected and thus benefits levels can't be cut. Politicians and bureaucrats threaten to cut instead a range of services to communities to make the budget work. Community-wide resistance to cuts in police staffing and education then leads to the state or local government borrowing more in the municipal debt market and raising property, sales, and income taxes. Only so much tax revenue can be squeezed from an already pressed taxpayer base.[i] The appropriation by tax, coupled with pending cuts in services, erode quality of life and drive over 850,000 residents out of state over a decade, exacerbating the crisis. The point of insolvency is reached, and the local government defaults on its debt payments. Individual investors who committed their savings to purchase municipal bonds lose their money. The road to ruin ends with clueless credit rating agencies, a day late and dollar short, downgrading the state's and municipality's debt and telling everyone what we already know.

Yet government default is not supposed to happen. In fact, these local and state governments issue bonds to the public marketing ultra-low-risk and little-to-no chance for default. Credit rating agencies keep pumping out investment-grade stellar ratings for most municipal bonds. Savers and citizens flock to these investments despite paltry yields because of the perceived minimal risk along with tax shielding benefits. Depending on the locale, savers are investing in a ticking time bomb.[j]

Moreover, until recently, states and cities that issue financial statements used by municipal bond investors and taxpayers to assess risk could shroud the true magnitude of retiree healthcare obligations.

---

i   According to the *Wall Street Journal*, Harvey suffers a crushing poverty rate of 36% and property tax rates that are 600% higher than the average in nearby Indiana.

j   As noted, financial writer Jim Grant has pointed out bondholders can't participate in gains, only in losses.

Those future retiree healthcare obligations are akin to debt, and the Pew Charitable Trust estimates that, in the aggregate, states have retiree healthcare obligations of $693 billion and only $48 billion in assets set aside to cover the retiree healthcare obligations.[68] An investor accustomed to disclosure norms and rules for public corporations (the same corporations public pension fund managers and comptrollers criticize and attack with their gadfly proxy proposals) would think these unfunded liabilities would be disclosed by states and cities on their balance sheets. Yet states report only a fraction of these deficits on their balance sheets and instead bury the true amounts in financial footnotes that very few people read and understand. In the case of New York State, full disclosure of retiree healthcare liability increases the official liability of $17 billion up to a whopping $72 billion.[69] That is ten times larger than the state's pension liability. While New York clouds its true financial condition, it eagerly presses public companies for greater disclosure standards. A disappointing, yet not atypical, hypocrisy: government bureaucracy demanding a standard of candor from Creators, Enablers, and Servers that it will not follow.

When public pension plans hit the wall of insolvency, a taxpayer bailout will without question be part of the solution. That bailout will surely come with a corresponding reduction in services to the taxpayer via less road maintenance, dwindling resources for public schools, etc., so that more taxpayer dollars can be poured into the broken pension plans.

Savers could be bigger losers than taxpayers. Bond rating agencies continue to spit out A-ratings for scores of financially shaky municipalities, cities, and states. All those mom and pop savers who put their net worth into supposedly safe and low return municipal bonds to protect life savings are going to wake up one day to the stark realization they were investing in the equivalent of a pump-and-dump stock scheme.

Poorly led cities, municipalities, and states have a record of borrowing from savers to shore up pension gaps and then defaulting, leaving the savers who lent the governments money with little to nothing. The playbook is one where risk of default in the pension plans shifts from workers and retirees to the savers. Politicians get the added benefit of delay, when they use money raised in bond markets to flush down an underfunded pension plan drain. This delays the day of reckoning past the next election or beyond the political life of the politician, yet the day of reckoning does come, as seen in Detroit, Puerto Rico, and Stockton.

The city worker, local cop, or state employee reading this may be thinking what's bad or risky for the taxpayer and saver might be good for the worker or retiree. Certainly, that is what public union bosses and politicians looking to curry their favor tell them. Sadly, these government workers and retirees are being misled. There are millions of public sector workers and retirees out there counting on future pension income that will not be there when they need it. The social contract of loyal years of service in exchange for a future benefit is about to be invalidated across droves of municipalities, cities, and states. The current public worker is hit twice. First, the current worker must contribute his wages into a sick pension fund to support current retirees even though the worker is unlikely to receive an equal benefit in retirement. Second, the worker must set aside more of his wages to save outside of the collapsing pension plan to replace lost income once retirement comes.

There is, however, a small cadre of winners in all this mess. Those ever-resilient elected officials and the bureaucratic army. The politicians will be retired or termed-out before the breaking point. The bureaucrats will cloud and delay a clear view of these pension plans to the public.

AIDING CHINESE AGGRESSION WHILE
IGNORING FIDUCIARY DUTY

Nearly every large public pension fund boasts on its website and in its glossy publications a commitment to sustainability and ESG doctrines. From CalPERS listing climate as one of its three top priorities to New York City committing to divest its fossil fuel holdings, a pension investing in Exxon these days is *verboten*.

Yet most pensions eagerly finance a much more real, current, and existential threat: Chinese oppression and militarism. There are hundreds of Chinese public companies listed in the United States and countless Chinese private companies that U.S. private equity firms own interests in; these Chinese companies help the communist government imprison millions of Muslims, crack down on thousands of Hong Kong protestors, build military bases in the South China Sea, develop surveillance technology to deploy in suppression of its people, and construct a wide-range military arsenal ranging from ballistic missiles to aircraft carriers. Any large pension fund, mutual fund, foundation, or college endowment inevitably invests in these entities, directly or indirectly, making Chinese aggression possible. Yet you won't find any disclosure, mention, or commitment not to invest in these entities from public pensions and their similarly ESG-minded brethren. We should deny public pension funds the manufactured moral high ground of sustainability for tomorrow when they knowingly finance epic oppression today.

Milton Friedman published in 1970 the article "The Social Responsibility of Business Is to Increase its Profits."[70] Friedman realized profits were the single best measure of a company's value to the market, consumers, and, ultimately, society. Once certain entities pushed their leftist values or political agenda onto companies, it forced investors owning shares in those companies to support those values too, directly, or indirectly. Eventually, companies engaged in politically correct business decisions were likely to be undermining free enterprise.

There is a close contemporary theorem to Friedman's position on public companies that holds for public pension plan managers. The social responsibility of a pension fund manager is to maximize the plan's return on assets and to minimize fund risk for the plan's retirees and current workers. Deviating from this core mission to pursue other agendas or indulge ancillary interests is a failure of fiduciary duty. That is especially true when you consider public workers and retirees are captive to their retirement plan and cannot vote with their feet by leaving the pension like private investors can by selling a stock. What is most worrisome is that this failure is both conscious and intended by the pension fund bureaucracy.

Instead of the best possible returns for their retirees, growing ranks of public pension fund managers are placing activities to support various endeavors and interests ahead of their funds' financial health. While these bureaucrats promote their ideology, the true financial health of the funds are clouded by a bevy of arcane assumptions that obscure decrepit conditions—a good example of what Warren Buffet was talking about when he said, "Forecasts usually tell us more of the forecaster than of the future."[71]

Bureaucracy within such public pensions grows not to improve service to the retirees but instead to bleed more financial resources from the fund. As the performance of funds continues to languish because of the fund managers' broken fiduciary compass, hundreds of thousands of retirees and workers come closer to a financial day of reckoning that they don't even know exists. Adding insult to that injury, the retirees and workers subsidize and pay for the distracted escapades indulged in by these bureaucrats. The clock is ticking; it's time to reform.

LEECH POWER CENTERS:

URBAN HELL

"A city has no sense, no sentiment, no soul."

AMIT KALANTRI

BIG CITIES' SHINY FAÇADE VERSUS STARK REALITY

Big cities are where the Leech way has been implemented over the longest period. Yet American big cities are brutal environments. Unless you work 9 to 5 in the shiny office tower and commute home to the burbs or can afford to live in exclusive city neighborhoods, day-to-day life in American urban areas is an unforgiving grind.

But, from a distance, most major American cities appear glitzy and polished. Most cities boast shiny airport terminals, sleek downtown skyscrapers, and breathtaking skylines. But up close, the reality can be quite different: homeless struggling to survive, abandoned streets, and graffiti. The image of most major American cities from afar is different from the gritty reality on the ground. And the people that pay the steepest price are the poorest and most disadvantaged of our society.

Yet the Leech ecosystem touts urban America as an exemplary standard for the rest of us in rural, small town, and suburban America.

Hillary Clinton in 2018 blamed her defeat by President Trump on a flawed electoral college system that didn't weigh higher-income urban areas over Middle America. She stated, "I won the places that represent two-thirds of America's gross domestic product. So, I won the places that are optimistic, diverse, dynamic, moving forward."[1] Clinton's views run shockingly counter to American core values, which is one reason she lost the Electoral College.

Politicians like Hillary Clinton claiming major cities are drivers of American GDP, job growth, and most things positive in the country cite numerous statistics, books, and academic studies in support.[a] However, these studies are ignorant of two factors about the supposed economic and innovative vitality of America's cities.

First, urban centers enjoy endless resources funneled into them. Policies are designed to embody a massive transfer of wealth from one geography and demographic to another. Pennsylvania, my home state, is an excellent example. Every time a new sports stadium or arena is built in Pittsburgh or Philadelphia, along with it comes yet another incremental transfer of wealth from rural and suburban Pennsylvanians in tax dollars to urbanites. Philly and the Steel City have influential local media outlets producing steady propaganda about how great each city is. The propaganda's goal is to direct or redirect resources to them. Rural and suburban areas don't have anything close to such propaganda resources. As the biblical adage goes, "For unto whomsoever much is given, of him shall be much required" (Luke 12:48).

Second, the lion's share of jobs and GDP in urban centers is hollow, because it directly correlates to activity with zero-to-negative net economic benefit. Large urban areas are hot zones of bloated government bureaucracies, public sector union bureaucracies, outdated academia, litigious law

---

a   Even smart people working for class organizations can fall prey to this false narrative. Check out "Why Cities Boom While Towns Struggle" in the May 13, 2018 issue of the *Wall Street Journal* by William A. Galston for an example of how this groupthink is effortlessly magnified into even more flawed, entrenched thinking.

firms, malignant environmental groups, and obsolete print media. Despite being advertised as drivers of GDP and the economy, the truth is that these activities are not net contributors but are growing and unsustainable drags on cities, regions, and the nation.

BAD POLICY MAKES URBAN AREAS DEADLY

Millions of honest and hard-working urbanites, many of them minority and poor, must endure dangerous streets every day. Crime in urban areas, particularly violent crime, hit crisis levels and now has moved beyond crisis to something worse. The twenty-five most dangerous zip codes in the United States consist exclusively of medium-sized and large-sized cities.[2] In certain areas of Chicago, Memphis, Baltimore, and Kansas City, you run a one-in-ten risk of becoming a victim of a crime within a year.[b] Property crime rates are exceedingly high in Memphis, San Francisco, Oakland, St. Louis, Portland, and Seattle.[c] Minneapolis police, stressed with rising crime and stagnant staffing levels, were unable to respond quickly to over 6,000 priority-one 911 calls (which include sexual assault, shootings, and robberies) over a twelve-month period.[3, d]

Chicago is in the news repeatedly when it comes to violent crime. The numbers are mind-blowing, especially for such an iconic American city. The Chicago Police Department reported an astonishing 771 homicides in 2016, where for much of the year an average of one shooting every two hours occurred.[4] Things are so bad that 2017 was considered a victory with over 1,100 new police officers hired and only 650 homicides, despite the July 4th weekend that year when more than

---

b   The company Neighborhood Scout annually aggregates the data. Crimes consist of property and violent categories. The list of the top twenty-five murder capitals boasts a roster of big city names.

c   Before the death of George Floyd, homicides and arson were up 60% in Minneapolis, shootings increased 50% in Philadelphia, and carjackings were up over 60% in New York City (first five months of 2020 compared to first five months of 2019).

d   Perhaps more troubling is 2,600 complaints were filed against Minneapolis police since 2012. Only twelve resulted in officer discipline, the most severe being a 40-hour suspension.

100 people were shot and 14 died.[5] Just over a year later things were not much better. Citizens took to the streets in early August of 2018, shutting down Lake Shore Drive to protest the out-of-control cycle of violence. The protest did not help: over the following weekend the Windy City saw 74 people shot, 12 of them fatally.[6] May 31, 2020 was Chicago's deadliest day in sixty years, with 18 murders (25 murders over the three-day weekend that also brought widespread looting). For the first half of 2020, Chicago posted a 40% increase in shootings and homicides compared to the prior year period.

The situation is so intense in Chicago that corpsmen about to be deployed with combat Marine units go through a Navy pre-deployment program where they work at Chicago's Stroger Hospital trauma center. About 30% of the Stroger's trauma center cases are gunshot wounds, far exceeding the normal national rate of just over 4% for trauma centers.[7] The Navy has come to the conclusion that corpsmen who make it in Chicago will have no problem dealing with what they later experience in Iraq, Afghanistan, or anywhere else.

Understand that for urban violent crime, it is not just the overall numbers and rates that matter but also the distribution of these crimes across different areas of the city. Chicago Police Department data from 2015 show the homicide rate of roughly 19 per 100,000 residents was composed of certain districts in the northern end of town having a low rate under 5, and other districts in the western and southern areas of town posting frightening rates in excess of 50.[8] A heat map for homicides in the city shows the usual high densities in west and south Chicago. So it's not just the city, but also the section of the city that one lives in, that determines how violent the environment is.

Indiscriminate killing in urban areas occurs across demographics. A quick look at the victims of shootings in Chicago offers startling revelations. Gangs shoot young girls crossing the streets. Drug dealers gun down old men watering their lawns. Young boys murder other young boys playing in their yards in broad daylight. Mothers waiting at bus stops take bullets to the head. Kids of cops are butchered while sitting on their porches. Grandkids of U.S. congressmen have been executed in their own homes. All of us are potential victims if we are in the high-incident areas and neighborhoods. There are no longer criminals' codes of conduct or unwritten rules when it comes to assaulting or killing. Murderers don't discriminate because of color, age, gender, or economic class.

The Chicago Police Department has changed tactics on quick moving, violent streets and are scaling back presence. This phenomenon is not unique to Chicago. Criminologist Richard Rosenfeld and former FBI Director James Comey point to police-community tension creating an environment in which police are less willing to proactively engage suspicious individuals or questionable activity.[9] The death of George Floyd in the summer of 2020 set the environment for policing and urban community trust of police to all-time lows.

The pressure police are experiencing is also coming from prosecutors' offices. This is especially the case where you have a politically elected head prosecutor. Consider Baltimore: the *Wall Street Journal* recently analyzed five years of court data in Baltimore and found that the rate of convictions for both felonies and violent crime dropped precipitously despite the homicide rate increasing sharply.[10] The team of prosecutors headed by Baltimore State's Attorney Mosby drops over 40% of felony cases before verdicts are entered.[11] The steady assault on law enforcement takes a cumulative toll: since 2015 when the city backed off on prosecution, homicides in Baltimore have exceeded 300 per year.[12] On a per capita basis, Baltimore's murder rate easily exceeds Chicago's.

Leftist prosecutors are popping up across major cities beyond Baltimore and Chicago. Philadelphia's District Attorney Larry Krasner made a career as defense attorney suing the police, elevating social justice over criminal justice, and enjoyed having classy supporters at his primary election victory party sing "Fuck the F.O.P." to him.[13] In late 2019, San Francisco did one better than Philadelphia when it elected as district attorney Chesa Boudin. Boudin's parents were members of the terrorist group Weather Underground and were imprisoned for the 1981 murders of two cops and a security guard. At Boudin's election party the crowd was led in a chant of "Fuck the POA!"[14] During the campaign, Boudin pledged not to prosecute crimes of prostitution, public urination, or public camping (that's code for vagrancy) if elected district attorney. [e]

The unintended consequences of less policing are playing out in California beyond San Francisco. Proposition 47 in 2014 reduced jail sentences in the state for nonviolent crimes such as drug use and petty theft. That resulted in police across California reducing efforts to apprehend individuals committing these types of crimes, since the police understood a quick release from custody would follow arrest. In the past decade, California's incarcerated population declined 25% while prison spending increased 100% (California spends over $80,000 per prisoner per year, exceeding the cost of tuition, room, and board at Stanford or USC).[15] Since the passing of Proposition 47, from 2014 to 2017, larceny is up 44% in San Francisco and 22% in Los Angeles.[16] Actual crime rates may be markedly higher, as many victims decide to not report the crime when they know there is little likelihood of police pursuing an arrest. The most affected neighborhoods are often the poorest. The official title of Proposition 47 was Orwellian: The Safe Neighborhoods and Schools Act.

New York City is also experiencing a spike in violent crime immediately following the implementation of a state bail reform law that eliminated cash bail. Under the statute, judges can no longer apply discretion on a case-by-case basis. The law, intended to prevent lengthy incarceration before trial of the accused who are unable to pay bail, has delivered the unintended consequence of a surge of violent crime in the city. The sharp increase is due to individuals who are arrested for a felony being placed right back in the streets, without posting bail, and then committing additional violent crimes.[f] Law-abiding citizens are

---

e   Boudin promptly followed through on his campaign promises by eliminating cash bail and stopping the upgrading of charges for repeat offenders.

f   A man who held up six banks in two weeks was released after each arrest. He expressed his surprise to a detective by stating, "I can't believe they let me out."

exposed to a revolving door of criminals, as they commit one crime, are released to the streets, and then commit another crime.

Urban bureaucrats and politicians utilized the virus crisis to impose unilaterally their version of criminal justice reform. New York City released inmates with health issues or who were doing time for minor charges; Los Angeles freed over 1,000 prisoners and backed off arrests; Philadelphia delayed arrest for crimes such as theft; and Denver reduced policing presence.[17] Criminals were released into streets that were no longer being policed. Urban violent crime soared as a result.

Chicago earns the most attention for its crime rates, but unfortunately there are cities experiencing worse. Detroit, St. Louis, Washington, D.C., Atlanta, Memphis, and Kansas City posted higher murder rates per capita than the Windy City. Baltimore suffered under a homicide rate of nearly 50 per 100,000 residents in 2015 and then blew by that rate in subsequent years.[18] St. Louis led the nation in 2015 with almost 60 homicides per 100,000 residents.[19] Both Detroit and New Orleans exceeded 40 homicides per 100,000 residents in 2015.[20] Keep in mind homicide statistics over time can mislead when one realizes trauma care has become impressively effective in saving lives; the trend in urban violent crime is much worse than what the trend in homicide rates indicates. Even with the advantage of world-class trauma care, depending on the year, these ultra-violent American cities post homicide rates above the notoriously dangerous cities of Kingston (Jamaica), Tijuana (Mexico), and Johannesburg (South Africa). Paradoxically, we may be the most powerful nation on earth, but our cities are far from the safest.

INFRASTRUCTURE SNAPS, CRACKLES, AND POPS

The infrastructure of urban centers is a mess, especially compared to suburban and rural areas. Spend a couple of hours in New York City and see the streets, bridges, walls, subway stations, airports, and sidewalks. The following words come to mind: *old, dirty, crumbling, creaky, dusty, fatigued,* and *neglected.*

Road conditions in urban areas versus rural areas are another striking contrast. The Transportation Department says that 35% of urban roads are in poor condition, compared to only 14% of rural roads.[21] Experts expect the gap to widen over time since urban roads experience heavier traffic volumes. The disparity between urban and rural road quality is not a coincidence; it reflects decades of mismanagement and a lack of attention to transportation hubs in and out of major cities.

The inefficiencies created by decaying infrastructure into and inside urban areas are imposing massive opportunity costs upon those working in, and commuting to, cities. Traffic congestion in and out of major cities defies what you learned in high school algebra. If you live in the suburbs, must travel 20 miles to downtown, and the roads have an average speed limit of 40 mph, most freshman high school students would be able to tell you the commute will take thirty minutes. In major American cities, that math will make you quite late. Urban commutes, for cities coast to coast, are a nightmare of jams, construction, closures, and unpredictability. San Francisco commuters have endured a 62% increase in weekday traffic delays over a six-year period.[22] Public transportation in Center City Philadelphia crawls at under four miles per hour during midday, which means walking across Center City beats the bus. Traveling into, within, and out of big cities requires excruciating investments of time. Early or late, you'll suffer lost productivity and a deteriorating quality of life, while fuel efficiency plummets and carbon emissions skyrocket.

A 2017 study by Inrix tells the story of America's urban traffic woes. New York, Los Angeles, San Francisco, and Atlanta ranked in the global top-ten worst cities for traffic congestion. Inrix estimates traffic congestion costs U.S. drivers over $300 billion in 2017, which works out to an average of over $1,400 per driver.[23] For Los Angeles commuters, traffic congestion cost totaled $9.7 billion, or over $2,400 per driver, with commuters wasting over 100 hours a year in peak traffic periods.[24] New York City's total cost topped all other cities at almost $17 billion in 2016.[25] Adding other intangible traffic jam costs, such as the effects of driver stress on health, makes these shocking numbers higher.

Crumbling infrastructure and inefficient congestion are not from lack of spending. No one spends more on infrastructure than New York City. Yet its third world transportation system is an embarrassment. The rail and subway systems are good examples. The MTA uses equipment and technology from the 1930s, which causes endless delays and serious accidents. Less than two out of three trains reach their destination on time. The subway system posts an astonishing 70,000 delays a month.[26] A commuter's experience on the MTA includes rats scurrying around stations, broken sewer pipes leaking human waste, and filth covering the floors of subway cars. A small, isolated incident anywhere in the system stands a good chance of creating a domino-effect of massive delays and bottlenecks across the wider network.

The disgrace that is the New York City subway system takes a heavy toll. The mental health of commuters subjected to the incompetently managed and decrepit subway system suffers. New Yorkers, who already carry a reputation of being gruff and grumpy, hit highly agitated levels before they get to work because of the misery of the network. There are also more tangible tolls. According to the city comptroller, if you are unlucky enough to be one of the 5.6 million weekday riders on the New York City system, there is a one in three chance you have experienced a work reprimand, a docked paycheck, or termination because of subway delays.[27] Projects take forever and overrun original budgets by multiples due to overwhelming regulations created to justify and protect the bureaucratic government and its allies.

The much-touted Second Avenue subway line was originally designed in the 1920s and was finally completed at a cost of over $2.5 billion per mile. The East Side Access subway line is years away from completion and already boasts a $3.5 billion per mile price tag. Unionized tunnel workers clock in at $111 per hour on New York subway projects, almost 300% more than rates elsewhere.[28] The Hudson River tunnel retrofit project required participation of nearly thirty government agencies and nearly twenty separate permits.[29] The project won't be completed until 2026 and the cost has nearly doubled from recent estimates. Expect the completion date to slide further and the cost to rise higher.

Not surprisingly, the decrepit New York City subway and wider metropolitan public transportation system are not the desired method of transportation for commuters. Even before the 2020 pandemic, public transportation ridership, especially in the outer boroughs from Manhattan where delays tend to be more frequent and severe, had been in decline.[9] Making the decline sharper is the rise of ride-hailing services from Uber and Lyft that offer an irresistible alternative. You couldn't ask for a starker contrast for residents choosing a transportation choice: costly, dirty, unreliable, communal, and time-consuming public transportation versus affordable, reliable, clean, customized, and immediate ride-hailing service. It's not a fair fight, which is why ride-hailing has grown exponentially in the Big Apple and residents for the first time in decades enjoy transportation options that cater to the customer.

New York City's politicians, bureaucrats, public transportation unions, and the Taxi and Limousine Commission will go all-in to stop ride-hailing Servers from growing. In the summer of 2018, the New York City Council passed legislation, which Mayor de Blasio quickly signed, that froze new ride-hailing licenses for one year so that the intrepid city government could study the impact of the technology. Everyone knows this has nothing to do with studying and everything to do with severely restricting ride-hailing's ability to serve customers. While this is bad for commuters, the legislation is great for public transportation unions, the politicians who obediently serve them, and government bureaucrats. The mayor shamelessly stated that growth in ride-hailing was a fundamental problem requiring the oppressive legislation.[30]

Although it is easy to pick on New York City, the Big Apple is not alone when it comes to subway and public transportation incompetence. Its rival to the north, Boston, suffers heavily with its mess of a

---

g   An MIT analysis concluded the New York MTA was a deadly spreader of the 2020 pandemic. When subway ridership dropped, new infections dropped.

public transportation system, the MBTA. The MBTA acknowledges the system's deficiencies and estimates over $10 billion and thirteen years will be needed for modernization.[31] As the MBTA's performance has degraded over the years, fares have steadily increased. Politicians and the public transportation union want to increase the gas tax and institute congestion pricing on cars so that good money can chase bad money down the subway tunnel.

What about the urban infrastructure we can't see? In certain instances, it is in worse shape than the crumbling messes we see. The most pressing danger must be water service, particularly where water and sewer authorities are run by urban public entities. Despite leftist politicians like Bernie Sanders and Elizabeth Warren misleading the public and advocating that government-run water systems are better and safer than for-profit systems, the opposite is true. Government-run water authorities lack scale; adopt cronyism instead of meritocracy to pick leaders; avoid the same scrutiny that for-profit water suppliers face; and rarely receive the customer rate hikes needed for capital improvements. Consequently, government-run water entities are 30% more likely to violate the Safe Drinking Water Act than for-profit water providers.[32] Yet 85% of Americans still get their drinking water from government-run utilities.[33] If you are an urban resident desiring safe, reliable, and reasonably priced water, the last thing you want is Senators Sanders' and Warren's solution.

The inept state of government-run water utilities covers the map of U.S. urban centers. In Baltimore, the pipe network for delivering fresh water to homes and businesses has reached a point of terminal decay. First, understand the scale of what Baltimore is dealing with. There are 5,000 miles of water pipes throughout the city and surrounding area. The age of the majority of those pipes is over eighty years.[34] The current pipe network is in such poor condition and so afflicted with leaks that city officials estimate roughly twenty percent of the water pulled from the reservoirs never makes it to the end user.[35]

That results in massive waste of precious water resources along with an elevated negative impact on the environment and carbon footprint. The city was until a few years ago replacing water pipe at the rate of five miles per year, or about 0.1% of the total pipe system. Even with a sharp increase in the rate of replacement, officials expect it will take up to a century to replace the current pipes. Leaky water pipes don't just waste valuable water resources but also contaminate the water that makes it to the house or business. It is just as easy for dirt and debris to enter the water pipe through a crack and end up in your faucet as it is for water inside the pipe to escape through the crack. Said differently, in and around older, eastern U.S. cities, the water quality for an urban resident is likely to be worse than that for a homeowner in a newer suburban area.[h]

What do Flint (Michigan), Pittsburgh (Pennsylvania), Newark (New Jersey), Milwaukee (Wisconsin), Providence (Rhode Island), and Portland (Oregon) have in common? All currently have lead levels in their drinking water that exceed the federal EPA health limits.[36] The problems and hurdles these cities must overcome to follow EPA lead limits are massive. Solutions to compliance will take years, or decades, to achieve. The investment required tallies in the billions of dollars, with already stressed finances of water authorities and cities challenged or unable to secure funding. The management of so many of these water authorities responsible for fixing the problems is incompetent and reflects decades of promoting non-accountable, political hacks. For the time being, if you live in one of these cities, either buy bottled water or invest in a high-end filter.

Also don't wait for urban politicians and government bureaucrats to acknowledge lead in drinking water. The federal government is a willing accomplice in helping cities shirk accountability and avoid transparency. Despite the Centers for Disease Control (CDC) stating there is no such thing as an acceptable, safe level of lead in the blood for children, the

----

[h]   A note of caution is needed, however, in situations like the one in and around Baltimore, where the city water authority supplies drinking water to surrounding areas. In those situations, the city's problems may also be the suburbs' problems when it comes to water quality concerns.

EPA asks that school districts voluntarily test their drinking water for lead and consider replacing equipment where the tests results exceeded somewhere between 5-to-20 parts-per-billion (ppb) of lead (it is not clear what level of lead in school drinking water EPA considers a health risk).[37, 38] The voluntary aspect creates the opportunity for denial by school districts and the 5-20 ppb range applied to schools exceeds the standard EPA mandate for water authorities of 15 ppb. That's right: the government allows higher levels of lead in kids' drinking water at school than in adults' drinking water at home. Too many urban school districts are taking advantage of this by avoiding known problem spots when voluntarily testing for lead and by avoiding repairs to improve water quality. In the meantime, urban kids risk harm at the water fountain.[i]

The most egregious behavior of urban leadership in the face of a public drinking water health crisis is in Newark, New Jersey. Residents are subjected to a bureaucratic combination of arrogance, denial bordering on lying, and incompetence. First the incompetence: the city water authority misapplied a water treatment process that corroded aged pipes, resulting in lead leaching from the pipes into the water supply of homes. Sure enough, when the city performed EPA-mandated testing of the drinking water in mid-2017, more than 10% of the homes reported back lead levels over twice the safe limit.[39] After failing two more lead tests, the city distributed over 40,000 water filters to residents. The city then failed additional lead tests, including locations where water filters were being used. Newark began distributing bottled water to residents in August 2019 and, adding insult to injury, did not notice that much of the bottled water was past its best-use-by date.

Now for the denial bordering on lying: in the middle of this mess and after failing a number of lead tests, city hall posted on Facebook in April 2018 that, "NEWARK'S WATER IS ABSOLUTELY SAFE TO DRINK."[40] It wasn't long before that post was supplanted with a more

---

i   At the start of the 2018–2019 school year, the Detroit public school system shut off the water due to high lead and copper levels. The 47,000 kids in the system drank bottled water instead.

somber series of public service announcements asking residents to avoid drinking the water. The mayor continued his nuanced manipulation of words by saying there was nothing wrong with Newark's water and instead the problem was with poor infrastructure.[41]

We end our Newark water crisis case study with the arrogance: at the end of 2018 the mayor, shunning accountability and leadership, blamed border wall funding and the federal government not giving Newark more money for fixing its water health crisis. This was followed by the state's governor in August 2019 demanding that the federal government "step up."[42] Accountability for a health crisis created, obfuscated, and exacerbated by the urban leadership and bureaucracy is conveniently evaded by pinning the blame on others.

Newark's water woes are, unfortunately, not unique. Across the country, expect water bills to rise well above the rate of inflation while urban residents wait for needed fixes. Since the late 1990s, cost inflation for urban consumers of water, sewer, and trash collection services has more than doubled, far outpacing general inflation and the consumer price index over the same period.[43] The bigger the city, the higher the cost inflation for water and sewer services. Baltimore's water rates doubled in fewer than ten years and the city expects over 10% rate increases annually for the coming years as it goes about complying with the EPA settlements to fix leaky pipes and overwhelmed sewer infrastructure.[44] The city won't be in compliance for years to come, meaning residents won't enjoy acceptable water quality either. The hyper-inflating financial burden hits already struggling families every time they receive a bill. That creates a downward spiral where uncollected bills and arrears skyrocket further, degrading the financial health and performance of the utility. In six short years, Baltimore's water receivables have increased by over 150% while the wastewater receivables have increased by more than 1400%. [45] Those trends will materially affect utility performance for all customers.

While Baltimore residents cope with skyrocketing utility bills, city workers are enjoying life in the slow lane while getting paid. A city inspector general report tracked GPS data from city vehicles and found that water meter readers engaged in the practice of driving around doing nothing or going home instead of reading meters, all while paid on the clock.[46] The city gave a thought to bringing charges against the workers but then decided not to, using the rationale that the behavior of the workers was endorsed and encouraged by the supervisors and water department management. Anyone who has experience with urban municipal work knows this is far from an isolated incident. Crumbling services coupled with an inefficient, disinterested, and unaccountable workforce is an unenviable combination for the customer.

Airports serve as entry points and linkages between major cities and reflect especially acute wreckages of despair. If you want to kill time during inevitable flight delays at one of the major New York City airports, engage in a debate with travel companions about which of the big three Big Apple airports is the worst—LaGuardia, Newark, or JFK. Only time will fly during that debate and a consensus will be nearly impossible since all three airports inflict passenger pain in unique ways.

LaGuardia is my personal favorite, with its unique combination of car traffic jams, clogged security lines, leaking roofs, and dirty restrooms. The slightest weather or logistical problem triggers hours of delays, extending your suffering in the purgatorial terminal. Don't be fooled by the current $8 billion rebuild of the airport, for it is nothing more than an exceedingly expensive facelift that doesn't change anything fundamental to the airport's inefficiencies. In ten years, the facelift project will be done. The restrooms may be nicer (for a while) and the food court may have more selections, but the rebuild does not include a new runway, and the current runways are a core airport obstacle. Thus, expect the same congestion, bottlenecks, and loss of productivity associated with flying into and out of LaGuardia to persist when the construction crews finally leave.

Urban infrastructure is often neglected because the money is being spent elsewhere. So-called leadership in big cities is more concerned with glitzy stadiums and arenas for professional sports teams than fixing water pipes, roads, or track beds. Examples abound in every major American city these days, with no better example than New York City. Despite the failed state of the Big Apple's infrastructure, the city managed to throw billions of precious dollars at a new Yankee Stadium, a new stadium for the Mets, a completely refurbished Madison Square Garden, a new arena in Brooklyn, a massive new stadium for the Jets and Giants, and an over-the-top exterior façade for the new subway station near the Freedom Tower. Billions of dollars that could have been invested into improving core infrastructure to help everyone are instead squandered on what only a miniscule, wealthy fraction of the population can enjoy.[j] In major cities, the ego and vanity of the few prevail over the urgent needs of the many.[k]

THE PLIGHT OF URBAN SCHOOLS

Graduating high school with competency in basic skills is becoming increasingly difficult in America. The U.S. public education system has been in terminal decline for decades. From 1970 to 2010, inflation-adjusted spending per student from K–12 has nearly doubled while math, science, and reading test scores have remained flat. That serves as a sobering forty-year indictment for the U.S. public education system run by bureaucrats and public unions while enjoying a government-sanctioned monopoly.

Challenged school districts' problems are exacerbated when policy reduces student accountability for poor behavior. In 2014, the Obama Education Department sent "Dear colleague" guidance letters to school administrators that threatened investigation and loss of federal funding if suspension rates for African American students were not reduced. The basis to drop suspension rates of African American kids was not without

---

[j]   Publicly financed sports venues often constitute a disproportionate share of municipality debt. In Glendale, Arizona, two-thirds of the city's debt is for its pro sports venues. When the pandemic shuttered commerce and travel, tax revenues tied to these venues and tourism evaporated, which will further stress the already fragile finances of municipalities like Glendale.

[k]   Although it is tough to beat New York City's spendthrift ways on sports stadiums, runners-up mention goes to Los Angeles, with its direct and indirect subsidy of a $5 billion football stadium, and Las Vegas, with its new, heavily subsidized, $1.8 billion football stadium.

merit: statistics showed they were more likely to be suspended than peers; excessive suspensions might harm the progress of students facing the discipline; and a new approach to an ill-behaved student might be more appropriate than traditional suspension. The problem was that the guidance was taken to an extreme. Certain risk-averse public school administrators got the message loud and clear and eventually applied it to all students, not just African Americans. Oklahoma City principals instructed teachers to forgo suspension for fighting, "unless there was blood."[47] Across urban public schools, groping a teacher, bullying, and bringing hollow-point bullets to class were more likely to land a delinquent in a talking circle than in suspension.[48] As suspensions fell across major public school districts such as Los Angeles and Chicago, it is not coincidental that academic proficiency dropped with it.

When Broward County, Florida, ignored violent student behavior, it resulted in a national tragedy. Nikolas Cruz, while attending middle school and high school in Broward, built an extensive rap sheet that included killing animals and bringing them to school, vandalizing school facilities, threatening to kill teachers and students, engaging in hate speech, assaulting students, and bringing knives to school.[49] Cruz went so far as to tote into school a backpack filled with bullets. Over the course of several years, Broward County sheriff's deputies made forty-five visits to Cruz's home responding to various calamities, one of which was Cruz punching his mother in the mouth and knocking her teeth out.[50] Law enforcement, the school district, and students recognized Cruz as a sociopath.

What were the consequences Cruz faced because of his sociopathic actions? Next to nothing, since Broward County schools and its sheriff avoided student discipline and juvenile arrests. In middle school, Cruz required adult supervision but remained in class. When Cruz brought to school that bullet-filled backpack, his only punishment was never to bring backpacks to school again. These omens went unreported to the police by school administrators. Cruz enjoyed a clean record since none of the forty-five visits by sheriff's deputies to Cruz's home resulted in a single arrest. That clean record allowed him to pass a background check and purchase a gun after he turned eighteen. Then in February 2018, Cruz returned to his old high school, Marjory Stoneman Douglas, and massacred seventeen people. The policies employed by Broward administrators and police are applied across scores of major public school systems.

Students in large and small public schools engaging in poor, indulged behavior does not occur in isolation. Teachers' unions and school administrators are accomplices. Regrettably, despite the dysfunctional crisis seen across public school systems, the trend has been moving away from accountability for teachers and administrators. You see it mostly everywhere you look.

A poignant exemplar is the nation's biggest city and largest school district: New York City. Disgrace might be too lenient of a term for New York City public schools. Barely over a third of students in grades 3–8 passed 2016 proficiency tests in math and English.[51] The percentages drop to 20% in math and 27% in English for African American students.[52] It wasn't too long ago that meaningful school reform was a top priority of then Mayor Bloomberg. Starting in 2007, the district issued annual Progress Reports with the goal of holding individual schools and the district accountable to students, parents, and taxpayers. Student progress was the metric most heavily weighted in the grading, with added metrics of student performance and school environment factored in. Comparing a school's score to the overall district score and to schools in the district with similar student populations, these scores and weightings were then used to produce a final letter grade (A–F) for each school. The findings and letter grades were published. Under Bloomberg's Progress Reports, a parent knew exactly where their child's school stood and how its scores were calculated.

All of that changed when Bill de Blasio succeeded Mayor Bloomberg in 2014. A systematic and methodical deconstruction of the accountability system Bloomberg introduced quickly ensued. Progress Reports were immediately scrapped and replaced with School Quality Reports that stopped assigning letter grades to schools. In 2015, the parent survey of questions was revamped to remove questions about parental satisfaction with the academic expectations of the school. Also, in 2015, the Department of Education stopped publishing the data that would allow parents or others to calculate what the letter grades would have been for each school if the grades were still assigned. If you described the Progress Report approach of the Bloomberg administration, you would use *accountability, results, progress, transparency,* and *performance.* In fewer than three years, Progress Reports morphed to School Quality Reports and the descriptors changed to *subjective, opaque,* and *hidden.* It is no longer about students' academic growth. Instead, the School Quality Reports system is about protecting bureaucrats, politicians, and the teachers' union from accountability.

Another illustration of how beyond repair the New York City public schools are is the Absent Teacher Reserve (ATR). The ATR started out as an attempt at reform during the Bloomberg administration. The idea was to offer principals more control over the choice of teachers at their schools. If you had a teacher that was unmotivated, excessively absent, or written-up for sleeping on the job, he should not land in a school with an opening simply because of union rules or seniority. If a poorly performing teacher was not picked by a school, he would go into the ATR where he could sit for years collecting full pay, filling in as a substitute as needed across the system, and potentially being reassigned to a permanent slot. The teachers' union vehemently opposes any deadlines for tenure on the ATR before a teacher would be let go and at times 25% of the teachers on the ATR have been there for six years or more. The ATR is neither small nor cheap. The average ATR teacher has eighteen years of experience, collects a salary just shy of $100,000 per year, and receives annual raises and bonuses.[53] Annual costs of the program hover around $150 million.[54]

At the start of the 2013 school year, close to 2,000 teachers sat in the ATR; the number fell to 1,200 at the start of the 2018–2019 school year.[55] Shelling out $150 million per year to have thousands of poorly performing teachers sit around and do little or nothing for years is bad policy and shows lack of leadership. The optics forced city government to do something to reduce the size of the ATR pool; yet firing incompetent ATR teachers was a non-starter with the all-powerful union. Mayor de Blasio managed to make the situation worse when he capitulated to union pressure and forced teachers in the ATR into schools that have trouble recruiting and retaining staff. Unfortunately, the schools within the New York City system that have the most trouble recruiting and keeping talented teachers are the ones with highest proportions of low-income and minority students, accelerating an already downward spiral of educational chaos for the students most in need of help.

The precious few New York City public schools that excel at building student skills, base admission on achievement tests and often specialize in areas such as the arts and sciences. These schools, just over half a dozen, brandish an alumni list of over a dozen Nobel laureates. One such high-performing school, Stuyvesant High, has a student body that is over 70% Asian and posts an impressive track record of excellence.[56] So, what does Mayor de Blasio do? Instead of trying to emulate the high-performing school at other schools, he pushes to scrap the admissions testing. The move was originally applauded by scores of city bureaucrats and politicians until a massive backlash hit from Asian New Yorkers.[1] De Blasio and other like-minded bureaucrats breaking what's clearly working while trampling on the Fourteenth Amendment's racial discrimination protections.

The effect of New York City's attempts at social engineering is parents send their kids to Catholic or charter schools, which post far superior academic results for minority students. That's why there are now over 200 charter schools in the city, with an enrollment of over 100,000 kids. The current backlog of students looking to gain admission into New York City charter schools is approaching 50,000.

---

[1] Brooklyn Borough President Eric Adams gloated in June 2018, "For years we tried to get rid of this darn test and we're finally getting rid of this test!" Adams reversed his position within two weeks.

As expected, de Blasio attacks charter schools every chance he gets, notably when charter schools attract less affluent kids. Politically, he has to keep the public school bureaucracy and the teachers' union happy, even if it sacrifices the ability of parents to choose what is best for their children. De Blasio, by his strict limits on charter schools coupled with his lenient approach to affluent parents paying private tuition, is telling middle-class and poor parents that they don't know what is best for their kids and bureaucrats must decide it for them.[m] Despite the failing system, spending in New York City public schools is among the highest in the nation and exceeds $23,000 per student per year.[57]

While New York is a wasteland of urban school district account-ability, Detroit is the obscenest example. The Detroit school system ranks dead last out of twenty-seven large urban districts for student proficiency, with only 5% and 7% of fourth graders being proficient in math and reading, respectively.[58] But when faced with competition or the threat of accountability, the district will fight to the death.

This happened in 2017, when the natural enemy of any urban public school system, a charter school, wanted to buy an old, abandoned Detroit public school building from a developer so that it could expand a suc-cessful program for kindergarten to second grade kids.[n] Many of the students are African American and low-income. The cherry on top is that the public school system, which by its own admission is starved for money, would receive $150,000 of proceeds from the charter school purchase, which could then be used to help fund gaps in a host of at-risk activities.

Yet all these benefits appear irrelevant to the way the Detroit public school system views things. The superintendent held up the sale of the building by arguing that certain deed restrictions applied, in violation

---

m   This arrogance is not exclusive to New York City. A representative of the Louisiana Association of Educators union had the gall to state in the New Orleans *Times-Picayune* in 2012, "If I'm a parent in poverty, I have no clue because I'm trying to struggle and live day-to-day."

n   The Detroit public school system is such a broken mess and charters are so adept at teaching children that more Detroit students attend charter schools than the public school system.

of the law. Regardless of budget shortfalls, the superintendent was stopping $150,000 from going into his school system and created unnecessary legal expenses. A familiar and rational stance for a Leech looks irrational to other people. Fortunately, after a prolonged battle in the courts, media, and legislature, Detroit Prep prevailed and bought the abandoned building in the summer of 2018.

A situation that mirrors Detroit's is found in the equally broken Milwaukee Public School (MPS) system. Over 40% of MPS students fail to graduate high school.[59] Math and reading proficiency levels hover at or below 20%.[60] Every parent who can find a charter school or move to the suburbs is doing so, which is driving declining MPS class sizes and enlarging budget deficits. The MPS in late 2018 had nearly a dozen vacant buildings and over forty schools operating at less than 70% of capacity.[61] The MPS expects that trend to continue, with a 63% increase in empty seats projected within the next decade.[62] These are desperate times for the MPS, which faces a certain death spiral unless performance improves.

So, where do the city bureaucrats, teachers' union, and MPS spend their time and effort these days? Mostly in resisting Wisconsin state law that requires MPS to sell vacant school buildings to successful charter schools that need space to accommodate growing demand. Five years ago a highly successful charter school, Saint Marcus Lutheran, offered to buy an abandoned MPS building complex for one million dollars. Sale of these vacant buildings would not only help kids wanting to enter charter schools, but would also help kids stuck in the MPS system since the building sale proceeds would be available to fill the system's gaping budget shortfalls. Yet MPS refused to sell to the charter school. An ill-advised sale to a construction syndicate failed and then MPS spent $10 million to relocate MPS students from an existing middle school to the vacated complex. Like Detroit, Milwaukee is experiencing what happens when Leech interests supersede the law, taxpayer interests, and student welfare: a school system that collapses, prompting greater exoduses out of the city and condemning children to failing schools whose parents can't afford to flee.

The tactics of public teachers' unions are not limited to cities but are found in state capitals too. Take the case of New Jersey. Democratic Governor Phil Murphy won the election in 2017 with the full-throated endorsement and support of the teachers' unions. One of the first things the governor did in early 2018 was fire the state's African American Assistant Commissioner at the Department of Education, Paula White. Democrat Mrs. White not only served a crucial role within the department before becoming assistant commissioner, she is also highly educated with a long, successful résumé in the field of education.

Despite her accomplishments, the New Jersey Education Association, the state's biggest teachers' union, viewed her as a threat. In the past, Mrs. White founded a charter school in Newark and served as an in-state head of a Democratic education reform group. These were two mortal sins when it comes to most teachers' unions. The governor was pushed to help the Leech and hurt taxpayers, kids, and parents. The governor fired Paula White as assistant commissioner hours after her unanimous approval by the state school board for the position. Sadly, no one in New Jersey batted an eye, understanding who really runs the state.

Providence, the capital of Rhode Island, recently underwent a third-party review of its public school system. The scathing report documents rats, lead paint, dirty drinking water, and exposed asbestos across the school district's facilities. Students regularly assault teachers, other students, and damage property without consequence, in part because in 2016 the Rhode Island legislature passed a law limiting school suspensions. The teachers' union has been known to defend teachers who sleep during class, fabricate grades, and excessively miss work. Absenteeism runs rampant for both students and teachers. The cumulative result of the Providence public school system is found with 5% math proficiency and 8.5% English proficiency for eighth graders. Yet Providence spends $18,000 per student, which is 50% more than the national average. Students and parents rush for the exits and look to charter schools for salvation. Meanwhile the teachers' union pushes for more "investment" and so-called evergreen contracts that automatically renew beyond the contract expiration date, while conveniently ignoring the dismal state of the public schools.

Teachers' unions, bureaucrats, and politicians in urban school districts are happy to abuse statistics to hide how bad conditions are and to avoid accountability. You hear these entities touting how four-year graduation rates in the United States increased from 79% in 2010–2011 to 84% in 2015–2016, which is an all-time high.[63] Although those numbers may be accurate on their face, they do not correlate to an improving situation for urban public school districts where the situation is quite the opposite: students are less prepared than ever for college and national test scores are flat. So, what gives?

One explanation is the recent embracing of "credit recovery" programs by major school districts. Credit recovery programs apply to kids who fail a class during the regular school year and look to replace the traditional summer school remediation route. In short, students who flunk, say, math or English work during normal school time on a condensed packet of material, typically online. The student doesn't need to retake the flunked class, doesn't need to attend summer school, and doesn't need to repeat the year/grade level. Credit recovery takes a fraction of the time as these other traditional routes and the content is easier. Teachers' unions and district bureaucrats love credit recovery because it drives graduation rates higher. Major urban public school districts, including those in New York City and Los Angeles, heavily embrace credit recovery. In the end, students and their families are the losers. Easier homework does not make better high school seniors or college freshmen. Over one million students in over 15,000 U.S. public high schools took credit recovery courses in the 2015–2016 school year.[64] That is an epic price to pay to inflate a misleading statistic used to make the administrators and teachers' unions look good.

URBAN FINANCE: BROKE, BUSTED, AND DESTITUTE
Major American cities are running under unsustainable budgets and broken financing. Unfortunately, this problem is not unique to large cities: aggregate pension and debt liability of approximately 1,000 U.S. cities have increased a startling 25% from 2013 to 2018.[65] "Our

foundation is rocky at best," said Dane Hutchings of the League of California Cities. "It's crunch time, and quite frankly, we simply cannot stand another market slowdown or substandard returns."[66] At the center of all these contributing factors sit the politicians and bureaucrats placing Leech ideology ahead of what is best for their city.

The highest debt-laden cities per capita in America are a who's who of our largest and best-known metropolises: Washington, D.C., Atlanta, San Francisco, New York City, Denver, Detroit, and Chicago. Many of these cities present debt burdens that defy actionable solutions: Chicago residents carry over $38,000 in city debt and city pension liability per taxpayer, which balloons to over $119,000 per taxpayer once allocations for debt associated with city public schools, county, state, public transportation, and the like are added.[67] New York City clocks in at over $16,500 per person, while residents of the California cities of San Diego, Los Angeles, and San Jose are weighted down by $6,500 or more per person.[68] Like Chicago, these cities face even more frightening, unmanageable, and unsustainable debt burdens when calculated on a per-taxpayer basis and when including the debt of affiliated government entities such as the county, state, public transportation, and public school district. These debt loads will inevitably lead to cuts in city worker retirement benefits (an uncertain outcome given union dominion over city governments) or eventual city default; those are the only long-term paths to meaningfully address the undeniable math.

This dire fiscal situation is even more frightening since the federal government already feeds massive infusions of dollars into these fiscal dumpster fires. In 2016, over $25 billion in taxpayer money was sent to major cities. Until the Trump tax reform of late 2017, federal tax policy offered fat subsidies to cities in the form of unlimited state and local tax deductions for individual filers. The more a city spent and taxed, the more the federal government subsidized that city by allowing individual taxpayers to deduct uncapped local and state property and income taxes from federal tax filings. A lower federal tax burden resulting from the local and state tax deductions helped to dull taxpayer's pain.

When you assess the fiscal prospects of large cities, especially when inevitable rising interest rates increase borrowing costs, you find a situation where either substantial cuts in already bare-bones services, significant increases in already high taxes, or both will be needed to keep the creditor wolves at bay in the shorter term. If New York Mayor de Blasio must choose between feeding tax revenue into higher wage rates of transit workers to cover bloated and unsustainable pension and healthcare costs or into needed track and equipment maintenance upgrades, you know what the answer is. That's because payroll costs for subway workers grew over 25% under his tenure, to an all-in average compensation level exceeding $150,000 per year, while the reliability of the subway has terminally declined.[69] Under de Blasio the city worker headcount has reached nearly 300,000, the highest on record. You don't want to be a resident, passenger, or homeowner in these cities when the music stops.

Paul Volcker, the former Chair of the Federal Reserve, once called out cities and other governments for using shady accounting and slimy math to, "obscure their true financial position, shift current costs on to future generations, and push off the need to make hard choices."[70] So, many cities utilize deceptive tactics to hide their true financial troubles. Leech leaders in these financial houses of cards will purposely low-ball pension and healthcare liability measurements, willingly suspend needed funding for services, and eagerly continue to borrow more money to pay the interest on money they've already borrowed. Chicago employed such a playbook for years, culminating in a $1 billion projected deficit for 2020, over $40 billion in pension liability, and interest expense of nearly $2 billion every year. That's why Chicagoans are strapped with a net city financial burden of over $38,000 per taxpayer and face continual, dual pressure from higher taxes and reduced public services.[71] What urban politicians and bureaucrats will not do is lead and institute needed reforms to spending, excessive giveaways to public unions, or punishingly high tax rates; what they will do is cover their tracks through various means including questionable financial disclosure documents. The size of the municipal bond market is massive, and it is funded predominantly by individual taxpayers. You would think the federal government through the SEC would not tolerate local governments misleading people on the nature of towns' finances. But then again, expecting a federal bureaucracy to police a city bureaucracy to protect the interests of Creator, Enabler, and Server investors is improbable. Don't anticipate it to happen except under the most egregious situations, such as with New Jersey in 2010 when the SEC was forced to charge the Garden State with securities fraud for misleading municipal bond investors. The SEC finally got around to this charge, but only after the state raised $26 billion across 79 offerings over five-plus years using misleading projections about pension funding needs.

A *Wall Street Journal* analysis of Merritt Research Services data for police and firefighter pension plans at cities of over 30,000 people shows a median coverage of only 71 cents for every dollar of liability in these plans.[72] As recently as 2001, the median for police pension plans was over 100 cents of assets for every dollar of liability, meaning the plans were overfunded. But in a few short years poor leadership in major cities created a financial crisis for police pensions that will only get worse if left unaddressed. More taxpayer dollars get poured into shoring up these pension plans instead of going to hiring more cops or investing in schools, infrastructure, and traditional services.

When taxpayers demand at last that something be done to stop a city from driving off the pensions' fiscal cliff, it often leads to undesirable outcomes. Memphis, Dallas, and San Jose experienced the resignation and retirements of hundreds of their police officers when pension plans were changed to match market and fiscal realities. Experience plummeted, morale drooped, and response times increased. Worse, the rates of serious and violent crime often increased, including homicide rates. San Jose's auditor reported that just after approval of police pension changes, officer staffing dropped and response times to incoming citizen calls ballooned. In Memphis, police morale got so bad after pension changes that the police union erected billboards in the city saying, "Welcome to Memphis: 228 homicides in 2016, down over 500 police officers."[73] Across many American cities we see a financial crisis in pensions catalyzing a more serious crisis in public safety.

Los Angeles exemplifies how endless giveaways culminate in ratcheting down public services. The city is facing annual structural deficits, which is bureaucrat code for spending more than you take in. Pension costs for police, firefighters, and city workers continue to climb beyond levels that already break the city's financial back. In the short term, city leadership reacts to the rising entitlement costs by deferring, delaying, and cutting spending on general fund services. The knee-jerk reaction by the city bureaucracy to the cycle is to squeeze as much revenue as possible across an entire spectrum of Creator, Enabler, and Server commerce. We all know, including bureaucrats, that you can't move real estate. That makes it an irresistible target to squeeze to fund gaping pension and retiree healthcare gaps. The situation results in a stealth mortgage on homes and other real estate that can be substantial. Recent studies estimate these unfunded liability gaps are equivalent to 20% of real estate values on average, nationwide.[74] The hidden mortgages in the form of inevitably rising property taxes will be paid by homeowners and renters as the cost is reflected in home market values and rents. Markets in fiscally undisciplined large cities and states will bear the worst of the impact, as we saw play out in Detroit and Puerto Rico.

While mayors and city government bureaucrats are using this self-inflicted and growing crisis to raise taxes across a broad spectrum of business, there is one part of the tax base they are willingly reducing taxes for: Mayor Garcetti secured a reduction in business taxes for lawyers and other professional services firms in Los Angeles. The tax cuts for the attorneys and friends will total over $40 million per year, all of it further reducing spending on city services, increasing taxes on others, or increasing the budget deficit.

URBAN LEADERSHIP VOID CONSEQUENCES
Although one could cite dozens of current examples of inept urban leadership, we start with my hometown of Pittsburgh. Mayor Bill Peduto

doesn't want to spend his time and attention on the tangible problems plaguing the day-to-day functioning of the city. Instead, he chooses to abuse his mayoral position to attend climate conferences across the globe and to lecture residents, businesses, and local communities on how they should live their lives and what their beliefs should be. That creates interesting juxtapositions. In September 2019, the mayor was signing permission slips for Pittsburgh Public Schools students to skip class in support of a national "climate strike."[75] While he was using kids as props for the cameras to strengthen his green label, the Pittsburgh Public Schools system was dealing with a forced shutdown that same day due to a water main break creating a drinking water crisis. Those are the same kids, by the way, who endure attending a school district where eighth grade math proficiency is at 19.5%.[76] The following month, the mayor was speaking at a climate action conference and calling for the banning of any future petrochemical development in the region.[77] That same week, a transit bus in the middle of downtown and during morning rush hour collapsed into a massive sinkhole while sitting at a red light.

In June 2017, the United States Conference of Mayors passed a unanimous resolution that committed to a target of 100% renewable energy by 2035.[78] In their eyes, wind, solar, and geothermal are renewable while natural gas and nuclear are not. The flowery language of the resolution spouted all kinds of platitudes about the technological advances of renewables, the dropping costs of renewables, all the health benefits of renewables, and so on as justification for the 100% target by 2035. The resolution received major press from the echo chamber of friendly media, and dozens of mayors went home to their cities thumping their chests over their newly found green cred.

The realities of physics, chemistry, and the power generation grid expose this resolution for what it is, a gimmick. Other energy forms will be needed, including natural gas or nuclear. When a mayor doesn't want to answer to the current realities of rampant homicides, drug addiction epidemics, crumbling infrastructure, homelessness, or failed schools, he or she can fabricate a problem to (never) solve.

Grandstanding on politically correct issues creates new problems. Major American cities today inevitably deploy bike-sharing depots and dedicated bike lanes on roads. The obsession afflicts even Fairbanks and other Alaskan cities where it's usually too cold to ride bikes. The touted rationale is to reduce carbon emissions, enlarge public transportation ridership, and improve wellness. More bike lanes usually come along with stricter speed limits, narrower driving lanes, turning restrictions, and traffic light timing that collectively fall under the fad of cities going on a "road diet." Los Angeles labels their road diet gimmick Vision Zero. New York City bureaucrats, not to be outdone, have their own Vision Zero plan and refer to road diet silliness as "traffic calming." Road diets are presented as the magical silver bullet to make cities happier, healthier, safer, and more sustainable.

Just watch out for the unintended and fatal consequences of road diets and all the tricks that go with them. One unintended consequence of road restrictions to accommodate bicyclists is more auto congestion and traffic jams, contributing to the national $300 billion economic cost of traffic congestion. All the idling traffic stuck in jams makes air quality worse, not better. First responders stuck in self-induced road diet congestion take much longer to arrive at accident scenes and emergencies. Traffic congestion made worse by bike lanes and road diets increases driver frustration, which results in agitated drivers running lights, making illegal turns, and speeding to beat the next light that won't be green for as long as it once was. Before you know it, those pedestrians and bikers you wanted to encourage in your city are being hit, injured, and killed at substantially elevated rates than before the new rules. Most cycling fatalities occur in urban areas, and a slew of major cities that promote bikes to the point of absurdity, including Tampa Bay, Miami, Jacksonville, Orlando, and Sacramento, post fatality rates for bicyclists that exceed the average U.S. homicide rate of approximately four murders per 100,000 people.[79]

Consider this dynamic at play in New York City. When de Blasio and his predecessor Bloomberg closed areas of Manhattan to autos to create pedestrian-only walkways, lowered speed limits, created dedicated bike lanes, and used traffic light sequence timing to reduce traffic speed, a couple of consequences ensued. First, traffic congestion rose markedly. New York became the third most congested city in the world according to Inrix, resulting in nearly $17 billion of lost productivity of commuters.[80] Second, death by car collision for pedestrians and bikers rose to 162 in 2016, with data showing the majority of accidents to pedestrians occurred in crosswalks.[81] The mayor then used the self-inflicted congestion and fatalities to justify taxing residents who have the audacity to drive in their own city, with the tax being in the form of congestion pricing that will squeeze hundreds of millions of dollars from drivers. The ill-gotten tax revenue will then be marketed as needed investment in the failing public transportation system but in reality will be used to engorge already bloated public unions that the mayor and bureaucrats need for support.

The biggest problems with bike sharing and bike lanes are in urban areas that embraced them the longest. Paris, France, started its docking bike sharing network back in 2007 and served as the model for American cities such as New York. Paris is now ground zero in bike-sharing misery. After pouring and committing hundreds of millions of euros into its extensive bike share network, the French capital in less than a year went from over 1,000 functioning bike docking stations to less than 300.[82] Throughout the first four months of 2018, there were more docking stations that did not have power across the sharing network than there were that had power. Vandalism results in an 80% bike attrition rate in as little as two years.[83] Tossed abandoned bikes and electric scooters from these failed ride-sharing debacles fill the Seine River, creating an environmental problem, and stack into muddy carcasses on the river bank, creating an eyesore. The hollowed-out network is in terminal decay and has been referred to as an "industrial catastrophe" in France.[84]

As the mess with the docking station bike share network was starting to spiral out of control in the City of Lights, other European cities like Lille and Brussels were taking on a much ballyhooed dock-less bike program of their own. Under these programs, there were no docking stations and users simply used an app to find a bike. Guess what happened? The same as what happened with the Paris docking network, only more random and with a social behavioral twist. Within four months over 80% of the bikes were destroyed, stolen, or commandeered off the network and the sponsor of the network shut down in the winter of 2018.[85] Vandalizing and destroying the bikes became a form of perverse entertainment, with many perpetrators posting their illegal acts on social media.

The great George Carlin said it best in the 1990s when all this nonsense with bike lanes, bike-sharing, and bike trails was just getting started: "I'm tired of these self-righteous environmentalists, these white, bourgeois liberals who think the only thing wrong with this country is that there aren't enough bicycle paths."[86]

A kissing cousin to the bike fixation of major city leadership is the obsession with public transportation. Since 1970, U.S. taxpayers have subsidized public transportation to the tune of $1.3 trillion.[87] Yet as time goes on, ridership declines and conventional public transportation becomes increasingly obsolete with the growing presence of ride-hailing apps, automated driving, and related disruptive technologies. Bus trips, the most widely used mode of public transportation, experienced more than a 15% decline in passengers in ten short years.[88]

You see public transportation falling behind everywhere, including the most left-leaning cities with some of the worst traffic congestion in the country, where public transportation should be in huge demand. The Chicago Transit Authority is experiencing erosion of its bus and train ridership and publicly laments that such a trend is common to most major urban public transportation systems. The Los Angeles public transportation system, LA Metro, suffered a staggering 24% decline in bus rides from 2013 to 2018.[89] Buses in L.A. take up to three times as long for a commute compared to a car or ride-hailing service. Despite these realities, LA Metro is in the midst of a multi-decade, $120 billion expansion paid for by a hike in sales tax.

Grossly fabricated cost-benefit analysis is applied to create an aura of objective rationale for spending huge sums on dubious public transportation projects. Mass transportation is not crucial to the success of urban economies. In most cities, it supplies a small percentage of workers' travel. Increasingly, work sites, retail, and other activities are located outside the city centers. New projects cannibalize existing public transit options, supplying meager incremental benefit. Often, a new subsidized public transportation project such as a commuter rail line reduces ridership on existing bus lines. Massive subsidy of public transport also squanders valuable real estate useful for more efficient traffic flow. Innovative technology, including ride-hailing and cheaper gasoline due to the natural gas shale revolution make public transportation uneconomic and obsolete.[o] Wasting focus and money to build yesterday's technology for tomorrow's demands makes little sense other than to urban bureaucracies.[p]

Urban bureaucrats don't have anything personal against the car. The automobile is in the crosshairs because it gives people unrivaled freedom of choice. Leeches view individual freedom and choice as liberties to be suppressed, controlled, and ended. Take out the car and replace it with public transportation and a bureaucrat or academic suddenly has greater power over individuals. With the car, the individual decides where he goes. With public transportation, the bureaucrat decides where everyone goes.

Rivaling the big-city politicians' and bureaucrats' love for bike lanes and public transportation is their lust for recycling. The problem with recycling is that the entire proposition depends on poorer countries such as China, India, and Vietnam agreeing to take our unsorted trash. When China refused to continue doing so in 2018 due to local outcry

---

o   It is not a coincidence that Lyft focused much of its national marketing effort on ad placements in public subway and bus stations.

p   The death blow to urban public transportation may prove to be COVID-19 and how it exposed the serious health risks that communal travel via subway, rail, and bus presents. In late 2020, San Francisco reported a 70% decline in bus ridership and a 93% drop in public transit revenue, while Washington, D.C.'s Metro suffered 88% lower than normal weekday ridership.

and the desire to expand its domestic recycling effort, the economics of global recycling became more expensive and unhinged. Most urban residents are ignorant of the fact that their recyclables are increasingly incinerated or dumped with regular trash in landfills. Consequently, communities and businesses that continue to recycle are facing steep increases in trash collection fees.

But that doesn't stop big-city bureaucrats from doubling down on nonsensical recycling endeavors. L.A. supplies a cautionary story. In 2017, Los Angeles instituted the catchy RecycLA program, which mandated a host of rules and regulations all in the name of nurturing sustainability, combating climate change, and improving worker safety.[90] Fees have risen and quality of service has declined. Residents not happy with their service or rates no longer can fire their hauler and find a new one, due to a newly created monopoly. An unvirtuous circle of life takes full form as city bureaucrats create the program, accommodating haulers seize monopolies and fleece residents via higher fees, and government hires more public workers to administer the dysfunctional program.

Flaunting sanctuary city status is another favored gimmick of urban leaders. We discussed the homicidal meat grinder of Chicago. With over one hundred people shot over the weekend of July 4, 2017, Mayor Rahm Emanuel (and his successor Mayor Lightfoot) should have been focused on ending the massacre and asking for any help available from the federal government. Instead, Mayor Emanuel chose to spend his time suing the federal government for sanctuary city rights.

Chicago is a leadership dream compared to the politician running Portland, Oregon. Ted Wheeler is not just the mayor of Portland but also acts as the police commissioner. In the summer of 2018, a violent, drug-infested leftist mob converged in the city to lay siege to a federal office building that housed U.S. Immigration and Customs workers. The mayor-police commish somehow managed to have Portland police officers stand down and not protect or rescue the federal workers or anyone else stuck in the general vicinity. Wheeler's rationale was that he did not agree with U.S. immigration policy, thus he refused to deploy city cops to do their job of restoring peace and upholding law and order. The police union president alleged that Wheeler ordered cops not to respond to 911 calls from the site and no arrests were made during the initial demonstration.[91] Federal workers were eventually evacuated and the building was reopened days later, but only after federal and out-of-state police came to the rescue. In total, the attacks and siege lasted for over thirty days, leaving nothing but a trail of destruction, human feces, drug needles, and lost confidence in the city's ability to maintain law and order. The mayor faced no consequences despite encouraging a mob mentality, destruction of property, assaults, drug use, terroristic threats, and a collage of various forms of harassment to law-abiding citizens. So, it happened again, in October 2018 when street thugs masquerading as social justice warriors took to the streets blocking traffic and assaulting innocent drivers while police sat idly watching blocks away. Law and order are dead in Portland.[q]

Distorted priorities are also to be found in the San Francisco mayor's office. At the top of city hall's agenda are sanctuary city status and various costly, feckless environmental sustainability initiatives. In the meantime, residents must live with filth and a mounting health crisis. A recent investigation of over 150 blocks in downtown San Francisco found disgusting and dangerous levels of human feces, used needles, and trash.[92] Most of the waste is created by the growing homelessness epidemic; the Bay Area combo of San Francisco and Oakland boast the highest per capita unsheltered homeless rates in the nation. The San Francisco Health Department estimates the city has more injection drug addicts (24,500) than kids in public high schools (16,000).[93] Kids navigate around the open cesspools to get to school. This being

---

q   Law and order have died in Seattle, too. The Emerald City's mayor during the summer 2020 unrest ordered police to abandon a Capitol Hill station, canceled curfew, banned use of tear gas, and promised no arrest for anyone violating prior curfew. Armed anarchists proceeded to seize the abandoned police station and occupy the Capitol Hill area for weeks. The incompetent mayor applauded the lawlessness, labeling it, "democracy," "peaceful expression," and "the Summer of Love."

San Francisco, there is a city government app (SF-311) and a private enterprise app (Snap Crap) that allow citizens to report and track human excrement across the city. Commuters constantly watch where they walk and ride their bike-shares. Visitors and tourists smell indescribable odors as they step out of hotel lobbies. Everyone runs the risk of contracting airborne viruses by inhaling particulate dried feces or HIV by accidentally stepping on used needles.

The drug and homeless crisis and associated filth affect the city budget. The 2017–2018 fiscal year saw $54 million spent for street environmental services, with about half going for cleaning up needles and feces on sidewalks. Staff for the street cleanup effort is 300 strong and expenditures are expected to rise to $60 million in the coming years.[94] That means less money for maintaining crumbling streets. To address the filth crisis, the city must address the homeless epidemic seriously, which may require more permanent housing or shelters. City officials estimate an additional 1,000 beds for the homeless are desperately needed and would cost $25 million.[95] Officials estimate the city spends $380 million on homelessness and will need hundreds of millions of more dollars to solve the plight.[96] Raising that kind of money will require increasing taxes, cutting expenditures in other parts of the city budget, or both.[r]

The start of 2020 saw the head of the San Francisco Public Works arrested by the FBI on charges of public corruption. A raging self-induced homelessness epidemic and the preoccupation with sustainability, sanctuary status, and a menu of socialist causes distracted leadership and provided the unsupervised head of public works the opportunity allegedly to engage in illegal and unethical activity with other bureaucrats, developers, and contractors.[97] The 2020 arrest casts a cloud over not only the accused, but also over the wider San Francisco leadership.

To the south, the City of Angels has been spending millions of dollars building new shelters for the homeless. The chronically homeless population is skyrocketing, and it's currently above 50,000 people.

---

[r] In November 2018 San Francisco voters approved Proposition C, which imposes a gross receipts tax on corporations with over $50 million in annual revenue to raise money for addressing the homeless epidemic.

What was already a shortage of beds in shelters has become a crisis. Today, the city needs nearly 20,000 more units to pull thousands of homeless from the streets and tent cities. Despite taxpayers ponying up over $350 million for shelters through various enacted ballot measures including the approval of a $1.2 billion bond issuance, experts estimate a shortfall of anywhere from $70 million to $250 million per year starting as soon as 2021.[97] Not surprisingly, the ballot measures, bond offering, and spending were justified with an assumption of the shelters decreasing the homeless population, but since all that spending the homeless population has grown by double digits.

In California, homelessness goes beyond raw numbers. The homeless population is getting younger and more aggressive, and is unhesitant to commit property crimes. Due in large part to Proposition 47, which effectively stopped police from arresting people for drug use, shoplifting, and other petty crime, the hands of police are tied in dealing with homeless problems and everyone, including the homeless, knows it. Drug abuse is rampant in plain view. People live in their cars on residential streets. Metro trains and public libraries are teeming with the displaced. Business storefronts are magnets for panhandlers.

Just to the south of L.A., Orange County and its cities are in outright rebellion when it comes to mandates to create homeless camps or shelters in the area. Orange County has been experiencing its own homeless epidemic for years, with camps springing up along dry river beds, street people living on sidewalks, and tents popping up around schools. A recent cleanup of a homeless encampment in Anaheim yielded the following disturbing bounty: over 400 tons of trash, almost 14,000 needles, and over 5,000 pounds of hazardous waste, including human feces.[98] When lawmakers announced plans to establish three temporary shelters in the county to house the homeless, the pushback was severe.[s]

---

s   The temporary shelters proposal happened after a judge ordered the county to house the homeless. At first the county offered the homeless 30-day vouchers in motels. As the 30 days ended, lawmakers proposed the temporary shelters as a fix.

Cities within the county refused to help or volunteer to house one of the shelters. Large groups of residents protested at county board meetings, expressing anger at how the government was more than willing to damage the quality of life in their neighborhoods in exchange for doing the politically correct thing. After feeling the residents' pushback, county lawmakers backed down from the proposal.

The hypocrisy of urban mayors and bureaucrats has been on display during the pandemic as they lectured one thing yet did the opposite. The mayor of Chicago, who closed salons in the city, managed to visit with her stylist for a haircut.[99] The mayor of New York, who scolded citizens to stay home, was driven to his public gym for a workout.[100] A UK government advisor, who advocated for a country-wide shut-down, was caught meeting with his married mistress in London.[101] All are clear, indelible illustrations of the double standard in the most trying of times.

THE LEECH CREATES A TALE OF TWO CITIES

Increasingly, one sees only two classes in American urban areas: the 1% well-to-do and the abject poor. There is no middle class. Where segregation in cities used to be defined by race, now it is mostly by income.

The New York City borough of Manhattan is the ultimate urban setting. You see two classes of people living on the island: the ultra-wealthy in enclaves like Midtown or the Upper East or West Sides and the destitute poor in places like Harlem. A 12,000-square-foot "apartment" atop a Park Avenue skyscraper sold for $91 million at the end of 2017. Many of the multi-million-dollar condos in Manhattan are owned by absent or part-time resident millionaires and sit vacant most nights. Midtown and upper Manhattan boast the highest concentration of opulence in the world.

From the $91 million palace, a short walk to the north into Harlem or a couple of subway stops to the south into lower Manhattan will place you in some of the worst public housing complexes in the nation. The New York City Housing Authority, Nycha, is responsible for maintaining the shelter of hundreds of thousands of residents and oversees over 175,000 units that are in need of $25 billion in repairs. Disastrous

Nycha is the largest public housing agency in America.

In these Big Apple housing complexes, drug use is rampant, homicides abound, and lawlessness rules. The roofs leak, elevators are not working, mold is prevalent, roaches are everywhere, and nothing works. Nycha critic and the Trump administration's regional administrator for Housing and Urban Development (HUD), Lynne Patton, spent four weeks sleeping on the floors of Nycha apartments and saw rats as large as possums that have no fear of humans.[102] During the winter of 2017–2018, over 300,000 residents in Nycha units were left without heat or hot water when boilers and other equipment failed. The affected residents had the unenviable choice of going without heat or using their kitchen ovens to heat the apartment.[103]

For years, inspections for lead paint required by law were unperformed and then falsely certified by the city as completed. When inspectors showed up, Nycha staff would turn off water to hide leaks and put up danger signs to reroute the inspectors away from problem areas. Nycha staff had the audacity to publish "quick tips" instructing workers how to mislead federal inspectors.[104] The state's health watchdog reported over 80% of inspected Nycha units had a hazardous condition.[105]

The ongoing deceit and neglect take a heavy toll on Nycha tenants. Lead poisoning serves as an illustration. At first, Nycha stated that nineteen children were found to have been lead poisoned since 2012, which on further review saw the number grow to 820 kids, and then in the summer of 2018 saw the number revised yet again to 1,160 children.[106] Follow-up inspections of homes were not performed where kids registered elevated lead levels and Nycha applied a threshold tolerable lead level of 10 micrograms per deciliter that was twice what the Centers for Disease Control applied. No one should be surprised if the numbers provided by this corrupt and incompetent entity change for the worse again. In 2016, over 38,000 complaints were filed related to lead paint or plaster issues.[107]

After filing a civil complaint against Nycha, in 2018 the U.S. Attorney entered into a consent decree taking the housing authority to task for neglect, deception, and ineptitude. A federal judge later in 2018 subsequently rejected the settlement as unsatisfactory, described Nycha living conditions as akin to "the biblical plagues of Egypt," and estimated New York City's current capital commitments to Nycha would not address current needs until 2166.[t]

Is Mayor de Blasio concerned about these deplorable Nycha conditions? No; Nycha has an all-important goal of attaining a 30% reduction in greenhouse gas emissions by 2027. One of the tactics to achieve the 30% reduction is replacing conventional light bulbs with more efficient LED lighting. But under Nycha's labor pact, all of those light bulbs must be replaced by union electricians making $81 an hour in base pay and $51 an hour in benefits (overtime clocks in at time-and-a-half).[108] When you do the math, Nycha is spending over $33 million to change light bulbs at twenty-three housing complexes, which works out to $1,973 per apartment.[109] De Blasio changes light bulbs while Nycha burns.

De Blasio using Nycha to enrich various special interests at the expense of tenant quality of life doesn't stop with climate change shenanigans. Nycha employees are represented by thirteen separate unions and many of the private contractors who do work for Nycha are also unionized.[110] This leads to a list of predictable problems. New York's poorest pay a heavy price to keep public unions, government bureaucrats, and Mayor de Blasio feeding at the trough.

De Blasio's distractions from Nycha misery don't stop at pursuing wasteful climate change red herrings or enriching public unions. While tenants freeze in winter without heat or hot water, the progressive mayor focuses on developing a proposal and then taking a victory lap for raining over $3 billion in subsidies to Amazon so that it would locate an office campus in Long Island City, Queens. The site of the new Amazon campus was to sit next to one of Nycha's largest complexes. That was until Amazon canceled the massive project due to a spectrum of New York

---

t   Judge Pauley delivered a 52-page scathing opinion that serves as a sober indictment of Nycha. Read it at http://nysd.uscourts.gov/cases/show.php?db=special&id=670.

Leech interests assaulting it from every direction. That included de Blasio himself who bragged, "There is tremendous pressure on Amazon to allow unionization and I will be one of the people bringing that pressure . . . I believe that ultimately that pressure will win the day."[111] Instead of winning the day, that pressure scuttled the opportunity for the Big Apple. New York and its leadership managed to transform the absurd ($3 billion in handouts to Amazon) into the obscene (siting the subsidized corporate headquarters next to a derelict Nycha complex) and then back into the absurd (ruining the bought opportunity by attacking it).

Economists have a new name for this striking urban housing dichotomy: the rich areas are called racially concentrated areas of affluence, or RCAAs. These are areas of a city where the population is mostly white, and the income level is far above the poverty level for that city. Cities scoring high on RCAA inequalities are those that have embraced Leech-endorsed policies: Boston, Baltimore, Chicago, Los Angeles, New York, Philadelphia, and Minneapolis.

As you might expect, government meddling can make things worse on the RCAA spectrum. The cumulative impact of bureaucratic incompetence over time is reflected in surprising statistics: for example, in 1970 the African American community comprised 13% of San Francisco's population while today it comprises only 5%.[112] The harder government tries to close this inequality gap in major cities, the more it ends up widening the gap or exacerbating problems. In many instances, government policy ends up subsidizing the rich in RCAA neighborhoods.

One of the trusty fallbacks of city hall bureaucrats is the tax-the-rich approach. This blunt policy instrument has been used so often that many cities have reached the point of tax exhaustion. Data from 2014 show that in New York City the top 1% of wage earners contributed close to 50% of income tax revenues.[113] That is too much concentrated risk in far too small of a demographic segment. Is it any wonder that in the very same year New York State led the nation in people who made more than $200,000 per year moving out? Even though much of the state exodus was made up of Big Apple residents, Mayor de Blasio isn't letting up. His view on how to pay for the embarrassing state of the city transportation network is to increase taxes on the wealthy by $700 million. That will worsen the stampede of taxpayers leaving.

Cities bifurcate into two classes of wealthy and poor, because new housing prices are driven to higher levels by costly and prohibitive regulations. Yet major cities keep adopting more onerous building codes for new construction. The growing list includes the leftist bastions of New York, Seattle, San Francisco, Portland, and Los Angeles. Adding to the complexity are a mosaic of laws, such as California's Environmental Quality Act, that allow just about anyone to object to and stop new development projects on vague grounds.[u]

In 2016, Los Angeles voters easily approved requirements for new projects that require between 25% (rentals) and 40% (for-sale) of the units meet affordability guidelines. These affordability guidelines, however, go against the laws of economics, making it less likely more housing will be built and shrinking the inventory of new and affordable housing on the market. In March 2017, Los Angelinos voted on Measure S, the Neighborhood Integrity Initiative. Measure S would have required a two-year delay for any development in the city that requires a modification to the existing maze of city planning rules. In the City of Angels, modifications to the complex city planning code are the rule and not the exception, which means Measure S would have served as an unofficial, yet effective, ban on new housing. Fortunately Measure S was defeated.[v] Los Angeles and California bureaucrats were not deterred by the defeat and imposed wage standards on new build projects that could double the hourly wage for some skilled trade slots. This only compounds the problem, raising the project costs even higher,

---

u   A San Francisco Russian bathhouse owner used this law to sue and hold up a 1,500-unit apartment project by arguing the development posed an environmental hazard to naked customers.

v   The election day turnout of Los Angelinos was a paltry 11%. Besides Measure S, the mayor was also up for re-election. To see such a level of voter apathy where so much was at stake for the city should cause concern.

which diminishes supply of housing further.

In May 2018, the state's energy commission decided to mandate solar panels for all new homes built in California. The mandate adds thousands of dollars to the cost of a new home and adds hundreds of dollars each year to the homeowner's maintenance costs. The bureaucrats justified the mandate by referencing a biased consultant study using assumptions for the cost of the panels and the energy savings that were fabricated, iffy, or highly suspect. Panel costs were lowballed by thousands of dollars.[114] Savings in monthly electric bills are a mirage since the savings are nothing more than the impact of massive renewable subsidies created by the bureaucrats, which simply siphon a dollar from one citizen to the other. This is not exactly improving affordability of homes, in a state where affordability is already excruciatingly painful.

Of course, the bureaucrat regulators justify the decision by hiding behind the green-washing of pending climate change doom and sustainability.[w] The real driver of this assault to affordable housing is cronyism: more government mandates means more control for bureaucrats, a larger subsidized and protected market for entities that built business models on such government subsidy, and a larger drain on Creator, Enabler, and Server taxpayers to pay for the subsidies and mandates. Do not forget the cherries on top of this mess: less affordable housing and no discernable impact on climate.

Philadelphia is one of the largest cities in the United States. The City of Brotherly Love boasts an unenviable statistic from the recent census: one quarter of its residents live below the poverty line.[115] That's the highest level in the country for a top-ten city. Philadelphia experienced a significant run-up in housing prices, with certain traditional working-class neighborhoods undergoing gentrification seeing price increases of 50+ percent in that period. Faced with this reality, the geniuses on

---

w   For a sense of the monster that the California Energy Commission bureaucracy has become, check out its organization chart at: *http://www.energy.ca.gov/commission/orgchart/California_Energy_Commission_org_chart.pdf*.

Philadelphia's City Council proposed to mandate that 10% of all new housing units be set aside for the poor at below-market rates. This type of simple-yet-dumb restriction makes new housing more expensive to build, thus reducing the supply of new units coming onto the market. Prices were driven up further.

Requiring builders to redistribute a portion of their new units to sell or rent at lower prices to low-income individuals or families is labeled with the altruistic sounding term "inclusionary zoning." Nearly 900 communities have adopted inclusionary zoning, and not surprisingly almost 80% of those communities fall in states where policies for inclusionary zoning exist: California, Massachusetts, and New Jersey.[116] As the inevitable math of inclusionary zoning and data-informed behavior of builders take their toll, expect a net reduction in new unit construction, net increases in housing scarcity, and less affordable housing for all those not designated as low-income in communities fool enough to embrace such nonsensical policies.

Major cities that took progressive stances on welcoming, accommodating and, in certain instances, enabling the homeless are starting to feel the repercussions of these policies. Homeless often gravitate to areas where commercial businesses exist because they offer a target-rich environment to panhandle and hustle. That is what is happening in progressive cities like Portland, Denver, and Berkeley. Large numbers of homeless in these commercial retail areas, especially when they set up encampments, are starting to create a health and safety risk, perceived or real, to shoppers. That means fewer shoppers, which hurts the bottom line of all those stores, restaurants, and businesses.

At a certain point business owners and customers say enough is enough. In 2015, more than 60 cities had laws banning public camping and around 100 cities prohibited sitting or lying down in public places, which were a 60% and over 40% increase from 2011, respectively.[117] Of course, these laws solve nothing if not enforced due to the growing unwillingness of law enforcement to do its job because of increased risk. And even if laws are enforced, the homeless are going to move just outside the peripheral boundary of the enforced commercial area and set up camp around the corner. The problem hasn't been solved; it has only migrated from a retail business address to some other address in the city.

FLEEING THE LEECH: INEVITABLE URBAN EXODUS

Often you hear pundits offer up the solution to urban America's problems of having more suburban residents move into the city. If you do that, the argument goes, commute times shorten, the urban tax base improves, and everything is better. This solution ignores one glaring flaw in the logic: people do not want to live in the city. Why? Because their kids will not develop in the substandard schools. Because they don't want to increase their chances of being a victim of violent crime. Because they don't want noise pollution exposure. Because they don't want to be taxed to death. Because they want a yard. There is an array of compelling reasons why people are subjecting themselves to the longer work commute and will continue to do so even if commute time grows longer.

Of course, until the harsh realities of urban living are tackled by city authorities and livable neighborhoods expanded, there is little guarantee families will move into the city. Data from the U.S. Census Bureau show that people living in the most expensive urban areas are in fact moving out, outpacing people moving in. Data for 2010 to 2014 show that more people left the ten most expensive metro areas in the nation, including Los Angeles, New York City, San Francisco, Boston, and Chicago, than those who moved in. This trend was especially pronounced for lower-income residents and for residents under forty years of age. New York City keeps losing people, year after year, in the all-important twenty-five to thirty-nine age demographic, bleeding close to 38,000 in just 2018.[118] The pandemic, civil unrest, and the defund the police movements will rapidly accelerate urban exodus.

The drivers of the exodus from the most expensive metro areas were not identified by the Census Bureau, but common sense tells us they include cost of living, cost of housing, crime, quality of schools, and greater opportunities. A study assessed what it would cost to build a modest 2,000-square-foot home in lower Manhattan and downtown San Francisco on property that is on the market. The answers were staggering: over $60 million in New York and over $25 million in San Francisco.[119]

Remember, the Leech never sleeps. He can find ways to suck you dry without you even realizing it. New York and Mayor de Blasio are trying to get U.S. taxpayers from Idaho to Mississippi to pay $15 billion for replacing a dilapidated transit tunnel under the Hudson River. Big-city mayors across the map are lobbying for similar transfer payment subsidization of pet projects in their area codes, many using their own ineptitude at managing the 2020 pandemic, the resultant shutdowns, and civil unrest as justification. Balance of tax dollar payments increasingly favors the bloated, failing, and violent ecosystems that are America's urban cities.

PROFILE #1: POPE FRANCIS

"Blessed are those who protect and care for our common home."

PROPOSED CONTEMPORARY BEATITUDE FROM POPE FRANCIS

"[W]ho am I to judge?"

POPE FRANCIS ON JULY 28, 2013

"A person who only thinks of building walls, and not building bridges, is not Christian."

POPE FRANCIS JUDGING PRESIDENTIAL CANDIDATE

DONALD TRUMP ON FEBRUARY 17, 2016

THE RAPID TRANSFORMATION OF FRANCIS
FROM HOPE TO ANTIPOPE

The Catholic Church boasts a two-thousand-year legacy of faith. Church history, however, is not perfect. Between periods of great inspiration there have been other periods where popes and the Catholic Church were flawed. Popes have not been immune from wrongdoing, poor decisions, and weak leadership. Whenever the Church changes popes, great opportunities and risks follow. Pope Francis succeeding Pope Benedict has been no different.

In a brief period, my view of Pope Francis has changed drastically. Like many, I watched the events in Saint Peter's Square unfold when Cardinal Jorge Bergoglio was chosen pontiff in March of 2013 after Pope Benedict's rare papal renunciation. The new Pope Francis appeared a humble pontiff, who would reinvigorate Catholicism, which added to my excitement.

Pope Francis has squandered the goodwill of those early days. His embracing of climate change ideology and anti-capitalist collectivism has created a virulent strain of Catholicism whereby in the words of Ayn Rand, "today you are supposed to apologize…because we are more prosperous."[1] When you add obvious instances of hypocrisy in both Francis's and the Church's teachings and history, faith itself is challenged.

We were taught in history class that there were times when individuals laid claim to the papacy in direct conflict with a legitimate, sitting pope. These interlopers were labeled "antipopes." Francis has managed to put a modern-day spin on the antipope phenomenon. Francis, who started out as a legitimately elected pope, has consistently betrayed and abused the roles and responsibilities of his office. Francis has tainted and sullied the papacy with a one-two punch of losing moral authority in the arena of traditional responsibilities and suffering a crisis of credibility in his crusade to expand the scope of Church authority beyond competency. Francis has tragically collapsed his reign from pope into antipope.

CATHOLIC VS PAPIST

Let me emphatically state: I am a Catholic, not a papist. There is a huge difference.

The pope, as head of the Church, serves as a living guardian of established truth. The pope's job is to preserve and guard existing Catholic doctrines and to spread the Gospel across the globe. A papist is someone who blindly adheres and subscribes to what the guy with the big hat in Rome says you should do. Certain Catholics refer to this devout following of the pope as *ultramontanism,* where everything the pope says goes.

Pope Francis is obsessed with expanding his power and authority into subject matters far beyond traditional Catholic beliefs: areas such as energy policy, global finance, and climate change science. One of Francis's media advisors, Father Rosica, brags that Francis, "breaks Catholic traditions whenever he wants," because he is, "free from disordered attachments."[2] Francis desires to redefine his position from one of humble steward to megalomaniacal oracle. Perhaps Pope Francis likens himself God.

While Francis expands his scope of authority to issues far beyond traditional Catholic doctrine, he also unilaterally dilutes and confuses the Church's position on a host of core Catholic values. No matter what your personal views are on abortion, gay marriage, contraception, and divorce, the Catholic Church offers clear positions on them. That has changed under the reign of Francis.

The pope's mealy-mouthed handling of core value positions coupled with his aggressive expansion of the scope of papal authority into non-traditional areas creates concern, disdain, and visible resistance within the Church. American Cardinal Burke is an outspoken critic of the pope. Burke requested clarification from Francis on the status of divorce and remarriage and was ignored by Francis. Then Burke went public with his concerns. Cardinal Burke took the brave and exceptional course of publicly calling out Francis's unilateral power-mongering of authority. Burke went so far to remind us that if the pope utilizes his power in a sinful manner, there is a duty for Catholics to disobey. Cardinal Burke is not alone in the Church.

The difference between Catholicism and papism has never been plainer than in the decades of sexual abuse of children by priests. The tragedy and scandal of the powerful abusing the young and weak show Rome, and this pope, as far from infallible. Pope Francis lost the moral and ethical high ground with the Vatican's response to the sex abuse scandals. Although Francis talks a good game of zero tolerance of sex abuse by clergy, his actions have left much to be desired.

FRANCIS AS CEO OF SALVATION INC.

The long-term existence of the Catholic Church is under threat. In the developed world, individuals have become less religious generally while Catholics have been shifting from devout to non-practicing. In both the United States and the developing world, the rise of Evangelical Christians has blocked Catholic Church growth. In Pope Francis's home continent of South America, Brazil is a striking example. Although Brazil still holds the most Catholics of any nation on earth, the percentage of the population that is Catholic dropped substantially from over 90% in 1970 to just 65% in 2010.[3] This drop coincides with a rise in Protestant Evangelical followers as well as those holding no religious affiliation. In the coming decades, Catholics will be a religious minority in Brazil. Shifting global demographics and trends pose an epic risk to the Vatican's business model.

Pope Francis has placed profit and loss over the core tenets of Catholicism. Francis's willingness to sacrifice Vatican credibility in exchange for short-term financial benefit played a leading role in the Peter's Pence embarrassment. Peter's Pence is the primary charity of the Pope. It solicits donations from the faithful by promising that proceeds will go to help the most needy across the globe. The sales pitch is effective marketing: donate to Peter's Pence and you will be acting vicariously through the pope to help the downtrodden. Historically popular, Peter's Pence enjoyed even more status early in Francis's tenure when he committed to heading a "poor church . . . for the poor."[4]

Unfortunately, that talk was cheap when Francis faced the financial reality of the Vatican. In late 2019, it was reported that for years most of the donations (in excess of $50 million annually) to Peter's Pence went to plug gaping holes in the Vatican's administrative budget and only about 10% of the donations went to help the poor.[5] Worse yet, the assets of the charity shrank by over $100 million due to poor investment decisions.[6] Francis has proven to be a poor steward of the charity, both financially and morally, and has demonstrated the financial needs of the Vatican bureaucracy surpass the critical needs of the poor, homilies to the contrary.

Growth and survival plans require more than money; they also require leadership and restoring trust. A change in strategy for any business or organization, especially one like the Catholic Church where values are viewed as unchangeable, requires first building support within your management team. The management team for the pope is the bishops, cardinals, and Vatican staff.

History shows an effective technique for influencing a palace, government, or corporation is to influence the inner circle of the leader. Popes and the Vatican have not been immune from this technique. Enter George Soros. He has well-documented views on what the values and strategy should be of the Catholic Church. So many of those views are close to Francis's views. Documents from WikiLeaks exposed the efforts of Soros to influence Francis on certain issues, including abortion and same-sex marriage. At the same time, Soros convinced Francis to elevate the topics of income equality and global warming as the centerpieces of the pope's visit to the United States.[7] The documents show how Soros and affiliated wealthy groups worked closely with the pope's closest advisers, including two U.S. bishops and one Latin American cardinal. Was Church leadership willing to push traditional morality aside to further the Vatican's earthly agenda?

Like a new CEO entering a corporation, Francis is not afraid to purge the ranks of those in upper management who are not on board with his views and replace them with those who toe the line. Francis stacks the College of Cardinals with leftists aligned with his views. Since the cardinals select future popes from within their group, filling the ranks with like-minded advocates increases the chances of future popes embracing leftist policy views. The appointment of cardinals in November 2016 illustrates this strategy. Francis passed over the leaders of the two largest archdioceses in the United States, Los Angeles and Philadelphia, most likely because the bishops leading those dioceses are conservative. Instead, Pope Francis elevated the leaders of the Chicago and Indianapolis dioceses to cardinal-elect, both of whom are well established voices from the left.

Those within Church leadership who echo Francis's views and adopt his agenda are elevated in rank, even if the individual is engulfed in accusations of wrongdoing. Much of Francis's sex abuse reform team ended up mired in controversy themselves. The pope is more than willing to stick with an individual accused of wrongdoing or moral failure as long as that individual remains politically loyal and ideologically aligned.

Holding steady to the Church's core traditional values can prove to be a recipe for disaster under Pope Francis. Francis tapped Cardinal Sean O'Malley in the early days of the Pope's reign to lead the Church's effort on sexual abuse. That was until O'Malley took Francis at his word of wanting zero tolerance and desiring serious reform. For when Cardinal O'Malley started to press for meaningful change within the Church, Francis changed members of the sex abuse panel O'Malley headed, ordered the panel to shift from proposing changes to holding academic conferences, and failed to mention O'Malley as an organizer for a 2019 summit on sex abuse. Cardinal O'Malley's demise shows even the most noble individuals dealing with the most sensitive of topics risk peril if their paths deviate from Francis's machinations.

Like Cardinal O'Malley, the Sovereign Order of Malta found out the hard way what happens when you follow Catholic doctrine that conflicts with Pope Francis's ambitions. The 900-year-old religious Order, commonly referred to as the Knights of Malta, is the Catholic Church's largest chivalric order and, more importantly, is a massive humanitarian army of over 100,000 volunteers worldwide who provide aid and care to thousands. The Order is well respected, has diplomatic relations with over one hundred nations, and is wealthy.

But there is one problem. This old, well-respected, wealthy, and influential organization has habit of sticking to traditional Catholic teachings. On top of that, the Order has had a degree of autonomy from the Vatican since the beginning, which inevitably brought it into conflict with Francis in 2015.

The Order's grand master demanded the member in charge of the Order's humanitarian efforts resign when it came to light that some projects were distributing condoms.[8] Catholic doctrine prohibits the use of artificial contraceptives. Nevertheless, Pope Francis found his excuse to strike. When the battle was finally over in early 2017, the Vatican announced that the grand master was resigning and that the Vatican would appoint its personal delegate to the Order to oversee spiritual and moral reform, which is code for tearing down the leadership and culture of the Order and then rebuilding it in Francis's vision. A new grand master now sits atop the Order; for how long will be decided by how well he takes orders from Rome.

Now, the Order of Malta is nothing more than a puppet state of the Vatican. The extent to which the current Order kowtows to Francis was on display when the Order's Grand Magistry suspended from its membership historian Henry Sire. Sire's mortal sin was criticizing the pope through a book he authored under a pen name. The press release from the Order serves as a blanket and thorough denunciation of Sire and reads as if the words came directly from the Vatican.[9]

The lesson provided to the rest of the Catholic Church is a stark one: fall in line with whatever the pope says or face dire consequences. Attempting debate or dialogue with the current pope runs serious risks. Don't let the gentle smile and fawning media fool you. Pope Francis's style is more strongman than Saint Francis.[a]

FRANCIS STRETCHES INFALLIBILITY DOCTRINE TO GROTESQUE EXTREMES

"When someone is honestly 55 percent right, that's very good and there's no use wrangling. And if someone is 60 percent right, it's wonderful, it's great luck, and let him thank God. But what's to be said about 75 percent, right? Wise people say this is suspicious. Well, and what about 100 percent right? Whoever says he's 100 percent right is a fanatic, a thug, and the worst kind of rascal."

The passage above, from *The Captive Mind's Old Jew of Galicia*,

---

a   Pope Francis has a sharp tongue when it comes to publicly criticizing other leaders within the Catholic Church whom he is not pleased with. His 2017 pre-Christmas address serves as a rich trove of Francis insults. The more colorful and mean-spirited words and terms include "cancer of plotting," "degenerate logic," "betrayers of trust," and "vainglory." North Korean dictator Kim Jong-un, a lover of unique and creative forms of insult, would do well to pay attention to the pope's command of abusive language.

raises important questions about the authority of the pope. On which areas and subjects does he speak authoritatively? Which areas and subjects are beyond his authority or competence? The answers to these questions hinge on the Catholic concept of papal infallibility.

Papal infallibility was defined by the Vatican Council as "the Roman Pontiff, when he speaks ex cathedra—that is, when in the exercise of his office as pastor and teacher of all Christians he defines, by virtue of his supreme Apostolic authority, a doctrine of faith or morals to be held by the whole Church—is, by reason of the Divine assistance promised to him in blessed Peter, possessed of that infallibility with which the Divine Redeemer wished His Church to be endowed in defining doctrines of faith and morals."[10]

Not everything the pope says or writes falls under the aura of infallibility. Note one of the requirements for infallibility is for the pope to speak *ex cathedra*. Speaking ex cathedra requires that certain conditions be met. Think of it this way: if you are going to speak infallibly and not be subject to questioning from the flock, you better go through an accepted process. Even the pope inside the Catholic Church has rules he needs to abide by, just like a CEO in a public corporation or a governor of a state has rules and processes she needs to follow.

When the pope speaks infallibly, the teaching is limited to doctrines of faith and morals. Francis's power grab is far from infallible and beyond the traditional scope of faith and morals, like the last decade in U.S. politics. The United States just experienced President Obama using executive orders relentlessly to plow beyond the limits of constitutional checks and balances and the doctrine of separation of powers to push an agenda in healthcare, energy, and financial policy without the consent of Congress. Not coincidentally, President Obama and Pope Francis hit it off famously and admire one another. Don't let the funny hat fool you; the current pope is as ruthless as they come in the brutal world of power politics.

FRANCIS ALLOWS CATHOLICISM TO BE HIJACKED BY ENVIRONMENTALISM

Papism, expanding the Church's power, funneling more money into the Church's coffers, and the abuse of papal infallibility converge in environmentalism and particularly climate change. The pope combines his instinctive dislike for capitalism and his fondness for environmentalism so that climate change becomes an integral part of, and falls within, the pope's and the Church's zone of authority. Once the pope declares expertise in this arena, he is free to create a business opportunity for the Church. This is the same model used to catalyze a rise to power by despots and tyrants for centuries.

To create a myth where followers respond for their own salvation, one needs a core document laying out a false, yet compelling, call to action. Pope Francis issued an encyclical letter in 2015, *Laudato Si*, where he discusses environmentalism, climate change, and the behaviors and thoughts appropriate for Catholics on these topics.[11] An encyclical is a papal document typically sent to the bishops or other Church leaders. Think of it as a leader's memo on a certain topic to the wider management team. You may wonder if an encyclical is infallible. Generally, using an encyclical as a vehicle to communicate does not constitute an infallible ex-cathedra pronouncement. But you might have infallibility with an encyclical, depending on a wide range of subjective considerations, from the language used, the timing of the letter, and a range of other factors.

The Vatican is no glass house and the pope has never sinned because Francis left no stones un-thrown in his environmental encyclical. The rambling document is a starkly blunt manifesto well beyond the traditional established bounds of faith and morals. Yet the encyclical's veneer is a thin, sweet wrapping of Saint Francis of Assisi walking among an unspoiled landscape with his wildlife friends. Excerpts, quotes, and positions in *Laudato Si* speak for themselves.

Francis is no fan of technology, science, and engineering advancement, saying, "Rather than a problem to be solved, the world is a joyful mystery to be contemplated with gladness and praise."[12] And, "It cannot be maintained that empirical science provides a complete explanation of life."[13] Francis would be happier, it appears, to see mankind revert back to the Dark Ages, where things were much more dismal, life was much more brutal, but where the Church enjoyed much more control over its flock.

The pope's disdain for technological advancement is not surprising considering the Catholic Church has a shameful record of suppressing scientific brilliance. The Church has been the enemy of science and objective thought for centuries. Galileo wasted under arrest because of his audacity in putting forth the concept of the earth revolving around the sun and not the other way around. History repeats itself and the Catholic Church continues its long legacy of scientific denial as Francis ignores the tremendous incalculable benefits that technology bestows on mankind.

Pope Francis doesn't place much stock in recent breathtaking developments of science and technology since he feels we are coming off, "a period of irrational confidence in progress and human abilities."[14] Although it is not clear from the encyclical what recent period of time the pope is referring to, what is clear is that the past few decades delivered more technological advancement, across a wider swath of the developed and developing world, that benefited more people (including Catholics), than the prior two centuries. Life expectancies are longer, infant mortality rates are lower, and education is more widely available than ever—all due to technology, human ability, and their applications across the globe in fossil fuels, finance, chemicals, GMOs, and capital markets. Confidence in man's ability is hardly irrational.

Francis laments our throwaway culture and completely misses the mark when it comes to the causes and solutions. "We have not yet managed to adopt a circular model of production capable of pre-serving resources for present and future generations, while limiting as much as possible the use of non-renewable resources."[15] Francis has consistently doubled down beyond his encyclical on this ridiculous rhetoric. In 2018, the Vatican held a climate change conference and, with the leaders of Exxon and BP in the audience, the pope criticized the continued search for fossil fuels and their ongoing extraction and consumption.[16] The pope presents a fool's choice: the continued use of fossil fuels and pending global climate catastrophe or the adoption of abundant renewable energy using green financing. Both scenarios are fantasy and ignore science.

Pope Francis suffers a fundamental misunderstanding of renewable and non-renewable resources. With electricity generation, for example, which the pope likes, there is no such thing as a renewable resource. In addition, "non-polluting energy" simply does not exist.[17] Solar generation requires the construction of solar panels, which consist of a range of rare earth elements and complex compounds, all of which exist in only finite amounts on the planet, just like oil, natural gas, and coal. In addition, the elements and compounds needed to build the solar panels are mined and processed, requiring substantial energy consumption, and carrying a significant environmental footprint. On a MWh-to-MWh basis, the cumulative environmental impact of a solar panel far exceeds that of a natural gas power plant. Solar and wind are far from renewable, as forms of electricity generation. The pope lives in his own world of hocus-pocus.

Francis demands we limit the use of non-renewable resources (using his flawed terminology). Although he's not clear why, one can infer from his words that we should restrict them because we might want to preserve these resources for the next generation. Once again, the pope is not paying attention to the world around him. The natural gas shale revolution sparked in the United States is now affecting the world. Because of technology, mankind has figured out ways to increase the amount of economically extractable natural gas for current and future generations. The world consumes more natural gas than ever, we discover more of it and make it available more than ever, and the cost is unimaginably lower. Fossil fuel in the form of natural gas is a blessing for Catholics across the globe.

To assess how impactful new sources of affordable and abundant fossil fuel are to mankind, look at the past 150 years. In the 1870s, atmospheric carbon dioxide was hovering around 285 ppm and there were over 1,400 global deaths per 100,000 people due to famine. By the 1940s, despite World War II, carbon dioxide levels rose to 310 ppm while global famine deaths dropped to 785 per 100,000 people. In the current decade, carbon dioxide crossed 400 ppm while famine deaths are 3 per 100,000 people. What makes these data more impactful is that from the 1940s to today, global population has tripled and GDP per capita has quadrupled. These facts, which conveniently elude Francis, prove the unquestionable benefit of fossil fuels to humans, whether found in large reductions in famine deaths, increased economic well-being, or both despite much larger global population.

The pope is possessed by the political rhetoric and dogma spewed by the extreme environmental movement. Francis jumps into the embrace of a seriously flawed concept: that of scientific consensus. "A very solid scientific consensus indicates that we are presently witnessing a disturbing warming of the climate system. In recent decades, this warming has been accompanied by a constant rise in sea level and, it would appear, by an increase of extreme weather events, even if a scientifically determinable cause cannot be assigned to each particular phenomenon."[18]

What exactly constitutes a scientific consensus? It is an illogical question. Science is about disproving consensuses not building them. When Einstein developed his theory of relativity, he did not worry that all the other physicists would disagree with him. When Columbus sailed to the New World, he didn't listen to the 50+ percent of explorers who said the world was flat. When Marie Curie discovered radioactivity, she wasn't bothered that it upended the major theories of physics at the time. When truth loses to the majority, both science and society will suffer.

Sigmund Freud has been lauded and criticized, but one thing he got right was the foolishness of relying on a scientific consensus. Freud surmised that, "People complain of the unreliability of science—how she announces as a law today what the next generation recognizes as an error and replaces by a new law whose accepted validity lasts no longer. But this is unjust . . . a rough approximation to the truth is replaced by a more carefully adapted one, which in turn awaits further perfecting."[19] Freud saw the ridiculous, inconsistent logic of people thinking they have a perfectly accurate and complete understanding of one theory, hypothesis, or phenomenon forever.

The scientific consensus flaw, whether it's of the pope's "very solid" variety or of the plain vanilla variety of settled science, was best articulated by the brilliant author Michael Crichton: "Let's be clear: the work of science has nothing whatever to do with consensus. Consensus is the business of politics. Science, on the contrary, requires only one investigator who happens to be right, which means that he or she has results that are verifiable by reference to the real world. In science consensus is irrelevant. What is relevant is reproducible results. The greatest scientists in history are great precisely because they broke with the consensus. There is no such thing as consensus science. If it's consensus, it isn't science. If it's science, it isn't consensus. Period."[20]

How about Pope Francis tagging blame for extreme weather events on climate warming even if there is no scientifically determinable cause? Climate models have proven repeatedly that they do not work and do not accurately predict temperatures. That should not come as a shock: if the local weatherman can't get tomorrow's weather right and if hurricane trackers can't provide anything but a wide cone of uncertainty for where the storm will be in two days, why would we expect to predict with any accuracy the earth's climate in fifty years? Not surprisingly, attempts to date have failed miserably.[b] We also witness questionable data presentation from so-called climate scientists, as evidenced by Climategate.[21] If these climate scientists and their models were held

b   The Chinese believe and showed that man can directly control weather. The China Meteorological Weather Association uses 1,500 weather professionals, thousands of workers, artillery, and supercomputers to control weather. This army was used during the 2008 Beijing Olympics to keep the games rain free and continues to be tasked with supplying rainfall to dry regions and avoiding severe weather in other regions. The days of only God controlling the weather may be over, even though man is feeble in predicting the weather. (*https://www.technologyreview.com/s/409794/weather-engineering-in-china/*)

accountable for work product and results anywhere beyond academia and politics, they would have some answering to do.

The pope has bumbled into an incredibly complex technical field, far removed from anything remotely resembling Catholic faith and morals. Francis defends his positions on climate change by making it an article of faith instead of a scientific fact. Francis cherry picks a subsection of public opinion on a complex scientific matter and then stamps it with a banner of illegitimate papal infallibility. Sadly, while he seeks to grow power through scientific subjects outside the traditional scope of faith and morals, it leaves less time for him to invest in addressing and healing from the sexual abuse scandals.

The pope, like many in the radical environmental movement, uses a debatable scientific argument of global warming being an existential threat, caused by increases in trace amounts of atmospheric carbon dioxide from human activity, and then pivots to what he really wants. "Humanity is called to recognize the need for change of lifestyle, production and consumption, in order to combat this warming or at least the human causes which produce or aggravate it."[22] Francis not only knows next to nothing about carbon dioxide concentrations and their impact on the global climate's complex system, despite his much ballyhooed chemistry background, but he also likely doesn't care much about carbon dioxide and its impact on climate. If he genuinely cared, he would not be traveling by private plane and tolerating a Vatican organization spewing a massive carbon footprint in its day-to-day operations.

BETRAYING THE POOR TO GROW THE BRANDS OF POPE AND CHURCH

Over the past decades, things changed rapidly for the Catholic Church. Technology and education proved a powerful duo of disruption to the Catholic Church business model that had thrived over hundreds of years. For example, it wasn't so long ago when the most educated Catholics toed the Church line of creationism and shunned evolution theory. Nor was it so long ago when few Catholics would dare to question publicly the Church's views on the banning of contraceptives and its prohibitions on premarital sex. But the Church's demands are increasingly out of touch with contemporary values influenced by rapid social and technological change. Not surprisingly, across the developed world the Catholic Church today commands less power and influence than at any time in its history.

With the Church's business model cracking under the relentless pressures of these disruptors, the pope as CEO needs to find a way to stop the bleeding. What he needs is a cause to energize the base. His answer is to hijack a page out of the radical environmental movement's playbook: create a boogeyman of an existential crisis for humanity (climate change), pin the culprit as something that is ubiquitous and impacts everyone (CO_2), develop a methodical and relentless ground game of messaging (employ a range of environmental groups, fund political parties, indoctrinate kids from an early age in the classroom, woo academia with research dollars), pound any dissent with the hammer of scientific consensus, and then offer up salvation via social engineering that imposes top-down decision-making across all facets of daily life (fuel economy standards, mandated renewable energy portfolios, new light bulbs, carbon taxes, etc.). Francis, with *Laudato Si*, appropriates climate change to help the Church reconquer its lost dominion over personal decision-making and daily life.

The pope commits grave error in the encyclical with the convergence of climate change, fossil fuels, and the commitment to serve the developing world's poor. Francis states, "[Climate change's] worst impact will probably be felt by developing countries in coming decades. . ."[23] and "We still have not solved the problem of poverty."[24] This is one of the popular banners of climate change religion: having a call to arms to limit fossil fuels and the pace of global electrification under the banner of protecting the poor and the developing world.

Yet slowing down the pace of affordable electrification and attacking the use of fossil fuels has a devastating impact on the developing world's poor. Study after study, in country after country, and time after time have proven beyond a doubt that an increased level of affordable and reliable electrification in societies yields lower infant mortality rates, longer life expectancies, and higher levels of education. Such benefits lead to the follow-on benefit of empowerment of women. The converse is also true: whenever a society experiences a decrease in electrification things get worse for its citizens, often much worse. Vast areas of the developing world have little to no access to electricity. Life for poor Catholics without electricity, notably in Latin America and Africa, is short, brutal, and unforgiving. The pope performs an immoral dis-service to his flock and to the poor of the world when he chides those wishing to expand the use of fossil fuels, technology, and electricity. The unfortunate results are to keep the poor in the developing world barefoot, in the dark, and uneducated so that the Church can better control its current flock and recruit its future flock. All while cloaking oneself in doing what's best for the global environment.

Papal hypocrisy is found in a discussion on how consumption patterns and climate change can create scarcity in water resources. The anti-capitalist Francis feels obliged to take a shot at the market economy by stating, "It is also conceivable that the control of water by large multinational businesses may become a major source of conflict in this century."[25] This coming from the CEO (pope) of a multinational business (Catholic Church) whose legacy is riddled with centuries of being the source of conflict (Crusades, the Inquisition, French Wars of Religion, Thirty Years' War, and so on). Another facet of the hypocrisy in this statement is that the pope is arguing how allowing the few to control water resources will create conflict while he is in the middle of a dissertation whose thesis is that we should allow the few (a different few, mind you) to control energy resources to avoid conflict.

FRANCIS WANTS TO REDISTRIBUTE WEALTH AND RETURN TO THE DARK AGES

Pope Francis suffers from an ideology that has been on display across a wide range of failed movements and flawed philosophies, not the least of which is collectivism. Pope Francis fully embraces the concept of wealth redistribution throughout his encyclical when he babbles euphemisms such as "inequitable distribution,"[26] references to the few or the minority having higher consumption levels than others, talking about "differentiated responsibilities,"[27] and, my favorite, the notion of an "ecological debt"[28] that the rich north of planet Earth owes the poor south.

Upside-down priorities riddle the encyclical. Consider the statement, "Clearly the Bible has no place for a tyrannical anthropocentrism unconcerned for other creatures."[29] That's a fancy way of saying the Bible has great respect for animals. One may also infer from the wording that the pope believes anthropocentrism, or the belief that human beings are the most significant entity in the world, is tyrannical. Such views are ridiculous. In Catholic teaching, people have souls, donkeys do not. People can go to heaven, rabbits cannot.

Francis doubles down on the animals-are-equal-to-humans position when he states, "Every act of cruelty toward any creature is 'contrary to human dignity.'"[30] Were priests performing their temple duties acting "contrary to human dignity" when they engaged in gratuitous sacrifice of animals at the altar or to atone for sins? Does this mean that large chunks of the Old Testament are now heresy? Jesus believed in this "heresy" too.

When the Pope backtracks later in the encyclical on his view that animals should enjoy the same moral standing as humans, he does so only to make another point. Those who get all worked up about protecting animals should be placing the same passion and intensity on protecting the poor of the world.

Pope Francis believes that humans, especially in the developed world, should willingly retreat from hard-earned progress and take steps backwards. "A fragile world, entrusted by God to human care, challenges us to devise intelligent ways of directing, developing, and limiting our power."[31] "We have the freedom needed to limit and direct technology."[32] This hints to one of the primary, dark philosophical tenets of the current pope: that people and human progress are inherently bad. Under Pope Francis, the Church is a secular instrument to tell us how to behave, which technology advancements not to use, and who deserves restitution.

After reading the encyclical, one comes away with the impression that Pope Francis is a full-blown socialist and a staunch anti-capitalist. All the talk of Mother Earth, the natural balance of things, and Saint Francis are nothing more than a smoke screen for income and wealth redistribution, with the Church sitting at the head of the decision-making table and in the middle of the money flow, like moneychangers in the temple.

If this view of the pope seems harsh, contemplate the following quotes from the encyclical:

> "Christian tradition has never recognized the right to private property as absolute or inviolable."[33]

> "[T]he Church teaches there is always a social mortgage on private property."[34]

> "This calls into serious question the unjust habits of a part of humanity."[35]

Like all views on collectivism, communism, socialism, and income/ wealth redistribution through history, Francis wants to level a playing field by dragging down those doing the best and achieving the most.

Positing mankind and society are ruining Mother Earth exposes the Church to a criticism: that it bans contraception. It doesn't take an environmental scientist or a pope to figure out that if you are concerned about high levels of consumption, exhaustion of natural resources, pollutants, poverty, and other environmental crises, one of the biggest drivers in all these is population growth. A study conducted by the East-West Center and Berkeley published in *Science* correlated birth rate and economic data from forty countries and showed that a birth rate less than the replacement birth rate (2.1 children per woman) improves standards of living.[36] But Francis is in a state of holy denial by shooting down any notion of reduced birth rates being a solution to improving the state of the poor. The Church will never have an ounce of credibility on the environment as long as it continues to demand that followers keep having children at a rate above what poor families, developing societies, and the environment can reasonably support in terms of food, shelter, and healthcare.

FRANCIS'S TROUBLING HISTORY WITH OPPRESSIVE REGIMES

If you are a dictator in a banana republic presiding over a collapsed society, you love Pope Francis. If you are a reclusive despot looking to instigate nuclear confrontation on the Korean peninsula, you adulate Pope Francis. If you are a hard-line ayatollah in the Mideast scheming the demise of Christianity, Pope Francis is the best pope you've had in your lifetime. If you are a smiling, new-age communist strongman in the world's most populous country looking to tighten your grip over domestic freedoms and desiring to flex your muscle globally, Francis is a dream come true. Dictators, communists, socialists, and warmongers the world over are ardent supporters of the current pontiff.

The pope's views on nuclear proliferation run counter to common sense, evidenced by this from the encyclical: "We need but think of the nuclear bombs dropped in the middle of the twentieth century . . . In whose hands does all this power lie, or will it eventually end up? It is extremely risky for a small part of humanity to have it."[37]

Francis is making a case for nuclear proliferation across the globe. His position could be interpreted to be that it is safer and better for mankind if everyone has nuclear weaponry instead of just a certain few (albeit now growing) responsible players. Thus, two big fans of Pope Francis should be the leaders of Iran and North Korea. This is particularly ironic considering North Korea intensely suppresses religious freedom and Iran systemically works to eradicate Christianity inside and outside its borders. Nevertheless, Pope Francis backs their nuclear ambitions. Intentionally or unintentionally, he argues that the world will be a safer place with Iran, North Korea, and others in the nuclear club, because the United States is the bigger nuclear threat, not them.[38]

Modern-day Venezuela under the legacy of the late Hugo Chávez and current dictatorship of Nicolas Maduro is one of the most oppressive countries on the planet. The people of Venezuela have suffered badly under both dictators. Security forces regularly assault and kill protestors, employing tactics of shooting into crowds, running over people with armored vehicles, gang beatings, and extended torture. The assaults occur at hospitals, schools, private homes, malls, and even the National Assembly. Food shortages force people to queue up in lines at 3:00 A.M., forage through garbage, eat cats and dogs, suffer widespread malnutrition, and starve. The rule of law has broken down, power blackouts are common, and anarchy reigns in the streets with people left to fend for themselves against crime and gangs. Healthcare is nonexistent and infant mortality rates are horrific.

Venezuela is also overwhelmingly Catholic. You would think a pope who is a native of South America and concerns himself with the plight of poor Catholics would be a vocal and outspoken critic of the Venezuelan regime. Yet despite Venezuelan bishops speaking out repeatedly in support of civil rights and the need for order, Francis and his envoy to Venezuela have been somewhere between silent to accommodating to the Venezuelan dictatorship. When the Church makes a request to Maduro for releasing political prisoners or holding fair elections, he simply ignores them and Pope Francis refuses to continue to push the issues. The pope has been supportive of the dictator by hosting him at the Vatican and describing the opposition as divided.[39]

Why is the pope so reluctant to take a strong stance in opposition to the Venezuelan regime? Why at times does he come across as blatantly supportive? The reason ties directly to Francis's preferences for socialism and communism. This is a pope who accepted from Bolivian dictator Evo Morales a crucifix adorned with a hammer and sickle; who considers Fidel Castro a great ecologist; and illogically keeps within his inner circle advisors who view China as the epitome of Catholic teachings in action.[40, 41, 42]

Chinese President Xi Jinping has a plan to tighten and limit domestic reforms and freedoms, both economic and social, despite the Chinese constitution granting religious freedom. President Xi, like any good communist, is an avowed atheist and has publicly stated his view that religion is a threat to the Chinese state.[c] He proudly proclaims a goal of Sinicizing all religions, which means the government controls all forms of religious thought, freedoms, and doctrine to the point where all religion is snuffed out.

Meanwhile, Chinese Catholics are enduring everything from imprisonment to the tearing down of churches. Catholics who have stayed true to their faith often hide in underground churches, instead of following the anti-Vatican and government-backed Chinese Patriotic Catholic Association. In early 2018, the government instituted new laws that require religious institutions to get state approval for teaching curriculum and a host of other activities.

Key to the Chinese government's strategy to destroy Catholicism is the state naming bishops in defiance of the Vatican's choices for those slots. President Xi understands that if one usurps the pope's fundamental authority in naming the leaders of the Church inside China, the government gains two advantages. The first is the state can place bishops who are more than eager to enforce communist doctrine across the Catholic Church inside China. The second advantage is the government challenges and debases Pope Francis's authority by defying one of the most fundamental powers the pope has in naming Church leaders.

Vatican-appointed bishops and cardinals, such as the retired bishop of Hong Kong, Cardinal Zen, have begged Francis to stand up to the Communist Party and to back increasingly oppressed Catholics in China.[d] Cardinal Zen, whose nickname "tiger" comes from his ability to articulate zingers and sharp one-liners, knows what he is talking

---

c   In a 2016 speech at a state-sponsored conference on religion, Xi stated that party members should, "never find any of their beliefs in any religion," and be, "firm Marxist atheists."

d   Cardinal Zen in an open letter to the pope stated that he believed the Vatican was selling out to the state-controlled Catholic Church in China.

about when it comes to the Chinese government oppressing Catholicism and Catholics. As far back as the 1980s he has worked to bring the government along a path to reasonable coexistence with the Vatican and Catholicism. Years of experience led him to conclude the atheist government's only interest in Catholicism was to control any organized religion, including Catholicism.

Pope Francis turned a deaf ear and a blind eye to Cardinal Zen. Frustratingly, Francis not only refused to stand up to President Xi, he shockingly moved to appease him. In February 2018, the Vatican indicated it would accept as legitimate seven bishops who were originally placed by the government, in defiance of and without the approval of the Vatican. Reports allege that two of these seven state-selected bishops engaged in relationships with women and may have children. What Francis has agreed to with Xi is conjecture since the Vatican refuses to release the text of the original 2018 agreement or the renewed October 2020 agreement. Meanwhile, the pope refused to meet with the octogenarian Cardinal Zen, who traveled to Rome to plead the case for millions of Chinese Catholics. Rather than meet him, the pope left the 86-year-old cardinal standing in the winter cold of Saint Peter's Square, holding his letter to Francis in his numb, frail hands.[e]

Why is Francis so eager to appease a clear anti-Catholic communist state? There are two potential reasons. The first is Francis's apparent sympathies toward socialism and communism and his negative views of capitalism and free enterprise.

The second potential reason for the pope's China appeasement is less complex. Francis may be willing to sell out millions of oppressed Chinese Catholics in exchange for a deal with the communist government whereby he can raise his global profile. Francis's profile would gain from announcing détente with the Chinese government on the naming of bishops; a historic trip to China that would garner global

---

[e]   Italian media reported that although Pope Francis refused to hold an audience with Cardinal Zen, he promised to read the letter.

attention by slobbering global elites; and reestablishing official Vatican diplomatic relations with China that were severed in the early 1950s. Pope Francis may not be able to resist the lure of, and the epic photo-op created by, holding mass in Tiananmen Square. Francis is obsessive about his personal image and legacy. President Xi understands him and is prepared to extract maximum leverage.

Pride is the most serious of the seven deadly sins; it is a dangerously corrupt selfishness combined with putting one's own desires before the welfare of others. Sadly, Francis has committed the sin of pride when it comes to the appeasement of the Chinese communist state.[43] Francis's shameful appeasement of the most anti-religious regime on earth mirrors two earlier decisions by the Vatican: accepting the Iron Curtain's religious oppression during the Cold War, and making a deal with Hitler in the 1930s that helped increase his power. Abandoning Chinese Catholics in the coming years is something Francis will have to answer for in the afterlife. For now, antipope Xi leads the Catholic Church in China.

THE ENEMY OF HUMAN PROGRESS

To fortify the case against modern man, capitalism, and technology the pope says, "Men and women have constantly intervened in nature, but for a long time this meant being in tune with and respecting the possibilities offered by the things themselves. It was a matter of receiving what nature allowed, as if from its own hand. Now, by contrast, we are the ones to lay our hands on things, attempting to extract everything possible from them while frequently ignoring or forgetting the reality in front of us."[44]

This view defies history. First, mankind has a long and storied history of understanding nature as something to be tamed by brute force, not by gently orchestrating a sustainable ballet with Mother Nature. Think about how Americans cleared forests, leaving no tree standing, ran buffalo herds off cliffs indiscriminately, dammed rivers, and drained wetlands. Later, interstate highways wiped out everything in their paths. Today, man is more in touch with nature than was the case in most of modern human history.

Second, situations where mankind accepts what nature has to offer is a recipe for disaster. Sometimes, nature gives us disease and pestilence. Without modern medicine we would have had to receive what nature dealt us in the form of epidemics and widespread death. Here and there, nature gives us extreme cold. Without fossil fuels we would freeze to death or be forced to abandon colder climates altogether. At times, nature delivers drought. Without fertilizers, chemicals, and irrigation we would starve. Anytime man is placed in a position where he must accept what nature offers, he is randomly exposed to the prospect of a miserable, short life.

Francis assures us that, "Nobody is suggesting a return to the Stone Age."[45] That's likely true since there was no Catholic Church during the Stone Age and therefore no need for a pope. No, Pope Francis is suggesting a return to a time of ignorance where mankind followed the papacy blindly.

THE SOCIALIST GOSPEL ACCORDING TO COMRADE FRANCIS

Francis appears to fancy himself a socialist economics professor instead of a spiritual leader, when he writes, "It is essential we prioritize the goal of access to steady employment for everyone."[46] Pope Francis is stealing a line from his predecessor Pope Benedict here. Someone should tell Pope Francis of the economic devastation that environmental extremism in the form of U.S. federal regulations has cast upon Appalachia the past ten years. Environmental zealots relegated a generation into government reliance and worse. Pope Francis is well-advised to heed his own belief that, "the disappearance of a culture can be just as serious, or even more serious, than the disappearance of a species of plant or animal."[47]

The pope also seems to prefer subsistence farmers using a donkey and hand tools working smaller plots of land, so we would eat less and potentially starve. He writes, "Economies of scale, especially in the agricultural sector, end up forcing smallholders to sell their land or to abandon traditional crops."[48] Economies of scale, coupled with technology in the form of genetically modified crops and chemical fertilizers, drastically increase crop yields, which increase the availability of food and lower the cost of food. Both are excellent news for the poor of the world, but not for Francis.

Finally, the pope writes, "To ensure economic freedom from which all can effectively benefit, restraints occasionally have to be imposed on those possessing greater resources and financial power."[49] Workers of the world unite! That's the same pretense used by socialism and communism, jointly boasting a history of persecuting and murdering Catholic priests, nuns, and faithful around the world.

Francis's disdain for capitalism should not come as a shock and is consistent with many of his predecessors. The Catholic Church has always been a command-and-control entity dictating how you converse with God, how you procreate, and what you do with your money. Inevitably, followers revolted, who became frustrated with the denial of personal freedom. That's what happened with Martin Luther in 1517. The Protestant Reformation, sparked by Luther, served as a genesis for Western capitalism and free enterprise. It is ironic that the very thing Francis despises is the same thing his predecessors enabled.

FRANCIS RESURRECTS INDULGENCES

The Catholic Church once used indulgences to allow Catholics to absolve their sins or those of deceased loved ones by performing good acts or by making donations to the Church. Absolving sins meant the avoidance of punishment after death or an early release from purgatory for the deceased. An indulgence was the spiritual equivalent of an institutionalized "get-out-of-hell-free card."

Any religion that sets out to define for its followers what is sin and then turns around and accepts money from its followers to erase that sin is in trouble spiritually. Poor light cast by the heavy use of indulgences cloaked the Catholic Church in the Middle Ages up to Martin Luther's Ninety-Five Theses in 1517 and has for some time since. Martin Luther made indulgences a flash point when he referenced the use of them by Pope Leo X to help build the Basilica of St. Peter: "Why does not the pope, whose wealth today is greater than the wealth of the richest Crassus, build the basilica of St. Peter with his own money rather than with the money of poor believers?"[50] A key underpinning of the Protestant Reformation was that indulgences were unethical and that earthly religious authorities are not in a position to sell salvation that God alone can give.

Pope Francis resurrected the practice of selling indulgences, marketing it with the shiny and sleek wrapping of climate change. Today, Original Sin is reborn in any developed Western country with a high living standard that is enjoying abundant energy and the quality of life it delivers. And, once again, indulgences for these sins are offered in exchange for good acts and money.

Good acts indulgences include making regular denouncements of fossil fuels, self-imposition of energy efficiency mandates, policies to require renewable portfolios in power grids, and CO_2 caps. These good acts indulgences, however, are only a pathway to the pope's preference for monetary indulgences.

Monetary indulgences can be as small as a few hundred dollars per year for a U.S. citizen through higher electric and gas bills, or as much as hundreds of billions of dollars a year for a nation through carbon taxes and transfer payments between developed and undeveloped nations under various climate change treaties, frameworks, and accords.

A FADING CHURCH LED BY A FLAWED POPE

Catholicism in the United States and across the globe is in terminal decline. Less than 40% of American Catholics attend mass regularly, with attendance declines experienced across all age groups.[51] The terminal decay has been accelerated with the revelations of thousands of sexual assaults by priests against children that were covered up by the Church for years. Cardinals knew and did nothing or, even worse, continued to promote the sexual predators into higher posts or simply shifted them from one diocese to another.

Pope Francis espouses a deeply flawed·ideology that is destroying the Catholic Church. His personal aversion to liberty, capitalism, and freedom are poisons. Climate change extremism, socialist ideology, and dictator appeasement have been arrogantly wrapped in a cloak of papal infallibility. They will speed both Francis's spiritual end and Catholicism's decline.

Lord Acton keenly understood the difference between being a Catholic and a papist. Lord Acton was a practicing British Catholic throughout his life, always doing his best to follow the faith. But he also was willing to step up, take on, and challenge the papacy. Lord Acton's squabbles with the Vatican started in 1870 when Pope Pius IX established the dogma of papal infallibility, the same dogma that Pope Francis employs today much like an American president making excessive use of executive orders to expand his power grip. Acton saw that papal infallibility was an instrument that would be used to place popes beyond any accountability for their actions. Looking back to the behavior of popes throughout history, many Catholics know popes can never be infallible.

Acton's fight against papal tyranny and the doctrine of papal infallibility gave rise to his most famous quote, "All power tends to corrupt and absolute power corrupts absolutely."[52] The less famous, but most applicable part of this quote from 1887 was Acton's statement that, "There is no worse heresy than that the office sanctifies the holder of it."[53] An infallible pope is as flawed as the rest of us.

The encyclical *Laudato Si* is a dangerous and misleading document that poses great harm to everyone. Francis is calling for an abandonment of science, reason, and human ingenuity. To be anti-carbon is to be anti-human. *Laudato Si* is a step backward. Francis concludes all the suffering that would be inflicted on humans is a reasonable price to pay so long as the Catholic Church resurrects its lost power and global influence. The pope summed up his aims best in tortured prose:

> Environmental education has broadened its goals. Whereas in the beginning it was mainly centered on scientific information, consciousness-raising and the prevention of environmental risks, it tends now to include a critique of the "myths" of a modernity grounded in a utilitarian mindset (individualism, unlimited progress, competition,

consumerism, the unregulated market). It seeks also to restore the various levels of ecological equilibrium, establishing harmony within ourselves, with others, with nature and other living creatures, and with God. Environmental education should facilitate making the leap toward the transcendent which gives ecological ethics its deepest meaning. It needs educators capable of developing an ethics of ecology, and helping people through effective pedagogy, to grow in solidarity, responsibility and compassionate care.[54]

The papacy must focus on lifting the human condition and not on being a global high priest to Leeches. The current antipope must exit Saint Peter's in Rome for this to happen.

PROFILE #2: BONO

In general people put too much faith in the rich, the famous, the politicians, and not enough faith in themselves.

BONO

WHAT CELEBRITIES SAY VERSUS WHAT THEY DO

There are countless rock bands and entertainers who parade hypocrisy on a grand scale and enable the Leech to thrive. No one does hypocrisy better, bigger, or has been at it longer than U2. U2 has been my favorite band from high school in the early 1980s through to this day. *Achtung Baby* is one of the ten greatest rock albums of all time. The four Dubliners continue to reinvent themselves, take artistic risks instead of playing it safe, and remain relevant musically.[a] If only they would stick to the music.

U2 has always been a politically active band, going back to the Amnesty International days in the 1980s, Live Aid, and Band-Aid. Cue the mullet-laden Bono wailing, his lines from, *Do They Know It's Christmas?*[1] Through the years, U2 and Bono evolved from focusing their activism on specific areas where they led by example to preaching

---

a   Despite my love of U2's music, I must say some of the band's best work sounds similar to the talented acts of Simple Minds and INXS. Lots of *The Unforgettable Fire* (released 1984) sounds like Simple Minds' *New Gold Dream* (released 1982) while certain tracks on *Achtung Baby* (released 1991) echo INXS' *Kick* (released 1987) and *X* (released 1990) albums.

today about global idealistic concepts where Bono refuses to lead by example. More distressingly, Bono lives his personal life and runs his career counter to what he is lecturing the rest of us to do.

There's the long-standing joke that goes something like: What's the difference between God and Bono? *God doesn't strut around Dublin all day thinking he's Bono.* Go up to any music fan and say "U2" or "Bono" and ask for impressions. You will likely hear *activists, common good, charity, saving Africa,* and *for the people.* These impressions have been part of the U2 media machine for decades. We have been conditioned to think of Bono as the idealist kid who was waving a white flag around Red Rocks in the name of Irish peace years ago who morphed into the thought-provoking black leather-clad global populist in the odd eyewear.

But the reality is something altogether different. Old-fashioned self-interest seems to drive Capitalist Bono. His veneer is nothing more than a Madison Avenue schtick that is employed to help sell more albums, downloads, concert tickets, and merchandise. U2, with Bono as captain, is a corporate behemoth that uses the faux wrapping of "doing good" to simply make more money, much like Starbucks, Apple, and Whole Foods of the business world. It is not a sin to be successful, despite what Pope Francis says. Capitalism is good. But for a global celebrity to portray and preach to the masses one thing while practicing the opposite behind the scenes is hypocrisy.

A telling quote from the bard with the colored glasses can be found in the book titled *Bono on Bono* (really), "Losing money was not a nice feeling, and you've got to be careful because nothing begins the love of money more than the loss of money."[2] I'm not certain as to whether Bono has lost money in his early business dealings. I'm not convinced Bono has an unhealthy love of money. But I am sure that U2 has more than made up for any potential losses and bad experiences from the past and that today, as a business entity, the band looks to rationally grow profit and wealth—not that there is anything wrong with that. What is wrong is saying or singing one thing into the mic and doing something different when no one is looking.

Bono refers to himself as a "factivist" in his TED Talk.[3] Yes. Bono gives TED Talks. Yet let's lay out the facts on Bono. The culmination of his and U2's actions through the years tell an interesting story.

HAVE YOU SEEN THE SIZE OF BONO'S CARBON FOOTPRINT?

Despite climate change being a complicated issue that perplexes even the most advanced computer simulation models, Bono has developed an impressive set of positions on it, and he has not been shy about articulating those positions, as shown by the following quotes.

Speaking in Tokyo in 2008 Bono said, "My prayer is that we become better in looking after our planet."[4]

Bono at Davos in 2008: "Turns out that the climate crisis is going to exacerbate that inequality. And in fact, undo all of the work that we've been trying to do over the years. So now we have to take that into our world view, that's what I'm going to do with Al Gore's tutelage and others, and try to figure out coherence, so that we have a real plan for how we can leave behind a better planet than what we were born into."[5]

The following gem is from *Time* in 2012: "The extraction of oil, coal and minerals brought, and still brings, a cost to the environment."[6] Along with: "When a nation is over-reliant on one or two commodities like oil or precious minerals, corrupt government ministers and their dodgy associates hoard profits and taxes instead of properly allocating them to schools and hospitals."[7]

Bono carefully constructed those statements to prove the conviction he and the band have for their eco-warrior props. But let's look at U2's 360° world stadium tour in 2009–2011 and the logistical organization required to put on the show. It would be an understatement to say that the band's stage and equipment requirements have come a long way from what they needed to perform in the early 1980s at small clubs like Pittsburgh's Decade.[b] Bono needed a statement that flaunted how

---

b   This was during the *Boy* tour on April 21, 1981. For the set list, check out http://www.u2gigs.com/show292.html.

the band was the biggest in the world. Bono's megalomania physically manifested itself with the 360° stage, which checked in at a weight of 190 tons, a height of 165 feet, and a surface area over 28,000 square feet.

Bands like U2, beguiled by the mega-stadium tours, typically use multiple stages that they sequence in advance. The 360° tour simultaneously deployed multiple behemoths. Each stage required 120 semi-trucks to transport. To move between continents, the stage at times was transported via faster, but more carbon-intensive, air instead of sea. Tour manpower totaled 137 traveling production crew and 120 local crew. The band members during the tour flew over 70,000 miles in their private jet. The jet was stationed in southern France, near the band's Cote d'Azur holiday villas.

The equipment, crew, and band members are transported using engines that run on carbon. The electricity used during the show approaches the demand for a small city. The massive, cumulative electricity appetite of the 360° tour is generated from the power grid, the majority of which comes from fossil fuel energy. Add in the carbon emissions from concert goers traveling to attend the shows and you have an epic carbon footprint. A large part of that carbon footprint is tied to nothing more than window dressing glitz that doesn't change a single note or improve sound quality by a decibel. This egregious carbon footprint satisfies the ego and vanity of the band alone.

U2 is more than happy to cover up its massive carbon footprint with a film of chic, politically correct sustainability. U2 announced that it would purchase carbon offsets as penance for the environmental impact of the large production, estimated to be up to 65,000 metric tonnes of carbon dioxide (nearly 72,000 standard U.S. tons).[8] That's approximately the same amount emitted in flying a passenger plane 34 million miles, or flying the band to Mars and back. In addition to the carbon offsets, the band also set up a page on PickupPal so that people could carpool to concerts in an attempt to lower the tour's carbon footprint. An environmental consultant calculated that to offset the tour's first-half 2009 emissions, the band would have had to plant over

20,000 trees.[9] In an interview with BBC Radio, U2's guitarist, the Edge, sounded exasperated at the scrutiny the band's excess was drawing and had the audacity to state, "We'd love to have some alternative to big trucks bringing the stuff around but there just isn't one."[10] How about a smaller stage?

There is also Bono's pet cause of fighting developing world poverty. Bono has been a vocal advocate of African poverty eradication, aid, and debt relief. He dedicated an entire TED Talk to the subject in 2013, which was chock-full of cute and glib one-liners rolled together with flashy data graphics. To his credit, Bono starts out on an accurate roll in the talk, highlighting significant progress in the developing world, sub-Saharan Africa included, reflected over the past few decades via lower child mortality rate, reduced extreme poverty levels, and increased numbers of AIDS patients receiving drug treatments.

Bono goes off the rails in his TED Talk, however, when he starts to attribute causes of these improvements in the developing world's quality of life. In Bono's mind, the drivers are debt relief and social media. And, in Bono's view, the biggest threats to sustaining the positive momentum are evil oil companies and U.S. budget cuts to aid programs.

Bono's view is lamentable because he woefully mis-assigns credit for what drove all this improvement over the past decades. The most important driver of the improved quality of life in the developing world has been access to affordable and reliable electricity generated by fossil fuels. The data speak unequivocally across the developing world: as carbon consumption and carbon dioxide emissions increase, infant mortality rate declines, life expectancy increases, education increases, and healthcare improves. The tandem of carbon use and carbon dioxide emissions is the most effective determinant of global quality of life.

Bono's view is ironic because he vilifies oil companies that work end-lessly, only in his imagination, to hide the payments of massive bribes to corrupt developing world governments. Companies that extract fossil fuel don't slow progress; they catalyze it. The answer to keeping the quality of life improving in the globe's poorer corners is simple:

accelerated access to affordable electrification. That only happens by extraction of fossil fuels like natural gas.

Converting more carbon in Africa into the magical electron would quickly improve the lives of millions. Even ONE, the lobbying organization Bono co-founded in 2004 and currently is a director of, states on its website that six out of ten people in sub-Sahara Africa live without access to electricity.[11] Yet, here is Bono talking about all the harm that fossil fuels do to the world. Bono unwittingly helps to keep hundreds of millions in the developing world in misery.

And he shamefully does so as one of the largest individual carbon dioxide emitters on the planet. Massive stages, sprawling mansions, and private jets all feed personal vanity and spew carbon dioxide. Urban legend, such as the popular yet unsubstantiated story of when he forgot his hat and had it chauffeured via taxis and flown first-class to catch up with him, is broadcasted to demonstrate how cool he is despite the carbon footprint that such an act would produce. Ridiculous excesses, such as a massive carbon dioxide belching yacht, are enjoyed in private, beyond the public eye.[12] With Bono, and his supposed environmental cred, hollow words and artificial image convolute truth and reality.

Such escapades can culminate in the billions of dollars. Bono, at times, is prone to associate himself with people of questionable character in the Wall Street world of environmentally conscious investing. In 2016, Bono teamed up with San Francisco–based investment giant TPG to create the cool-sounding Rise Fund. The $4 billion fund boldly touts its ability to grow companies to further the UN's sustainable development goals, and to improve the world.[13] The fund's founding executive, William McGlashan, is Bono's buddy and enjoyed a bit of rock-star status himself with favorable media attention showered on the politically correct Rise Fund. That is, until TPG parted ways with him in disgrace due to his alleged involvement in the national college admissions fraud scandal of 2019. McGlashan is accused of paying $50,000 to a college admissions consultant for fixing his son's standardized test scores and for creating a fake athletic profile of his son in order to secure admission to the University of Southern California.[14] If Bono or his eco-warrior partners can't behave socially-consciously on a personal level, why should we consider them authorities on much larger issues?

BONO MINIMIZES TAX WHILE HE LECTURES YOU TO PAY TAX

Bono does not suffer from a lack of confidence. Speaking at Expo 2015 in Milan, Bono stated, "These are big questions: can we face the problem of hunger in the world, can we fix the problem of poverty in the world, can we fix the problem of conflict in the world? With regard to the first two of those three, I can speak with confidence when I say yes, absolutely."[15]

Bono has been a huge advocate of rich countries, such as the United States and European nations, forgiving debt obligations of African nations. He has readily attached his name to efforts that include Jubilee 2000, a coalition of dozens of countries that in the 1990s strove for third world debt forgiveness by the year 2000. Bono also threw his support into Jubilee 2000's offshoot effort Drop the Debt, a celebrity platform for the debt relief movement. Bono's attention on debt relief didn't stop there. He was all-in on the UK-centric Make Poverty History campaign, which reached its crescendo in 2005 with its cute little wristbands, and the American version of Make Poverty History, the ONE campaign. The Make Poverty History campaign embraced as a core tenet the need to combat tax avoidance by the rich and powerful, which we will see shortly sits in ironic contrast to U2's tax planning.

Writing about his support for Jubilee 2000 in the January 1999 issue of the British magazine Q, Bono said, "Such debt relief would give crippled nations a chance to get up off their knees and walk again."[16] He called Jubilee 2000 one of, "the most inspirational thought[s] I bumped into."[17] At about the same time, in February of 1999, he was at the rock pulpit again, this time penning an editorial for the *Guardian* titled "World Debt Angers Me." In it he said, "Africa owes $227 billion to western creditors—$379 for every man, woman and child in Africa. She can do with spending that just on her children. . . . Consider: for every $1 the

West gives in aid to developing countries, $9 comes back in debt service."[18]

Debt forgiveness went from glib talk to reality. In 2005–2006, rich nations committed to forgive $100 billion in debt for poor nations meeting certain criteria, with most of the debt forgiveness earmarked for African nations that included Ghana, Mozambique, and Zambia. The $100 billion in debt forgiveness was on top of the aid rich countries had already provided to Africa through the years.

Consider the continent of Africa in total. Over the past fifty years, developed nations contributed over $1 trillion in some form of aid. Despite the vast sum, Africa today remains a basket case of inadequate government, rule of law, living conditions, health, and capital markets. Aid has not solved these issues, and some argue it has made things worse by creating and reinforcing a vicious cycle of inescapable dependency. For a compelling discussion on how conventional aid can deter development of the third world, read economist Dambisa Moyo's *Dead Aid*.[c] Interestingly, one of the supporting quotes on the book jacket comes from historian Niall Ferguson: "This reader was left wanting a lot more Moyo, and a lot less Bono."

Now, how about two country examples of debt forgiveness? Mozambique was one of the biggest beneficiaries of debt forgiveness, with its debt slashed from 86% of gross domestic product in 2005 to 9% the next year.[19] The country has built its debt back up and then some since then, currently sitting at over 100% of GDP.[20] Ghana's debt was 82% of GDP in 2005 just before the international community forgave about half of it. It's now up to 60% of GDP and growing.[21] In 2003 terms, Ghana's debt stood at $7.5 billion. The debt level, in today's dollars, is now nearly $40 billion.[22] We forgave the debt, Africa did not forget how to borrow or outspend, and we've rewarded poor fiscal discipline.[d]

---

c   Ms. Moyo's excellent work and courageous positions became the target of attacks from economist Jeffrey Sachs. The next chapter is on Sachs, a friend of Bono.

d   Making matters worse, opportunistic China swoops in, lending over $140 billion to African nations since 2000 with terms often demanding ownership of vital assets such as mines and ports to be turned over to the communist state in the event of default.

Let's lay the groundwork of today's situation with a bit of Irish history. Back in 1969, Irish Finance Minister Charles J. Haughey proposed a tax exemption for artists. The exemption applied to the income of artists, writers, and composers derived from the sale of their works. Artists, whether musical, literary, or visual, paid no income tax from the sale of their work if they set up shop in Ireland. Sure, there was paperwork and approvals needed, and the tax-exempted works had to be original and of cultural or artistic merit. (The thought of Irish government bureaucrats debating whether paint splotches on a canvas are original or have artistic merit should give you the chills).

If you were an artist, Ireland was the place to go or stay. The intent of the law was to help artists struggling to make ends meet. Guess what happened? Scores of artists moved to Ireland and enjoyed paying zero income tax from their earnings on their works. We are not talking about starving artists, mind you. We are talking about a who's who of celebrity stardom, especially those from the neighboring United Kingdom such as author Fredrick Forsyth, members of rock group Def Leppard, singer Lisa Stansfield, *Trainspotting* author Irvine Welsh, and alt-punk, new wave legend Elvis Costello.

Irish tax law also helped U2. Staying in Ireland, U2 avoided paying taxes to support needed programs for Ireland's less fortunate. Suffice to say that Ireland lost tens of millions of euros each year in tax revenues from wealthy celebrity artists, including Bono. All of this changed in 2006, when Minister of Finance Brian Cowen capped the tax exemption for artists at €250,000 a year. For incomes above that cap, a 41% rate plus additional levies would be applied on income from song royalties. As soon as the ink was dry on the new rules, guess what happened? U2 decided to move its publishing company to the Netherlands later that year.[23] Why the Netherlands? Because the Netherlands levied only a 5% tax on music royalties. Interestingly, the Rolling Stones had moved their publishing arm to the Netherlands years earlier. Rumor has it the Rolling Stones set the tax planning example that turned U2, Dutch.

In 2010, U2 Ltd. reportedly paid €16,500 in corporate tax in

Ireland to cover a modest book income, while between mid-2009 and mid-2011 U2 the band grossed hundreds of millions of dollars, primarily from the largest moneymaking tour in history.[24, 25] No one other than those running the U2 machine knows the true and full extent of what all the corporations, subsidiaries, and trusts earn, what they loan and borrow from each other, and what they pay in tax. U2's business structure and finances, although legal and compliant, are complex and not transparent.

The shadowy and opaque structure of U2's finances does not stop Bono from shamelessly promoting transparency in other industries. Recall Bono is a co-founder and director of ONE, the world-wide lobbying organization whose mission is to eradicate poverty in Africa by advocacy and public relations efforts. Part of ONE's agenda is, "helping secure legislation in the U.S., Canada and EU on transparency in the extractives sector to help fight corruption and ensure more money from oil and gas revenues in Africa is used to fight poverty."[26]

In Bono's 2013 TED Talk on extreme poverty, he smugly stands on a glitzy California stage calling for increased corporate and government transparency. He touts how he is an "evidence-based activist" that celebrates open data and number crunching.[27]

ONE, with Bono as co-founder and a director, is pushing the energy industry, corporations, and governments to be more transparent and to pay their fair share to fight poverty. Meanwhile, Bono and the U2 machine show us little when it comes to what they pay in tax and where they pay it. A founder, sitting on the board of a transparency advocacy group, who lectures on the topic, doesn't listen to his own admonitions.

While all this tax planning and offshoring by U2 was occurring behind the scenes, Bono was in full hypocritical regalia at a Croke Park concert in Ireland in 2005. The concert was just before the Irish government capped the artist exemption at €250,000 per year. Prime Minister Bernie Ahern had earlier pledged 0.7% of Ireland's GDP to African aid by 2007. The prime minister later changed the target date to 2012 so he could shift more money into needed domestic programs. At the concert,

Ahern was in attendance and Bono did not miss a perfect opportunity to embarrass the prime minster in front of thousands of Irish. Bono stated, "I am aware An Taoiseach Bertie Ahern is in the crowd here tonight. He has promised to give 0.7 per cent of our GDP to Africa and I urge him not to break that promise."[28] Bono didn't stop there, adding, "I know it's hard to build a hospital in Abuja, Nigeria, when you need to build hospitals here."[29] As you might expect, the mini lecture by Bono put the Prime Minister in a tough spot. All this posturing at Croke Park occurred while Bono and U2 were enjoying millions in tax-free royalty income. Picture thousands of working blokes in the audience paying income tax to pay for African and Irish hospitals, a Prime Minister in the audience pushing for 0.7% of Irish GDP to go to African aid, and a guy onstage with a mic lecturing all of them, milking most of them on ticket prices, and paying little in Irish taxes.

Irish comedian Graham Norton put it best when he said, "People like Bono really annoy me. He goes to hell and back to avoid paying tax. He has a special accountant. He works out . . . tax loopholes. And then he's asking me to buy a well for an African village. Tarmac the road outside your house, you tight-wad!"[30] Irish singer Sinead O'Conner had a to-the-point quote on the subject with her now famous tweet of, "I pay my taxes in Ireland, Bozo."[31]

If all the U2 tax machinations weren't enough for you, consider the Paradise Papers. The Paradise Papers are a trove of documents from the elite offshore law firm Appleby that were hacked and released to the media in 2017. On release, the public became aware of numerous celebrities and organizations that were secretly (but legally) avoiding taxes by sheltering profits in offshore tax havens, such as Malta and the British Bailiwick of Guernsey. I mention Malta and Guernsey because they happened to be the havens that an investment entity, that Bono was a minority owner of, used to avoid paying tax on profits from a Lithuanian shopping mall, one acquired in 2007. The extent of the activities unveiled by the Paradise Papers was impressive: an entity named Nude Estates was established in Malta. Nude Estates proceeded to pay five million pounds for the shopping mall in Lithuania, and then Nude Estates transferred its ownership in the mall to another entity, Nude Estates 1, which was established in Guernsey.[32] Malta touts an ultra-low tax rate for foreigners of 5% of company profits while Guernsey doesn't tax profits at all. When Bono was outed with the release of the Paradise Papers, he deflected by sheepishly saying he was distressed, unaware of the tax avoidance machinations, and that he was a relatively small investor in the Nude Estate entities.[33]

Bono's history of public posturing and U2's private financial actions are troubling because of what happened while all of this was unfolding. An especially nasty recession hit Ireland in the second half of 2008. The stock market crashed, property values collapsed, Irish banks had to be rescued by the EU and IMF, the government collapsed in elections, and unemployment skyrocketed. It was an economic perfect storm, not seen in Ireland in generations. If there was ever a time a nation needed its most famous and wealthy native sons to step up and simply pay their fair share, it was during the post-2008 recession period. Unfortunately, that never happened. By then, U2's royalty income was being safely shielded in the Netherlands. As a giant protest balloon by Art Uncut at the Glastonbury Festival in 2011 asked, "U Pay Tax 2?"[34]

HOW BONO GROWS HIS BRAND AND WALLET
UNDER COVER OF "DOING GOOD"

Bono found the time to continue leveraging his public posturing of doing good to help launch Product Red in 2006 at the World Economic Forum in Davos, Switzerland.[35] Product Red couples well-established global corporate brands and products with a range of global health initiatives funded through the Global Fund to Fight AIDS, Tuberculosis, and Malaria. Product Red is housed underneath ONE. The idea of Product Red is devilishly tempting: what if you linked some of the best brands in the world with charitable giving to pursue things like an HIV cure? You could persuade the consumer that by buying these goods or services the consumer wasn't being selfish and deaf to those less fortunate. Quite the opposite; suddenly an enlightened consumer was making a true difference!

Product Red brings serious brands to the table: you can do your part of saving the world by buying Converse shoes, upgrading Apple devices, riding your Vespa, gulping down your Starbucks, playing the special version of *Angry Birds*, writing with your Mont Blanc pen, listening to music on Beats headphones, and using the AMEX card.[e] If you have any doubt about the legitimacy of your warm and fuzzy feelings coexisting with your consumerism, don't worry because a slew of celebrities are there to tell you just how awesome Product Red is. At the head of the celebrity pack sits one of the founders of Product Red: Bono.

But it's never simple with Bono. We need to look a little closer at Product Red to see if there is something different going on from the marketing façade. A fundamental concern about Product Red is a lack of transparency. Product Red is not a typical charity or not-for-profit. Instead, it is property owned by a private company, known as The Persuaders LLC.[36] A private company that is hard to delve into. It is not clear who owns The Persuaders LLC. You can't tell how much each company pays Product Red to be part of the product line, and you can't see the cash flows between partner companies, The Persuaders LLC, and Product Red.

Another concern is simple math, even though the math is hard to come by due to the lack of transparency. At issue is the amount of money Product Red eventually kicks up to the Global Fund relative to the amount of money the product sponsors and Product Red spend on marketing the campaign. The best data out there is from 2007, but it is telling. At that time, it was estimated that over $100 million was spent on Product Red marketing while only about $18 million was sent up to the Global Fund.[37] You don't have to be a Madison Avenue ad executive to realize that the math is troubling. The Product Red website quotes a $650 million cumulative contribution to the Global Fund, yet data verifying that statement were not found.

---

e   Product Red brands come and go often. For a current list of affiliated brands, go to www.red.org.

Now that people are buying more products due to the Product Red campaign, doesn't anyone have an issue with exploitation of the developing world by mining more minerals for consumer electronic products and by working more people for longer hours and at outrageously poor wages to make fashionable clothes? Bono one day is lecturing us on the need to reduce the consumption of things like fossil fuels and minerals and for the need for fair commerce with the developing world. Then, the next day he turns around and encourages us to spend more of our money buying stuff we really don't need—stuff manufactured and consumed to the detriment of the developing world.

The biggest worry about Product Red is the negative impact it has on direct contributions to charities by consumers. When you think about it, Product Red is a vehicle that allows consumers in rich countries to spend more on stuff, conspicuously consume more stuff, have less disposable income to donate to charity, have a convenient excuse to not donate to a charity, and to feel really good about all of it (*I gave when I bought the high end vodka*). Product Red muscled out true charities and not-for-profits using the most powerful celebrity public relations and corporate marketing machines on earth.

So why are corporations and Bono doing it? For Bono, two potential reasons come to mind: his ego and his wallet. Product Red has corralled the biggest brands in the world. Those brands and participating products directly or indirectly enlarge the demand for U2 products, whether it be CDs, books, downloads, concert tickets, or other merchandise. Bono gets a seat at the big-boy table of global corporations and gets to hitch U2 offerings to the sales platforms of multi-billion-dollar corporations. Product Red successfully exposes U2, its brand, and products to a wider audience than ever before.

All the networking and cross-business interests via Product Red helps Bono to cash in. Louis Vuitton serves as a good example. In 2010, a print advertisement for Louis Vuitton titled "Every Journey Began in Africa" featured Bono and Mrs. Bono. None other than famed photographer Annie Leibovitz shot the ad. You've probably seen it if you are either a

U2 or Louis Vuitton fan: Bono and wife walking from a small vintage propeller airplane that landed in the middle of the African bush; Bono toting nothing but his weathered guitar case and an expensive bag. This was just one ad in a series of celebrity Louis Vuitton shots that constituted the luxury bag maker's Core Values campaign from 2007 to 2012. The ads featured celebrity jocks, rockers, artists, three astronauts, and Mikhail Gorbachev. Bono and wife donated their fees to appear in the campaign to TechnoServe (a nongovernmental organization that fosters enterprise in the developing world), the Conservation Cotton Initiative (supports sustainable farming in Africa), and Chernobyl Children's Project International. Louis Vuitton said a portion of their proceeds from bag sales would go to the same charities. Each bag had a price of around $5,000.

If this was for charity, how did Bono personally gain? In the ad, both Bono and his wife were wearing clothes that were part of a clothing line named Edun. Guess who created Edun? Mrs. Bono. Guess who bought 49% of Edun in 2009 from Mrs. Bono? The parent of Louis Vuitton, LVMH. What's good for alleviating African poverty is good for bag sales. What's good for bag sales is good for Edun. What's good for Edun is good for LVMH and Bono. The trusty formula was at work: talking up a sympathetic cause (African poverty), finding a multi-billion dollar retail giant to partner with (LVMH), plastering himself in media globally pushing all that luxury gear (Core Values ads), convincing consumers to shell out thousands of dollars for a handbag to save the world (proceeds were donated to…), and then discreetly getting deals done in conference rooms (selling 49% of Edun and retail sales of Edun clothes resulting from the ad campaign). The formula is a beneficial one for Bono.

If you have a smartphone or MP3 player, chances are you experienced first-hand how the relationship with the behemoth of big business, Apple, was used to pull dollars from consumers' pockets into U2's pockets. The first way was clever. The second way was anything but clever.

The clever episode occurred in 2004 when Bono approached Apple founder Steve Jobs about featuring U2 in the now-famous silhouette commercial for the Apple MP3 player. This was a clear break for U2 from its past stances on promoting products. U2 was one of those bands that looked down on other artists who took money in exchange for product endorsements or were featured in ads. U2 and Bono were above that form of prostitution. They had principles and artistic integrity! Well, when Bono saw what Jobs and Apple were up to with the iconic MP3 player commercials, he wanted in. What happened was the featuring of U2 playing their single "Vertigo" across TVs, the internet, and billboards globally. Sales of MP3 players went up. Sales of U2 song and album downloads went up.

The band was quick to point out that Apple didn't pay it for appearing in the ads. What money was made was earned without U2 sacrificing their artistic integrity and principles. Well, sort of. As part of the "Vertigo" advertisement, Apple offered a limited edition U2 MP3 player, complete with all the regular bells and whistles but also emblazoned with engraved autographs of the four band members. U2 received a royalty on every one sold. Apple made U2's new album at the time, *How to Dismantle an Atomic Bomb,* and the first single "Vertigo," available exclusively through its website for about a month before being available in stores. Apple and U2 unveiled a digital box set of 400 U2 tracks (dubbed *The Complete U2*) that U2 aficionados could own with a click of the mouse and $149. For those shelling out the $349 for the U2 special edition MP3 player, you were rewarded with a $50 coupon that could be used if you decided to purchase *The Complete U2* digital box set.

If you want to see a classic roasting of Bono, U2, and the Apple scheme, watch Bruce Springsteen's speech for U2 at their hall of fame induction (can be found on YouTube, search "Bruce Springsteen inducts U2 into Hall of Fame"). The Boss was spot-on in his induction speech.

THE *SONGS OF INNOCENCE* DOWNLOAD DEBACLE

The not-so-clever episode of U2 and Apple teaming up to separate consumers from their wallets was one of the most famous global invasions of privacy ever. In 2014, a decade after the silhouette "Vertigo" commercials, U2 was preparing to release the album *Songs of Innocence*. Over the decade, Apple had come a long way with the ubiquitous introduction of the smart devices and digital downloads. Such a long way that users tallied somewhere around half a billion and the traditional modes of music promotion and sales were demolished by digital media creative destruction. One thing that had not changed was Bono's and U2's willingness to take a high road of righteousness publicly and then turn around and do something contrary to that position.

Bono once quipped that, "Until it's on the radio or online, it's not real. With U2, our album isn't finished until it's in the stores."[38] He wasn't joking. In fact, he was being modest because in 2014 U2 and Apple had millions of users all over the world wake up to find *Songs of Innocence* downloaded into accounts and onto devices without consent.[39] To make matters worse, it was far from obvious to most account holders how to remove the album from the millions of smart devices. The event was on a scale of a state-sponsored cyberattack.

The band was ecstatic at first, bragging that the event represented the biggest release and largest "ownership" of an album in the history of music.[40] A week after the forced ownership, Apple and U2 were in full damage control and offered up a process to remove the music from devices. Bono tried to downplay the situation by acting as if simple spam or harmless junk mail happened. Of course, these were not great analogies since the forced downloads bypassed security firewalls. The amount of precious bandwidth needed to make room for the force-fed album and the time spent to remove the product from smart devices was cumulatively astounding. The invasion of privacy to users who had a reasonable expectation of privacy for the content of their smart devices was egregious. The arrogance that both Apple and U2 displayed was disturbing.

Why did U2 do it? No one outside the band may ever know. Regardless, the *Songs of Innocence* fiasco was the climax of hypocrisy in the book of Bono. Can you imagine how Bono would feel if suddenly anyone or any corporation could invade his privacy at a whim? Do you think Bono would agree that a company or a government could dictate to the masses which artist or art is acceptable and which is not? The incident, although lawful, was hypocritical and a violation of the norms of modern society.

ANTI-GUN RANTS ON STAGE AND GUN VIOLENCE PROFIT OFFSTAGE

There is one last glorious example of the "Bono rules" in action: the issues of gun control and gun violence. Bono has always been a proponent for stricter gun control laws, including participation in the celebrity-stacked Voices Against Violence Global Partnership, which advocates for tighter gun control laws. There is a bevy of U2 concert performances where Bono appropriated songs in the U2 catalog to put a gun violence and gun control spin on them. The most prevalent example is *Bullet the Blue Sky* where Bono would play a video at the intro of the song mocking Charlton Heston's views on guns, showing images of little kids playing with guns, and then later in the song Bono would shout out statistics and projections on how many more deaths will occur from gun violence in the United States over the coming years.[41] There's also the little-known tidbit that, according to producer Steve Lillywhite, the song "Vertigo" was originally intended by Bono to have a gun control theme and was originally titled "Native Son."

Bono was a co-founder of Elevation Partners, a multi-billion-dollar private equity firm that invested in media and technology-focused companies. Elevation's focus was to help new media and technology companies apply their technology and build valuable businesses. One of Elevation's key investments was made in 2005 when it acquired Bioware/Pandemic Studios, which was an alliance between two videogame makers. What types of videogames does Bioware/Pandemic create and market to mostly young and impressionable minds? Ones like *Mercenaries: Playground of Destruction*, *Full Spectrum Warrior*, *Saboteur*, and *Mass Effect*. As the names imply, these games are classic first-person, shoot-em-up fare where you try to destroy as many things

or people as you can, usually with some form of a firearm. In 2007
Elevation sold Bioware/Pandemic Studios to Electronic Arts for a cool
$620 million in cash.[42]

BONO'S UNITED NATIONS MOMENT

The vast majority of Bono's actions in pursuing his self-interests are what
makes free enterprise hum: creating great music, enjoying high quality
of life through energy consumption, minimizing tax, promoting the
brand, guarding privacy, and making money through shrewd business
transactions. The problem is the hypocrisy that manifests when you
superimpose Bono's words over these actions. That hypocrisy was on
display a couple of years ago in New York.

In the summer of 2018, Bono donned his tinted glasses and spoke at
the United Nations to lobby for Ireland being added to the 15-member
Security Council in 2021 as a non-permanent member. In his speech
he made the case for Ireland by emphasizing how the Emerald Isle is
a nation of storytellers and how it fully understands the importance of
compromise. Bono believes both of those traits would be critical to the
United Nations in the coming years.

Bono then went on to emphasize how the international world
order was facing an existential crisis. Which institutions facing crises
did Bono feel Ireland could save? He ran off a murderer's row of
Leech-dominated institutions including the United Nations, the
European Union, the G-7, and the World Trade Organization. The
speech even threw in an obligatory climate change tantrum on the
United States' astute withdrawal from the Paris Climate Agreement
with, "Paris . . . fuck!"[43]

This staged Bono-rambling on global matters he knows little about
in front of elitist bureaucrats working for global organizations covered
by a fawning leftist-dominated media is nothing new for the front man.
One line in the speech sticks out. Picked up across the global media,
Bono said, "You can count on Ireland to do its part in that work." [44]
This statement is the pinnacle of a career opportunist's sanctimony.

Bono breathlessly speaks for Ireland and tells the world that the Irish will do their part.

Yet it serves another purpose. Bono advocating to save failing global institutions is the Leech use of a naïve, attention-addicted celebrity and is right out of the Leech way playbook.

PROFILE #3: JEFFREY SACHS

"There's nothing more distasteful than an academic having to, like, trot out his credentials. You really come off as a jerk when you do that."

REZA ASLAN

"[Intellectuals are those] who talk and write about subjects outside of their professional competence ... have no direct responsibility for practical affairs ... [and] cannot help nibbling at the foundations of capitalist society."

JOSEF SCHUMPETER

EXEMPLAR OF ELITIST PRETENSION

Dr. Jeffrey Sachs is an elitist. His website sports a bio that runs nearly 2,000 words (see www.jeffsachs.org). Why? Because he is just that damn impressive. Sachs lives in a bubble of privilege, having spent his adult life in academia. Not just in run-of-the-mill academia mind you, but in two of the most insulated, out-of-touch bastions this nation has to offer: Harvard and Columbia Universities.

His official title when he joined Columbia in 2002 was the Quetelet Professor of Sustainable Development. How many working stiffs would love to hold a highly paid, tenured, and cushy job where the title defies any objective and consistent measure of accountability? Dr. Sachs spends his time traveling the world, giving interviews, delivering speeches, collecting praise, sitting on panels with do-nothing elites, and trying to figure out more efficient ways to suck resources from the Enablers, Creators, and Servers.

MODUS OPERANDI

Sachs's description of his modus operandi for his favorite theme of solving African poverty says a lot: "The way I look at it, it doesn't cost anything to ask for money. So I advise Africa's governments to come right out and demand money from the donor agencies—and then demand it again. And again. That's what I do. I write a letter. Then an op-ed. And then I throw a tantrum. In the end, the money may appear—if only so they can get rid of me."[1]

Jeff Sachs is far from a stereotypical professor who is content to publish obscure pieces in journals that no one outside of a small cadre of academics will read. If there are camera lights, a live microphone, a reporter, or a crowd, Sachs runs toward it like a moth to a flame. His brand is continually projected, whether it is in an entertainment magazine (*Vanity Fair*) or at a rock concert (he and Bono from U2 are bosom buddies).[2] He's everywhere, and it's not by accident. You can even read in the *New York Times* how Sachs likes to spend his leisurely Sunday hour-by-hour.[3]

Sachs is at the confluence of a number of this book's subjects: Pope Francis and how his flawed encyclical on the environment is harming the poor; the lack of rigor in today's academia; public pension fund bureaucrats' penchant for clouding their fund's true financial health to focus on pushing favored ideology and others' transparency; and a rock star lecturing the rest of us on how to behave while he follows none of his own advice. Whether by chance or design, Sachs shares many of the same attributes.

Jeffrey Sachs has procured hundreds of millions of dollars under the banner of doing good for the global poor. Much of the money is used to feed bureaucratic organizations.

And, Sachs benefits from his endeavors. Look no further than the home he had when jumping from Harvard to Columbia. Columbia felt Dr. Sachs needed the right sort of digs to call home if he was going to build a bureaucratic organization. With Sachs's rhetoric on income inequality, his views on taxing the rich more, his support for Occupy Wall Street, and his shallow math, which argues African poverty could be eliminated with a small amount of Western wealth redistribution, you might think the good professor required nothing more than a log cabin.

The truth is quite the opposite. Columbia paid millions of dollars for a palatial pad in one of the toniest sections of Manhattan to give the Sachs family a home.[4] The university was careful to point out that the bottom two floors of the palace were to be used as a conference center for the Earth Institute and that Sachs would pay rent in return for his family occupying the upper three floors (yes, the total is five floors). If you try to find how much Sachs paid in rent and whether it reflected fair market value for such luxurious uptown accommodations, you will encounter the mysterious phrase "normal faculty rate."[5] Subsequently, Sachs moved to a multi-million dollar pad in the Upper West Side that is equipped with direct elevator access, a media room, fireplaces, terrace, chef's kitchen, and wine storage.[6] But don't worry; the building is LEED-certified, so it's green! It is comical how a person can walk out of a multi-million dollar house that only the top 0.1% of Americans can afford and commute with a straight face to a rally only blocks away to shout support to Occupy Wall Street.

Columbia and its affiliates promote Sachs. The process is linear and repeatable: use Columbia's or an affiliated organization's public relations machine to shine the media spotlight on him. Of course, he makes sure that message is only about poor Africans and a guy just wanting to help them. Then, go convince certain entertainment celebrities like Bono and Angelina Jolie or heads of state to promote your personal image to a wider audience. Then, start writing books and giving speeches, making sure that the books have a quote or foreword from your celebrity or heads of state friends, whom you can then name-drop in a speech. With all that hype, find a way to get mentioned in *Time* (back when people actually read the magazine) as one of the world's most influential people and encourage impressionable acolytes to create a Jeff Sachs fan club website that supports a presidential run (thankfully, the website went dark).[7] Then, repeat.

THE EARTH INSTITUTE

Sachs built a massive organization that sucks in huge sums of money by proclaiming moral imperatives. The money is then allocated to a cadre of affiliates connected to the host organization. If you look past the glossy, feel-good public relations of these entities, you will find a focused machine with the Earth Institute at Columbia University at the center.

Sachs sat at the helm of the Earth Institute, or EI, for fourteen years until he stepped down in 2016. The EI is a bureaucratic monster. It starts with the organization's mission: "Columbia's Earth Institute blends research in the physical and social sciences, education and practical solutions to help guide the world onto a path toward sustainability."[8] What is research in the social sciences and how does it blend with physical science? How about those practical solutions? Who gets to decide what is practical? Which metrics must one apply to discover something is a solution? How is sustainability quantified? Besides being massively condescending, this mission statement sets limitless boundaries and zero accountability.

The Earth Institute is not a small operation. This bureaucratic machine rakes in vast amounts of money and uses it to fund individuals, entities, and initiatives. The website of EI lists over 1,400 faculty and staff.[9] A sampling of titles will leave you bewildered: Research Scientist, Adjunct Research Scientist, Senior Research Scientist, Adjunct Associate Research Scientist, Special Research Scientist, Adjunct Associate Research Scholar, Senior Research Staff Assistant, Postdoctoral Research Fellow, Graduate Research Assistant, Scholar in Residence, Research Fellow, Senior Lecturer, Senior Technical Consultant, Post-Doctoral Research Scientist, and so on. Over time there have been staff on the payroll of this bureaucratic beast too that have the title of Curator (one can only wonder what they are curating), Anesthesia Technician (who or what is being drugged?), and Ordinary Seaperson (What's a seaperson? What do you have to achieve to graduate to the position of Ordinary Seaperson?). These ridiculous staff positions consume precious resources.

How do you pay for all these critical positions with their impressive titles? The revenue of the Earth Institute was over $120 million in fiscal 2014.[10] Two-thirds of that revenue came from government (i.e., your tax dollars) and the rest was from a combination of foundations, gifts, and endowment income. The tentacles of the Earth Institute burrow into those organizations through these money flows.

HOW THE EI FEEDS

The Earth Institute applies a crafty circular logic in the form of a proven recipe to keep the money flowing. First, you need a motivated actor. The motivated actor in this case is Columbia University and its various social science and humanities programs. Columbia is constantly on the prowl for nourishment. To sustain itself and grow, Columbia must find new and more efficient ways to procure funding. It's a four-step process.

Step 1. Start with the premise that there is an epic disaster, crisis, or Armageddon facing humankind—the larger the calamity, the better. Ideally, you want something that could strike within a generation, or better, one that currently exists where you argue that it could spread to affect your current or potential stakeholders. Scare the stakeholders but don't make the crisis too imminent or you will be exposed when the end of the world doesn't arrive on time. Climate change, excessive consumption, egregious consumerism, and peak food-oil-clean water are perfect calamities for this ploy. They are universal, looming disasters that aren't here now of course. Manhattan isn't under water; Whole Foods is well stocked; and oil is plentiful. But the threat will be at our doorstep soon, if we don't act. In thirty years, Manhattan will be under water, the grocery shelves will be empty, and we will have run out of oil. The Earth Institute has a history of embracing these types of boogeymen.

Step 2. Offer hope to a hyped problem through an expensive and unworkable solution. At this stage, everything is in place to allow the entity to start nourishing and propagating.

Step 3. It's feeding time. Dr. Sachs and the Earth Institute convince others to fund their activity. Funding sources include the government, foundations, organizations, and individuals via donations and grants.

The focus is on marketing a crisis so that people and organizations will provide more money.

Step 4. Once the Earth Institute/Sachs complex is up and feeding, it creates offspring. At first, these offspring may be substantively dependent on the Earth Institute, but after a while they grow to where they can also self-sustain and start sucking resources on their own. These offspring can range from a person to something as large as a multi-million-dollar program. The offspring can return the favor to the Earth Institute by coordinating the procuring of resources and perhaps sending a portion back.

For all this to succeed, one must constantly turn up the rhetoric no matter what, otherwise the effort dies.

THE MILLENNIUM VILLAGES PROJECT: SPAWN OF THE EI

What would happen if you took a motivated actor like Sachs, placed him in the academia culture of Columbia, had him build a bureaucratic organization called the Earth Institute, had the EI combine forces with other well-established elitist organizations like the United Nations, and then followed the time-tested recipe to grow and feed the organization under the auspices of saving Africa's poor? The answer, the Millennium Villages Project (MVP). The MVP is the ultimate example of what happens when unaccountable bureaucracies incubate.

Once created, the MVP promise of solving all of Africa's poverty problems needed money. So, Sachs focused on where the money was. Soon, he convinced billionaire George Soros into committing millions of dollars of his foundation's money to jump-start the MVP in 2006.[11] Soros, a man who isn't a billionaire by accident, overrode his foundation board's recommendation to deny Sachs funding.

Sachs also swayed global, multi-billion-dollar corporations. Ericsson ponied up the money to provide cell phones and charging stations for one of the first villages targeted by the MVP, Dertu in northern Kenya. The solar-powered cell phone charging stations didn't work and a diesel generator had to be brought in to charge the phones.[12] Thank God for carbon and less so for renewables.

The MVP shunning carbon-based power generation has led to severe consequences. In the Ugandan village of Ruhiira, the MVP invested millions of dollars into hospital and operating facilities to improve healthcare and reduce infant mortality. Unfortunately, the EI adhered to environmental fundamentalism, with a reliance on solar power and a de-emphasis of fossil fuels for energy in remote, poor villages and clinics. When General Electric donated two advanced incubators for the natal care facility at Ruhiira, they sat unused, wrapped in plastic in a corner because there was no reliable power to run them.[13] Blood transfusions were also not an option because the refrigerators to store the blood would not run when the solar power broke, which was often. It was common to see doctors more concerned about power reliability, whether they had enough diesel, and if the generators were working than they were about equipment, patients, and staff. We can only wonder if GE knew how its contributions of equipment failed because of a toxic combination of incompetence and radical environmental ideology.

Undeterred, before one could spell "sustainable," Sachs and his team were pounding on more doors of existing and potential new donors, marketing the MVP's supposed accomplishments. They blamed program failures and shortfalls on a lack of more funding, which served as a selling point for that added funding. Sachs's effort led to the pouring of even more money into the MVP and EI. All that added money did not improve performance of the MVP and certainly did not eradicate poverty in Africa.

Nevertheless, Sachs loved to make a huge splash when he showed up at one of the MVP locations. He would typically roll into the village in an air-conditioned SUV with security (oh my, the carbon footprint of that endeavor).[14] Then Sachs would gather the residents around him and he would start his typical speech, laden with all those catch-phrases and impressive data points. He might imply things were working and getting better, that the best days were ahead, or that there was more success to come. And then after he received applause and appreciation from the naïve crowd to fuel his ego, he'd depart from the village.

USING AFRICAN POOR AS A CONVENIENT MEANS TO AN END

Sachs and the EI would use data when it bolstered their rhetoric and would ignore the same data when it made the case for something inconsistent with their rhetoric. For example, Sachs and the MVP argued that the malaria incident rate and the economic growth of a country displayed an inverse correlation: the higher the incident rate of malaria, the lower the economic growth rate of the country.

There were millions of dollars in opportunity with malaria. The Bill and Melinda Gates Foundation was already investing hundreds of millions of dollars into malaria prevention though research and the distribution of mosquito nets across Africa.[15] Sachs wanted to get in on the action, but he needed to offer something different and better than what the other foundations were already doing. So, he began to argue that the way to go with mosquito nets was to allow the MVP to take control over distribution instead of allowing established nonprofits to continue to make inroads.

To seize the opportunity, Sachs needed to discredit the rival efforts and create a buzz about the MVP approach. First, he used old data to show malaria is not a good thing for economies (I guess you needed a Harvard degree to figure that out).[16] Then he would broadcast how the cost to arm the entire poor population of Africa with mosquito nets would equate to small sums for rich Western economies. Sachs was not beyond taking incomplete data and applying dubious assumptions to produce catchy but flawed cost numbers. Things like the cost would be much less than Wall Street's Christmas bonuses, that the cost would equate to a cup of Starbucks coffee a year for each person in the rich Western world.[17]

Sachs would also attack his perceived competition of charity organizations doing tangibly good work in Africa with mosquito net distribution and education by proclaiming that the market-based, sustainable programs already in place were unethical.[18] But these other organizations had more experience than Sachs. They were building a system that grew on its own as time went on. Mosquito net manufacturing and distribution took root across Africa. These were the real experts, the people on the ground in Africa, the ones who were knowledgeable. Nevertheless, Sachs continued his criticism.

What happens to someone who dares to call out Sachs on his questionable positions? Those from the donor community who made a logical, reasoned defense of why a local, market-based approach to making mosquito nets was working, might experience the professor's temper. Measured and intelligent positions were rebutted by Sachs with the words "reprehensible" and "ignorant."[19] He even went so far as to call the distinguished parasitologist Christian Lengeler a "punk" when Lengeler had the nerve to disagree with Sachs.[20] When things don't go Sachs's way, he may go straight to the gutter.

Pamela White, who was the USAID head for Tanzania, summed up best how Sachs dealt with dissenting views when she said: "I don't want to argue with you Jeff, because I don't want to be called ignorant or unprofessional. I have worked in Africa for thirty years. My colleagues combined have worked in the field for one hundred plus years. We don't like your tone. We don't like you preaching to us. We are not your students. We do not work for you."[21]

Sachs is also seemingly unaware of data discrediting his positions. Remember that brilliant analysis Sachs touted that showed higher malaria incident rates correlated to lower economic growth? Guess what? That same data shows a strong correlation of carbon footprint to economic growth. In other words, the more carbon a country uses per person, the higher the quality of life, the lower the infant mortality rate, and the longer the life expectancy. Electrification through carbon-based power generation of poor African nations would not only charge economic growth, it could also quickly and decisively eradicate malaria. If the poor had power, they would live in better homes, use air conditioning, have powered schools, enjoy internet access, and access better healthcare. All of which drastically reduce the incident rates and effects of malaria, saving millions of lives.

But the MVP and EI have made it a point to shun fossil fuel development in their efforts and instead to insist on a reliance on so-called renewable power like solar and wind. As is often the case, these power sources are expensive, unreliable, and subject to logistical challenges. The MVP is full of examples where half-hearted commitments to renewables have outright failed or never materialized. Yet renewables fit the image the EI and MVP desired. Renewables sell and the EI needs funding to thrive.

Sachs and the MVP stepped in it again when they shifted gears from mosquito nets in places like Tanzania to increasing agriculture yields in Uganda as the latest way to lift Africa out of poverty. Sachs and his New York team decided that the best crop to impose on Ugandans was corn, even though people in Uganda, particularly southern Uganda, don't care for corn.[22] So corn it was and Sachs spouted about how this was going to be a game-changer. When the first harvests hit in the test village of Ruhiira in 2007, the result was a significant increase in corn crop yields.

Yet, there was a problem: the team didn't think beyond the first step of improving crop yields. So, when the bumper crop led to excess inventory, there were no storage facilities. People stacked corn everywhere in the villages, including their homes. Then came the rats who fed off the poorly stored corn (and also chewed holes in stored unused mosquito nets), which created the threat of disease.[23] Making matters worse, Ruhiira was far from demand centers for the corn and the road network added heavy cost and time burdens to get the corn to the demand centers. Villagers and farmers holding the corn inventory panicked and sold their inventory at steep discounts, collapsing the market price.[24] To add insult to injury, the MVP pushed the choice of corn on Ruhiira instead of helping the village grow the popular and faster-growing matoke. Not only did the corn harvest fall to waste, but it also distracted and diminished attention and resources from the more profitable and sustainable matoke farming.

The MVP had a penchant for doubling down on riskier bets and ignoring unwelcomed news. When things weren't unfolding well across the MVP, certain local villages under pressure instituted an agricultural credit program. Despite predictions of disaster from people who knew Africa, the MVP imposed on three villages low-interest loans to local farmers and other villagers, where the loan proceeds were supposed to be put to use to improve crop yields, markets, and equipment. The effort saw default rates running as high as 90+ percent for one of the villages and two-thirds in another village.[25] Simple math would have told Sachs there was no conceivable way the farmers could have met their loan obligations to repay their debts. The MVP handed out loans in these three villages without sufficiently screening ability to repay, without the need to post collateral, and without the need to supply documentation of creditworthiness. Moreover, a considerable number of those who took out the loans failed to use the proceeds for their farming and used them instead for other unrelated needs.

Incidentally, the MVP made little mention of this epic fail in their annual reports, except for a mention of one of the villages (the one in Tanzania with the 90+ percent default rate) having lower than expected repayment rates.[26] The excuses cited? A combination of variability of rains and grasshoppers (translation: blame climate change).

After years and millions of dollars spent on the MVP, the results were sobering. The MVP did not lift the villages from poverty. The MVP was unable to hit many of the key goals announced by Sachs and often made things demonstrably worse. The village of Dertu in Kenya offers a compelling example. Touted by the MVP as a major success, the reality of Dertu in 2010 was something entirely different. Dertu had no running water, was without power, had human waste overflowing from unkept latrines, saw garbage built up everywhere, and suffered from no property rights. The money that the MVP pumped into the village attracted poor from surrounding areas, which led to the village becoming a giant shanty town. Buildings constructed by the MVP fell into disrepair. Residents lost hope. One of the leaders in the village published a fourteen-point complaint of how the MVP failed his village. The complaints ranged specifically from no lights in the delivery room, so babies were delivered in the dark, to broadly incompetent staff.[27] The overriding themes (and two of the fourteen points) were a lack of accountability and no sense of ownership of the project.

THOSE WHO DARE TO CHALLENGE SACHS

After five years or so of making bold claims, falling short of achieving them, continuing to spend millions, and making even bolder claims, there were true experts out there who began to question the MVP and Sachs. Of course, those who dare question Sachs face the threat of public attack. Recall from our Bono discussion Dambisa Moyo, the Oxford- and Harvard-educated economist who authored *Dead Aid: Why Aid Is Not Working and How There Is a Better Way for Africa*. She is smart, probably smarter than Jeff Sachs. When she had the gall to question the approaches and the results of efforts like the MVP, Sachs launched a lengthy response in the *Huffington Post*.[28] Beyond the *Huffington Post* piece, Moyo was accused of hypocrisy and betraying her fellow Africans; she was happy to accept financial aid for her education but now wanted to deny others the same.[29] It was even suggested she wanted to deny African children protection from malaria.

Moyo's arguments center on the belief that true and lasting elevation from poverty requires economic development and jobs for the afflicted. She sees a big difference between dumping piles of mosquito nets into the village squares and leaving versus developing mosquito net factories within the poor regions so that malaria is prevented, and the economy grows at the same time.

Moyo's views did not sit well with Sachs. There were two hundred million cases of disease and one million preventable deaths per year in Africa, Sachs said. He used the statistics to argue that Moyo's view is flawed because with these numbers it doesn't matter where the nets come from or how they are made; simply get nets into the hands of as many poor Africans as you can the quickest. If aid is the quickest way, then so be it and don't let ideology interfere with a life and death, quality of life opportunity for millions of poor. Sachs's view, that how mosquito nets get to Africans doesn't matter when saving lives are at stake, is ironic since it contradicts his position on energy. Immediate access to reliable electricity through fossil fuels would save millions of lives in Africa. Yet Sachs opposes the practicality of fossil fuels in favor of the ideological purity of so-called renewables.

Like Moyo, others had the courage to step up and speak out when it came to Sachs's flawed project and questionable conclusions. Michael Clemens and Gabriel Demombynes from the Center for Global Development (CGD) and the World Bank published an in-depth analysis of the MVP's claimed accomplishments and the procedures used to measure and develop them.

The CGD study went through a detailed statistical analysis of MVP sites in Kenya, Ghana, and Nigeria compared to the surrounding regions. Everyone from UNICEF to the World Bank was issuing reports and findings that quality of life was improving across all of Africa at the same time Sachs was taking credit for improvements at sites falling within the MVP.[30] The CGD study found that when assessed under the more objectively rigorous impact evaluation methodology, the discernible benefits ascribed to the MVP were often lowered, sometimes by half, from what Sachs and team professed.[31] And even that was only a rough estimate since the core design of the MVP was constructed in a way where objective assessment was rendered impossible.

The critique of the MVP didn't stop there, however. The study also highlighted how the MVP lacked a credible control group in the project, a fundamental flaw of any analysis looking to measure performance over time. Other weaknesses of the MVP approach that were called out in the CGD study included selectively choosing which sites to include in the before-and-after comparisons, subjectively picking comparison locations to measure the MVP villages against, lack of baseline data, too short of a time horizon, and small sample sizes.[32] Basically, the CGD study concluded that the MVP made fundamental mistakes and embraced significant flaws when designing its project and assessing its impacts.

CONTRASTS IN EXCEPTIONALISM

One of Sachs's recent attention-seeking endeavors is railing against the concept of American exceptionalism. To Sachs, the concept of America dictating affairs and saving the planet is ludicrous. Yet Sachs is an ardent advocate when it comes to pressing the concept of his own exceptionalism as it relates to flawed prescriptions to end global poverty and to save us from climate change—another example of an academic economist who thinks he is in the problem-solving business when he is in the problem-creation business.

EPILOGUE:

DEFILING THE NOBLE LIE

"...a time to keep silence, and a time to speak..."

ECCLESIASTES 3:7

FOUNDER OF MORAL PHILOSOPHY, SOCRATES was one of the greatest minds on earth. His student Plato was no less of a beacon of philosophy and moral thought, followed by Plato's best and brightest student, Aristotle. That's one heck of a philosophical coaching tree. No writings of Socrates are known to exist; thus, we rely on the writings of his student Plato and other contemporaries, who recorded his thoughts and actions. The legacies of Socrates, Plato, and Aristotle resonate today, for good and bad, millennia after their deaths.

Despite Plato's clear brilliance, I struggle to understand him. Plato believed a great society should be ruled by an enlightened authoritarian king or class, and individual liberty is second behind society's collective need. This reminds me of modern-day Leechdom. For what it's worth, I'm more of an Aristotle fan, who elevated reason over authority and identified it as the true source of happiness.

Aside from my misgivings about Plato, he stands as a mighty pillar of Western thought. Seeing a concept created by Socrates and refined by Plato taken by modern-day Leeches to suit their anti-democratic agenda angers me. The soiled concept from Socrates is the "noble lie," which appears in Plato's *Republic*. Plato believed a noble lie, which isn't a true lie but has truth within it, if applied appropriately, serves to bind society together. A noble lie with no truth, is just an ignoble lie.

When put to worthwhile aims, the noble lie is a powerful guide for improvement. Think of the concept of heaven. Many of us are willing to live a life of faith in the hope of going to heaven after death, despite having no way to know if it really exists. Would the United States have the status it enjoyed the past hundred years if Americans did not embrace the concept of Lincoln's "Of the people, by the people, for the people" despite years of slavery and racial discrimination? A series of noble lies has built our shared American experience, one after another.

Since World War II, the Leech has increasingly used the noble lie to undermine much of what built America. The Leech ripped out the pages from Plato's *Republic* and used them to bring our country to the tipping point.[a] Nothing in nature is limitless or perpetual, including American liberty. The Leech is becoming the "single hand" that Hayek spoke of, exercising control and power over the rest of us.[1]

American higher education created a noble lie that a college degree was the hallmark of good parenting and necessary for a successful adult life. Academia then used that noble lie to create an indoctrination system where students are subjected to four-plus years of propaganda that solidify Leech control from one generation to another.

Public pension fund managers borrowed the noble lie of responsible corporations being sound investment opportunities. The managers then

---

a   Malcolm Gladwell's *The Tipping Point* is most often associated with understanding how new products and societal fads/trends spread. But the same concepts in the book also apply to the wider acceptance of the message from, and the growth in the ranks of, the government bureaucracy, the media, academia, and environmental groups.

misappropriated the noble lie to convert their considerable fund assets into weapons to attack those corporations found incompatible with Leech dogma. Sacrificed before the Leech altar was the bureaucrat's fiduciary duty of making sure he maximized returns on fund assets for retirees.

Pope Francis commandeered the noble lie of papal infallibility as it pertains to traditional Catholic doctrine. He then used the noble lie to shove radical environmentalism ahead of traditional Catholic values to further his personal socialist ideologies.

Government bureaucrats twisted the noble lie of government looking out for the interests of ordinary citizens. The bureaucrats then applied the noble lie to use government agencies to oppress, intimidate, and drain valuable resources from our economy to feed and expand the Deep State.

Humanities professors and college administrators grabbed onto the noble lie that a well-rounded engineer, doctor, or coder is superior to one narrowly trained. The entrenched faculty then used the noble lie to subvert the traditional, rigorous STEM curricula and make STEAM. The quality of the STEM programs and graduates have been diluted on purpose.

The Federal Reserve used the noble lie of government intervention during severe economic distress to save the country from ruin. The Fed pressed the noble lie during and well beyond the 2008 financial meltdown and the 2020 pandemic shutdown to dictate capital allocation across national and global economies. While spendthrift governments and the elite class benefit, the Fed punishes savers and creates asset bubbles over a wide spectrum, fanning dangerous sparks of future economic firestorms.

What happens to our country once the misappropriation of all these noble lies takes cumulative effect? Unfortunately, there is an answer to that question readily available today in the state of Illinois and city of Chicago.

The Illinois crisis emanates from Leech-induced policies and leadership. A life-long career politician and lawyer from Chicago, Mike

Madigan, had served as Illinois House of Representatives speaker since the early 1980s, which is an all-time achievement for any state, as well as Congress (he abruptly stepped down in early 2021). Speaker Madigan is certain things, but a Creator, Enabler, or Server is not one of them.

Speaker Madigan has presided over the methodical destruction of both Illinois and Chicago. Both the city and state face massive deficits and huge funding gaps for pensions and other entitlements. The state has a credit rating just one notch above junk and is a contender to become the first state in the Union to fall into junk status. Chicago is already there and loses ground every quarter.

With Madigan's tight hold over the legislature for years, it is common to see up to two-thirds of the seats in Illinois state elections not have an opponent to a Madigan endorsed candidate. Gerrymandering allows Madigan and the Democrats to draw complicated district lines designed to assure perpetual Leech-friendly victors. Elected judges are ones who typically receive the most money and support from the Madigan machine and the plaintiffs' bar, an obvious conflict for a branch of government that is supposedly there to keep the legislative and executive branches in check. An Illinois utility is investigated for allegedly bribing Madigan associates with jobs, contracts, and board seats so that the speaker-influenced legislature approves customer rate adjustments desired by the utility. Democracy as we think of it is dead in Illinois, with policy, legislatures, and judges being determined by the elite class and not the people. Once in power, they feed the Leech as opposed to serving the people.

Crime in Chicago continues to spiral out of control in a violent orgy of assault, robbery, and murder while city and state leaders focus on distractions. Kids can't safely get to school, don't stay in school, and even if they did would not be afforded a real prospect of becoming proficient in basic reading and math skills. Taxes of all forms and types continue to grow, increasing an already heavy burden on individuals and enterprise. Homeowners in modest areas of Chicago are paying over 10% of their property value annually in the form of property taxes. Businesses of

Creators, Enablers, and Servers have been rushing the exits for years to leave the Windy City and the Land of Lincoln, adding to an epic crisis.

Madigan gains from this. He is a partner in a Chicago law firm that bears his name, Madigan and Getzendanner, whose specialty is property tax appeals. Madigan leads the legislature in enacting huge spending bills and raising taxes, including property taxes. When homeowners and businesses reach the breaking point with their tax bills, they hire Madigan's firm to represent them in court to argue for lower taxes, personally enriching Speaker Madigan. The judges presiding over the tax hearings are often recipients of political contributions from Madigan and his network. Former reform-minded Governor Bruce Rauner, a sworn enemy of Madigan, refers to the situation as a Mafia protection racket, albeit a sickeningly legal one.[2] Facing a Madigan-concerted political blitzkrieg, Rauner lost the governorship in 2019. Illinois and Chicago are the future that awaits us if we continue to allow the Leech to misappropriate the noble lie to achieve its aims.

AUTHOR'S NOTE

"There are decades where nothing happens; and there are weeks where decades happen."

VLADIMIR LENIN

DURING MY FREE TIME, I worked on this book. With kids, work, and life intervening, whittling away free time, it is not surprising that the effort took a couple of years to complete. And everything changed in those couple of years.

When I began my first chapter, Barack Obama was in the White House, coming down the home stretch of an eight-year relentless campaign to embed forever the Leech philosophy across government, academia, and the media into American society. What Franklin Roosevelt created with the New Deal and Lyndon Johnson nurtured with the Great Society, Barack Obama took to dizzying levels with the Deep State. We saw government target the three most vital organs of our economy and way of life: healthcare, energy, and finance/banking. Congress aided and abetted, enacting Obamacare and Dodd-Frank. When the voters booted out Democrat majorities in the House and

Senate, Obama simply shifted his lines of attack through the administrative state and judicial branches.

The cumulative impact of decades of bureaucratic creep and wealth redistribution policies reached an apex under Obama. The data prove it.[a] Hard-working, middle-class Americans worked four times as much and earned six times as much as the bottom 20% of Americans, yet enjoyed only 20% more in spendable income due to the government redistributing wealth through unending social programs and a rigged tax code.[1] The lower middle class, just above the bottom 20%, worked two-and-a-half times as much and earned three times as much as the bottom 20%, yet had about the same spendable income.[2] The high earners in the top 20%, which the middle class aspires to enter, made twenty-six times that of the bottom 20% but enjoyed only three times the spendable income.[3] Under Obama, hard work was punished; success and achievement were vilified; and dependency, resentment, and victimhood were celebrated.

All indications were that President Obama was about to smoothly pass the baton to his former colleague, Hillary Clinton, who would finish the job. She had the support of a sitting president with the bully pulpit; the support of a popular ex-president who happened to be her husband; the opportunity for the public to elect the first woman president; the use of a campaign war chest second to none; and the support of the media that bordered on hysterical full-throated rapture. If those advantages were not enough, she was also up against Donald Trump, whom most experts and pundits thought of as a bad joke.

If you were a Leech working in government, the media, or academia, you had the entire country at your feet in the eight years leading up to 2016. Better yet, the next four years under a Clinton presidency offered even more opportunity to tighten your control over the rest of us. If

---

a   Check out John F. Early's work at the Cato Institute on this subject. Not surprisingly, the U.S. Census data on income distribution ignores transfer payments via social programs as well as tax payments. That creates grossly skewed results to justify policies favored by the federal bureaucracy. Early does the data justice by accounting for these major impacts and showing a much different conclusion across income groups.

you were a Creator, Enabler, or Server, the summer and fall of 2016 were dark days indeed. One had the feeling that as a nation we were crossing a point of no return.

Then election night arrived on November 8, and Donald Trump had won the election. The result shocked so many, especially the self-proclaimed experts in government and the media. But more shocking was how he accomplished the feat: by easily winning traditional red states that the experts claimed were in play for Clinton, while at the same time busting down the much-touted, but in the end brittle, blue wall of Midwestern states including Pennsylvania, Wisconsin, Ohio, and Michigan. The middle class had enough of seeing its hard-earned wealth and freedom appropriated, consumed, and redistributed by government bureaucrats. Americans rejected vilification of success and hard work.

The Trump victory spun many into an all-out nation-wide tantrum. Reporters and journalists punched away at their keyboards with a shrillness of angst that laid bare whatever meager semblance of objectivity they tried to portray to the rest of us prior to the election. Senior management at a tech giant was caught on video somberly pouting about the election outcome and trying to figure out what to do about it (they settled on asking all employees in the audience to hug one another). "Fake news" went from a catch phrase to something all too real as bias and negativity levels toward the president reached peaks never seen in the history of the modern mainstream media.

Government bureaucrats huddled to find ways to throw roadblocks into a coming transition of power that promised to drain the swamp that is the administrative state. For four years, Trump administration policy was consciously ignored and fought from within as thousands of bureaucrats worked endlessly to undermine what their publicly elected bosses directed them to do. Blatant obstruction by government bureaucrats not only went unpunished but received praise. Certain officials showed no respect for the law as they allegedly leaked classified national security material to the mainstream media, strengthening our enemies and placing us at greater risk.

Even the most esteemed institutions the country has to offer succumbed. The U.S. Supreme Court is now unfortunately no exception, after years of a leftist legal press inciting and demanding outcome-based rulings and positions from the nation's highest court. Justice Ruth Bader Ginsburg fell under the trance of the cacophony. The trailblazing justice dropped the ethical mores of judges not intervening in political campaigns by going on the record to criticize candidate Trump. Justice Ginsburg also saw fit to weigh in with an endorsement of Obama nominee Merrick Garland for the Supreme Court, another no-no when it comes to a judge's ethical compass and the Code of Conduct for U.S. Judges.[b]

The elites at once went on the offensive to fabricate the story of why and how President Trump won. You know the story-lines well by now: a flawed electoral college system that came up with a different result than what a national popular vote system would give; horrible timing on a reversal by the FBI Director on investigating Clinton's emails; ignorant, or "deplorable," voters who didn't have the intelligence necessary to vote for the obvious choice; Hillary's off-the-charts unlikable index and her campaign's botching of the election; and the most fantastic of all, the Russians hacking and stealing the election. An army of professors, students, journalists, and government bureaucrats threw everything it had at the public to delegitimize Trump's victory before he could even deliver an inaugural address (sadly, Trump returned the favor after the 2020 election when he sought to delegitimize the Biden victory).

The situation amped up heading into the inauguration to go beyond rhetoric and words. The Resist movement came into being with a philosophy that if you didn't like what the Trump presidency had to offer, you could simply burn Washington, D.C., and the country down. Rocks flew; fires were set; punches were thrown. Members of Congress, the intelligence services, urban city governments, and administrative branch bureaucrats ignored laws and too often disobeyed their oaths of office. The

---

b   For an excellent explanation of how Supreme Court Justice Ginsberg's behavior had morphed over time, give a read to Judge Silberman's op-ed article titled "A 'Notorious' 2016 for Ginsburg and Comey" published late February 2016 in the *Wall Street Journal*.

federal judiciary piled on by shooting down over 90% of Trump administration attempted rollbacks of onerous administrative state regulations.[4] All the while, the media was pumping a steady stream of propaganda to discredit the Trump administration.

With all this premeditated fraying of the American fabric, one wonders why it has come to this. The answer is quite simple. Trump not only ended an epic, eight-year run of the Leech class in our society but also clearly articulated an intention and a plan to loosen its grip. You heard it in his rhetoric about draining the swamp of Washington, D.C., which strikes at the heart of the Leech ecosystem. You saw it in tactics with the withdrawal from the harmful Paris Climate Agreement and the rollback of crushing regulations that hurt just about everyone and benefited no one except the government bureaucrat, the rent seeking corporation, and the radical environmental group. You realized it with the historic tax reform bill of 2017 that for the first time started to chip away at subsidies that rewarded out-of-control spending by leftist mayors and governors through the capping of the state and local tax deduction. You viewed it in the personal standoffs the president had with some of the marquee standard-bearers of the Resist movement: Pope Francis, Senators Schumer and Warren, Hollywood (Meryl Streep, Robert DeNiro, Susan Sarandon, Kathy Griffin, to name only a few), and various mayors of broken big cities. You heard it when the president was booed at a Washington Nationals World Series game (the tax-subsidized stadium filled with well-to-do bureaucrats and entities feeding off of us at the swamp's trough) and being cheered at the Army-Navy football game (the seats filled with the brave men and women of our armed forces who voluntarily serve to protect us).

And you measured it when the cumulative impact of Trump's policies took effect. By early 2020, labor participation rate and wage growth were markedly higher than during the Obama years. The minority poverty rate was the lowest on record, and national unemployment sat at a fifty-year low. Hundreds of thousands of manufacturing jobs were unfilled as hiring demand exceeded the supply of workers. These data are a scoreboard to gauge the efficacy of Trump administration policies, and a government-induced economic coma justified on a virus emanating from China, Trump's maddening inability to exercise decorum on social media, his hyping of conspiracy theories, or his regrettable lack of leadership as a lame duck won't change that.

Before his meltdown after the 2020 election, President Trump was an existential threat to the Leech class. Despite his obvious flaws, Trump was a singular force of creative destruction and disruptive innovation that could change the Leech ecosystem permanently. Trump's use of Twitter to communicate to the public versus the traditional means of a press conference makes the traditional, heavily biased, news media irrelevant. The push toward deregulation equates to less government bureaucrats. The president's outsider status and unconventional campaign made obsolete the political establishment, both Democrat and Republican.

Even dictionaries joined the fray. Merriam Webster's shortlist for word of the year in 2017 included *complicit, recuse, empathy,* and *dotage.*[5] The winner was *feminism.* The dictionary company explained why this word list was chosen. *Complicit* was on the shortlist because of Russian interference in elections and a *Saturday Night Live* skit making fun of Ivanka Trump. *Recuse* made the list because of Jeff Session's reversal on investigations. *Empathy* was there because of a Hollywood director's protest of Trump's proposed rules on immigration. *Dotage,* which means a state or period of senile decay marked by decline of mental poise and alertness, also made the esteemed list because North Korean dictator Kim Jong-Un insulted President Trump with this word. *Feminism* took the top prize as word of the year in part because the dictionary found presidential counselor Kellyanne Conway's remarks on feminism controversial.

The Merriam-Webster editor produced a video not just to disclose the shortlist and the winner, but also to tie each word to a creative assault on the character, intelligence, or ethics of the Trump administration.[6] Of course, the editor calmly claimed the list was developed using highly scientific methods. The methodology, however, is anyone's guess outside of Merriam-Webster.

With the Biden administration now in power, do not expect the Leech to go quietly in the night. Mark Twain nailed it long ago, lamenting, "How easy it is to make people believe a lie, and how hard it is to undo that work again."[7] This fight is far from over. The brutal Leech is anti-individual, anti-libertarian, and anti-freedom.

These traits were on full display during the pandemic crisis and the subsequent self-induced economic coma. A small cadre of bureaucrats commanded all free enterprise to halt, using the justification of "common good" and "public interest." Economic pain ensued, triggering a $2 trillion relief package. Although $2 trillion divided by 330-odd million Americans works out to just over $6,000 for every man, woman, and child in the United States, only $1,200 was provided to each adult. The massive difference fed a cornucopia of other interests, including: migrant and refugee assistance, NASA's bureaucracy, the Endowment for the Arts, the Endowment for the Humanities, public radio, museums and libraries (that we couldn't access), Social Security administrative costs (not retiree benefits), higher salaries for Smithsonian staff, the Kennedy Center, the Peace Corps, raises for congressmen, and Amtrak.

Hugely benefiting from the pandemic, the Leech grew exponentially during the crisis and it does not intend to recede. Now the Leech determines the value and quality of our lives, instead of us making our own decisions. The ultimate manifestation of individual rights, the ability to self-determine actions, is more heavily dampened than ever by the Deep State, bureaucrats, media talking heads, and academia.

Two quotes to contemplate as we move forward. First, a line from Christopher Hitchens: "May you keep your powder dry for the battles ahead, and know when and how to recognize them."[8] Indeed, the coalition of the willing Creators, Enablers, and Servers shall require dry powder for the coming battles. Second, a thought from Horatio Nelson in his memorandum to British naval officers before the victorious Battle of Trafalgar: "No Captain can do very wrong if he places his Ship alongside that of an Enemy."[9] We know who the enemy is; let us engage in public discourse so that good prevails over evil.

ENDNOTES

INTRODUCTION

1   "Quote by Dennis Miller," SComedy, accessed August 1, 2020, from http://scomedy.com/quotes/4950.

2   Wikipedia, s.v. "Ronald Reagan," accessed July 28, 2020, https://en.wikipedia.org/wiki/Ronald_Reagan.

3   Mario Cuomo, 1984 Democratic National Convention keynote address.

4   James Burke, "Speech on Conciliation with America," in *The Speeches of the Right Honorable Edmund Burke* (London: Duffy, 1853), 71–122.

5   Wikiquote, s.v. "Milton Friedman," accessed August 1, 2020, https://en.wikiquote.org/wiki/Milton_Friedman.

6   Miles Davis, jazzquotes, accessed August 1, 2020, http://jazz-quotes.com/artist/miles-davis/.

7   Friedrich A. von Hayek, *Road to Serfdom* (University of Chicago Press, 1944).

8   Thomas Jefferson, letter to William Roscoe, December 27, 1820.

9   *The Two Killings of Sam Cooke*, Netflix documentary, 2019.

10   George Orwell, *Why I Write* (n.p.: 1946).

11   Abraham Lincoln, Gettysburg Address, given at the dedication of the Soldiers' National Cemetery, November 19, 1863.

12   "War Correspondent and Journalist," International Churchill Society, accessed August 1, 2020, https://www.winstonchurchill.org/the-life-of-churchill/life/man-of-words/war-correspondent-and-journalist/.

13   Golda Meir obituary, *New York Times*, December 9, 1978.

14   John Ruskin, *The Two Paths* (n.p. Parlor Press, 2004).

15   Amity Shlaes, "Techies: Join the Side You're On," *Forbes*, April 19, 2016.

16   William D. Montalbano, "Vatican Finds Galileo "Not Guilty'," *Washington Post*, November 1, 1992.

17   Malcolm X, *Malcolm X Speaks; Selected Speeches and Statements*, ed. George Breitman (n.p.: Grove Press, 1966).

THE AWESOMENESS OF CREATORS, ENABLERS, AND SERVERS AND HOW TO DEFINE THE LEECH

1   Ayn Rand, *Letters of Ayn Rand*, ed. Michael Berliner (n.p.: Dutton Adult, 1995).

2   Calvin Coolidge, Address to the American Society of Newspaper Editors, January 17, 1925, https://www.presidency.ucsb.edu/documents/address-the-american-society-newspaper-editors-washington-dc.

3   Charlotte Gibson, "Who's the Highest-Paid Person in Your State?," ESPN.com, March 20, 2018, http://www.espn.com/espn/feature/story/_/id/22454170/highest-paid-state-employees-include-ncaa-coaches-nick-saban-john-calipari-dabo-swinney-bill-self-bob-huggins.

4   Heaven's Door, accessed August 1, 2020, https://www.heavensdoor.com/.

5   Robin Murray, "John Lydon Defends Butter Adverts," Clash, November 13, 2011, https://www.clashmusic.com/news/john-lydon-defends-butter-adverts.

6   "Experience Il Palagio," Il Palagio website, accessed August 1, 2020, http://www.il-palagio.com/.

7   Chris Kornelis, "Jeremy Renner's Favorite Tools for Making Music and Flipping Homes," *Wall Street Journal*, June 6, 2018.

8   Interagency Working Group (IWG), "Remarks before the Nazi War Criminals Interagency Working Group," National Archives, accessed August 1, 2020, https://www.archives.gov/iwg/research-papers/weitzman-remarks-june-1999.html.

9   W. D. Richter, *Invasion of the Body Snatchers*, directed by Philip Kaufman (Los Angeles, CA: Republic Pictures, 2002), motion picture.

10   Immanuel Kant, "An Answer to the Question: What Is Enlightenment?," September 30, 1784, https://www.marxists.org/reference/subject/ethics/kant/enlightenment.htm.

11   Calvin Coolidge, speech to Massachusetts Senate, Boston, Massachusetts, January 7, 1914.

12   Margaret Thatcher, interview by William F. Buckley, *Firing Line*, episode S0288, July 25, 1977.

13   Franklin Roosevelt, Fireside Chat 3: On the National Recovery Administration, July 24, 1933.

14   Wikipedia, s.v. "Iron triangle (US politics)," accessed August 1, 2020, https://en.wikipedia.org/wiki/Iron_triangle_(US_politics).

15   Dirk von Koch, *Die Brüsseler Republik*, Der Spiegel, December 27, 1999.

16   Martin Luther King Jr., *Strength to Love* (New York: Harper and Row, 1963).

17   CNBC's Rick Santelli's Chicago Tea Party, YouTube video, posted February 19, 2009, by the Heritage Foundation, https://www.youtube.com/watch?v=zp-Jw-5Kx8k.

18   Thomas Paine, "Letter Addressed to the Addressers," 1792, http://thomaspaine.org/essays/french-revolution/letter-addressed-to-the-addressers.html.

19   Robert Bellafiore, *Summary of the Latest Federal Income Tax Data, 2018 Update*, Tax Foundation Fiscal Fact No. 622, November 2018. See https://taxfoundation.org/summary-latest-federal-income-tax-data-2018-update/.

20   Franz Oppenheimer, *The State* (Indianapolis: Bobbs-Merrill, 1914).

21   Howard Moore Jr., "The Court's Relationship to Black Liberation," in Robert Lefcourt, *Law Against the People: Essays to Demystify Law, Order, and the Courts* (New York: Random House, 1971).

THE LEECH MOTHERSHIP: THE DEEP STATE

1   Brad Hershbein, David Boddy, and Melissa S. Kearney, "Nearly 30 Percent of Workers in the U.S. Need a License to Perform Their Job: It Is Time to Examine Occupational Licensing Practices," Brookings, January 27, 2015, https://www.brookings.edu/blog/up-front/2015/01/27/nearly-30-percent-of-workers-in-the-u-s-need-a-license-to-perform-their-job-it-is-time-to-examine-occupational-licensing-practices/.

ENDNOTES

2 Kevin Kosar, "The Lost Genius of the Post Office," Politico, June 8, 2017, https://www. politico.com/agenda/story/2017/06/08/us-post-office-technical-difficulties-000449/.

3 "U.S. Postal Service Reports Fiscal Year 2018 Results," U.S. Postal Service press release, November 14, 2018, https://about.usps.com/news/national-releases/2018/pr18_093. htm.

4 "Postal Service Employment by State," Governing.com, accessed August 1, 2020, https://www.governing.com/gov-data/public-workforce-salaries/postal-service-usps-employment-number-of-employees-by-state.html.

5 *Collective Bargaining Agreement between American Postal Workers Union, AFL-CIO and U.S. Postal Service*, May 21, 2015–September 20, 2018, https://apwu.org/sites/ apwu/files/resource-files/2015-2018%20APWU%20Collective%20Bargaining%20 Agreement.pdf.

6 Joshua J. Mark, "Ancient Egyptian Taxes and the Cattle Count," *Ancient History Encyclopedia*, February 7, 2017, https://www.ancient.eu/article/1012/ ancient-egyptian-taxes--the-cattle-count/.

7 Thomas Jefferson, Inaugural Address, March 4, 1801.

8 John Locke, *Second Treatise of Civil Government*, section 141, 1690.

9 Michael E. Parrish, *The Hughes Court: Justices, Rulings, and Legacy* (n.p.: ABC-CLIO, 2002).

10 Maurice W. Lee, *Economic Fluctuations: An Analysis of Business Cycles and Other Economic Fluctuations* (n.p.: R. D. Irwin, 1955), 236.

11 Franklin Delano Roosevelt, First Inaugural Address, March 3, 1933.

12 Administrative Procedure Act (APA), Pub. L. No. 79–404, 60 Stat. 237 (1946).

13 Immigration and Naturalization Service v. Chadha, 462 U.S. 919 (1983).

14 Chevron U.S.A., Inc. v. Natural Resources Defense Council, Inc., 467 U.S. 837 (1984).

15 Ethics in Government Act, Pub. L. 95–521 (1978).

16 Lyndon Johnson, 1964 State of the Union Address, January 8, 1964.

17 John C. Goodman, "Why We Lost the War on Poverty," *Forbes*, January 23, 2014.

18 United States Census Bureau, Current Population Survey, 1960 to 2016 Annual Social and Economic Supplements.

19 Bruce D. Meyer and James X. Sullivan, *Annual Report on U.S. Consumption Poverty: 2016*, American Enterprise Institute, https://www.aei.org/research-products/report/ annual-report-on-us-consumption-poverty-2016/.

20 Robert Hall and Nicolas Petrosky-Nadeau, "Changes in Labor Participation and Household Income," FRBSF Economic Letter, website of the Federal Reserve Bank San Francisco, February 1, 2016, https://www.frbsf.org/economic-research/publications/ economic-letter/2016/february/labor-force-participation-and-household-income/.

21 Diane Katz, "Red Tape Receding: Trump and the High-Water Mark of Regulation," *Backgrounder* (Heritage Foundation), November 8, 2017, https://www.heritage.org/ sites/default/files/2017-11/BG3260.pdf.

22 "Obama Cabinet Mtg—I've Got a Pen and a Phone," YouTube video, posted by CNN, March 31, 2016, https://www.youtube.com/watch?v=EnmDqlvQD0s.

23 Bureau of Labor Statistics, "Table R-1, All Consumer Units: Annual Detailed Expenditure Means, Standard Errors, Coefficients of Variation, and Weekly (D) or Quarterly (I) Percents, 2018," Consumer Expenditure Survey, 2018, https://www.bls. gov/cex/2018/research/allcuprepub.pdf.

24   Erica York, Madison Mauro, and Emma Wei, "Tax Freedom Day 2019 is April 16th," Tax Foundation, https://taxfoundation.org/publications/tax-freedom-day/.

25   Eric Yoder, "Q&A for federal workers: Annual Hiring Rates," *Washington Post*, April 3, 2018, https://www.washingtonpost.com/news/powerpost/wp/2018/04/03/qa-for-federal-workers-annual-hiring-rates/?utm_term=.47183f4cf888.

26   Robert Longley, "The Complicated Process of Firing a Government Employee," ThoughtCo., updated May 2, 2020, https://www.thoughtco.com/why-its-hard-firing-government-employees-3321489.

27   Susan E. Dudley and Jerry Brito, *Regulation: A Primer* (Arlington, VA: Mercatus Center/Washington DC: George Washington University Regulatory Studies Center, 2012), https://www.mercatus.org/system/files/RegulatoryPrimer_DudleyBrito_0.pdf.

28   U.S. Bureau of Labor Statistics website, https://data.bls.gov/pdq/SurveyOutputServlet. (August 6, 2020).

29   See the Bureau of Labor Statistics website, https://www.bls.gov/.

30   Andrew G. Biggs and Jason Richwine, "Comparing Federal and Private Sector Compensation" (working paper 2011-02, March 4, 2011, American Enterprise Institute for Public Policy Research, rev. June 2011), https://www.aei.org/wp-content/uploads/2011/10/AEI-Working-Paper-on-Federal-Pay-May-2011.pdf.

31   Biggs and Richwine.

32   Terence Jeffrey, "Per Capita Federal Spending Up Sevenfold Since 1941," CNSNews, October 18, 2017, https://www.cnsnews.com/commentary/terence-p-jeffrey/capita-federal-spending-sevenfold-1941.

33   Drew DeSilver, What Does the Federal Government Spend Your Tax Dollars On? Social Insurance Programs, Mostly," *Facttank* (Pew Research Center), April 4, 2017, http://www.pewresearch.org/fact-tank/2017/04/04/what-does-the-federal-government-spend-your-tax-dollars-on-social-insurance-programs-mostly/.

34   Chapman University, "America's Top Fears 2017: Chapman University Survey of American Fears," *The Voice of Wilson* (Wilson College blog), October 11, 2017, https://blogs.chapman.edu/wilkinson/2017/10/11/americas-top-fears-2017/.

35   "National: Public Troubled by 'Deep State,'" Monmouth University Poll (West Long Branch, NJ), March 19, 2018, https://www.monmouth.edu/polling-institute/documents/monmouthpoll_us_031918.pdf/.

36   James Broughel, "New Rule Exposes the Regulatory Watchdog That Wasn't," *The Hill*, May 20, 2019, https://thehill.com/opinion/finance/444528-new-rule-exposes-the-regulatory-watchdog-that-wasnt.

37   Ronald Reagan, speech at the Neshoba County Fair, August 3, 1980 (transcript), http://neshobademocrat.com/Content/NEWS/News/Article/Transcript-of-Ronald-Reagan-s-1980-Neshoba-County-Fair-speech/2/297/15599.

38   Alexander Hamilton, *The Federalist Papers*: No. 79.

39   Pacific Legal Foundation, "Arbitrary Federal Vaping Regulations Threaten Businesses, Consumers—and Constitutional Rights," press release, January 30, 2018, https://pacificlegal.org/press-release/arbitrary-federal-vaping-regulations-threaten-businesses-consumers-and-constitutional-rights/.

40   Steve Forbes, "IRS Illegality," *Forbes*, April 4, 2014, https://www.forbes.com/sites/steveforbes/2012/04/04/irs-illegality/#58cacc7d346a.

41   Jason J. Fichtner, "The Hidden Costs of Tax Compliance," Mercatus Center website, May 20, 2013, https://www.mercatus.org/publication/hidden-costs-tax-compliance.

42   Leon Trotsky, *The Revolution Betrayed: What Is the Soviet Union and Where Is It Going:* (n.p.: Pathfinder Press, 1937, 1972).

43   Bentley Coffey, Patrick A. McLaughlin, and Pietro Peretto, *The Cumulative Cost of Regulations,* Mercatus Research Paper 2016, available online at https://papers.ssrn.com/sol3/papers.cfm?abstract_id=2869145.

44   Clyde Wayne Crews Jr., *Ten Thousand Commandments* (Washington, DC: Competitive Enterprise Institute, 2018), https://cei.org/sites/default/files/Ten_Thousand_Commandments_2018.pdf.

45   Crews.

46   John Buckner, "Trump and Greitens Pre-Election Promises Crucial for Rolla's Growth," *Rolla Daily News*, December 23, 2016.

47   Friedrich A. von Hayek, *Road to Serfdom* (University of Chicago Press, 1944).

48   Danielle Kertzleben, "Rep. Alexandria Ocasio-Cortez Releases Green New Deal Outline," NPR, February 7, 2019, https://www.npr.org/2019/02/07/691997301/rep-alexandria-ocasio-cortez-releases-green-new-deal-outline.

49   Mary E. McLeod to the Senior Leadership Team, CFPB, November 25, 2017, https://www.politico.com/f/?id=0000015f-fbe7-d90d-a37f-fff74f280000.

50   Supreme Court of the United States, "Syllabus: LUCIA ET AL. v. SECURITIES AND EXCHANGE COMMISSION," accessed August 6, 2020, https://www.supremecourt.gov/opinions/17pdf/17-130_4f14.pdf

51   Copyright, worldwide rights ©Salvador Dalí. Fundació Gala-Salvador Dalí (Artists Rights Society), 2017 / In the USA ©Salvador Dalí Museum, Inc. St. Petersburg, FL 2017.

52   European Commission, "COLLEGE (2019–2024): The Commissioners: The European Commission's Political Leadership," official website of the European Commission, accessed August 6, 2020, https://ec.europa.eu/commission/commissioners/2014-2019/vestager/announcements/market-works-consumers_en.

53   Felix Richter, "EU ANTITRUST FINES: Google Hit with Another Antitrust Fine in Europe," Statista, March 20, 2019, https://www.statista.com/chart/14752/eu-antitrust-fines-against-tech-companies/.

54   European Commission, "COLLEGE (2019–2024)."

55   "Obama: 'If You've Been Successful, You Didn't Get There on Your Own,'" Real Clear Politics Video, July 15, 2012, https://www.realclearpolitics.com/video/2012/07/15/obama_if_youve_got_a_business_you_didnt_build_that_someone_else_made_that_happen.html.

LEECH-TARGETED CALLINGS BEYOND THE GOVERNMENT BUREAUCRAT

1   Ilya Shapiro, Trevor Burrus, and Thomas A. Berry, "*Mann v. National Review*," CATO Institute Legal Briefs, January 19, 2017, https://www.cato.org/publications/legal-briefs/mann-v-national-review.

2   MTMP (Mass Torts Made Perfect), "Who We Are," MTMP website, accessed August 6, 2020, https://mtmp.com/about-mtmp/.

3   Daniel J. Capra et al., "Tobacco Litigation and Attorneys' Fees," *Fordham Law Review* 67, no. 6 (1999): 2827–58, https://ir.lawnet.fordham.edu/cgi/viewcontent.cgi?article=3580&context=flr.

4   Tim Loh and Jef Feeley, "Bayer's Roundup Headache Grows as Plaintiffs Pile into Court," Bloomberg, October 30, 2019, https://www.bloomberg.com/news/articles/2019-10-30/bayer-is-now-facing-42-700-plaintiffs-in-roundup-litigation.

5   Sarah Randazzo and Jacob Bunge, "Mass-Tort Machine Powers Wave of Roundup Lawsuits," *Wall Street Journal*, November 27, 2019.

6   Hamilton Lincoln Law Institute, "In Re Google Referrer Header Privacy Litigation," HLLI, accessed August 6, 2020, https://cei.org/litigation/re-google-referrer-header-privacy-litigation.

7   Hamilton Lincoln Law Institute.

8   Jonathan Stempel, "Google's 'Cookie' Privacy Settlement That Paid Users Nothing Was Just Voided by a U.S. Appeals Court," *Business Insider*, August 6, 2019, https://www.businessinsider.com/us-appeals-court-voids-google-cookie-privacy-settlement-that-paid-users-nothing-2019-8.

9   John Steele Gordon, "A Short History of American Medical Insurance," *Imprimis* 47, no. 9 (September 2018), https://imprimis.hillsdale.edu/short-history-american-medical-insurance/.

10   Grafton Partners L.P. v. Superior Court, 36 Cal.4th 944 (2005).

11   Fact sheet: Sargent Shriver Civil Counsel Act (AB 590) (Feuer), Judicial Council of California, August, 2012.

12   Adam Brinklow, "SF Voters Guarantee Lawyers for Evicted Tenants," Curbed, June 7, 2018, https://sf.curbed.com/2018/6/7/17437548/san-francisco-prop-election-eviction-lawyer.

13   Robert Lefcourt, *Law Against the People: Essays to Demystify Law, Order, and the Courts* (New York: Random House, 1971).

14   Dr. Stephen J, Gerras and Dr. Leonard Wong, "Lying to Ourselves: Dishonesty in the Army Profession," U.S. Army War College Strategic Studies Institute, February 2015, available for download at https://ssi.armywarcollege.edu/lying-to-ourselves-dishonesty-in-the-army-profession/.

15   Franklin D. Roosevelt, Letter on the Resolution of Federation of Federal Employees Against Strikes in Federal Service, August 16, 1937 at the Presidency Project, http://www.presidency.ucsb.edu/ws/index.php?pid=15445.

16   Wikipedia, s.v. "Labor unions in the United States," accessed August 6, 2020, https://en.wikipedia.org/wiki/Labor_unions_in_the_United_States.

17   Alexander Russo, "Maps: Collective Bargaining, State by State," *This Week in Education* (blog), November 24, 2015, https://scholasticadministrator.typepad.com/thisweekineducation/2015/11/maps-collective-bargaining-state-by-state.html#.XEyVY01YbWM.

18   Pew Charitable Trusts, "The State Pension Funding Gap: 2016," Pew, April 12, 2018 http://www.pewtrusts.org/en/research-and-analysis/issue-briefs/2018/04/the-state-pension-funding-gap-2016#0-overview.

19   James Sherk, "Unelected Unions: Why Workers Should Be Allowed to Choose Their Representatives," Heritage Foundation, August 27, 2012, https://www.heritage.org/jobs-and-labor/report/unelected-unions-why-workers-should-be-allowed-choose-their-representatives.

ENDNOTES

20   Wikipedia, s.v. "United Federation of Teachers, accessed August 6, 2020, https://en.wikipedia.org/wiki/United_Federation_of_Teachers.

21   Jeffrey S. Solochek, "Florida Teachers on Edge as New Law Threatens Their Unions," *Tampa Bay Times*, March 16, 2018, https://www.tampabay.com/news/education/teachers/Florida-teachers-on-edge-as-new-law-threatens-their-unions_166405203.

22   "6440 UNIVERSITY OF CALIFORNIA: ISSUE 1: UC BUDGET PACKAGE," accessed August 6, 2020, https://abgt.assembly.ca.gov/sites/abgt.assembly.ca.gov/files/6440%20University%20of%20California.pdf.

23   "6440 UNIVERSITY OF CALIFORNIA."

24   Mike Antonucci, "Teachers Unions at Risk of Losing 'Agency Fees,'" *Education Next* 16, no. 1 (Winter 2016), https://www.educationnext.org/teachers-unions-risk-losing-agency-fees-friedrichs-california/.

25   "SUPREME COURT OF THE UNITED STATES: Syllabus: JANUS v. AMERICAN FEDERATION OF STATE, COUNTY, AND MUNICIPAL EMPLOYEES, COUNCIL 31, ET AL.," June 27, 2018, https://www.supremecourt.gov/opinions/17pdf/16-1466_2b3j.pdf.

26   Kris Maher, "Unions Take Hit After Court Ruling," *Wall Street Journal*, August 6, 2018.

27   Jessica Barnett, "Union Leaders: Resignation Denied," Commonwealth Foundation policy blog, December 11, 2018, https://www.commonwealthfoundation.org/policyblog/detail/union-leaders-resignation-denied.

28   California Senate Bill No. 285, approved by Governor Brown October 7, 2017.

29   See the Battelle for Kids website at http://www.p21.org/storage/documents/FINAL_REPORT_PDF09-29-06.pdf.

30   Battelle for Kids.

31   Michael F. Lovenheim and Alexander Willen, "A Bad Bargain: How Teacher Collective Bargaining Affects Students' Employment and Earnings Later in Life." See the ERIC website at https://eric.ed.gov/?id=EJ1084123.

32   Neal McCluskey, "Show Me the (Education) Money!" *CATO at Liberty* (blog, CATO Institute), April 20, 2018, https://www.cato.org/blog/show-me-education-money.

33   Table 208.20. Public and Private Elementary and Secondary Teachers, Enrollment, Pupil/Teacher Ratios, and New Teacher Hires: Selected Years, Fall 1955 through Fall 2026, *Digest of Education Statistics*, IEC/NCES, https://nces.ed.gov/programs/digest/d16/tables/dt16_208.20.asp?current=yes.

34   "Enrollment Trends," Fast Facts, IEC/NCES, accessed August 6, 2020, https://nces.ed.gov/fastfacts/display.asp?id=65.

35   Frederick M. Hess, "Year of the Strike," *National Review*, October 29, 2018.

36   Allysia Finley, "L.A. Teachers Union Can't Do Basic Math," *Wall Street Journal*, January 5–6, 2019.

37   The Editorial Board, "Unions in La-La Land," Opinion, *Wall Street Journal*, January 15, 2019, https://www.wsj.com/articles/unions-in-la-la-land-11547511666.

38   The Editorial Board.

39   The Editorial Board.

40   Austin Beutner, "L.A. Schools Have a Math Problem," *Wall Street Journal*, January 15, 2019.

41   Jonathan Moody and Anthony Randazzo, "Hidden Education Funding Cuts," *Equable* report, March 2020.

42 Chad Aldeman, "West Virginia and the Problem with Average Teacher Salary Rankings" *Teacher Pensions Blog*, March 6, 2018, https://www.teacherpensions.org/blog/west-virginia-and-problem-average-teacher-salary-rankings.

43 Finley, "L.A. Teachers Union Can't Do Basic Math."

44 The Editorial Board, "Unions in La-La Land."

45 "From Thomas Jefferson to Edward Carrington, 16 January 1787," Founders Online, National Archives, https://founders.archives.gov/documents/Jefferson/01-11-02-0047. Original source: *The Papers of Thomas Jefferson*, vol. 11, *1 January–6 August 1787*, ed. Julian P. Boyd (Princeton: Princeton University Press, 1955), 48–50.

46 Society of Professional Journalists, "Our Mission," SPJ, accessed August 6, 2020, https://www.spj.org/mission.asp.

47 James Barron, "A. M. Rosenthal Is Remembered for 'Tender Ferocity'," *New York Times*, May 15, 2006, https://www.nytimes.com/2006/05/15/nyregion/15rosenthal.html.

48 Joanne Griffith, ed., *Redefining Black Power: Reflections on the State of Black America* (San Francisco: City Lights, 2012), 115.

49 Susan Lehman, "Times Editor Dean Baquet on Calling Out Donald Trump's Lies," *New York Times*, September 23, 2016, https://www.nytimes.com/2016/09/23/insider/times-editor-dean-baquet-on-calling-out-donald-trumps-lies.html.

50 "*Ethical Journalism: A Handbook of Values and Practices for the News and Editorial Departments*: Introduction and Purpose," *New York Times*, accessed August 6, 2020, https://www.nytimes.com/editorial-standards/ethical-journalism.html#introductionAndPurpose.

51 Rachel Smolkin, "Justice Delayed," *American Journalism Review,* August/September 2007.

52 Michael Barthel and Amy Mitchell, "Americans' Attitudes about the News Media Deeply Divided along Partisan Lines," Pew Research Center, May 10, 2017, http://www.journalism.org/2017/05/10/americans-attitudes-about-the-news-media-deeply-divided-along-partisan-lines/.

53 Gallup, "Confidence in Institutions," accessed August 6, 2020, https://news.gallup.com/poll/1597/confidence-institutions.aspx.

54 Jonathan Wai and Kaja Perina, "Expertise in Journalism: Factors Shaping a Cognitive and Culturally Elite Profession," *Journal of Expertise* (2018).

55 Brett T., "'This Thread Is a Home Run': James Hasson Reminds Us of Journalists Coordinating with the Clinton Campaign," Twitchy, August 19, 2019, https://twitchy.com/brettt-3136/2019/08/19/this-thread-is-a-home-run-james-hasson-reminds-us-of-journalists-coordinating-with-the-clinton-campaign/.

56 Jane C. Timm, "'It's Irresponsible and It's Dangerous': Experts Rip Trump's Idea of Injecting Disinfectant to Treat COVID-19," NBC News, updated April 24, 2020, https://www.nbcnews.com/politics/donald-trump/it-s-irresponsible-it-s-dangerous-experts-rip-trump-s-n1191246.

57 Daniel Funke, "In Context: What Donald Trump Said about Disinfectant, Sun and Coronavirus," PolitiFact, April 24, 2020, https://www.politifact.com/article/2020/apr/24/context-what-donald-trump-said-about-disinfectant-/.

58 Wikipedia, s.v. "Corporation for Public Broadcasting," accessed August 6, 2020, https://en.wikipedia.org/wiki/Corporation_for_Public_Broadcasting.

59   Timothy Karr, "Gov. Phil Murphy Signs New Jersey Civic Info Bill into Law," *Free Press*, August 27, 2018.

60   Adam Gabbatt, "New Jersey Pledges $5m for Local Journalism to Boost State's 'Civic Health'," *Guardian* (UK), July 6, 2018, https://www.theguardian.com/us-news/2018/jul/06/new-jersey-journalism-local-news-civic-information-consortium.

61   Free Press Action Fund, Proposal for the New Jersey Civic Information Consortium, Free Press, April 2017, https://www.freepress.net/sites/default/files/legacy-policy/proposal_for_the_new_jersey_civic_information_consortium.pdf.

62   Jeffrey A. Trachtenberg, "Cardi B, Live Events, Fewer Issues: Meet the New Rolling Stone," *Wall Street Journal*, July 2, 2018, https://www.wsj.com/articles/cardi-b-live-events-fewer-issues-meet-the-new-rolling-stone-1530529320.

63   Pulitzer, "Announcement of the 2018 Pulitzer Prize Winners," Pulitzer.org, April 15, 2018, https://www.pulitzer.org/news/announcement-2018-pulitzer-prize-winners.

64   James Piereson and Naomi Schaefer Riley, "A Battle over a Capitalist's Legacy," *Wall Street Journal*, January 30, 2018.

65   Southern Poverty Law Center, *Annual Report 2017*, https://www.splcenter.org/sites/default/files/com_splc_annual_report_2017_web_final-1.pdf.

66   Dennis Prager, "The Bad Hate the Good: The Southern Poverty Law Center Vs. Prager University," *Prager's Column*, June 19, 2018, https://www.dennisprager.com/the-bad-hate-the-good-the-southern-poverty-law-center-vs-prager-university/.

67   Maria Puente, "George, Amal Clooney donate $1M to Southern Poverty Law Center to Combat Hate Groups," *USA Today*, August 22, 2017, https://www.usatoday.com/story/life/2017/08/22/george-amal-clooney-donate-1-m-southern-poverty-law-center-combat-hate-groups/590033001/.

68   Southern Poverty Law Center, "SPLC Statement on Generous Donation from Apple," SPLC, August 17, 2017, https://www.splcenter.org/news/2017/08/17/splc-statement-generous-donation-apple.

69   Bob Moser, "The Reckoning of Morris Dees and the Southern Poverty Law Center," *New Yorker,* March 21, 2019.

70   Planned Parenthood Federation of America, "Services," accessed August 6, 2020, Planned Parenthood, https://www.plannedparenthood.org/uploads/filer_public/bd/bb/bdbb30b1-4ca3-4c98-8c36-d533c3acbb25/services_feb_2017.pdf.

71   Alexandra Desanctis, What Planned Parenthood's Annual Report Proves, National Review, January 4, 2018.

72   Planned Parenthood, *2016–2017 Annual Report*, plannedparenthood.org, https://www.plannedparenthood.org/uploads/filer_public/71/53/7153464c-8f5d-4a26-bead-2a0dfe2b32ec/20171229_ar16-17_p01_lowres.pdf.

73   Christopher C. Horner, "Law Enforcement for Rent," Competitive Enterprise Institute, August 28, 2018, https://cei.org/AGclimatescheme.

74   Horner.

75   "State AGs for Rent," Opinion, *Wall Street Journal*, November 7, 2018.

76   Casey Tolan, "Gov. Brown on GOP Tax Plan: Republicans 'Acting Like a Bunch of Mafia Thugs'," *Mercury News*, updated December 5, 2017, https://www.mercurynews.com/2017/12/04/jerry-brown-tax-plan-gop-congress/.

77   Adam Andrzejewski and Thomas W. Smith, *National Foundation on the Arts and Humanities: Open the Books Oversight Study* (Burr Ridge, IL: openthebooks.com, July 2017), https://www.openthebooks.com/assets/1/7/OpenTheBooks_Oversight_Report_-_National_Foundation_on_the_Arts_and_Humanities_FINAL.pdf.

78   Benjamin Elisha Sawe, "Richest Counties in the United States," WorldAtlas, April 25, 2017, https://www.worldatlas.com/articles/richest-counties-in-the-united-states.html.

79   Tom Warren, "Google fined a record $5 billion by the EU for Android antitrust violations," The Verge, July 18, 2018, https://www.theverge.com/2018/7/18/17580694/google-android-eu-fine-antitrust.

80   Felix Richter, "Google Hit with Another Antitrust Fine in Europe," Statista, March 20, 2019, https://www.statista.com/chart/14752/eu-antitrust-fines-against-tech-companies/.

81   European Commission, "COLLEGE (2019–2024): The Commissioners: The European Commission's Political Leadership," official website of the European Commission, accessed August 6, 2020, https://ec.europa.eu/commission/commissioners/2014-2019/vestager/announcements/market-works-consumers_en.

82   Verizon Communications Inc. v. Law Offices of Curtis V. Trinko, LLP (02-682) 540 U.S. 398 (2004).

83   47 U.S.C. § 230.

84   Winston Churchill, *The World Crisis*, vol. 1, *1911–1914* (n.p.: Thornton Butterworth, 1923).

85   PragerU.com, "Adam Carolla: Don't Make Things Worse," YouTube video, June 4, 2018, https://www.youtube.com/watch?v=8i6LA-7mi9M.

TRAINING GROUNDS PART 1: WHO RUNS ACADEMIA

1   Wikipedia, s.v. "academic integrity," accessed August 6, 2020, https://en.wikipedia.org/wiki/Academic_integrity.

2   "The Park & the Four Freedoms," Four Freedoms Park Conservancy, accessed August 6, 2020, https://www.fdrfourfreedomspark.org/fdr-the-four-freedoms/.

3   Douglas Belkin, "Votes on Leaders Spread at Colleges," *Wall Street Journal*, May 21, 2018.

4   Mitchell Langbert, Anthony J. Quain, and Daniel B. Klein, "Faculty Voter Registration in Economics, History, Journalism, Law, and Psychology," *Econ Journal Watch* 13, no. 3 (September 2016): 422–51, https://econjwatch.org/File+download/944/LangbertQuainKleinSept2016.pdf?mimetype=pdf.

5   Dian Schaffhauser, "Who's Worth More: The Administrator or the Professor?" *Campus Technology,* August 9, 2017.

6   National Center for College Students with Disabilities website, accessed August 6, 2020, http://www.nccsdonline.org/.

7   Matt Pickles, "Shouldn't Lectures Be Obsolete by Now?" BBC, November 23, 2016, https://www.bbc.com/news/business-38058477.

8   Harvard University, "The Graduating Class of 2018," *Harvard Crimson*, 2018, https://features.thecrimson.com/2018/senior-survey/national-politics-narrative/.

9   Sahar M. Omer, "Libraries to Extend Loan Periods, Eliminate Standard Late Fees," *Harvard Crimson*, May 1, 2017, https://www.thecrimson.com/article/2017/5/1/library-eliminates-standard-fees/.

10   Mara Silvers, "MRC Student Coalition Demands," iPetitions, accessed August 6, 2020, https://www.ipetitions.com/petition/mrc-student-coalition-demands-2.

11   Judith Shulevitz, "In College and Hiding from Scary Ideas," Opinion, *New York Times*, March 22, 2015, https://www.nytimes.com/2015/03/22/opinion/sunday/judith-shu-levitz-hiding-from-scary-ideas.html.

12   "Students protest Heather Mac Donald at Claremont McKenna," YouTube video of Bill O'Reilly's *The O'Reilly Factor*, posted by Fox News, April 10, 2017, https://www.you-tube.com/watch?v=Qw6ZEnUdLKs.

13   Jesús Treviño, "Diversity and Inclusiveness in the Classroom," Office for Diversity and Inclusive Excellence, University of Arizona, https://humanities.arizona.edu/sites/humanities.arizona.edu/files/Classroom%20Dialogue%20Guide%20.pdf.

14   Helen Lauterbach, "Speak UP organizes panel event as an alternative option to Mac Donald lecture," *Bucknellian*, November 22, 2019, https://bucknellian.net/96161/news/speak-up-organizes-panel-event-as-an-alternative-option-to-mac-donald-lecture/.

15   University of California, Irvine, "Message from UCI Chancellor about Current Admission Issues," UCI, August 2, 217, https://news.uci.edu/2017/08/02/message-from-uci-chancellor-about-current-admission-issues/.

16   Richard Vedder, "College Wouldn't Cost So Much If Students and Faculty Worked Harder," *Wall Street Journal*, April 13, 2019.

17   Melissa Korn, "You Graduated Cum Laude? So Did Everyone Else," *Wall Street Journal*, July 3, 2018.

18   Tawnell D. Hobbs, "University of Chicago Plays Down Test Scores," *Wall Street Journal*, June 14, 2018.

19   Nathan Kuncel and Paul Sackett, "The Truth about the SAT and ACT," *Wall Street Journal*, March 8, 2018.

20   Dana Bolger et al., "Open Letter from Yale Law Students, Alumni, and Educators Regarding Brett Kavanaugh," updated July 18, 2018, https://docs.google.com/forms/d/e/1FAIpQLScUrOBy5sPzw1VGusbYr2VqVqPiNmO5adNdo8mlcsryvgOfrw/viewform.

21   Shera S. Avi-Yonah and Jamie D. Halper, "Students Filed Title IX Complaints Against Kavanaugh to Prevent Him from Teaching at Harvard Law," *Harvard Crimson*, October 2, 2018, https://www.thecrimson.com/article/2018/10/2/students-file-title-ix-against-kavanaugh/.

22   Fire, "Student Rights on Campus Guides," accessed August 6, 2020, https://www.thefire.org/first-amendment-library/special-collections/fire-guides/bias-response-team-report-2017/.

23   Eric Owens, "University Of Florida Urges Students To Report Politically Incorrect Halloween Costumes As BIAS INCIDENTS," *Daily Caller*, October 12, 2016, https://dailycaller.com/2016/10/12/university-of-florida-urges-students-to-report-politically-incorrect-halloween-costumes-as-bias-incidents/.

24   Grace Gottschling, "Prof Exposes $11 Million Payroll for "Diversicrats" at UMich," Campus Reform website, June 6, 2018, https://www.campusreform.org/?ID=10991.

25   The Editorial Board, "Adios, Bias Response Team," Opinion, *Wall Street Journal*, October 30, 2019.

26   Dean of Students Office, University of Michigan, "Campus Climate Support," accessed August 6, 2020, https://deanofstudents.umich.edu/campus-climate-support.

27   Iowa State University, "Process," Campus Climate, accessed August 6, 2020, https://www.campusclimate.iastate.edu/system/process.

28   WSN Editorial Board, "NYU Bias Hotline Offers Constructive Resolutions," *Washington Square News* (NYU), September 19, 2019, https://nyunews.com/2016/09/19/nyu-bias-hotline-offers-constructive-resolutions/.

29   Center for Race and Gender, University of California Berkeley, "Islamophobia Reporting App," Berkeley.edu, August 3, 2016, https://www.crg.berkeley.edu/news/islamophobia-reporting-app/.

30   Peter Van Voorhis, "'Virtual Safe Space': Smartphone App Records Campus Microaggressions," *The College Fix,* December 2, 2016, https://www.thecollegefix.com/virtual-safe-space-smartphone-app-records-campus-microaggressions/.

31   Colleen A. Sheehan and James Matthew Wilson, "A Mole Hunt for Diversity 'Bias' at Villanova," *Wall Street Journal*, March 29, 2019.

32   Anemona Hartocollis, "A Campus Argument Goes Viral. Now the College Is Under Siege," *New York Times*, June 16, 2016, https://www.nytimes.com/2017/06/16/us/evergreen-state-protests.html.

33   Abby Spegman, "Evergreen Professor at Center of Protests Resigns; College Will Pay $500,000," *Seattle Times*, updated October 5, 2017, https://www.seattletimes.com/seattle-news/evergreen-professor-at-center-of-protests-resigns-college-will-pay-500000/.

34   Jillian Kay Melchior, "Rough Social Justice at Evergreen State," *Wall Street Journal*, May 23, 2018.

35   Yale University Office of the President, "Committee to Establish Principles on Renaming," Yale, accessed August 6, 2020, https://president.yale.edu/advisory-groups/presidents-committees/committee-establish-principles-renaming-0.

36   Joe Parkinson and Emre Peker, "In University Purge, Turkey's Erdogan Hits Secularists and Boosts Conservatives," *Wall Street Journal*, August 24, 2016, https://www.wsj.com/articles/after-failed-coup-turkeys-erdogan-is-purging-universities-of-potential-enemies-1472053608.

37   Wikipedia, s.v. "Sino-British Joint Declaration," accessed August 6, 2020, https://en.wikipedia.org/wiki/Sino-British_Joint_Declaration.

38   Reuters, "China's Xi calls for universities' allegiance to the Communist Party," Reuters, December 8, 2016, https://www.reuters.com/article/us-china-education/chinas-xi-calls-for-universities-allegiance-to-the-communist-party-idUSKBN13Y0B5.

39   Raymond Yeung and Ng Kang-chung, "Watch What You Say about Hong Kong Independence, CY Leung Warns Local Schools," *South China Morning Post*, August 16, 2016, https://www.scmp.com/news/hong-kong/politics/article/2004621/watch-what-you-say-about-hong-kong-independence-cy-leung.

40   Yeung and Kang-chung.

41   Wikipedia, s.v. "Moral and national education controversy," accessed August 6, 2020, https://en.wikipedia.org/wiki/Moral_and_National_Education_controversy.

42   The Editorial Board, "China's Brutal 'Boarding Schools'," Opinion, *New York Times*, March 17, 2019, https://www.nytimes.com/2019/03/17/opinion/china-uighurs.html.

43 Ben Blanchard, "China Says Pace of Xinjiang 'Education' Will Slow, but Defends Camps," Reuters, January 6, 2019, https://www.reuters.com/article/us-china-xinjiang-insight/china-says-pace-of-xinjiang-education-will-slow-but-defends-camps-idUSKCN1P007W.

44 Fire, "Spotlight on Speech Codes 2017," Fire website, https://www.thefire.org/spotlight-on-speech-codes-2017/.

45 Philip Wen, "China Draws Fire Over Academic Controls," *Wall Street Journal*, December 19, 2019.

46 Abigail Thompson, "The University's New Loyalty Oath," *Wall Street Journal*, December 20, 2019.

47 William F. Buckley and Ronald Reagan, *Firing Line,* Episode S0401, 1980.

48 OpenSecrets.org, 2012 Presidential Race, Barack Obama (D), Contributors, https://www.opensecrets.org/pres12/.

49 Anthony Gockowski, "Evergreen Profs Asked to Make 'Accommodations' for Protesters," Campus Reform, July 6, 2017, https://www.campusreform.org/?ID=9398.

50 See Yale, *Bulldogs' Blogs*, https://admissions.yale.edu/bulldogs-blogs.

51 Hannah Mendlowitz, "In Support of Student Protests," Yale, February 23, 2018, https://admissions.yale.edu/bulldogs-blogs/hannah/2018/02/23/support-student-protests.

52 United States Department of Education Office for Civil Rights, Assistant Secretary, letter dated April 4, 2011, https://www2.ed.gov/about/offices/list/ocr/letters/colleague-201104.pdf.

53 Nicholas Wolfinger, "Op-ed: Frivolous Title IX Investigations Are an Insult to Real Sexual Assault Victims," *Deseret News*, October 14, 2017, https://www.deseret.com/2017/10/14/20621493/op-ed-frivolous-title-ix-investigations-are-an-insult-to-real-sexual-assault-victims.

54 Yale University, "Yale Sexual Misconduct Policies and Related Definitions," Sexual Misconduct Response & Prevention, accessed August 6, 2020, https://smr.yale.edu/find-policies-information/yale-sexual-misconduct-policies-and-related-definitions.

55 Ingrid Jacques, "Jacques: False Title IX Complaint Stalls Female UM Prof's Career," Opinion, *Detroit News*, February 28, 2018, https://www.detroitnews.com/story/opinion/columnists/ingrid-jacques/2018/02/28/false-title-nine-complaint-um-female-professor/110956612/.

56 Jacques.

57 Jacques.

58 Laura Kipnis *Unwanted Advances: Sexual Paranoia Comes to Campus* (New York: Harper, 2017).

59 Federal Reserve Bank of St. Louis, "Student Loans Owned and Securitized, Outstanding," FRED, Economic Research, updated July 8, 2020, https://fred.stlouisfed.org/graph/?id=SLOAS,#0.

60 "Student Loans Will Cost Taxpayers $36 Billion: Thanks, Obama," *Investor's Business Daily*, February 9, 2018, https://www.investors.com/politics/editorials/student-loans-will-cost-taxpayers-36-billion-thanks-obama/.

61 U.S. Government Accountability Office, "Federal Student Loans: Education Needs to Improve its Income-Driven Repayment Plan Budget Estimates," GAO-17–22, November 2016.

62 "The Great Student-Loan Writedown," Review & Outlook, *Wall Street Journal*, February 13, 2020.

63   Josh Mitchell, "Student Loan Losses Seen Costing U.S. More Than $400 Billion," *Wall Street Journal*, November 21, 2020.

64   United States Government Accountability Office, "Public Service Loan Forgiveness: Education Needs to Provide Better Information for the Loan Servicer and Borrowers," Report to Congressional Requesters, September 2018, https://www.gao.gov/assets/700/694304.pdf.

65   The Editorial Board, "The Great Student-Loan Scam," Review & Outlook, *Wall Street Journal*, August 21, 2019, https://www.wsj.com/articles/the-great-student-loan-scam-11566343674.

66   *Federal Student Loans: Actions Needed to Improve Oversight of Schools' Default Rates*, GAO-18-163, April 26, 2018.

67   Adam Andrzejewski and Thomas W. Smith, *Open the Books Oversight Report: Ivy League, Inc.*, March, 2017, https://www.openthebooks.com/assets/1/6/Oversight_IvyLeagueInc_FINAL.pdf.

68   National Science Board, "Expenditures and Funding for Academic R&D," Science & Engineering Indicators 2018, https://www.nsf.gov/statistics/2018/nsb20181/report/sections/academic-research-and-development/expenditures-and-funding-for-academic-r-d.

69   See the website of the U.S. Department of Labor, https://www.dol.gov/.

70   William J. Bennett, "Our Greedy Colleges," *New York Times*, February 18, 1987.

71   David O. Lucca, Taylor Nadauld, and Karen Shen, *Credit Supply and the Rise in College Tuition: Evidence from the Expansion in Federal Student Aid Programs*, Federal Reserve Bank of New York, Staff Report no. 733, July 2015, revised February 2017, https://www.newyorkfed.org/medialibrary/media/research/staff_reports/sr733.pdf.

72   Kari Travis, "U.S. Rep. Foxx Talks PROSPER Act, Modern Challenges for Higher Education," *Carolina Journal*, February 2, 2018, https://www.carolinajournal.com/news-article/rep-virginia-foxx-talks-prosper-act-modern-challenges-for-higher-education/.

73   John Villasenor, "Views Among College Students regarding the First Amendment: Results from a New Survey," Brookings, September 18, 2017, https://www.brookings.edu/blog/fixgov/2017/09/18/views-among-college-students-regarding-the-first-amendment-results-from-a-new-survey/.

74   Eric L. Dey et al., *Engaging Diverse Viewpoints: What Is the Campus Climate for Perspective-Taking?* (Washington, DC: Association of American Colleges and Universities, 2010), https://tools.bard.edu/wwwmedia/files/6796486/1/Engaging_Diverse_Viewpoints.pdf.

75   "Student Attitudes Free Speech Survey," 2017, *Fire*, https://www.thefire.org/publications/student-surveys/student-attitudes-free-speech-survey/student-attitudes-free-speech-survey-full-text/.

76   Abby Ohlheiser, "Ray Kelly Was Booed off the Stage at Brown University," *Atlantic*, October 29, 2013, https://www.theatlantic.com/national/archive/2013/10/ray-kelly-gets-booed-stage-brown-university/354606/.

77   Valerie Strauss, "Scripps College Uninvites George Will Because of Column on Sexual Assault," *Answer Sheet* (*Washington Post* blog), October 8, 2014, https://www.washingtonpost.com/news/answer-sheet/wp/2014/10/08/scripps-college-uninvites-george-will-because-of-column-on-sexual-assault/?utm_term=.96b9b9ea3cf5.

78   Madison Park and Kyung Lah, "Berkeley Protests of Yiannopoulos Caused $100,000 in Damage," CNN, February 2, 2017, https://www.cnn.com/2017/02/01/us/milo-yian-nopoulos-berkeley/index.html.

79   Juan Prieto, "Violence Helped Ensure Safety of Students," *Daily Californian*, February 7, 2017, http://www.dailycal.org/2017/02/07/violence-helped-ensure-safety-students/.

80   Fire, "Email from the Intercultural Affairs Committee," Fire, October 27, 2015, https://www.thefire.org/email-from-intercultural-affairs/.

81   Yale, "Outstanding Students Honored at Class Day," YaleNews, May 19, 2015, https://news.yale.edu/2017/05/19/outstanding-students-honored-class-day.

82   Peter Salovey, "Actions to Address Discrimination, Harassment; Create More Inclusive Yale," YaleNews, April 9, 2019, https://news.yale.edu/2019/04/09/actions-address-discrimination-harassment-create-more-inclusive-yale.

83   Yale University, "Yale Receives $4 Million Mellon Foundation Grant to Support Race Studies Centers across Four Universities," *YaleNews*, January 4, 2020, https://news.yale.edu/2020/01/14/yale-receives-4-million-mellon-foundation-grant-support-race-studies.

84   University of California, Irvine, UCI Sustainability, accessed September 2, 2020, https://sustainability.uci.edu/teaching-climate-and-sustainability-a-faculty-curriculum-workshop/

85   Andrew Follett, "This Is an Actual Lecture at MIT: 'Is Islamophobia Accelerating Global Warming?'" *Daily Caller*, May 11, 2016, https://dailycaller.com/2016/05/11/this-is-an-actual-lecture-at-mit-is-islamophobia-accelerating-global-warming/.

86   Kate Hardiman, "Professors Tell Students: Drop Class If You Dispute Man-Made Climate Change," *The College Fix*, August 31, 2016, https://www.thecollegefix.com/professors-tell-students-drop-class-dispute-man-made-climate-change/.

87   Hardiman.

88   Susan Scafidi, *Who Owns Culture?: Appropriation and Authenticity in American Law* (Rutgers University Press, 2005).

89   Catherine Rampell, "Political Correctness Devours Yet Another College, Fighting over Mini-Sombreros," *Washington Post*, March 3. 2016, https://www.washingtonpost.com/opinions/party-culture/2016/03/03/fdb46cc4-e185-11e5-9c36-e1902f6b6571_story.html?utm_term=.365518c6fe6b.

90   Bowdoin Orient editorial board, "Listen and Learn," *Bowdoin Orient*, February 26, 2016, http://bowdoinorient.com/bonus/article/10975.

91   Jenna Scott, "Statement of Solidarity re: "Tequila" Party," BSG, February 24, 2016, http://students.bowdoin.edu/bsg/bsg/statement-of-solidarity-re-tequila-party/.

92   Pete Vanderzwet, "Study: Liberal-to-Conservative Faculty Ratio in Academia Will Blow Your Mind," *American Thinker*, February 11, 2017, https://www.americanthinker.com/blog/2017/02/study_liberaltoconservative_faculty_ratio_in_academia_will_blow_your_mind.html.

93   American Association of University Professors, "About: Mission," AAUP website, accessed August 6, 2020, https://www.aaup.org/about/mission-1.

94   American Association of University Professors, "American Association of University Professors," AAUP, January 31, 2017, https://www.aaup.org/file/2017-Harassment_Faculty_0.pdf.

95   Jennifer Kabbany, "U. Michigan Professor Rails against Voting Trump in Lengthy
      Classroom Rant (VIDEO)," *The College Fix*, November 8, 2016, https://www.thecolleg-
      efix.com/u-michigan-professor-rails-voting-trump-lengthy-classroom-rant-video/.

96   William Nardi, "Professors Call Founding Fathers 'Terrorists,' Founding Ideals a
      'Fabrication'," *The College Fix*, November 16, 2016, https://www.thecollegefix.com/
      professors-call-founding-fathers-terrorists-founding-ideals-fabrication/.

97   Fire, "Spotlight on Speech Codes 2017," Fire website, https://www.thefire.org/
      spotlight-on-speech-codes-2017/.

98   Fire.

99   Fire.

100   Thomas K. Lindsay, "Congress vs. Campus Speech Restrictions," *RealClear Politics*,
      August 24, 2015, https://www.realclearpolicy.com/blog/2015/08/25/congress_vs_
      campus_speech_restrictions_1399.html.

101   Kathleen Parker, "At Marquette, Conservatives Got it Wrong," Opinion, *Washington
      Post*, July 7, 2018.

102   McAdams v. Marquette, case number 2017-AP-1240.

103   Molly Beck, "Marquette Professor John McAdams Prevails: Five Takeaways from
      Wisconsin Supreme Court Decision," *Milwaukee Journal Sentinel*, July 6, 2018, https://
      www.jsonline.com/story/news/politics/2018/07/06/marquette-professor-john-
      mcadams-prevails-five-takeaways-wisconsin-supreme-court-decision/762921002/.

104   Marquette University, "McAdams Case: Get the Facts," Marquette.edu, Facts about the
      McAdams Case, accessed August 6, 2020, http://www.marquette.edu/mcadams-case-
      facts/mcadams-facts.php.

105   Joe Pinsker, "The Problem with 'Hey Guys'," *Atlantic*, August 23, 2018, https://www.
      theatlantic.com/family/archive/2018/08/guys-gender-neutral/568231/.

106   Fire, "RUTGERS UNIVERSITY – NEW BRUNSWICK," Fire School Spotlight, accessed
      August 6, 2020, https://www.thefire.org/schools/rutgers-university-new-brunswick/.

107   Guest Columnist, "University of Oregon's Bias Response Team needs open scrutiny
      (OPINION)," *Oregonian*, June 7, 2016, https://www.oregonlive.com/opinion/index.
      ssf/2016/06/university_of_oregons_bias_res.html.

108   Olivia Sylvester, "Students Remove Shakespeare Portrait in English dept., Aiming
      for Inclusivity," *Daily Pennsylvanian*, December 12, 2016, https://www.thedp.com/
      article/2016/12/shakespeare-portrait-removed.

109   Philip Sean Curran, "PRINCETON: University's Gender-Neutral Language Guidelines
      Come to Light," CentralJersey.com, August 18, 2016. URL not available.

110   Todd Starnes, "Call Me 'Ze,' Not 'He': University Wants Everyone to Use 'Gender
      Inclusive' Pronouns," *Townhall*, August 27, 2015, https://townhall.com/columnists/
      toddstarnes/2015/08/27/call-me-ze-not-he-university-wants-everyone-to-use-
      gender-inclusive-pronouns-n2044684.

111   The Citizen Lab.

112   Forbes Guest Contributor, "Business of Education," *Forbes*, September 28, 2011,
      https://www.forbes.com/global/2011/1010/thoughts-opinions-proverbs-business-
      education-forbes-staff.html#7638555231d4.

113   Carrie Dann, "Americans Split on Whether 4-Year College Degree Is Worth the
      Cost," NBC News, September 7, 2017, https://www.nbcnews.com/politics/first-read/
      americans-split-whether-4-year-college-degree-worth-cost-n799336.

114 CalPoly, "Collegiate Learning Assessment (CLA+)," Academics Programs and Planning, accessed September 2, 2020, https://academicprograms.calpoly.edu/cla.

115 Douglas Belkin, "Exclusive Test Data: Many Colleges Fail to Improve Critical-Thinking Skills," *Wall Street Journal*, June 5, 2017.

116 Jillian Berman, "Student Debt Just Hit $1.5 Trillion," *MarketWatch*, May 8, 2015, https://www.marketwatch.com/story/student-debt-just-hit-15-trillion-2018-05-08.

117 NextAdvisor, in partnership with Time, "Personal Loans," *Time*, accessed August 6, 2020, http://time.com/money/5169145/50000-dollars-student-debt-default/.

118 Josh Mitchell, "The Long Road to the Student Debt Crisis," *Wall Street Journal*, June 8–9, 2019.

119 The Editorial Board, "The Great Student-Loan Scam," Opinion, *Wall Street Journal*, August 20, 2019.

120 Abigail Hess, "American Women Hold Two-Thirds of All Student Debt—Here's Why," CNBC, March 13, 2018, https://www.cnbc.com/2018/03/13/american-women-hold-two-thirds-of-all-student-debt-heres-why.html.

121 Jaison R. Abel, Richard Deitz, and Yaqin Su, "Are Recent College Graduates Finding Good Jobs?" *Current Issues in Economics and Finance* 20, no, 1 (2014), https://www.newyorkfed.org/medialibrary/media/research/current_issues/ci20-1.pdf.

122 Andrea Fuller, "Student Debt Payback Far Worse Than Believed," *Wall Street Journal*, January 18, 2017.

123 Fuller.

124 Fuller.

125 Zachary Bleemer et al., *Echoes of Rising Tuition in Students' Borrowing, Educational Attainment, and Homeownership in Post-Recession America*, Staff Report No. 820 (Federal Reserve Bank of New York, July 2017), https://www.newyorkfed.org/medialibrary/media/research/staff_reports/sr820.pdf.

126 Tyler Durden, "US Government Caught Fabricating Student Loan Default Data," *Trading Report*, January 19, 2017, https://www.thetradingreport.com/2017/01/19/us-government-caught-fabricating-student-loan-default-data/.

127 Anna Maria Andriotis, "Student Debt at 65," *Wall Street Journal*, February 2–3, 2019.

128 Josh Mitchell, "The U.S. Makes It Easy for Parents to Get College Loans—Repaying Them Is Another Story," *Wall Street Journal*, April 24, 2017.

129 Mitchell.

130 Mitchell.

131 uAspire and New America, "Decoding the Cost of College, The Case for Transparent Financial Aid Award Letters," ECMC Foundation, June 5, 2018, downloadable at https://www.ecmcfoundation.org/informed/2019/decoding-the-cost-of-college-the-case-for-transparent-financial-aid-award-letters.

132 Stephanie Marken and Zac Auter, "Half of U.S. Adults Would Change at Least One Education Decision," Gallup, June 1, 2017, https://news.gallup.com/poll/211529/half-adults-change-least-one-education-decision.aspx.

133 Marken and Auter.

134 Stephen Ambrose, *Eisenhower: Soldier and President* (New York: Simon and Shuster, 1968), 484.

135 Preety Sidhu and Valerie J. Calderon, "Many Business Leaders Doubt U.S. Colleges Prepare Students," Gallup, February 26, 2014, https://news.gallup.com/poll/167630/business-leaders-doubt-colleges-prepare-students.aspx.

136   Brandon Busteed, "America's "No Confidence" Vote on College Grads' Work Readiness," Gallup, April 24, 2015, https://news.gallup.com/opinion/gallup/182867/america-no-confidence-vote-college-grads-work-readiness.aspx.

137   Brandon Busteed and Zac Auter, "Career-Relevant Education Linked to Student Well-Being," *Gallup Blog*, February 13, 2018, https://news.gallup.com/opinion/gallup/226934/career-relevant-education-linked-student.aspx.

138   Allie Grasgreen, "Ready or Not," *Inside Higher Ed*, February 2, 2014, https://www.insidehighered.com/news/2014/02/26/provosts-business-leaders-disagree-graduates-career-readiness.

139   Camille L. Ryan and Kurt Bauman, "Educational Attainment in the United States: 2015: Population Characteristics," March 2016, United States Census Bureau, https://www.census.gov/content/dam/Census/library/publications/2016/demo/p20-578.pdf.

140   Express Employment Professionals, "Blue Collar Workers: Career and Life Satisfaction High; Trust in Elected Officials Low," *America Employed*, August 29, 2019, https://www.expresspros.com/Newsroom/America-Employed/Blue-Collar-Workers-Career-and-Life-Satisfaction-High-Trust-in-Elected-Officials-Low.aspx.

141   Andrzejewski and Smith, *Open the Books Oversight Report: Ivy League, Inc.*

142   Farran Powell, "10 Universities with the Biggest Endowments," *U.S. News and World Report*, September 28, 2017.

143   Melissa Korn, "Giving to Colleges Hits $46.7 Billion," *Wall Street Journal*, February 11, 2019.

144   Tom Coburn, Thomas W. Smith, and Adam Andrzejewski, "Paid Advertising," a letter to President Donald Trump reprinting in *USA Today*, October 1, 2018, https://www.openthebooks.com/assets/1/7/USA_Today_Two-Page_Ad__1.pdf.

145   Financial Report, Fiscal Year 2019, Harvard University.

146   Korn, "Giving to Colleges Hits $46.7 Billion."

147   NSC Research Center, "Current Term Enrollment – Spring 2018," National Student Clearinghouse Research Center website, accessed August 6, 2020, http://nscresearch-center.org/currenttermenrollmentestimate-spring2018/.

TRAINING GROUNDS PART 2: HIJACKING STEM

1   "Best Global Universities for Engineering," *U.S. News & World Report*, accessed August 7, 2020, https://www.usnews.com/education/best-global-universities/engineering.

2   Jill Barshay, "U.S. Now Ranks Near the Bottom among 35 Industrialized Nations in Math," *Hechinger Report*, December 6, 2016, https://hechingerreport.org/u-s-now-ranks-near-bottom-among-35-industrialized-nations-math/.

3   Ellen Barry, "U.S. Accuses Harvard Scientist of Concealing Chinese Funding," *New York Times*, January 28, 2020, https://www.nytimes.com/2020/01/28/us/charles-lieber-harvard.html.

4   Organisation for Economic Co-Operation and Development, "China Headed to Overtake EU, US in Science & Technology Spending, OECD Says," OECD.org, http://www.oecd.org/newsroom/china-headed-to-overtake-eu-us-in-science-technology-spending.htm.

5   Mary Platt, "$15M+ Gift Establishes Smith Institute for Political Economy and Philosophy at Chapman University," *Newsroom* (blog, Chapman University), December 5, 2016, https://blogs.chapman.edu/news-and-stories/2016/12/05/15m-gift-establishes-smith-institute-for-political-economy-and-philosophy-at-chapman-university/.

6   Danielle Struppa, "'UnKoch' Attacks Academic Freedom," *Wall Street Journal*, May 20, 2018, https://www.wsj.com/articles/unkoch-attacks-academic-freedom-1526841292.

7   Pardes Seleh, "Stanford Faculty Advised to Drop Gendered Pronouns, Stop Calling on So Many Males in Class," *Daily Wire*, September 5, 2016, https://www.dailywire.com/news/stanford-faculty-advised-stop-using-gendered-pardes-seleh.

8   MacArthur Foundation, "About Us," accessed August 7, 2020, https://www.macfound.org/about/.

9   The White House, "President Obama Awards the Presidential Medal of Freedom," The Presidential Medal of Freedom website, accessed August 7, 2020, https://obamawhitehouse.archives.gov/campaign/medal-of-freedom.

10   Ben Guarino, "In Trump Budget Briefing, 'Climate Change Musical' Is Cited as Tax Waste. Wait, What?" *Washington Post*, May 23, 2017, https://www.washingtonpost.com/news/speaking-of-science/wp/2017/05/23/in-trump-budget-briefing-climate-change-musical-cited-as-tax-waste-wait-what/?utm_term=.a496a4fe4180.

11   Office of the Director, "Diversity Initiatives," National Science Foundation, accessed August 7, 2020, https://www.nsf.gov/od/odi/diversity.jsp.

12   Heather Mac Donald, "How Identity Politics Is Harming the Sciences," *City Journal*, Spring 2018, https://www.city-journal.org/html/how-identity-politics-harming-sciences-15826.html.

13   ACT Inc., *The Condition of College and Career Readiness: Nation 2018*, ACT, https://www.act.org/content/dam/act/unsecured/documents/cccr2018/National-CCCR-2018.pdf.

14   Rafi Eis, "The Conservative and Progressive Theories of Education," *National Review,* November 25, 2019.

15   American Academy of Arts & Sciences, "Indicator," Bachelor's Degrees in the Humanities, accessed August 27, 2020, https://www.amacad.org/humanities-indicators/higher-education/bachelors-degrees-humanities.

16   American Academy of Arts & Sciences, "Workforce," Humanities Indicators, accessed August 7, 2020, https://www.humanitiesindicators.org/content/indicatordoc.aspx?i=10.

17   Jaison R. Abel and Richard Deitz, "Do the Benefits of College Still Outweigh the Costs?" Federal Reserve Bank of New York, *Current Issues in Economics and Finance* 20, no. 3, (2014). https://www.newyorkfed.org/medialibrary/media/research/current_issues/ci20-3.pdf.

18   PayScale.com, "Highest Paying Jobs with a Bachelor's Degree," College Salary Report, updated for 2019, https://www.payscale.com/college-salary-report/majors-that-pay-you-back/bachelors.

19   Strada and Gallup, "From College to Life: Relevance and the Value of Higher Education," Strada Education Network, May 2018, available online at https://go.stradaeducation.org/from-college-to-life.

20   National Science Board, *2018 Science & Engineering Indicators*, NSF, https://www.nsf.gov/statistics/2018/nsb20181/assets/nsb20181.pdf.

21   Anthony P. Carnevale, Jeff Strohl, and Michelle Melton, *What's It Worth? The Economic Value of College Majors*, Georgetown University Center on Education and the Workforce (2014), accessed August 7, 2020, https://1gyhoq479ufd3yna29x7ubjn-wpengine.netdna-ssl.com/wp-content/uploads/2014/11/whatsitworth-complete.pdf.

22   Carnevale, Strohl, and Melton.

23   Anemona Hartocollis, "Harvard Rated Asian-American Applicants Lower on Personality Traits, Suit Says," *New York Times*, June 15, 2018, https://www.nytimes.com/2018/06/15/us/harvard-asian-enrollment-applicants.html.

24   Allen Cheng, "SAT / ACT Prep Online Guides and Tips: What Harvard's Asian Admissions Lawsuit Reveals About How You Should Approach College Applications," *PrepScholar* (blog), October 19, 2018, https://blog.prepscholar.com/harvard-asian-admissions-lawsuit-application-strategy.

25   Deirdre Fernandes, "Harvard Report Found Asian-Americans Faced Admissions Penalty," *Boston Globe*, June 15, 2018, https://www.bostonglobe.com/metro/2018/06/15/harvard-studies-revealed-concern-over-asian-american-admis-sions-rate/cZcvzgxFg9zZ6F2am5QeVP/story.html.

26   Daniel Golden, "Debate over Affirmative Action in College Admissions Could Be Disastrous for Legacy Students," *Pacific Standard*, July 16, 2018, https://psmag.com/education/affirmative-action-in-college-admissions.

27   UN, "Our Common Future, Chapter 2: Towards Sustainable Development," from A/42/427. *Our Common Future: Report of the World Commission on Environment and Development*, UN Documents website, accessed August 7, 2020, http://www.un-documents.net/ocf-02.htm; *Report of the World Commission on Environment and Development: Our Common Future* (1987), https://sustainabledevelopment.un.org/content/documents/5987our-common-future.pdf.

28   Rachelle DeJong, "An Ivy League Nudge-ucation," *Commentary* magazine, April 2014, https://www.commentarymagazine.com/articles/dejong-rachelle/an-ivy-league-nudge-ucation/.

29   Emory, "Make Your Personal Sustainability Pledge," Sustainability Initiatives, accessed August 7, 2020, http://sustainability.emory.edu/cgi-bin/MySQLdb?VIEW=/viewfiles/view_pledge.txt&pageid=1042.

30   Sustainability Council, minutes from December 8, 2011, meeting, p. 4, https://sustain-ability.siu.edu/_common/documents/2011-2012/2011-dec-minutes.pdf.

31   Rachelle Peterson and Peter W. Wood, *Sustainability: Higher Education's New Fundamentalism*, National Association of Scholars, March 2015, https://www.nas.org/storage/app/media/images/documents/NAS-Sustainability-Digital.pdf.

32   The Association for the Advancement of Sustainability in Higher Education, "Academic Programs," AASHE Campus Sustainability Hub, accessed August 7, 2020, https://hub.aashe.org/browse/types/academicprogram/.

33   Cornell Atkinson Center for Sustainability, Cornell Sustainability Courses, accessed August 7, 2020, http://www.atkinson.cornell.edu/education/curricula/index.php.

34   Blaine Friedlander, "Cornell Earns STARS Platinum Sustainability Rating," *Cornell Chronicle*, June 25, 2020, https://sustainablecampus.cornell.edu/news/cornell-earns-stars-platinum-sustainability-rating.

35   Peter Boghossian and James Lindsay, "The Conceptual Penis as a Social Construct; A Sokal-Style Hoax on Gender Studies," *Skeptic* magazine, 2017, https://www.skeptic.com/reading_room/.conceptual-penis-social-contruct-sokal-style-hoax-on-gender-studies/.

36   Charlotte Allen, "A Hoax and Its 'Human Subjects,'" *Wall Street Journal*, January 28, 2019.

37   Allen.

38   Carrie Mott and Daniel Cockayne, "Citation Matters: Mobilizing the Politics of Citation Toward a Practice of 'Conscientious Engagement,'" *Gender Place and Culture: A Journal of Feminist Geography*, June 2017.

39   Mark Carey, M. Jackson, and Alessandro Antonello, "Glaciers, Gender, and Science," *Progress in Human Geography* 40, no. 6 (2016), https://doi. org/10.1177%2f0309132515623368 .

40   Erin Palmer, "(Re)Figuring the World of General Chemistry: Possibilities for Participation, Learning, and Identity" (PhD diss., University of California, Berkeley, 2018), https://digitalassets.lib.berkeley.edu/etd/ucb/text/Palmer_ berkeley_0028E_18083.pdf.

41   Tian An Wong, "How Mathematics Can Be an Anti-Racist, Feminist Enterprise," *The Print*, February 6, 2020, https://theprint.in/opinion/ how-mathematics-can-be-an-anti-racist-feminist-enterprise/359842/.

42   Caltech, "Academic Preparation," Caltech Undergraduate Admissions website, accessed August 7, 2020, https://www.admissions.caltech.edu/apply/ first-year-freshman-applicants/academic-preparation.

43   American College for Physicians, "About ACP: Who We Are," accessed August 7, 2020, https://www.acponline.org/about-acp/who-we-are.

44   Heather Heying, "First, They Came for the Biologists," *Wall Street Journal*, October 2, 2017, https://www.wsj.com/articles/first-they-came-for-the-biologists-1506984033.

45   *Science: The Endless Frontier: A Report to the President by Vannevar Bush, Director of the Office of Scientific Research and Development, July 1945,* https://www.nsf.gov/od/ lpa/nsf50/vbush1945.htm.

FUNDING SOURCES PART 1: THE FED

1   "S&P 500: $100 Invested on Fed Days vs. Non-Fed Days Since 1995" (2016), http://fm.cnbc.com/applications/cnbc.com/resources/editorialfiles/ charts/2016/09/1474399854_Untitled.png.

2   Fred Imbert, "Bespoke: The S&P 500 Has Performed 10 Times Better on Fed Days," CNBC, September 20, 2016, https://www.cnbc.com/amp/2016/09/20/bespoke-the- sp-500-has-performed-10-times-better-on-fed-days.html.

3   Imbert.

4   Federal Reserve, "The Structure and Functions of the Federal Reserve System," FederalReserveEducation.org, accessed August 7, 2020, https://www.federalreserv- eeducation.org/about-the-fed/structure-and-functions.

5   Board of Governors of the Federal Reserve System, "What Are the Federal Reserve's Objectives in Conducting Monetary Policy?" federalreserve.gov, accessed August 7, 2020, https://www.federalreserve.gov/faqs/money_12848.htm.

6   John C. Williams, "The Future Fortunes of R-star: Are They Really Rising: Remarks to the Economic Club of Minnesota?" May 15, 2018, John C. Williams' Speeches, Federal Reserve Bank of San Francisco website, https://www.frbsf. org/our-district/press/presidents-speeches/williams-speeches/2018/may/ future-fortunes-r-star-are-they-rising/.

7   Bill Dudley, "The Fed Shouldn't Enable Donald Trump," Bloomberg Opinions,
     August 27, 2019, https://www.bloomberg.com/opinion/articles/2019-08-27/
     the-fed-shouldn-t-enable-donald-trump.

8   Dudley.

9   Federal Reserve, "Federal Reserve Reform Act of 1977," Federal Reserve
     History, November 16, 1977, https://www.federalreservehistory.org/essays/
     fed_reform_act_of_1977.

10   Wikipedia, s.v. "Federal Reserve Reform Act of 1977," accessed August 7, 2020,
     https://en.wikipedia.org/wiki/Federal_Reserve_Reform_Act_of_1977.

11   Anthony M. Diercks, The Reader's Guide to Optimal Monetary Policy, initial submission
     to JEL, June 2017.

12   Jerome H. Powell, chairman, Board of Governors of the Federal Reserve System, letter
     to April 18, 2019, https://www.schatz.senate.gov/imo/media/doc/Chair%20Powell%20
     to%20Sen.%20Schatz%204.18.19.pdf.

13   Mary C. Daly, "Why Climate Change Matters to Us, Federal Reserve Bank of
     San Francisco," Mary Daly's Speeches, November 8, 2019, https://www.frbsf.
     org/our-district/press/presidents-speeches/mary-c-daly/2019/november/
     why-climate-change-matters-to-us/.

14   Raphael Bostic, "A Moral and Economic Imperative to End Racism," Federal Reserve
     Bank of Atlanta, July 2020, https://www.frbatlanta.org/about/feature/2020/06/12/
     bostic-a-moral-and-economic-imperative-to-end-racism.

15   Lael Brainard, "Delivering Fast Payments for All," Federal Reserve Bank of Kansas City
     town hall speech, August 5, 2019, https://www.bis.org/review/r190812b.htm.

16   "Former Fed Chairman Alan Greenspan Speaks Extensively to Maria Bartiromo," CNBC
     interview, August 17, 2012, https://www.cnbc.com/id/20819918/.

17   Eric Levitz, "Fed Chair Warns Trump to Not Roll Back Wall Street Regulations,"
     Intelligencer, August 25, 2017, http://nymag.com/intelligencer/2017/08/fed-chair-
     implores-trump-to-keep-wall-street-regulations.html?gtm=top&gtm=bottom.

18   Elena Holodny, "FISCHER: Trump's push to deregulate Wall Street 'may be taking us
     in a direction that is very dangerous'," Business Insider, August 16, 2017, https://www.
     businessinsider.com/fed-stanley-fischer-on-unwinding-post-crisis-regulation-2017-8.

19   American Economic Association, AEA Presidential Address, accessed
     August 7, 2020, https://www.aeaweb.org/webcasts/2020/
     aea-presidential-address-twenty-first-century-monetary-policy.

20   François Villeroy de Galhau, "The Euro Area: Staying the Course Through
     Uncertainties," introductory remarks at the Bank of France Symposium & 34th
     SUERF Colloquium, March 28, 2019, https://www.banque-france.fr/en/intervention/
     euro-area-staying-course-through-uncertainties.

21   Lisa Beilfuss, "Fed Chief Touts Early Signs of Recovery, but Warns of Significant
     Uncertainty and Calls for More Congressional Support", Barron's, June 16, 2020,
     https://www.barrons.com/articles/fed-chief-touts-early-signs-of-recovery-but-warns-
     of-significant-uncertainty-and-calls-for-more-congressional-support-51592319158.

22   Federal Reserve, "Janet Yellen," Federal Reserve History, accessed August 7, 2020,
     https://www.federalreservehistory.org/people/janet_l_yellen.

23   Board of Governors of the Federal Reserve System, "Lael Brainerd," federalreserve.gov,
     accessed August 7, 2020, https://www.federalreserve.gov/aboutthefed/bios/board/
     brainard.htm.

24   Federal Reserve Bank of San Francisco, "Mary C. Daly Named Federal Reserve Bank of San Francisco President and Chief Executive Officer," news release, September 14, 2018, https://www.frbsf.org/our-district/press/news-releases/2018/mary-c-daly-named-federal-reserve-bank-of-san-francisco-president-and-chief-executive-officer/.

25   John Kenneth Galbraith, *U.S. News & World Report*, January 11, 1988.

26   Jeff Cox, "Janet Yellen Says Trump Has a 'Lack of Understanding' of Fed Policies and the Economy," Federal Reserve, CNBC, February 25, 2019, https://www.cnbc.com/2019/02/25/janet-yellen-says-trump-has-a-lack-of-understanding-of-fed-policies-and-the-economy.html.

27   Janet L. Yellen, "What the Federal Reserve Is Doing to Promote a Stronger Job Market," speech at the 2014 National Interagency Community Reinvestment Conference, Chicago, IL, March 31, 2014, https://www.federalreserve.gov/newsevents/speech/yellen20140331a.htm.

28   Brian Blackstone, "Negative Rates, Designed as a Short-Term Jolt, Have Become an Addiction," *Wall Street Journal*, May 20, 2019.

29   See the U.S. Debt Clock at http://usdebtclock.org/.

30   "U.S. Is Bankrupt and We Don't Even Know It: Laurence Kotlikoff," Bloomberg, August 10, 2010, https://www.bloomberg.com/news/articles/2010-08-11/u-s-is-bankrupt-and-we-don-t-even-know-commentary-by-laurence-kotlikoff.

31   Social Security and Medicare Boards of Trustees, "A Summary of the 2020 Annual Reports: A Message to the Public," Office of the Chief Actuary, Social Security website, accessed August 7, 2020, https://www.ssa.gov/oact/TRSUM/.

32   Federal Reserve Bank of St. Louis, "Federal Outlays: Interest as Percent of Gross Domestic Product (FYOIGDA188S)," FRED, accessed August 7, 2020, https://fred.stlouisfed.org/series/FYOIGDA188S.

33   Committee for a Responsible Federal Budget, "As Debt Rises, Interest Costs Could Top $1 Trillion," CRFB.org, February 13, 2019, https://www.crfb.org/blogs/debt-rises-interest-costs-could-top-1-trillion.

34   Committee for a Responsible Federal Budget.

35   Committee for a Responsible Federal Budget.

36   Christoph Gisiger, "James Grant: The Fed is now hostage to Wall Street," *Finanz und Wirtschaft*, August 22, 2016, https://www.fuw.ch/article/the-fed-is-now-hostage-to-wall-street/.

37   U.S. Debt Clock.

38   "Credit Ratings: How Fitch, Moody's and S&P Rate Each Country," *Datablog*, April 30, 2010, https://www.theguardian.com/news/datablog/2010/apr/30/credit-ratings-country-fitch-moodys-standard.

39   U.S. Debt Clock.

40   "Best-Run Cities in America," Wallet Hub, accessed August 7, 2020, https://wallethub.com/edu/best-run-cities/22869/#main-findings.

41   Raymond F. DeVoe Jr., quoted in "How to Find Safe Places to Invest Your Money," Barron's, updated April 2, 2019, https://www.barrons.com/articles/safe-places-to-invest-cash-51553898708.

42   Paul Kupiec and Edward Pinto, "The Government Creates Another Housing Bubble," *Wall Street Journal*, May 31, 2018.

43 Edward J. Pinto and Tobias Peter, "National Housing Market Index Release for Q4 2017," *AEIdeas* (blog), March 26, 2018, http://www.aei.org/publication/national-housing-market-index-release-for-q4-2017/?mod=article_inline.

44 "Milton Friedman Teaches Monetary Policy," video streamed on the Free to Choose Network, YouTube video posted May 30, 2013, https://www.youtube.com/watch?v=6LfUyML5QVY.

45 David M. Byrne and Carol A. Corrado, "The Increasing Deflationary Influence of Consumer Digital Access Services," Finance and Economics Discussion Series Divisions of Research & Statistics and Monetary Affairs Federal Reserve Board, Washington, D.C., 2020-021.

FUNDING SOURCES PART 2: UNWITTING RETIREES (AKA "OTHER PEOPLE'S MONEY")

1 Louise Sheiner, "Are State and Local Pension Funds Really in Crisis?" *Up Front* (blog, Brookings Institution), July 15, 2019, https://www.brookings.edu/blog/up-front/2019/07/15/are-state-and-local-pension-funds-really-in-crisis/.

2 Knowledge at Wharton podcast, "The Time Bomb Inside Public Pension Plans," August 23, 2018, https://knowledge.wharton.upenn.edu/article/the-time-bomb-inside-public-pension-plans/.

3 Pew Trusts, "The State Pension Funding Gap: 2017," Pew, June 27, 2019, https://www.pewtrusts.org/en/research-and-analysis/issue-briefs/2019/06/the-state-pension-funding-gap-2017.

4 U.S. Department of Labor, "Fiduciary Responsibilities," Department of Labor website, accessed August 7, 2020, https://www.dol.gov/general/topic/retirement/fiduciaryresp.

5 Kim, Crystal. "Sustainable Investing Assets Hit $12 Trillion - Thanks to Donald Trump," Barron's, November 1, 2018. https://www.barrons.com/articles/sustainable-investing-assets-hit-12-trillion-thanks-to-donald-trump-1540996295.

6 Alicia H. Munnell and Anqi Chen, "New Developments in Social Investing by Public Pensions," Center for Retirement Research at Boston College issue brief, no. 53, November 2016, http://crr.bc.edu/wp-content/uploads/2016/11/slp_53.pdf.

7 James Mackintosh, "Sustainable Funds Mostly Track the Market," *Wall Street Journal*, February 24, 2020.

8 J. D. Morris and Nanette Asimov, "PG&E Says Power Line Inspections Revealed 10,000 Problems—Some in Need of Immediate Repair," *San Francisco Chronicle,* July 16, 2019.

9 Richard Gonzales, "California Can Expect Blackouts for a Decade, Says PG&E CEO," NPR, October 18, 2019, https://www.npr.org/2019/10/18/771486828/california-can-expect-blackouts-for-a-decade-says-pg-e-ceo.

10 Grabien staff, "Gov. Gavin Newsom Blames Capitalism and Climate Change for the Wildfires," grabienews, November 1, 2019, https://news.grabien.com/story-gov-gavin-newsom-blames-capitalism-and-climate-change-wildfi.

11 Pippa Stephens, "PG&E Power Outage Could Cost the California Economy More Than $2 Billion," CNBC, October 10, 2019, https://www.cnbc.com/2019/10/10/pge-power-outage-could-cost-the-california-economy-more-than-2-billion.html.

12 Adam Neumann, "The Beginning of a New Story," WeWork, January 8, 2019, https://www.wework.com/newsroom/posts/wecompany.

13   U.S. Securities & Exchange Commission, "Investor Advisory Committee Meeting," SEC.gov, December 13, 2018, https://www.sec.gov/video/webcast-archive-player. shtml?document_id=iac121318.

14   Esther Whieldon, "SEC's Pierce: ESG Is Used Like a 'Scarlet Letter' to Shame, Misjudge Companies," *Market Intelligence,* June 18, 2019.

15   https://www.calpers.ca.gov/docs/forms-publications/calpers-at-a-glance.pdf. No longer accessible.

16   Timothy M. Doyle, "CalPERS and the Point of No Returns," American Council for Capital Formation, December 5, 2017, http://accf.org/2017/12/05/ calpers-and-the-point-of-no-returns/.

17   Dale Kasler, "CalPERS Rethinks Ban on Tobacco Stocks," *Sacramento Bee*, April 4, 2016, https://www.sacbee.com/news/business/article69836422.html.

18   Sarah Krouse, "New York Pension Fund Doubles Bet on Low-Carbon Companies," *Wall Street Journal*, January 30, 2018, https://www.wsj.com/articles/ new-york-pension-fund-doubles-bet-on-low-carbon-companies-1517320801.

19   https://www.revolvy.com/page/Scott-Stringer. No longer accessible.

20   Tim Doyle, "Politics over Performance: The Politicization of the New York City Retirement Systems" United Neighbors of NY website, January 1, 2018, https://unitedneighborsofny.com/latest-news/research-and-analysis/ politics-over-performance-the-politicization-of-the-new-york-city-retirement-systems/.

21   ValueWalk, "New Report on New York City Pension Funds Sounds Alarms," valuewalk.com, January 29, 2018, https://www.valuewalk.com/2018/01/ new-report-on-new-york-city-pension-funds-sounds-alarms/.

22   ValueWalk.

23   ValueWalk.

24   Edmund McMahon and Josh McGee, "The Never Ending Hangover; How New York City's Pension Costs Threaten Its Future," Manhattan Institute, June 2017, available for download at ScribD, https://www.scribd.com/document/351835419/ The-Never-Ending-Hangover-How-New-York-City-s-Pension-Costs-Threaten-Its-Future.

25   ValueWalk, "New Report on New York City Pension Funds Sounds Alarms."

26   Daniel Fischel, Christopher Fiore, and Todd Kendall, "Fossil Fuel Divestment and Public Pension Funds," June 7, 2017, available for download on the website of the Heartland Institute, https://www.heartland.org/publications-resources/publications/ fossil-fuel-divestment-and-public-pension-funds.

27   Justin Baer, "Former New York Pension-Fund Executive Sentenced to 21 Months in Prison," *Wall Street Journal*, updated July 12, 2018, https://www.wsj.com/ articles/former-new-york-pension-fund-executive-sentenced-to-21-months-in- prison-1531429910.

28   United States of America v. Navnoor Kang and Deborah Kelley, sealed indictment, accessed August 7, 2020, https://www.justice.gov/file/920006/download.

29   David Seifman, "Former State Comptroller Alan Hevesi Sentenced to 1 to 4 Years in Prison for Pension Scandal," *New York Post*, April 15, 2011, https://nypost. com/2011/04/15/former-state-comptroller-alan-hevesi-sentenced-to-1-to-4-years-in- prison-for-pension-scandal/.

30   Funston Advisory Services, *Fiduciary and Conflict of Interest Review of the New York State Common Retirement Fund*, June 16, 2016, https://www.osc.state.ny.us/reports/ pension/NYSCRF_Fiduciary_and_Conflict_of_Interest_Review_2016.pdf.

31   Marc Lifsher, "Former CEO of CalPERS Pleads Guilty to Fraud, Corruption Charge," *Los Angeles Times*, July 11, 2014, http://www.latimes.com/business/la-fi-calpers-guilty-plea-20140712-story.html.

32   Dale Kasler, "Former CalPERS Chief Sentenced to Prison in Bribery Scandal," *Sacramento Bee*, May 31, 2016.

33   AP, "CEO of California's $350B Pension Fund Has No Degree," AP News, September 14, 2018, https://apnews.com/73d743eb81eb441db0bb784b6e746536,

34   Yves Smith, "CalPERS' CEO Marcie Frost's Misrepresentations Regarding Her Education and Work History During and After Her Hiring," *Naked Capitalism*, August 27, 2018 https://www.nakedcapitalism.com/2018/08/calpers-ceo-marcie-frosts-misrepresentations-regarding-her-education-and-work-history-during-and-after-her-hiring.html.

35   Smith.

36   Smith.

37   Heather Gillers, "Calpers CEO Tackles Flurry of Challenges," *Wall Street Journal*, September 27, 2018.

38   "Willshire Trust Universe Comparison Service," as reported by Heather Gillers of the *Wall Street Journal*, March 6, 2020.

39   See the Public Plans Database, https://publicplansdata.org/public-plans-database/.

40   Joshua D. Rauh, "Hidden Debt, Hidden Deficits: 2017 Edition: How Pension Promises Are Consuming State and Local Budge," essay, Hoover Institution, https://www.hoover.org/sites/default/files/research/docs/rauh_hiddendebt2017_final_webread-ypdf1.pdf.

41   Heather Gillers, "Public Pension-Fund Losses Surpass Worst From '08 Crisis," *Wall Street Journal*, May 12, 2020.

42   Peter Vanham, "Global Pension Timebomb: Funding Gap Set to Dwarf World GDP," World Economic Forum, May 26, 2017, https://www.weforum.org/press/2017/05/global-pension-timebomb-funding-gap-set-to-dwarf-world-gdp/.

43   World Economic Forum, *We'll Live to 100–How Can We Afford It?* (white paper), May 2017, http://www3.weforum.org/docs/WEF_White_Paper_We_Will_Live_to_100.pdf.

44   Jason Zweig, "Can We Be Brutally Honest about Investment Returns?" *Wall Street Journal*, January 19, 2018, https://www.eur.nl/sites/corporate/files/2018-02/wsj_-_can_we_be_brutally_honest_about_investment_returns.pdf.

45   Zweig.

46   Spencer Jakab, "Public Pensions Are Stuck in the Clouds," *Wall Street Journal*, July 27–28, 2019.

47   Peter Bernstein, *Classics Collection: Capital Ideas, Against the Gods, The Power of Gold* (Wiley, 2005).

48   Pew Trusts, "The State Pension Funding Gap: 2016," Pew, April 12, 2018, https://www.pewtrusts.org/en/research-and-analysis/issue-briefs/2018/04/the-state-pension-funding-gap-2016.

49   Tyler Durden, "New Jersey Prepares to Raise Taxes on 'Almost Everything' as it Nears Financial Disaster," zerohedge.com, March 14, 2018, https://www.zerohedge.com/news/2018-03-13/new-jersey-prepares-raise-taxes-almost-everything-it-nears-financial-disaster.

50   Pew Trusts, "State Pension Funds Reduce Assumed Rates of Return," December 2019, https://www.pewtrusts.org/-/media/assets/2020/01/state_public_pension_funds_ lower_assumed_rates_of_returns_final_2020.pdf.

51   Zorast Wadia, Alan H. Perry, and Charles J. Clark, "2020 Corporate Pension Funding Study," Milliman.com, April 28, 2020, http://www.milliman.com/Solutions/Products/ Corporate-Pension-Funding-Study/#targetText=The%20FY2018%20funded%20 ratio%20of,2018%20Milliman%20Pension%20Funding%20Study.

52   Kilgore, Tomi. "GE Freezing Pensions for 20,000 Employees." MarketWatch, October 8, 2019. https://www.marketwatch.com/story/ ge-freezing-pensions-for-20000-employees-2019-10-07.

53   CalPers, "Discount Rate Frequently Asked Questions," accessed August 7, 2020, https://www.calpers.ca.gov/page/about/organization/facts-at-a-glance/ discount-rate-frequently-asked-questions.

54   Peter Mixon, "Estimating Future Costs at Public Pension Plans: Setting the Discount Rate," Pensions&Investments, April 29, 2015, https://www.pionline.com/article/20150429/ONLINE/150429853/ estimating-future-costs-at-public-pension-plans-setting-the-discount-rate.

55   Spencer Jakab, "Public Pensions Are Stuck in the Clouds," *Wall Street Journal*, July 27–28, 2019.

56   Barry S. Burr, "Actuarial leaders disband task force, object to paper on public plan liabilities," Pensions&Investments, August 3, 2016, https://www.pionline.com/article/20160803/ONLINE/160809964/ actuarial-leaders-disband-task-force-object-to-paper-on-public-plan-liabilities.

57   Burr.

58   Burr.

59   Government Accountability Institute, "Green Fog: The Coming Climate Change Bond Crisis," October 2019, available for download at https://www.g-a-i.org/investigations/.

60   Government Accountability Institute.

61   Associated Press, "New York City Sues 5 Major Oil Companies, Claiming They Contributed to Global Warming," *Chicago Tribune*, January 10, 2018, http://www.chi-cagotribune.com/news/nationworld/ct-new-york-sues-oil-companies-global-warming-20180110-story.html.

62   Supreme Court of the State of New York, New York County, Index No. 452044/2018, NYSCEF DOC. NO. 567, https://iapps.courts.state.ny.us/fbem/DocumentDisplayServle t?documentId=/N/2DxDTaU8Gqsq9IN5wOA==&system=prod.

63   John Schwartz, "Judge Dismisses Suit Against Oil Companies over Climate Change Costs," *New York Times*, June 25, 2018, https://www.nytimes.com/2018/06/25/cli-mate/climate-change-lawsuit-san-francisco-oakland.html.

64   "The Climate-Change Tort Racket," Opinion Page Review and Outlook, *Wall Street Journal*, June 9–10 2018.

65   Doyle, "CalPERS and the Point of No Returns."

66   California School Boards Association, "The Impact of Pension Cost Increases on California's Schools," CSBA, accessed August 7, 2020, https://www.csba.org/-/media/ 10A77157DED54E0BAC001F0718F23304.ashx.

67   Heather Gillers, "Many U.S. Cities See Downturn at Hand," *Wall Street Journal*, March 4, 2020.

68   Michael Rainey, "States Face a $645 Billion Hole for Retiree Health Care Liabilities,"
      Fiscal Times, September 20, 2017, http://www.thefiscaltimes.com/2017/09/20/
      States-Face-645-Billion-Hole-Retiree-Health-Care-Liabilities.

69   Heather Gillers, "States Need $645 Billion to Pay Full Health-Care Costs," *Wall Street
      Journal*, September 20, 2017, https://www.wsj.com/articles/states-need-645-bil-
      lion-to-pay-for-these-promises-and-thats-not-counting-what-they-owe-in-pen-
      sions-1505899801.

70   Milton Friedman, "The Social Responsibility of Business is to Increase its Profits," *New
      York Times Magazine*, September 13, 1970.

71   Warren Buffett, *Tap Dancing to Work: Warren Buffett on Practically Everything, 1966-
      2012: A Fortune Magazine Book*, comp. Carol Loomis (n.p.: Portfolio, 2012).

LEECH POWER CENTERS: URBAN HELL

1   Aaron Blake, "Hillary Clinton Takes Her Deplorables Argument for Another Spin,"
      Washington Post, March 12, 2018, https://www.washingtonpost.com/news/the-
      fix/wp/2018/03/12/hillary-clinton-takes-her-deplorables-argument-for-another-
      spin/?utm_term=.146960529fe7.

2   Dr. Andrew Schiller, "The Most Dangerous U.S. Neighborhoods of 2018,"
      Neighborhood Scout blog, November 21, 2018, https://www.neighborhoodscout.com/
      blog/25-most-dangerous-neighborhoods.

3   Law Officer, "Minneapolis Police Department Unable to
      Dispatch Officers to 6700 Priority Calls in the Last Year," lawof-
      ficer.com, July 29, 2019, https://lawofficer.com/news/
      minneapolis-police-department-unable-dispatch-officers-6700-priority-calls-last-year/.

4   Madison Park, "Chicago Police Count Fewer Murders in 2017, but Still 650 people Were
      Killed," CNN, January 1, 2018, https://www.cnn.com/2018/01/01/us/chicago-murders-
      2017-statistics/index.html.

5   Park.

6   Wikipedia, s.v. "Crime in Chicago," accessed August 7, 2020, https://en.wikipedia.org/
      wiki/Crime_in_Chicago.

7   American College of Surgeons, *National Trauma Data Bank 2016 Annual Report*, ed.
      Michael C. Chang, https://www.facs.org/~/media/files/quality%20programs/trauma/
      ntdb/ntdb%20annual%20report%202016.ashx.

8   Ford Fessenden and Haeyoun Park, "Chicago's Murder Problem," *New York Times*,
      May 18, 2016, https://www.nytimes.com/interactive/2016/05/18/us/chicago-murder-
      problem.html.

9   Kaitlyn D'Onofrio, "Police Afraid to do Their Jobs, Says FBI Director," DiversityInc., May
      17, 2016, https://www.diversityinc.com/news/james-comey-viral-video-effect-police.

10   Scott Calvert and Coulter Jones, "Baltimore Felony Conviction Rates Fall under State's
      Attorney Marilyn Mosby," *Wall Street Journal*, updated November 22, 2016, https://
      www.wsj.com/articles/baltimore-felony-conviction-rates-fall-under-states-attorney-
      marilyn-mosby-1479834018.

11   Justin Fenton and Tim Prudente, "Conviction Rate Has Dipped under Baltimore State's
      Attorney Marilyn Mosby, Giving Challengers an Attack Line She Once Used," *Baltimore
      Sun*, May 30, 2018, http://www.baltimoresun.com/news/maryland/crime/bs-md-ci-
      mosby-conviction-rates-20180410-story.html.

12   Tyler Durden, "A Tour Down Homicide Lane, as Baltimore Descends into Chaos,"
      ZeroHedge, May 9, 2017, https://www.zerohedge.com/news/2017-05-08/
      tour-down-homicide-lane-baltimore-descends-chaos.

13   Holly Matkin, "U.S. Attorney Blasts Anti-Police Philly DA After 6 Officers Shot, DA
      Backpedals," *Police Tribune*, August 15, 2019, https://defensemaven.io/bluelives-
      matter/news/u-s-attorney-blasts-anti-police-philly-da-after-6-officers-shot-da-back-
      pedals-pLzzoNqv2kiKINMFUDI-YA.

14   Evan Sernoffsky, "SF Supervisor Leads Anti-Police-Union 'F— the POA' Chant at DA
      Election Party," *San Francisco Chronicle*, November 6, 2019, https://www.sfchronicle.
      com/crime/article/SF-supervisor-leads-anti-police-union-F-the-14814220.php.

15   Allysia Finley, "The Troubles Beneath the Surface of California's Comeback," *Wall
      Street Journal*, June 29–30, 2019.

16   Allysia Finley, "Why California Leaves Its Homeless out in the Sun," *Wall Street Journal*,
      May 11, 2018.

17   Editorial Board, "Coronavirus and Public Order," Opinion, *Wall Street Journal*, March
      20, 2020, https://www.wsj.com/articles/coronavirus-and-public-order-11584745241.

18   Associated Press, "Baltimore Homicide Rate Is on a Record
      High, Deadlier Than Detroit and Chicago," *USA Today*, September
      25, 2018, https://www.usatoday.com/story/news/2018/09/25/
      baltimore-homicide-murder-rate-fbi-statistics-death-crime-killings/1426739002/.

19   "The 30 cities with the highest murder rates in the US," *Bismarck Tribune*, November
      13, 2017, #31, St. Louis, Missouri, https://bismarcktribune.com/news/national/the-
      cities-with-the-highest-murder-rates-in-the-us/collection_5a789407-4d43-5403-
      ad56-7c47880bda8e.html#31.

20   "The 30 cities with the highest murder rates in the US," #28. Indianapolis, Indiana,
      https://bismarcktribune.com/news/national/the-cities-with-the-highest-murder-rates-
      in-the-us/collection_5a789407-4d43-5403-ad56-7c47880bda8e.html#28.

21   "Rural Highways," EveryCRSReport.com, July 5, 2018, https://www.everycrsreport.
      com/reports/R45250.html.

22   Gregory D. Erhardt et. al., "Do Transportation Network Companies Decrease or
      Increase Congestion?" *Science Advances*, May 2019, https://advances.sciencemag.org/
      content/5/5/eaau2670.full.

23   "INRIX Identifies the Worst Traffic Hotspots in the 25 Most Congested U.S. Cities,"
      press release, INRIX, accessed August 7, 2020, http://inrix.com/press-releases/
      us-hotspots/.

24   INRIX, accessed August 7, 2020, http://inrix.com/scorecard-city/?city=Los%20
      Angeles%3B%20CA&index=1.

25   Gerald Schifman, "Congestion Cost New York $16.9 Billion Last Year," Crain's New
      York Business, February 23, 2017, https://www.crainsnewyork.com/article/20170224/
      TRANSPORTATION/170229928/congestion-cost-new-york-16-9-billion-in-2016.

26   Winnie Hu, "New York Subway's On-Time Performance Hits New Low," *New York
      Times*, March 19, 2018, https://www.nytimes.com/2018/03/19/nyregion/new-york-
      subways-on-time-performance-hits-new-low.html.

27   Allana Akhtar, "Riders Lost Wages, Jobs Due To Subway
      Delays: Survey," Jalopnik, July 10, 2017, https://jalopnik.com/
      riders-lost-wages-jobs-due-to-subway-delays-survey-1796776439.

28   Steven Malanga, "Why Service Is Lousy in High-Tax States," *Wall Street Journal*, February 20, 2019.

29   Hudson Tunnel, "Welcome," Hudson Tunnel Project, accessed August 7, 2020, http://hudsontunnelproject.com/index.html.

30   NYC, "Mayor de Blasio, City Council, Advocates Celebrate Passage of For-Hire Vehicles Legislation," NYC.gov, August 9, 2018, https://www1.nyc.gov/office-of-the-mayor/news/404-18/mayor-de-blasio-city-council-advocates-celebrate-passage-for-hire-vehicles-legislation#/0.

31   Jon Kamp, "Boston Can't Fix Its Trains Fast Enough," *Wall Street Journal*, July 12, 2019.

32   David M. Konisky and Manuel P. Teodoro, "When Governments Regulate Governments," *American Journal of Political Science,* September 18, 2015.

33   G. Tyler Miller Jr. and Scott Spoolman, *Living in the Environment: Principles, Connections, and Solutions*, 16th ed. (n.p.: Cengage Learning, 2009).

34   Joan Jacobson, "Keeping the Water On: Strategies for Addressing High Increases in Water and Sewer Rates for Baltimore's Most Vulnerable Customers," *Abell Report* 29, no. 4 (November 2016), https://www.abell.org/sites/default/files/publications/Keeping%20the%20Water%20On.pdf.

35   John W. Schoen, "The Trickle-Down Effect of Baltimore's Crumbling Infrastructure," CNBC.com, November 21, 2013, https://www.cnbc.com/2013/11/21/-down-effect-of-baltimores-crumbling-infrastructure.html.

36   Rachel Layne, "Lead in America's Water systems Is a National Problem," CBSN News, November, 21, 2018, https://www.cbsnews.com/news/lead-in-americas-water-systems-is-a-national-problem/; Olga Khazan, "The Trouble With America's Water," *Atlantic*, September 11, 2019, https://www.theatlantic.com/health/archive/2019/09/millions-american-homes-have-lead-water/597826/.

37   Centers for Disease Control and Prevention, Childhood Lead Poisoning Prevention Program, CDC.com, accessed August 7, 2020, https://www.cdc.gov/nceh/lead/default.htm.

38   United States Environmental Protection Agency, "Drinking Water Requirements for States and Public Water Systems: Lead in Drinking Water in Schools and Childcare Facilities," EPA, accessed August 7, 2020, https://www.epa.gov/dwreginfo/lead-drinking-water-schools-and-childcare-facilities.

39   Josiah Bates, "Newark Officials Providing Bottled Water to 15,000 Homes over Lead Contamination Concerns. Here's What You Need to Know about the City's Water Crisis," *Time*, updated August 27, 2019, https://time.com/5653115/newark-water-crisis/.

40   NRDC, "The Truth about Newark's Water," NRDC.org, accessed August 7, 2020, https://www.nrdc.org/truth-about-newarks-water.

41   NRDC.

42   Bates, "Newark Officials Providing Bottled Water to 15,000 Homes over Lead Contamination Concerns."

43   U.S. Bureau of Labor Statistics, Consumer Price Index for All Urban Consumers: Water and Sewer and Trash Collection Services [CUSR0000SEHG], FRED (Federal Reserve Bank of St. Louis), accessed March 18, 2018, https://fred.stlouisfed.org/series/CUSR0000SEHG.

44   "Changing the Way Baltimore Bills for Water Is not an Option," *Baltimore Sun* editorial, December 18, 2017, https://www.baltimoresun.com/opinion/editorial/bs-ed-1219-water-bills-20171218-story.html.

45   Roger Colton, "Baltimore's Conundrum: Charging for Water / Wastewater Services that Community Residents Cannot Afford to Pay," prepared for *Food and Water Watch,* November 2017.

46   Ian Duncan, "Baltimore Water Meter Readers Wasted $120,000 Driving around Aimlessly or Going Home Early, Probe Finds," *Baltimore Sun*, June 14, 2018, http://www.baltimoresun.com/news/maryland/investigations/bs-md-ci-water-meter-readers-20180613-story.html.

47   The Oklahoman Editorial Board, "School Discipline Reform Failed, Repeal Was Needed," *Oklahoman*, January 3, 2019, https://newsok.com/article/5619208/school-discipline-reform-failed-repeal-was-needed.

48   Paul Sperry, "How Liberal Discipline Policies Are Making Schools Less Safe," *New York Post*, March 14, 2015, https://nypost.com/2015/03/14/politicians-are-making-schools-less-safe-and-ruining-education-for-everyone/.

49   Tunku Varadarajan, "A Parkland Father's Quest for Accountability," *Wall Street Journal*, January 12–13, 2019.

50   Varadarajan.

51   New York State Education Department, "State Education Department Releases Spring 2016 Grades 3-8 ELA and Math Assessment Results," NYSED, July 29, 2016, http://www.nysed.gov/news/2016/state-education-department-releases-spring-2016-grades-3-8-ela-and-math-assessment-results.

52   New York State Education Department.

53   Christina Veiga, "New York City's Absent Teacher Reserve Could Get Pricier as Teachers Collect Raises, Bonuses," Chalkbeat New York, June 14, 2018, https://chalk-beat.org/posts/ny/2018/06/14/new-york-citys-absent-teacher-reserve-could-get-pricier-as-teachers-collect-raises-bonuses/.

54   David Cantor, "NYC Teachers Who Lost Their Jobs but Remain on the Payroll Receive Big Raises as Budget Watchdogs Call to Reform $136M Absent Teacher Reserve," *The 74*, June 18, 2018, https://www.the74million.org/article/nyc-teachers-who-lost-their-jobs-but-remain-on-the-payroll-receive-big-raises-as-budget-watchdogs-call-to-reform-136m-absent-teacher-reserve/.

55   Cantor.

56   Dennis Saffran, "To Make Elite Schools 'Fair,' City Will Punish Poor Asians," *New York Post*, July 19, 2014, https://nypost.com/2014/07/19/why-nycs-push-to-change-school-admissions-will-punish-poor-asians/.

57   Madina Touré, "New York City to Spend an Average of $17.5K Per Student This School Year," Politico, August 31, 2018, https://www.politico.com/states/new-york/albany/story/2018/08/31/new-york-city-to-spend-an-average-of-17-500-per-student-this-school-year-589344.

58   C.J. Szafir and Cori Peterson, "This Building Is for Sale (but Not to a Charter School)," *Wall Street Journal*, November 9, 2018.

59   Scott Anderson, "By the Numbers: Milwaukee Public Schools Graduation Rates Consistently Below State Averages in 2015," *Patch*, updated July 16, 2016, https://patch.com/wisconsin/waukesha/numbers-milwaukee-public-schools-graduation-rates-consistently-below-state.

60   Milwaukee Public Schools, "Student Test Results," WPS, accessed August 7, 2020, http://mps.milwaukee.k12.wi.us/en/District/About-MPS/School-Board/Office-of-Accountability-Efficiency/Student-Test-Results.htm.

61   Szafir and Peterson, "This Building Is for Sale."

62   Szafir and Peterson.

63   Moriah Balingit, "U.S. High School Graduation Rates Rise to New High," *Washington Post*, December 4, 2017, https://www.washingtonpost.com/news/education/wp/2017/12/04/u-s-high-school-graduation-rates-rise-to-new-high/?utm_term=.d6e7964024ba.

64   Tawnell D. Hobbs, "A New Way to Avoid Summer School for Failing Students," *Wall Street Journal*, June 10, 2018.

65   Heather Gillers, "Many U.S. Cities See Downturn at Hand," *Wall Street Journal*, March 4, 2020.

66   Randy Diamond, "League Urges CalPERS to Find Ways to Exceed 7% Return Projections," Chief Investment Officer, May 16, 2018, https://www.ai-cio.com/news/league-urges-calpers-find-ways-exceed-7-return-projections/.

67   Truth in Accounting, "City Combined Taxpayer Burden™ Report: Including Underlying Government Units," Taxpayer on the Hook, May 2019, https://www.truthinaccounting.org/library/doclib/City-Combined-Taxpayer-Burden-Report.pdf.

68   Gunjan Banerji, "Illinois, Chicago Seek Billions From Investors," *Wall Street Journal*, March 26, 2019.

69   "System Failure: How Politics and Bad Decisions Starved New York's Subways," *New York Times*, November 18, 2017, https://www.nytimes.com/2017/11/18/nyregion/new-york-subway-system-failure-delays.html.

70   Nicole Bullock, "Paul Volcker Warns on Health of US State Finances," *Financial Times*, June 8, 2015, https://www.ft.com/content/7c36c050-0e0b-11e5-8ce9-00144feabdc0.

71   Truth in Accounting, "Chicago, IL," DATA-Z, accessed August 7, 2020, https://www.statedatalab.org/state_data_and_comparisons/city/chicago.

72   Heather Gillers and Zusha Elinson, "Ill-Funded Police Pensions Put Cities in a Bind," *Wall Street Journal*, July 4, 2017, https://www.wsj.com/articles/ill-funded-police-pensions-put-cities-in-a-bind-1499180342.

73   Ryan Poe, "Strickland Chides Police Union for 'Harmful' Billboards," *Commercial Appeal*, February 8, 2017, https://www.commercialappeal.com/story/news/government/city/2017/02/08/police-union-defends-memphis-billboards/97651850/.

74   Rob Arnott and Lisa Meulbroek, "The Stealth Pension Mortgage on Your House," *Wall Street Journal*, August 6, 2018.

75   Pam Surano, "Pittsburgh Public Schools and Pittsburgh Mayor Bill Peduto Offer Conflicting Messages On Climate Strike," KDKA2 CBS Pittsburgh, September 19, 2019, https://pittsburgh.cbslocal.com/2019/09/19/pittsburgh-climate-strike-youth/.

76   Pittsburgh Public Schools, *2019 District Performance Results PSSA/PASA and Keystone Exams*, https://www.pghschools.org/cms/lib/PA01000449/Centricity/Domain/19/2019DistrictPerformanceResultsPSSAKeystone_083019.pdf.

77   Don Hopey, "Peduto: Fossil Fuel Industries Will Take Toll on Pittsburgh Region," *Pittsburgh Post Gazette*, October 31, 2019.

78   The United States Conference of Mayors, "Resolutions: 85th Annual Meeting: 100% Renewable Energy in American Cities," USMayors.org, accessed August 7, 2020, https://www.usmayors.org/the-conference/resolutions/?category=a0F6100000BKCxfEAH&meeting=85th%20Annual%20Meeting.

79   Scott Calvert and Max Rust, "America's Deadliest Place to Bike," *Wall Street Journal*, September 26, 2018.

80   INRIX, "INRIX 2019 Global Traffic Scorecard," INRIX.com, http://inrix.com/scorecard/.

81   The Perecman Firm, P.L.L.C., "New York City Reports over 160 Pedestrian, Cyclist Deaths in 2016," Perecman.com, March 1, 2017, https://www.perecman.com/blog/2017/march/new-york-city-reports-over-160-pedestrian-cyclis/.

82   Matthew Dalton and Sam Schechner, "Famed Parisian Bike Network Rolls into a Ditch," *Wall Street Journal*, April 26, 2018, https://www.wsj.com/articles/famed-parisian-bike-network-rolls-into-a-ditch-1524735000.

83   Chris Newens, Véliberté, Egalité, Fraternité: Is Paris's Seminal Bike Share Scheme Out of Date?," *Guardian* (UK), https://www.theguardian.com/cities/2017/dec/07/velib-paris-bike-cycle-share.

84   Dalton and Sam, "Paris Bike Network Rolls into a Ditch."

85   Camila Domonoske, "Bike-Share Firm Hits The Brakes in France After 'Mass Destruction' Of Dockless Bikes," WABE, February 27, 2018, https://www.wabe.org/bike-share-firm-hits-the-brakes-in-france-after-mass-destruction-of-dockless-bik/.

86   George Carlin, Jammin in New York, stand-up comedy concert, 1992.

87   Randal O'Toole, "Charting Public Transit's Decline," CATO Institute, November 8, 2018, https://www.cato.org/publications/policy-analysis/charting-public-transits-decline.

88   APTA, *2019 Public Transportation Fact Book, Appendix A*, American Public Transportation Association, https://www.apta.com/wp-content/uploads/APTA_Fact-Book-2019_FINAL.pdf.

89   Ethan Millman, "Los Angeles Bus Push Fails to Catch On," *Wall Street Journal*, August 26, 2019.

90   City of Los Angeles, "recycLA," Ware Disposal, accessed August 10, 2020, https://www.waredisposal.com/city-of-los-angeles-recycla/.

91   Everton Bailey Jr., "'Portland Mayor Has 'Failed Miserably' as Police Commissioner, Police Union President Says," Oregon Live, August 3, 2018. https://www.oregonlive.com/portland/index.ssf/2018/08/portland_mayor_has_failed_misc.html.

92   Bigad Shaban et al., "Survey of Downtown San Francisco Reveals Trash on Every Block, 303 Piles of Feces and 100 Drug Needles," NBC Bay Area, February 18, 2018, https://www.nbcbayarea.com/news/local/diseased-streets/166605/.

93   Phil Matier, "San Francisco—Where Drug Addicts Outnumber High School Students," *San Francisco Chronicle*, January 31, 2019.

94   Aria Bendix, "San Francisco Spent $54 Million This Year on Street Cleanup — Here's Why It's Shelling Out Way More Than Other Cities," *Business Insider*, September 12, 2018, https://www.businessinsider.com/san-francisco-spent-54-million-street-cleanup-2018-9.

95   Dominic Fracassa, "SF Mayor Breed Envisions Adding 1,000 Beds for the Homeless by End of 2020," *San Francisco Chronicle*, October 3, 2018, https://www.sfchronicle.com/bayarea/article/London-Breed-expected-to-set-goal-of-adding-1-000-13279982.php.

96   Jim Carlton, "City Tax Would Aid Homeless," *Wall Street Journal*, November 1, 2018.

97   Doug Smith, "L.A. County's Homeless Problem is Worsening Despite Billions from Tax Measures," *Los Angeles Times*, February 19, 2018.

98   Theresa Walker, "Thousands of Pounds of Human Waste, Close to 14,000 Hypodermic Needles Cleaned Out from Santa Ana River Homeless Encampments," *Orange County Register*, March 8, 2018.

99   Wilson Wong, "Chicago Mayor Lori Lightfoot Defends Hairstylist Visit amid Coronavirus Outbreak," NBC News, April 11, 2020, https://www.nbcnews.com/news/nbcblk/chicago-mayor-defends-hairstylist-visit-amid-coronavirus-outbreak-n1181546.

100   Eliza Relman, "New York City Mayor Bill de Blasio Violates His Own Government's Recommendations and Hits the Gym in Brooklyn amid the Coronavirus Shutdown," *Business Insider*, March 16, 2020, https://www.businessinsider.com/nyc-mayor-bill-de-blasio-goes-ymca-announcing-closure-gyms-2020-3.

101   Phil Bracchi, "Naked Hypocrisy: How Professor Lockdown's Mistress Was Telling the Public to Stay at Home Two Weeks before the Government Only to Be Caught in Secret Trysts with Her Lover," *Daily Mail* (UK), https://www.dailymail.co.uk/news/article-8294315/Naked-hypocrisy-Professor-Lockdowns-mistress-telling-public-stay-home.html.

102   Jillian Kay Melchior, "The Weekend Interview with Lynne Patton," *Wall Street Journal*, March 30–31, 2019.

103   Mara Gay and Laura Kusisto, "Public Housing Crumbles in New York," *Wall Street Journal*, March 20, 2018.

104   United States Attorney's Office, "Manhattan U.S. Attorney Announces Settlement with NYCHA and NYC to Fundamentally Reform NYCHA through the Appointment of a Federal Monitor and the Payment by NYC Of $1.2 Billion of Additional Capital Money over the Next Five Years," United States Department of Justice, June 11, 2018, https://www.justice.gov/usao-sdny/pr/manhattan-us-attorney-announces-settlement-nycha-and-nyc-fundamentally-reform-nycha.

105   Greg B. Smith, "City Finds 83% of NYCHA Units Pose 'Severe' Health Risks," *New York Daily News*, April 2, 2018, http://www.nydailynews.com/new-york/city-finds-83-nycha-units-pose-severe-health-risks-article-1.3911103.

106   Nolan Hicks, Yoav Gonen and Max Jaeger, "More Than 1K NYCHA Kids Tested Positive for Lead," *New York Post*, August 30, 2018, https://nypost.com/2018/08/30/nycha-developments-poisoned-nearly-1400-kids/.

107   United States of America v. New York City Housing Authority, 18 Civ. 5213, filed June 11, 2018 in Southern District of New York. https://www.epa.gov/sites/production/files/2018-06/documents/nycha-cp.pdf.

108   The Editorial Board, "$1,973 LEDs and the Green New Deal," Opinion, *Wall Street Journal*, February 16-17, 2019.

109   The Editorial Board.

110   Jillian Kay Melchior, *The Weekend Interview with Lynne Patton*, *Wall Street Journal*, March 30–31, 2019.

111   J. David Goodman, "Amazon's New York Charm Offensive Includes a Veiled Threat," *New York Times*, January 30, 2019.

112   Michael Gibson, "The Google Pinata," *National Review,* March 9, 2020.

113   Carl Campanile, "City's 1 Percent Pay Larger Income Tax Share Than Rest of US," *New York Post*, April 15, 2014, https://nypost.com/2014/04/15/citys-one-percent-pay-larger-income-tax-share-than-rest-of-us/.

114   Michael Shellenberger, "California's Solar Roof Law Will Raise Housing and Energy Prices but Do Little to Reduce Emissions," Forbes, May 10, 2018, https://www.forbes.com/sites/michaelshellenberger/2018/05/10/californias-solar-roof-law-will-increase-housing-energy-prices-and-do-little-to-reduce-emissions/#6ea4bf0e3199.

115 Pew Trusts, "Philadelphia's Poor: Experiences from Below the Poverty Line," Pew, September 26, 2018, https://www.pewtrusts.org/research-and-analysis/reports/2018/09/26/philadelphias-poor-experiences-from-below-the-poverty-line.

116 Patrick Sisson, "Affordable Housing and Inclusionary Zoning Study Examines Paths to Inclusive Communities," Curbed, October 10, 2017, https://www.curbed.com/2017/10/10/16454688/inclusionary-zoning-affordable-housing-study.

117 Mary Wisniewski, "As More Cities Ban Homeless Camps, Advocates Cry Foul," Reuters, December 23, 2014, https://www.reuters.com/article/us-usa-chicago-homeless/as-more-cities-ban-homeless-camps-advocates-cry-foul-idUSKBN0K11UY20141224.

118 Janet Adamy and Paul Overberg, "Millennials Continue Their Exodus From Big U.S. Cities," Wall Street Journal, September 26, 2019.

119 Adam Bonislawski, "Where a Single-Family House and 100+ Luxury Apartments Cost the Same," Wall Street Journal, December 12, 2018.

PROFILE #1: POPE FRANCIS

1 Ayn Rand interview with Tom Snyder, Tomorrow show, 1979.

2 Catholic Herald, "Pope Francis "Breaks Catholic Traditions Whenever He Wants," California Catholic Daily, December 31, 2016, https://cal-catholic.com/pope-francis-breaks-catholic-traditions-whenever-he-wants/.

3 Pew Research Center, "Brazil's Changing Religious Landscape," Pew Forum, July 18, 2013, http://www.pewforum.org/2013/07/18/brazils-changing-religious-landscape/.

4 Philip Pullella and Catherine Hornby, "Pope Francis Wants Church to Be Poor, and for the Poor," Reuters, March 16, 2013, https://www.reuters.com/article/us-pope-poor/pope-francis-wants-church-to-be-poor-and-for-the-poor-idUSBRE92F05P20130316.

5 Francis X. Rocca, "Vatican Uses Most Gifts for Budget, Not Charity," Wall Street Journal, December 11, 2019.

6 Rocca.

7 George Neumayr, "The Unholy Alliance Between George Soros and Pope Francis," American Spectator, May 3, 2017, https://spectator.org/the-unholy-alliance-between-george-soros-and-pope-francis/.

8 Jan Bentz, "Catholic Knights of Malta Remove Top Official amid Questions over Fidelity to Church Teaching," December 15, 2016, LifeSite, https://www.lifesitenews.com/news/order-of-malta-controversy-results-in-key-leadership-change.

9 "Author of 'The Dictator Pope' Henry Sire Suspended from Order of Malta Membership," press release, Order of Malta, March 23, 2018, https://www.orderofmalta.int/2018/03/23/henry-sire-the-dictator-pope-suspended/.

10 P. J. Toner, Catholic Encyclopedia (1912), s.v. "infallibility," Catholic Answers, https://www.catholic.com/encyclopedia/infallibility.

11 Pope Francis, Encyclical Letter: Laudato Si of the Holy Father Francis: On Care for Our Common Home, May 24, 2015, http://www.vatican.va/content/francesco/en/encyclicals/documents/papa-francesco_20150524_enciclica-laudato-si.html.

12 Pope Francis, par. 12.

13 Pope Francis, par. 199.

14 Pope Francis, par. 19.

15 Pope Francis, par. 22.

16   Elisabetta, Povoletto, "Pope Tells Oil Executives to Act on Climate: 'There Is No Time to Lose'," *New York Times*, June 9, 2018, https://www.nytimes.com/2018/06/09/world/europe/pope-oil-executives-climate-change.html.

17   Pope Francis, *Encyclical Letter*, par. 58.

18   Pope Francis par. 23.

19   Sigmund Freud, *The Freud Reader*, ed. Peter Gay (New York: Norton, 1995), 721.

20   Michael Crichton, *Aliens Cause Global Warming*, Caltech Michelin Lecture, January 17, 2003.

21   Wikipedia, s.v. "Climatic Research Unit email controversy," accessed August 10, 2020, https://en.wikipedia.org/wiki/Climatic_Research_Unit_email_controversy.

22   Pope Francis, *Encyclical Letter*, par. 23.

23   Pope Francis, par. 25.

24   Pope Francis, par. 27.

25   Pope Francis, par. 31.

26   Pope Francis, par. 46.

27   Pope Francis, par. 52.

28   Pope Francis, par. 51.

29   Pope Francis, par. 68.

30   Pope Francis, par. 92.

31   Pope Francis, par. 78.

32   Pope Francis, par. 112.

33   Pope Francis, par. 93.

34   Pope Francis, par. 93.

35   Pope Francis, par. 93.

36   East-West Center, "Global Study: Low Birth Rates Can Bring Surprising Economic Benefits," East-West Wire, October 9, 2014, https://www.eastwestcenter.org/news-center/east-west-wire/global-study-low-birth-rates-can-bring-surprising-economic-benefits.

37   Pope Francis, *Encyclical Letter*, par. 104.

38   Pope Francis, par. 104.

39   TeleSur, Opinion, "Venezuela Opposition Criticizes Pope's Call for Dialogue," *TeleSur*, April 29, 2017, https://www.telesurenglish.net/news/Pope-Francis-Venezuela-Opposition-Divided-Refuses-Dialogue-20170429-0013.html.

40   Cindy Wooden, "Hammer-Sickle Crucifix Raises Eyebrows during Pope Francis' Visit to Bolivia," *National Catholic Reporter*, July 9, 2015, https://www.ncronline.org/news/world/hammer-sickle-crucifix-raises-eyebrows-during-pope-francis-visit-bolivia.

41   Tommaso Perrone, "Francis and Fidel. A Historic Meeting to Talk about the Environment," Lifegate, September 21, 2015, https://www.lifegate.com/people/news/pope-francis-and-fidel-castro-environment-cuba.

42   Reggie Littlejohn, "Praise of China's Adherence to Catholic Social Doctrine Flies in the Face of Facts," *National Catholic Register*, February 9, 2018, https://www.ncregister.com/daily-news/praise-of-chinas-adherence-to-catholic-social-doctrine-flies-in-the-face-of.

43   Pope Francis, "Message of His Holiness Pope Francis to the Catholics of China and to the Universal Church, Vatican, September 26, 2018, http://w2.vatican.va/content/francesco/en/messages/pont-messages/2018/documents/papa-francesco_20180926_messaggio-cattolici-cinesi.html.

44 Pope Francis, *Encyclical Letter*, par. 106.

45 Pope Francis, par. 114.

46 Pope Francis, par. 127.

47 Pope Francis, par. 145.

48 Pope Francis, par. 129.

49 Pope Francis, par. 129.

50 Martin Luther, "The 95 Theses," www.LUTHER.de, accessed August 10, 2020, http://www.luther.de/en/95thesen.html, thesis 86.

51 Lydia Saad, "Catholics' Church Attendance Resumes Downward Slide," Gallup, April 9, 2018, https://news.gallup.com/poll/232226/church-attendance-among-catholics-resumes-downward-slide.aspx.

52 Online Library of Liberty, "Lord Acton Writes to Bishop Creighton That the Same Moral Standards Should Be Applied to All Men, Political and Religious Leaders Included, Especially Since "Power Tends to Corrupt and Absolute Power Corrupts Absolutely (1887)," Liberty Fund, accessed August 10, 2020, https://oll.libertyfund.org/quote/214.

53 Online Library of Liberty.

54 Pope Francis, *Encyclical Letter*, par. 210.

PROFILE #2: BONO

1 Trevor Horn and Midge Ure, "Do They Know It's Christmas," lyrics, Genius, https://genius.com/Band-aid-do-they-know-its-christmas-lyrics.

2 Michka Assayas, *Bono on Bono: Conversations with Michka Assayas* (n.p.: Hodder & Stoughton, 2006).

3 Bono, "The Good News on Poverty (Yes, There's Good News)," TED video, filmed February 2013, https://www.ted.com/talks/bono_the_good_news_on_poverty_yes_there_s_good_news.

4 Ben Hewitt, "U2 Wreak Havoc With 'Massive Carbon Footprint'," Quietus, July 7, 2009, http://thequietus.com/articles/02076-u2-wreak-havoc-with-massive-carbon-footprint.

5 "Bono Speaks Out about Climate Change at Davos Forum," Newshub, January 24, 2008, https://www.newshub.co.nz/world/bono-speaks-out-about-climate-change-at-davos-forum-2008012510.

6 Bono, "The Resource Miracle," *Time*, May 28, 2012, http://content.time.com/time/magazine/article/0,9171,2115044,00.html.

7 Bono.

8 Meghan Sweeney, "U2 Hits Back in Row over 360 Tour Carbon Footprint," Irish Central, August 18, 2009, https://www.irishcentral.com/culture/entertainment/u2-hits-back-in-row-over-360-carbon-footprint-237655351.

9 Belfast Telegraph, "Have U2 Created a Monster with Massive Carbon Footprint of 360 Tour?" *Belfast Telegraph*, July 7, 2009, https://www.belfasttelegraph.co.uk/entertainment/music/news/have-u2-created-a-monster-with-massive-carbon-footprint-of-360-tour-28491170.html.

10 Georgie Rogers, "U2 Defend Their Footprint: The Edge Brands Green Criticism of Their Extraordinary Stage 'Unfair'," BBC, August 14, 2009, http://www.bbc.co.uk/6music/news/20090814_u2.shtml.

11 "Affordable and Clean Energy," One, accessed August 10, 2020, https://www.one.org/us/issues/affordable-and-clean-energy/.

12   "INSIDE LOOK: Bono's Secret Yacht Is Called Kingdom Come!," Celebs
      on Yachts, August 24, 2015, http://www.celebsonyachts.com/
      inside-look-bonos-secret-yacht-is-called-kingdom-come/.
13   The Rise Fund website, accessed August 10, 2020, https://therisefund.com/.
14   Liz Moyer, "Private Equity Firm TPG Says It Fired Executive Charged in College
      Bribery Case, but He Says He Quit," CNBC, March 15, 2019, https://www.cnbc.
      com/2019/03/15/private-equity-firm-tpg-says-it-fired-mcglashan-charged-in-college-
      bribery-case.html.
15   Paddy Agnew, "We Have Enough Food to End World Hunger, Says Bono," *Irish
      Times*, September 7, 2015, https://www.irishtimes.com/news/world/europe/
      we-have-enough-food-to-end-world-hunger-says-bono-1.2342441.
16   Brian Hiatt, "Bono and U.K. Rockers Aid International Debt Relief,"
      MTV, February 15, 1999, http://www.mtv.com/news/512180/
      bono-and-uk-rockers-aid-international-debt-relief/.
17   Hiatt.
18   Bono, "World Debt Angers Me," Debt Relief, *Guardian* (UK), February 16, 1999, https://
      www.theguardian.com/world/1999/feb/16/debtrelief.development.
19   Matina Stevis, "Big African Debt Burdens, Written Off, Are Back Again," *Wall
      Street Journal*, updated November 17, 2015, https://www.wsj.com/articles/
      big-african-debt-burdens-written-off-are-back-again-1447705258.
20   Trading Economics, "Mozambique Government Debt to GDP," Tradingeconomics.com,
      2019, https://tradingeconomics.com/mozambique/government-debt-to-gdp.
21   Trading Economics, "Ghana Government Debt to GDP," Tradingeconomics.com, 2018,
      https://tradingeconomics.com/ghana/government-debt-to-gdp.
22   Moses Mozart Dzawu, "Ghana's Debt at Highest in Four Years
      as Revenue Undershoots," Economics, Bloomberg, May 28,
      2019, https://www.bloomberg.com/news/articles/2019-05-28/
      ghana-s-debt-at-the-highest-in-four-years-as-revenue-undershoots.
23   Tom Peterkin, "U2 Move Their Assets out of Ireland," *Telegraph* (UK), August 8, 2006,
      https://www.telegraph.co.uk/news/1525823/U2-move-their-assets-out-of-Ireland.html.
24   Donal O'Donovan, "U2 Firm Pays Tax Bill of Just €16,500 As Profits Plummet,"
      Independent.ie, December 2, 2011, https://www.independent.ie/entertainment/music/
      u2-firm-pays-tax-bill-of-just-16500-as-profits-plummet-26797909.html.
25   Ray Waddell, "U2's '360' Tour Gross: $736,137,344!" Billboard.com, July 29, 2011.
26   ONE, "About ONE," one.org, accessed August 10, 2020, https://www.one.org/
      international/about/.
27   TED, "Bono: Musician, Activist," TED.com, accessed August 10, 2020, https://www.ted.
      com/speakers/bono.
28   "When the Band Has No Shame," *Irish Times*, August 12, 2006, https://www.irishtimes.
      com/news/when-the-band-has-no-shame-1.1037586.
29   "When the Band Has No Shame."
30   Nick Shaxson, "Bono: Tax Haven Salesman for the Celtic Paper Tiger," Tax
      Justice Network, October 15, 2015, https://www.taxjustice.net/2014/10/15/
      bono-tax-haven-salesman-celtic-paper-tiger/.

31 James O'Shea, "Sinead O'Connor Slams Bono, Bob Geldof as "Bozo" and "Lily Livered Cowards," Irish Central, June 19, 2012, https://www.irishcentral.com/news/sinead-oconnor-slams-bono-bob-geldof-as-bozo-and-a-lily-livered-cowards-159543355-237511511.

32 Roisin O'Connor, "Paradise Papers: Bono Used Malta-Based Company to Invest in Lithuanian Shopping Mall, Tax Leak Reveals," *Independent* (UK), November 6, 2017, https://www.independent.co.uk/arts-entertainment/music/news/bono-paradise-papers-tax-leak-investments-u2-ireland-malta-guernsey-netherlands-haven-a8039716.html.

33 Hilary Osborne, "Bono Used Malta-Based Company to Invest in Lithuanian Shopping Centre," *Guardian* (UK), November 5, 2017, https://www.theguardian.com/news/2017/nov/05/bono-malta-firm-buy-lithuania-shopping-centre-u2-paradise-papers.

34 Adam Gabbett, "U2 Glastonbury Tax Protest: Activists Condemn 'Heavy-Handed' Security," *Guardian* (UK), June 25, 2011, https://www.theguardian.com/music/2011/jun/25/u2-bono-tax-protest-glastonbury.

35 World Economic Forum. (2006). "Bono and Bobby Shriver Launch Product Red to Harness Power of the World's Iconic Brands to Fight Aids in Africa." Retrieved September 15, 2020, from https://www.shopsplusproject.org/resource-center/bono-and-bobby-shriver-launch-product-red-harness-power-worlds-iconic-brands-fight.

36 William Easterly and Laura Freschi, "Cui Bono? The Murky Finances of Product Red™," *Aid Watch Blog*, December 8, 2009. No longer accessible.

37 Jack Doyle, "Product RED's Impact Is Shrouded in Vague Answers," *Nonprofit Times*, November 1, 2009, https://www.thenonprofittimes.com/npt_articles/product-red-s-impact-is-shrouded-in-vague-answers/.

38 Jason Newman, "9 Biggest Revelations in Bono's 'BBC' Interview About U2," *Rolling Stone*, February 4, 2014.

39 Wikipedia, s.v. "*Songs of Innocence* (U2 album)," accessed August 10, 2020, https://en.wikipedia.org/wiki/Songs_of_Innocence_(U2_album).

40 Visith Assar, "Apple's Devious U2 Album Giveaway Is Even Worse Than Spam," *Wired*, September 16, 2014, https://www.wired.com/2014/09/apples-devious-u2-album-giveaway-even-worse-spam/.

41 "Bullet the Blue Sky—Live From Boston 2001—U2," YouTube video, November 7, 2011, https://www.youtube.com/watch?v=ofVa5ob2mT0.

42 Tor Thorsen, "EA Buying BioWare/Pandemic for $860M," Gamespot.com, October 11, 2007, https://www.gamespot.com/articles/ea-buying-bioware-pandemic-for-860m/1100-6180818/.

43 Simon Carswell, "Ireland's UN Seat Bid: Bono Says Irish 'Storytellers' Vital," *Irish Times*, July 3, 2018, https://www.irishtimes.com/news/politics/ireland-s-un-seat-bid-bono-says-irish-storytellers-vital-1.3552171.

44 Associated Press, "Bono Says Existence of UN, EU and NATO Are Threatened: 'What They've Achieved Is at Risk," *USA Today*, July 3, 2018, https://www.usatoday.com/story/life/people/2018/07/03/bono-un-eu-nato-threatened/753908002/.

PROFILE #3: JEFFREY SACHS

1 Nina Munk, *The Idealist: Jeffrey Sachs and the Quest to End Poverty* (n.p.: Anchors, 2014), 140.

2   Nina Munk, "Jeffrey Sachs's $200 Billion Dream," *Vanity Fair*, June 5, 2007, https://www.vanityfair.com/news/2007/07/sachs200707.

3   John Leland, "Reveling in the Rites of the City," *New York Times*, January 18, 2013.

4   Karen W. Arenson, "For Professor, a Town House Fit for a King," *New York Times*, November 20, 2002.

5   Arenson.

6   Jennifer Gould, "Econo-Nerd Jeffrey Sachs Buys $6.25M UWS Condo," *New York Post*, October 14, 2015.

7   Munk, *The Idealist*, 35.

8   Earth Institute, Columbia University "Mission," accessed August 1, 2020, http://www.earth.columbia.edu/articles/view/1791.

9   Earth Institute, Columbia University, "Earth Institute Staff Directory," accessed July 1, 2020, http://www.earth.columbia.edu/eidirectory.

10   Earth Institute, Columbia University, Earth Institute 2014 Annual Report. See http://annualreport.ei.columbia.edu/.

11   Anita Snow, "George Soros Gives $27 Million to Africa Project," *Christian Science Monitor*, October 4, 2011, https://www.csmonitor.com/Business/Latest-News-Wires/2011/1004/George-Soros-gives-27-million-to-Africa-project.

12   Munk, *The Idealist*, 76.

13   Munk, 134.

14   Munk, 85.

15   *Newswire Newsletter*, "Gates Foundation Donates $258M to Malaria Fight," November 1, 2005, https://www.devex.com/news/gates-foundation-donates-258m-to-malaria-fight-47018.

16   John Luke Gallup and Jeffrey D. Sachs, "The Economic Burden of Malaria," *American Journal of Tropical Medicine and Hygiene*, January–February 2001.

17   Munk, *The Idealist*, 97.

18   Munk, 100–101.

19   Munk, 103, 171.

20   Munk, 102.

21   Munk, 106.

22   Munk, 127.

23   Munk, 128.

24   Munk, 129.

25   Munk, 178.

26   Earth Institute, Columbia University, *The Millennium Villages Project 2009 Annual Report*, https://irp-cdn.multiscreensite.com/6fae6349/files/uploaded/MVP%20 2009%20Annual%20Report%20-%20EIMPUNDP%20-%20General%20Public%20 Version%20-%20FINAL.pdf.

27   Munk, *The Idealist*, 201–2.

28   Jeffrey Sachs and John W. McArthur, "Moyo's Confused Attack on Aid for Africa," *Huffington Post*, May 27, 2009, https://www.huffpost.com/entry/moyos-confused-attack-on_b_208222.

29   Brian Stewart, "Is Dambisa Moyo Right about Cutting Aid to Africa?," CBC News, June 4, 2009, https://www.cbc.ca/news/world/is-dambisa-moyo-right-about-cutting-aid-to-africa-1.799680.

30   Kathleen Beegle et al, *Poverty in a Rising Africa: Africa Poverty Report* (International Bank for Reconstruction and Development / The World Bank, 2016), http://documents1.worldbank.org/curated/en/949241467996692059/pdf/103948-PUB-POVERTY-AFRICA-Box394870B-PUBLIC.pdf.
31   Michael A. Clemens and Gabriel Demombynes, "When Does Rigorous Impact Evaluation Make a Difference? The Case of the Millennium Villages," Center for Global Development, Working Paper 225, October 2010, see https://www.cgdev.org/publication/when-does-rigorous-impact-evaluation-make-difference-case-millennium-villages-working.
32   Clemens and Demombynes, "When Does Rigorous Impact Evaluation Make a Difference?"

EPILOGUE: DEFILING THE NOBLE LIE

1   Friedrich A. von Hayek, *The Road to Serfdom* (n.p.: Routledge, 1944).
2   James Taranto, "Bruce Rauner vs. the Illinois 'Mafia,'" *Wall Street Journal*, March 3–4, 2018, https://www.wsj.com/articles/bruce-rauner-vs-the-illinois-mafia-1520030669.

AUTHOR'S NOTE

1   John F. Early, *Reassessing the Facts about Inequality, Poverty, and Redistribution*, Cato Institute, policy analysis no. 839, April 24, 2018, https://www.cato.org/publications/policy-analysis/reassessing-facts-about-inequality-poverty-redistribution.
2   Early.
3   Early.
4   Institute of Policy Integrity, "Roundup: Trump-Era Agency Policy in the Courts," policyintegrity.org, last updated July 27, 2020, https://policyintegrity.org/trump-court-roundup.
5   Peter Sokolowski, on the 2017 Word of the Year (video), Merriam-Webster.com, accessed August 1, 2020, https://www.merriam-webster.com/video/2017-word-of-the-year-behind-the-scenes.
6   Sokolowski.
7   Mark Twain, autobiographical dictation, December 1906, in Twain, *Autobiography of Mark Twain*, vol. 2 (University of California Press, 2013).
8   Christopher Hitchens, *Letters to a Young Contrarian* (New York: Basic Books, 2005).
9   Horatio Nelson, *Trafalgar Memorandum*, 1805. Full text available online at https://archive.org/stream/nelsonmemorandum00nels/nelsonmemorandum00nels_djvu.txt.